Festivals & Daily Life in the Arts of Colonial Latin America, 1492–1850

Papers from the 2012 Mayer Center Symposium
at the Denver Art Museum

Edited by Donna Pierce

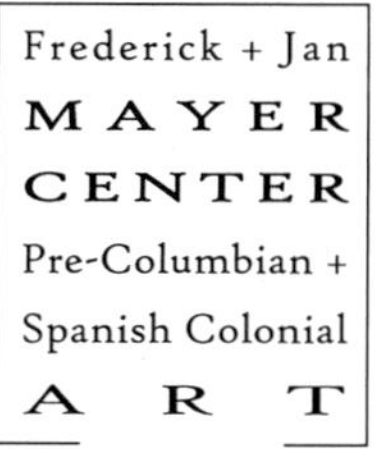

DENVER ART MUSEUM

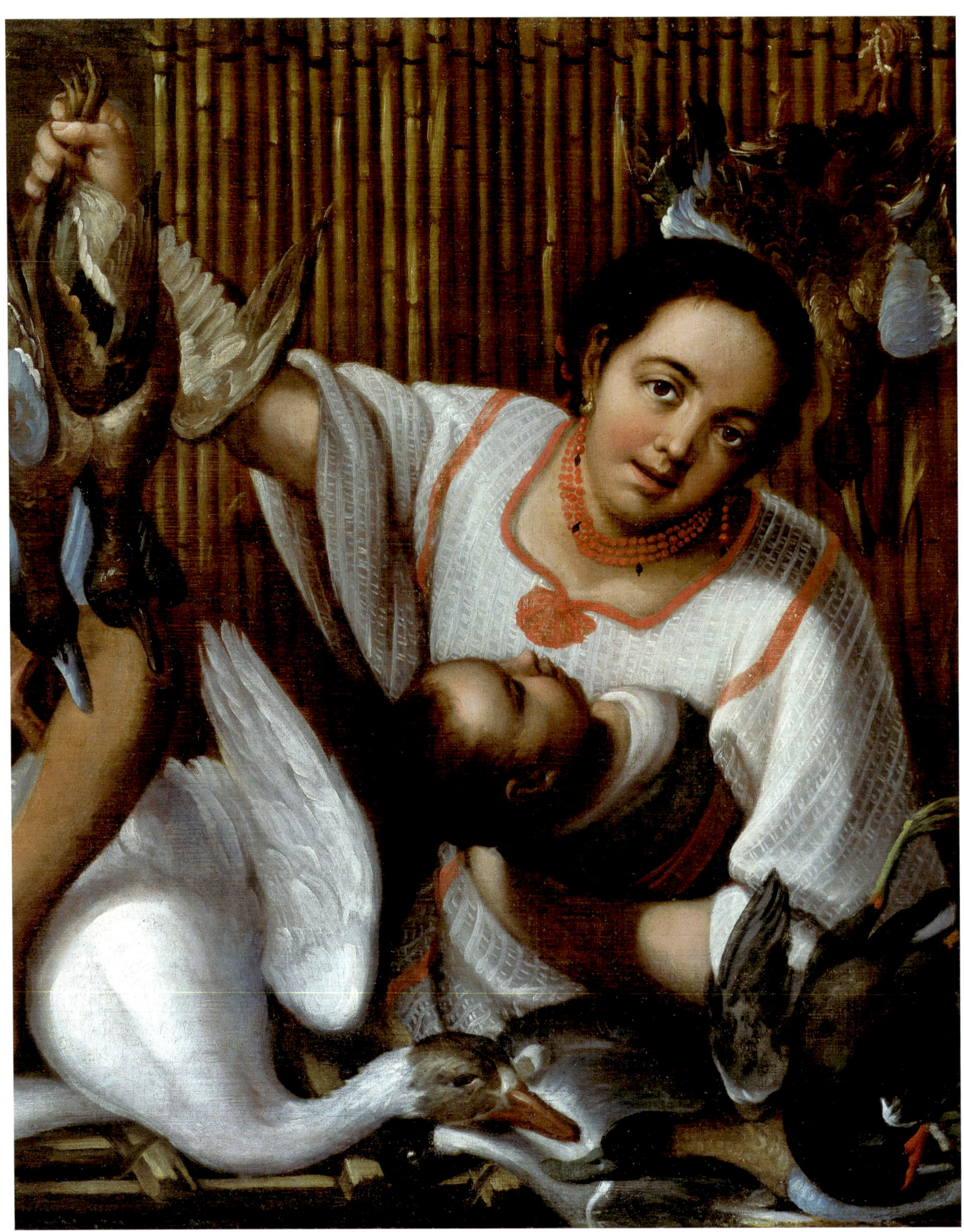

Dedicated with affection and gratitude
to Jan Mayer and to the memory of Frederick Mayer
for their vision, passion, and generosity.

Published by the Mayer Center for Pre-Columbian & Spanish Colonial Art at the Denver Art Museum

Library of Congress Cataloging-in-Publication Data

Mayer Center Symposium (12th : 2012 : Denver Art Museum)
Festivals and daily life in the arts of colonial Latin America : papers from the 2012 Mayer Center Symposium at the Denver Art Museum / edited by Donna Pierce.
pages cm
Includes bibliographical references.
ISBN 978-0-914738-98-5 (paperback)
1. Arts, Colonial--Latin America--Congresses. 2. Arts, Latin American--Congresses. 3. Festivals--Latin America--Congresses. I. Pierce, Donna, 1950- editor. II. Title.

NX501.5.M39 2012
700.98--dc23

2014018563

Mayer Center for Pre-Columbian & Spanish Colonial Art at the Denver Art Museum
100 West 14th Avenue Parkway
Denver, CO 80204
http://mayercenter.denverartmuseum.org
www.denverartmuseum.org

Editor: Donna Pierce, with the assistance of Nancy Mann
Project coordination, design, and production: Julie Wilson Frick

Cover illustrations: p. 132, fig. 4
Frontispiece: (detail) *De Indio y Mestiza, sale Coyote* (From Indian and Mestiza, Coyote). Mexico, mid 1700s. Oil on canvas, 31½ x 41 in. Denver Art Museum; Collection of Frederick and Jan Mayer, TL-32012.

Printed and bound by O'Neil Printing, Phoenix, AZ. Distributed by the University of Oklahoma Press, www.oupress.com

CONTRIBUTORS

Beatriz Berndt L. M.	*Independent Scholar (Mexico City, Mexico)*
Gustavo Curiel	*Instituto de Investigaciones Estéticas, Universidad Nacional Autónoma de México (Mexico City, Mexico)*
Kelly Donahue-Wallace	*University of North Texas (Denton, TX)*
Alexandra Kennedy-Troya	*Universidad de Cuenca (Cuenca, Ecuador)*
Susan Migden Socolow	*Emory University (Atlanta, GA)*
Barbara E. Mundy	*Fordham University (New York, NY)*
Frances L. Ramos	*University of South Florida (Tampa, FL)*
Jorge F. Rivas Pérez	*Colección Patricia Phelps de Cisneros (Caracas, Venezuela)*

Contents

Foreword

The Denver Art Museum is indeed fortunate in being able to count among its greatest resources a Spanish Colonial collection rich in art from all over Latin America. Although the museum's Spanish Colonial collection might be said to have begun with Anne Evans's 1936 gift of a group of *santos* from southern Colorado and northern New Mexico, its true genesis should probably be credited to Otto Bach, who began his successful thirty-year tenure as the museum's director in 1944. Ignoring the advice of eastern colleagues to carve out a special niche in regional art, Bach boldly set out to build an encyclopedic collection of world art. In 1952, the museum made its first purchase of Pre-Columbian art, and in 1968 Bach established a New World Department that brought Pre-Columbian and Spanish Colonial objects from Latin America together under the curatorship of Robert Stroessner. Today the combined collection of the New World Department covers a time span from about 1200 BCE to the present. More than five thousand objects from these collections are now displayed in the Jan and Frederick Mayer Galleries of Pre-Columbian and Spanish Colonial Art at the Denver Art Museum.

Within a year of its founding, the New World Department received the Frank Barrows Freyer Memorial Collection of seventeenth- and eighteenth-century colonial art from Peru and Bolivia. Assembled by María Engracia Freyer during the 1920s while her husband was chief of a United States naval mission to Peru, the collection received special export status in recognition of Freyer's contributions to the reorganization of the Peruvian navy. The New World Department flourished through the interest and support of longtime museum trustee Frederick Mayer and his wife Jan and the spirited curatorship of Stroessner. Cultivating collectors nationally as well as in the Denver area, Stroessner increased the holdings of the department dramatically before his death in 1991. Of special note was the 1990 gift of the Stapleton Foundation's extensive collection of colonial art from northern South America acquired between 1895 and 1914, a donation made possible by the Renchard family of Washington, D.C. In addition, an exemplary collection of Spanish Colonial silver from the Robert Appleman family and major gifts from the Mayers of important examples of Mexican colonial painting have greatly enriched the collection.

The growth of the New World collections and programs received a major boost with the enlightened endowment gift of Frederick and Jan Mayer. This gift made it possible to establish separate curatorial positions in Pre-Columbian and Spanish Colonial art and to underwrite the department's administrative costs, support staff, publications, and programs. In 1999, Donna Pierce and Margaret Young-Sánchez, came to the museum as the Frederick and Jan Mayer Curators of Spanish Colonial Art and Pre-Columbian Art, respectively. As a result of the Mayers' generosity, the Denver Art Museum has the only curator in the United States dedicated exclusively to colonial Latin American art.

The Mayers also founded the Frederick and Jan Mayer Center for Pre-Columbian and Spanish Colonial Art at the Denver Art Museum, dedicated to increasing awareness and promoting scholarship in these fields by sponsoring academic activities including annual symposia, fellowships, study trips, and publications. Since the first one in 2001, Mayer Center symposia have taken place nearly every year. During November 2–3, 2012, the Mayer Center hosted "Festivals and Daily Life in the Arts of Colonial Latin America, 1492–1850" with speakers from Latin America and the United States; those papers are presented in this volume.

Over the years, the Mayers generously supported the museum's larger mission at every turn. The untimely death of Frederick Mayer in 2007 was a great loss to the community. His generosity of spirit and infectious enthusiasm were an inspiration to all. We are blessed to have the ongoing support of his wife Jan, and offer warm thanks to her for her ongoing dedication to the museum as a whole and to the study of New World art in particular.

Christoph Heinrich
Frederick and Jan Mayer Director
Denver Art Museum

Introduction and Acknowledgments

The Frederick and Jan Mayer Center for Pre-Columbian and Spanish Colonial Art at the Denver Art Museum sponsors annual symposia alternating between these fields of art. Held in November 2012, the twelfth symposium in the series was titled "Festivals and Daily Life in the Arts of Colonial Latin America, 1492–1850." Specialists in the arts and history of Latin America traveled to Denver from Mexico, Ecuador, Venezuela, and throughout the United States to present recent research on topics ranging from discussions of ephemeral architecture, painting, and sculpture to engravings, decorative arts, and costumes and clothing of the period. The discussions covered art from the geographic areas of modern-day Mexico, Ecuador, Colombia, Venezuela, and Argentina, among others. The Mayer Center sponsors the publication of proceedings of the symposia. This volume presents revised and expanded versions of the papers presented at the 2012 symposium.

Barbara Mundy (Fordham University) opens the volume with a thought-provoking discussion of Pre-Columbian dance festivals and their associated costumes and accouterments, their continuation and reinterpretation in colonial Mexico, and their remaining vestiges in modern times. Gustavo Curiel (Universidad Nacional Autónoma de México) presents a moving discussion of the mourning activities performed in Mexico City to commemorate the 1665 death of Philip IV. He reconstructs a vision of the ephemeral monument erected by the Inquisition by comparing documentary sources, such as the artist's contract, with surviving engravings of a related monument.

Beatriz Berndt (Independent Scholar, Mexico) continues the festival theme by analyzing extant engravings, written descriptions, and political motivations in the ephemeral facade designed to celebrate the enthronement of Charles IV in Mexico City in 1789. Frances Ramos (University of South Florida) examines celebrations and art in honor of Saint Joseph in the city of Puebla, Mexico, and their associations with local politics. Kelly Donahue-Wallace (University of North Texas) closes the festival section with a discussion of ephemeral structures and related public art works in Mexico City under the direction of the newly-founded Royal Academy of Art of San Carlos in the late colonial era.

Jorge Rivas (Colección Cisneros, Caracas) begins the discussion of daily life by presenting recent research on a uniquely American furniture form, the *butaca* (easy) chair, tracing its origins in Venezuela and its eventual spread throughout pan-Caribbean Latin America. Historian Susan Socolow (Emory University) follows with an examination of women's quotidian clothing in colonial Argentina based on documentary evidence found in travelers' descriptions and estate inventories. Alexandra Kennedy-Troya (Universidad de Cuenca, Ecuador) closes the volume by tracing Ecuadorian *costumbrista* images of daily life from their origin in colonial-era Enlightenment discourse to their production for the tourist market and use by politicians in the nineteenth and early twentieth centuries.

We are grateful to these scholars for their participation in the symposium and their contributions to this publication. We hope that this volume, an interdisciplinary study bringing together new research on an understudied era and area, will serve as an important resource for scholars and enthusiasts of early modern history in general and Latin American art and history in particular.

I would like to acknowledge the staff of the New World Department for their efforts in organizing the symposium: Julie Wilson Frick, Mayer Center Program Coordinator; Trish Tomlinson and Jana Gottshalk, Curatorial Assistants in the New World Department; Anne Tennant, New World Research Associate; Michael Brown, former Mayer Center Fellow; and Sabena Kull, New World intern. Denver Art Museum Events, Audio-Visual, and Security staff led by Tony Fortunato and Terri Cross provided significant and cheerful support. As always, I thank my New World Department colleague, Margaret Young-Sánchez, Frederick and Jan Mayer Curator of Pre-Columbian Art, for her support.

In the preparation of this publication, I am grateful to Nancy Mann for her superb editing skills. Anne Tennant, Michael Brown, Jana Gottshalk, and Sabena Kull provided valuable bibliographic and editing assistance. Thanks are due to Laura Caruso, Senior Editor and Manager of Publications at the DAM, for ongoing advice and editing and to Carmella Padilla for her meticulous copy editing and proofing skills. Jeff Wells and Christina Jackson, Denver Art Museum photographers, were always quick to provide expert services. Digital mapmaker Fabrice Weexsteen enthusiastically offered his technical and scholarly knowledge in the creation of the maps, developed in collaboration with the New World Department. Thanks are due to the staff of O'Neil Printing for production of this volume and to the University of Oklahoma Press for distribution. My profound gratitude goes to Julie Wilson Frick, Mayer Center Program Coordinator, for book coordination, image gathering, compilation, map research, contract negotiation, and most importantly, for the elegant and clean design of this volume, and all Mayer Center symposia publications.

On behalf of all of us at the Denver Art Museum and those who participated in the symposium, I want to express our deepest gratitude to the late Frederick Mayer, and to his wife Jan, for providing the opportunity to bring such a distinguished group of scholars together from many parts of the world to share ideas. Creating an ongoing forum for scholarly exchange in the field, along with the ability to publish the results, was a major part of the Mayers' vision for the founding of the Mayer Center for Pre-Columbian and Spanish Colonial Art and its programming. The Mayers represent the ideal supporters, interested in all aspects of museums and the scholarship surrounding them. The DAM in general, and the New World Department in particular, have been blessed to have them as our guardian angels. We dedicate this publication to the memory of Frederick Mayer and to Jan Mayer in gratitude for her ongoing support, enthusiasm, and friendship.

Donna Pierce
Frederick and Jan Mayer Curator of
Spanish Colonial Art
Head of the New World Department
Denver Art Museum

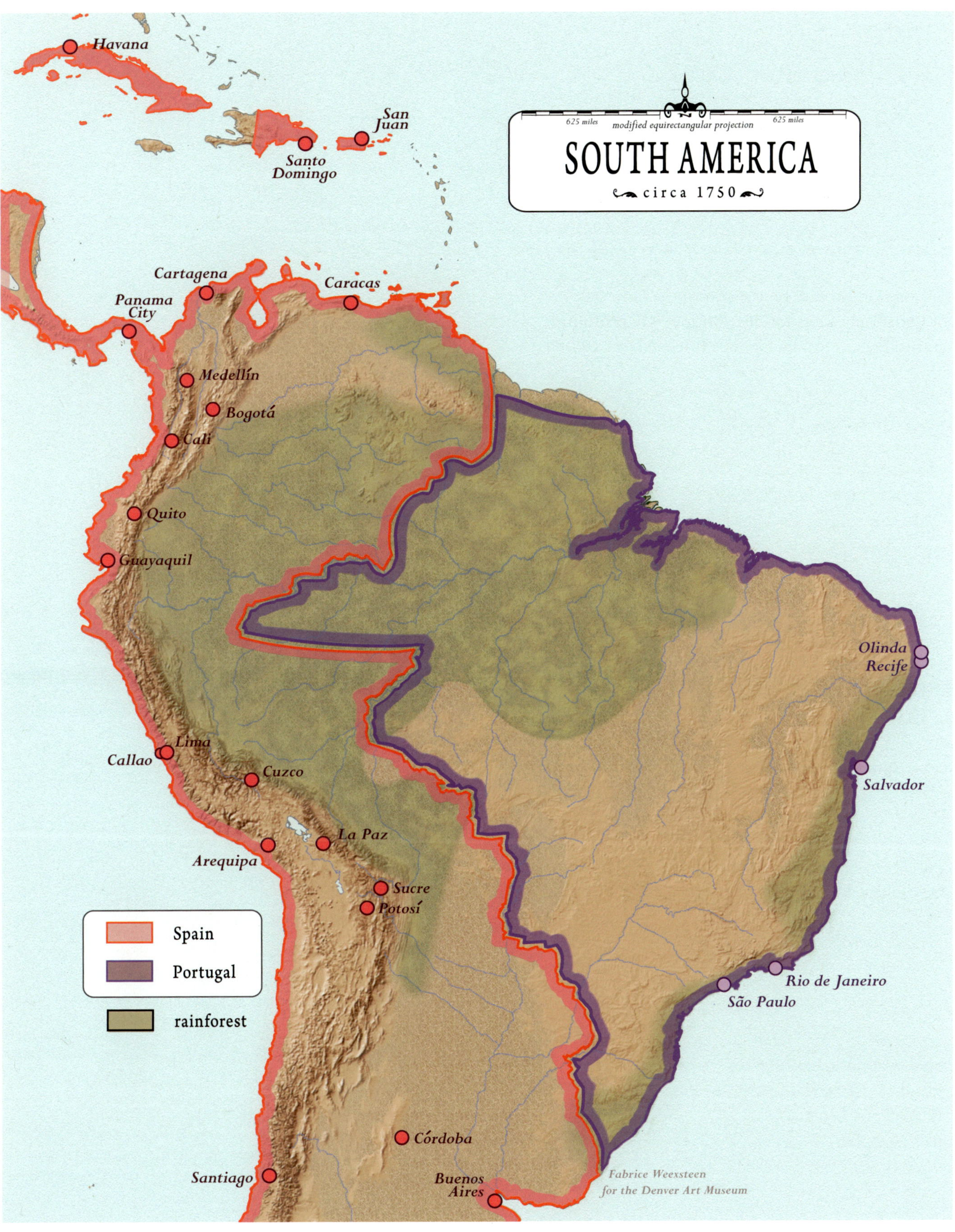
625 miles
modified equirectangular projection
625 miles
SOUTH AMERICA
circa 1750
Havana
San Juan
Santo Domingo
Cartagena
Caracas
Panama City
Medellín
Bogotá
Cali
Quito
Guayaquil
Olinda
Recife
Lima
Callao
Cuzco
Salvador
La Paz
Arequipa
Sucre
Potosí
Spain
Portugal
rainforest
Rio de Janeiro
São Paulo
Córdoba
Santiago
Buenos Aires
Fabrice Weexsteen
for the Denver Art Museum

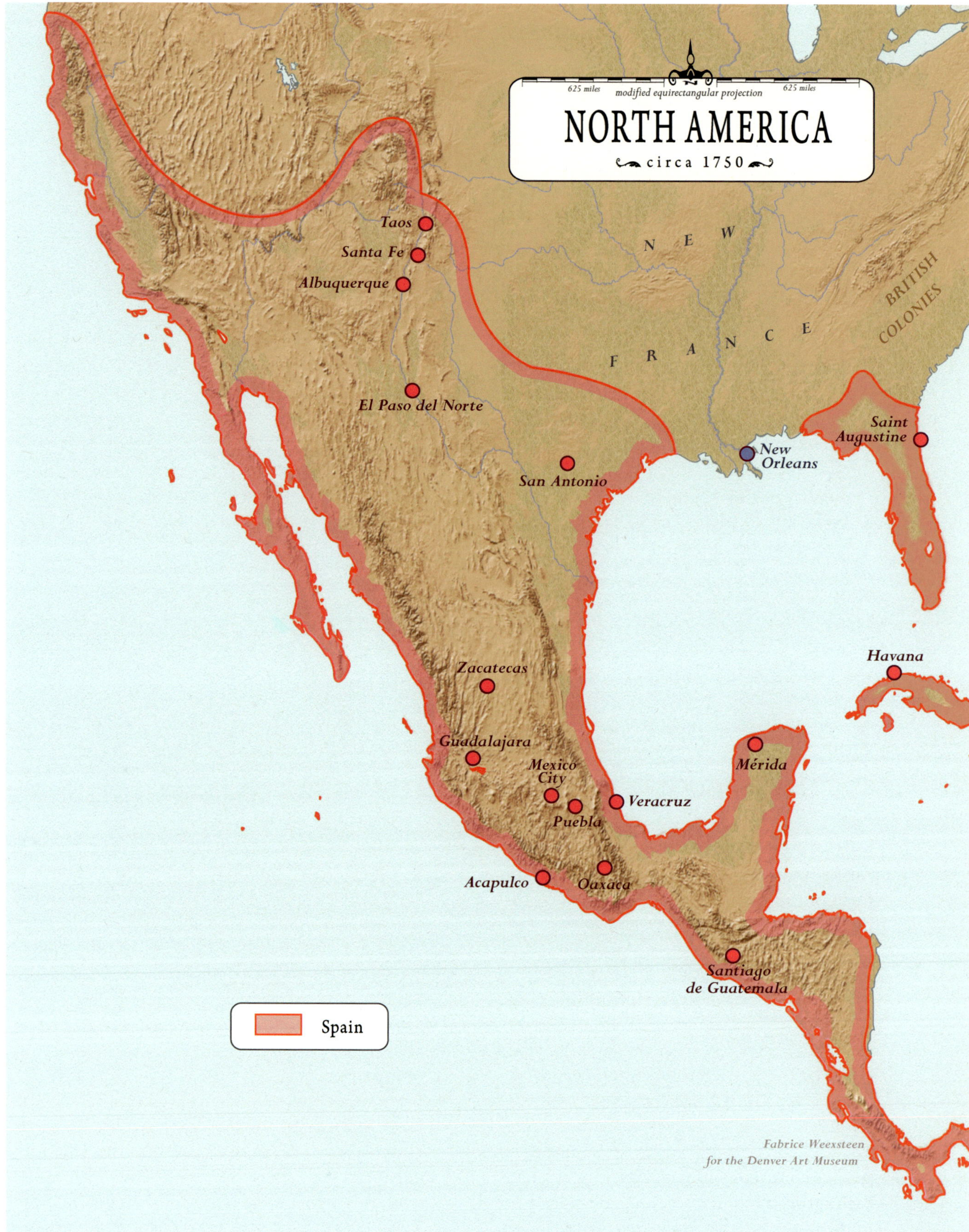

625 miles
modified equirectangular projection
625 miles
NORTH AMERICA
circa 1750
Taos
Santa Fe
Albuquerque
El Paso del Norte
San Antonio
NEW FRANCE
BRITISH COLONIES
New Orleans
Saint Augustine
Havana
Zacatecas
Guadalajara
Mexico City
Puebla
Veracruz
Mérida
Acapulco
Oaxaca
Santiago de Guatemala
Spain
Fabrice Weexsteen
for the Denver Art Museum

Indigenous Dances in Early Colonial Mexico City

Barbara E. Mundy

A spectacular *biombo*, or painted folding screen, created in Mexico City probably around 1690, lays before us the unique festival culture of one of the richest cities in the Habsburgs' global empire, a polyglot place where African slaves, Filipino craftsmen, and Spanish grandees jostled in the streets (fig. 1).[1] One of the largest ethnic groups in the city was its Nahuatl-speaking indigenes, who had dominated much of Mexico before the Spanish Conquest of 1519–1521. Indeed, Mexico City had once been Tenochtitlan, capital of the Aztec empire and, with 150,000 or so residents, one of the most populous cities in the world. These autochthonous peoples are the key players in this painted scene: the festivities are set off by an indigenous wedding, with the garlanded bride in a red and white *huipil*, a traditional woven shift, emerging from the church at the far right. The wedding sets off a series of other events that careen across the painted screen, including, along with a pole juggler, another indigenous spectacle, that of *voladores*, or "fliers," a performance well documented in colonial Mexico City and the surrounding Valley of Mexico. In it, trained acrobats would climb a high wooden pole with a set of ropes tightly wound around the top. After tying themselves by their feet, they would jump off, and in their slow gyring progress downward as the ropes unfurled, the audience below could enjoy their wheeling figures against the blue sky. But the focus of this essay is an important scene closest to the newly wedded couple: a *mitote*, a kind of dance carried out by performers costumed in festive versions of indigenous garb (fig. 1, right side).

The dancers wear distinctive costumes. They are masked and each wears a frontal miter tied at the back of the head—a seventeenth-century version of a royal crown, the *xiuhhuitzolli*, worn by pre-Hispanic rulers in the Valley of Mexico. The dancers wear wide-legged pants and loose, lace-sleeved shirts that emerge from under colorful short-sleeved tailored jackets. In one hand, each carries a fan made of long green feathers; in the other, a rattle. The *mitote* we see depicted here, like those shown on other *biombos*, has a clearly choreographed form: the two lines of four pairs of eight dancers have trained for these parts. Movements are limited, largely vertical, as the dancers are shown bowing or lifting arms and feet in time to the music. The coordination of their movements as they turn to new partners in front of or behind them, with echoing or mirroring movements, is emphasized by the plumes of their feather fans held in opposing hands. The central figure of the dance is a richly dressed individual at left, whose presence is emphasized by the elaborate green feather panache that a small page holds to form a halo behind his head. Behind him are the musicians, who play a Spanish guitar, identifiable by its small size, and a harp, hoisted up in an odd fashion on the musician's shoulder.[2]

Mitotes like this one appear not only in *biombo* paintings but also in descriptions of festivals in seventeenth-century New Spain, particularly in Mexico City, where they were often recorded as being performed at political events sponsored by Habsburg rulers. The presence of the *mitote* shows the pluralistic nature of festival culture in cities under Habsburg rule, as urban inhabitants took advantage of the frequent calls for commemoration of royal events like the birth of an heir or the accession of a monarch to fill these mandated celebrations with events of their own making.[3] On one hand, these multifold local appropriations, happening across the Habsburg-dominated globe, allowed political subjugation by distant rulers to take on a familiar festival face; on the other, they gave local elites a time and place to assert their presence and their unique history and identity within these public displays of Habsburg authority. While studies of global Habsburg festival culture often focus on the role of local Spanish authorities or Creoles (people of European descent born in the Americas), less attention has been paid to the role of key political players in the Americas: the indigenous elite.

In this essay I focus on this important "interpretative community," to borrow the idea popularized

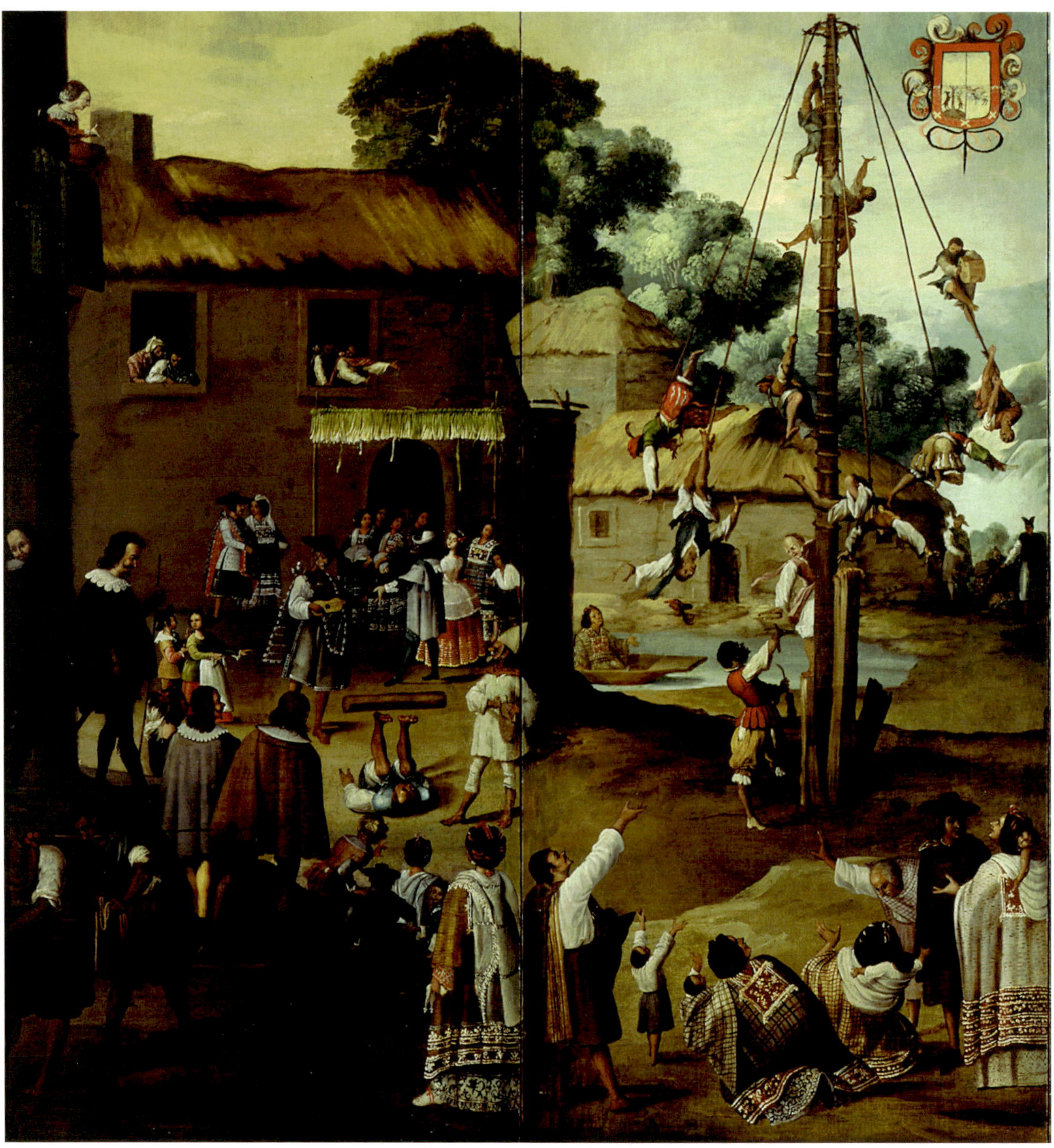

Fig. 1. *Biombo con desposorio indígena y palo volador (Folding Screen with Indian Wedding and Flying Pole)*. Mexico, c. 1690. Oil on canvas, 66 x 120 in. Los Angeles County Museum of Art, purchased with funds provided by the Bernard and Edith Lewin Collection of Mexican Art Deaccession Fund. Photo: © 2009 Museum Associates / LACMA / Art Resource, NY.

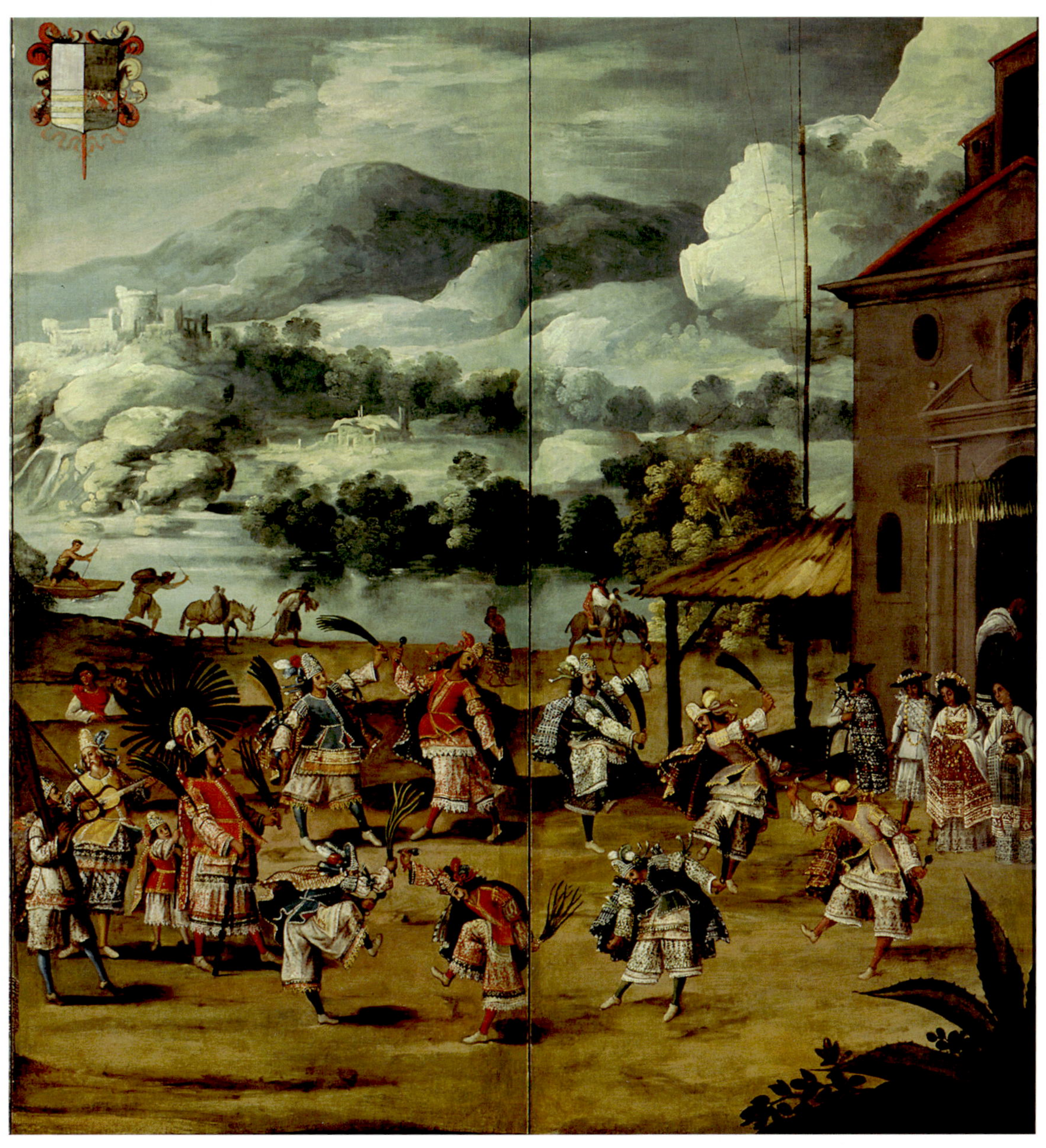

by Stanley Fish, to attempt to understand the meanings that Indian dances would have had in the early colonial period to the community that sponsored and performed them. I underscore the indigenous context of the *mitote*, a performance that had a long history in Mexico City, one predating the Conquest and deeply tied to indigenous rulers and rule. I survey both its pre-Hispanic context and the reasons why it, unlike other indigenous festivals, flourished in the colonial period. To explore its meanings in this indigenous context, particularly its political meanings, I end by discussing an important image created by and for indigenous elites in the 1560s, found in the Tlatelolco Codex.

Meanings of *Mitote*

The indigenous performance we see in the *biombo* was called a *mitote* by Spanish observers in the sixteenth and seventeenth centuries, and the origins of this word merit exploration. The root is from Nahuatl, the main indigenous language of central Mexico, and it is significant that rather than applying available Spanish vocabulary (*baile* or *danza*), European witnesses used a Nahuatl moniker—one indication that they saw the performance as something distinct from their own categories, needing to be marked by a specific vocabulary. But the word is not, strictly speaking, a correct Nahuatl form, and from my sampling of Nahuatl language sources, it was not used by Nahuatl speakers themselves. So it's probable that European observers heard a Nahuatl term and created a neologism that they would thenceforth use as a generic term to designate all such indigenous dances. "*Mitote*" comes from the Nahuatl root *i'totia* (when vowel lengths are marked, it is written *i'tōtiā),* a word translated in Alonso de Molina's 1571 Spanish-Nahuatl *Vocabulario* as "to dance." Since Nahuatl root words are not used in unmodified forms (that is, there is no spoken infinitive form), Europeans seem to have adapted their word *mitote* from *mi'totia* (also rendered *mitotia*, without the glottal stop) meaning "s/he dances." In contrast, Nahuatl texts like Bernardino de Sahagún's Florentine Codex nominalize the root in more grammatically standard ways, as in *netotiliztli,* meaning "dance" or "dancing."[4]

While the term *mitote* becomes a catch-all for indigenous dances in Spanish-language sources by the mid-sixteenth century, Nahuatl sources often use more specific names for songs and accompanying dances, signaling a rich repertory that is now lost to us. In describing the 1564 wedding of Luis de Santa María, then the native governor of Mexico City, an indigenous diary writer recorded the performance of the *chichimecayotl*, a dance named after the original tribes of the north, the Chichimec; the *atequilizcuicatl*, a song whose name means "the sprinkling of water"; and the dance of the Otomí, another northern ethnic group who also shared their name with a group of elite pre-Hispanic warriors.[5] Sahagún's informants offer us names of songs, which in other contexts also serve as names for dances, and they were often named for non-Mexica peoples: the song of "the drunkards of Cuextlan"; the *huexotzincayotl*, named after Huexotzinco, a traditional enemy of the Aztecs of Tenochtitlan; the *anahuacayotl*, named after Anahuac, often used as a metaphor for Tenochtitlan.[6] Given how much the ceremonial economy of pre-Hispanic Tenochtitlan depended on displays of military prowess, some of these song-dances, like the *cuextecayotl, nonohualcayotl, cozcatecayotl, tepetlacayotl, meztitlancalcayotl,* and *huexotzincayotl,* almost certainly originated in the exhausted passes of humiliated captives forced to perform dances of defeat.[7] Others, like the dance of the Otomí, may have been dances to mark military triumphs.

While words with the *i'totia* root are often translated with the English "dance" or the Spanish "*baile*" and "*danza*," there is an ill-fit between the terms, revealed by other vocabulary. One set of words in Molina's *Vocabulario* that derive from *i'totia* are all related to the dance, but in a second set of meanings created through agglutination, *i'totia* combines with "palm of the hand" to mean "robbery by use of sorcery." In this usage, the *i'totia* root is associated not with a dance, but with a specific kind of enchantment. The idea that dance had an enchanting function was also suggested by the Franciscan writer Gerónimo de Mendieta, who wrote, "one of the most important things that there was in this country [in the pre-Hispanic period] were the songs and dances, used to make sacred the feasts for their devils that they honored as gods."[8] That is, the combined effect of song and dance was "to make sacred," or, in other words, enchant the mundane.

Another root word used to describe dances, *macehua*, may relate to the root *ma'cehua* (when vowel lengths are marked, it is written *ma'cēhua*), a word also meaning "to obtain or to deserve what one desires, to do penance"; however, this association is not a secure one.[9] When Sahagún uses the term *macehualiztli*, he glosses it as "*baile, danza,*" and also adds "*que por otro nombre se llama areitos.*"[10] That term, *areito*, is not Spanish, but a Taíno loanword from the first New World encounters in the Antilles, another sign that Spanish observers, especially a sensitive one like Sahagún, understood a not-perfect fit between the indigenous word for dance and its Spanish translation.

Pre-Hispanic *Mitotes*, Costume, and Music

It is Sahagún who provides the most valuable explanation of why he and other observers did not easily map the Spanish terms of *danza* and *baile* onto the indigenous ceremonial dances. A student of Nahua history who gathered together a group of Nahua intellectuals over the course of three decades, Sahagún would eventually create the great three-volume encyclopedia about the Nahua world commonly known as the Florentine Codex (figs. 2–6). It comprises two columns of text, one in Nahuatl and the other a sometimes-parallel Spanish translation. In the Spanish discussion of the *macehualiztli*, Sahagún indicates that they were not just dances but also had accompanying songs, and were performed to the percussive musical accompaniment provided by two drums, the *teponaztli* and the *huehuetl*, as well as various rattles (*ayacachtli, tetzilacatl, omichicahuaztli*) and flutes.[11] Thus, it might be productive to think of these events as entire performances, rather than just dances.

Because the writers of the Florentine Codex focus on pre-Hispanic ritual events, it is clear from their text that *netotiliztli* and *macehualiztli*, terms they often used as a kind of couplet, were components of many important ceremonies, and scenes of dances are pictured in the text.[12] For instance, dances are described and pictured for the calendar feast of 1 Flower, and a section in Book 9 places heavy emphasis on the dances performed at the celebration of Huitzilopochtli, the Mexica tutelary deity (figs. 2 and 5). These latter dances were sponsored by the merchants (*pochteca*), long-distance traders who, in the pre-Hispanic period, traveled around what is now Mexico, bringing back luxury goods from the corners of the empire. The emphasis the text places on these *pochteca*-sponsored dances may have to do with the particular context of the Florentine Codex, which was composed mostly in the urban monastery of Santiago located in Tlatelolco, a former center of the *pochteca*. As patron deity of Tenochtitlan and Tlatelolco, Huitzilopochtli was important, as was his feast, celebrated yearly and running through the night. Dances were a key element of this feast, performed to the beat of a drum. Their solemnity was marked by an incense-bearing indigenous priest who would cense the drums before the dance began, just as the altar was censed during the Catholic Mass.

Most important is the connection between these dances and the military, bearing out my reading of the names of specific dances discussed above. The Huitzilopochtli dance was led by the *tlacateccatl*, who held one of the highest military ranks; after him came another warrior, the *cuacuachicti*, as well as warriors called Otomí and seasoned warriors called *tequihuaque*. Training for these dances was an important activity carried out in the *cuicacalli*, the "house of song," as young men being educated in a school called the *telpochcalli*, some of whom were destined to be warriors, were drilled in dance (figs. 3–4).[13] According to the Florentine Codex, dance training lasted into the night, accompanied by the loud beating of the drums, and like sleep-deprivation exercises by today's military, it may have functioned to train young warriors to go without sleep and maintain alertness should the city come under siege.

Sacred dances were also an important feature of consecration rituals for a ruler, and here too members of military orders put their training on display. The Dominican friar Diego Durán tells us how at the coronation of Tizoc (r. 1481–1486), the emperor-elect gave gifts to warriors, among them the Otomí warriors and the *tequihuaque*, before they began their dances; this celebration may have doubled as a display of military discipline. Following the martial dances, another set of dances began as the ruler-elect danced with dozens

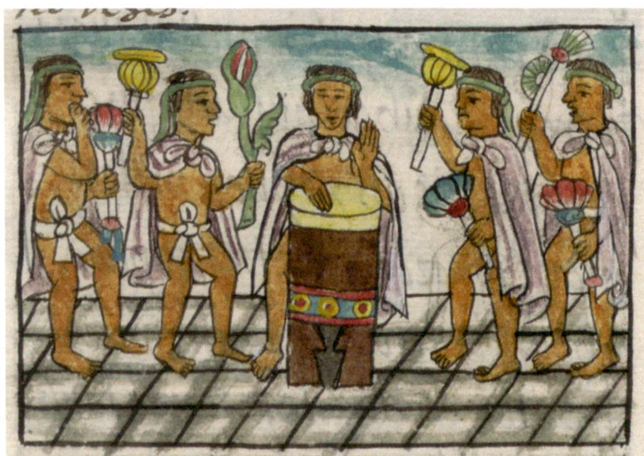

Fig. 2. Florentine Codex, book 9, chapter 8, dances of the merchants in honor of Huitzilopochtli. Mexico, c. 1575. Ink and pigment on paper. Biblioteca Medicea Laurenziana, Florence, vol. 2, book 9, fol. 30v.

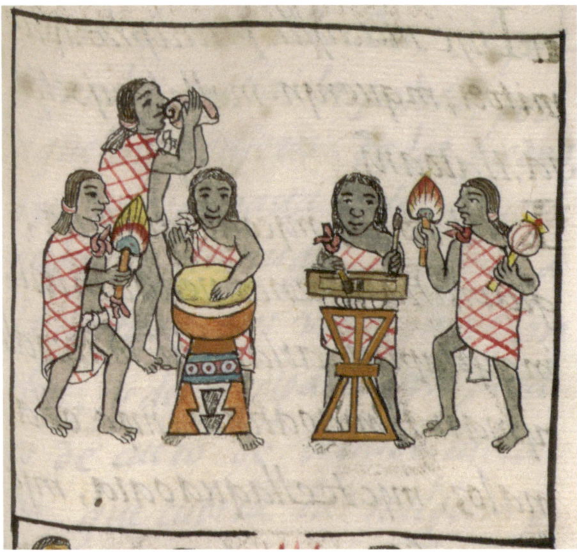

Fig. 3. Florentine Codex, book 8, chapter 17, dances of the priests of the *cuicacalli*. Mexico, c. 1575. Ink and pigment on paper. Biblioteca Medicea Laurenziana, Florence, vol. 2, book 8, fol. 41r.

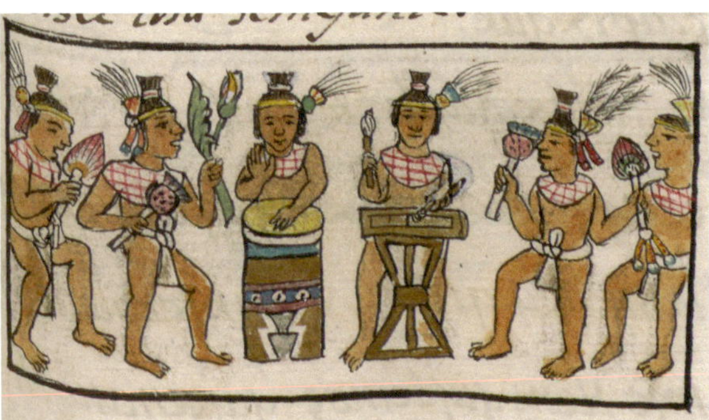

Fig. 4. Florentine Codex, book 8, chapter 16, youths dancing in the *cuicacalli*. Mexico, c. 1575. Ink and pigment on paper. Biblioteca Medicea Laurenziana, Florence, vol. 2, book 8, fol. 28r.

of rulers of surrounding cities who had been invited, and in some cases compelled, to come to Tenochtitlan for his consecration. Given their sometimes-compulsory nature, we can read these dances as part of the choreographed power plays in which the Mexica rulers of Tenochtitlan engaged with rulers from the surrounding cities and regions. To make the Mexica ruler's wealth and largess clear to all, the invited rulers were given elaborate gifts of jewelry and clothes, and then began a marathon of "dancing, feasting, and banqueting" that lasted for four days.[14] So successful were these events that Ahuitzotl (r. 1486–1502), who succeeded Tizoc, also sponsored four days of dancing for the rulers invited to his coronation, as did Moteuczoma (r. 1502–1520).[15] Such elite dances were not confined to Tenochtitlan but were a feature of ceremonial life across the Valley of Mexico. At the site of Texcotzinco, a hilltop retreat where the rulers of Texcoco were consecrated, they no doubt repeated the same display of largess as their Mexica relatives and competitors. A large plaza has been excavated at one side of the site, most likely used to host performances of the sacred dance.[16]

The images set into the text by the Florentine Codex artists offer a primer in the iconography of these dances. The most important feature in the depictions is the upright drum, the *huehuetl*, played by striking with the palms, which occupies the central axis in most of the images. Its name, from *hue*, meaning "great" or "old," both terms of veneration, also testified to its importance. A secondary accompaniment was the horizontal slit-drum, the *teponaztli*, set on an hourglass-shaped wooden frame, and cushioned by what appears to be an annular rope; this was played by wooden mallets wrapped in some kind of cord whose color suggests that the rope may have been coated with black rubber (figs. 3–6). While the merchants dancing for Huitzilopochtli and the lords dancing to celebrate the feast held on the day 1 Flower wear long cloaks over their conventional loincloths (figs. 2 and 5), the *cuicacalli* dancers wear black body paint marking their priestly status and cloaks with a red net-diamond pattern (as in fig. 3); students in the *tepochcalli* wear short neck stoles with the same pattern (fig. 4). The headgear of the dancers seems to be more closely associated with social status than with the iconography of the dance (lords wear quetzal feathers, merchants wear green head-ties, and warriors have knotted topknots and wear headbands with small sprays of uncolored feathers). However, the paraphernalia carried in the hands is part of the dance costume. In all the scenes, at least one of the figures carries a rattle (*ayacachtli*).[17] The codex also mentions the *tetzilacatl*, "twisted reed," which may refer to the mallets, and the *omichicahuaztli*, "strong bone," referring to the notched bones used to create rasping sounds, which are not directly pictured, but which we know from other contexts were likely battle trophies, made of the femurs of defeated enemies.[18]

The iconography associated with surviving examples of the *teponaztli* and *huehuetl* also underscores their bellicose nature. Wooden *teponaztli* and *huehuetl* are frequently carved in low relief with militaristic imagery; a surviving example found in the Mexican town, and former Mexica garrison, of Malinalco includes signs for *tlachinolli*, meaning "fire" or "burnt thing," combined with those of *atl*, or "water," which together form the couplet *atl tlachinolli*, meaning "warfare." The Malinalco drum also features singing and dancing jaguars and eagles, standing for the eagle and jaguar knights, the highest ranking of the Mexica military orders.[19]

Another characteristic of these dances is the presence of feather costumes and ornaments, an extraordinary art form perfected by indigenous craftsmen. To make the most elaborate feather objects, tens of thousands of individual feathers would be carefully sewn or pasted onto cloth or paper supports, creating suits of clothing or iridescent images. The most prized feathers—the green quetzal feather or brilliant parrot feathers—came from birds of the tropical rainforest and were acquired by long-distance trade. And feather objects were instrumental in the dance. According to the Florentine Codex, for instance, one of the key roles of the pre-Hispanic featherworkers was to create the dance costume of Moteuczoma.[20] In the codex's images of pre-Hispanic history, the dancing merchants carry bouquets made with feathers, and the one at far right carries a small feather standard (fig. 2); the dancing lord closest to the viewer in figure 5 carries a long fan made

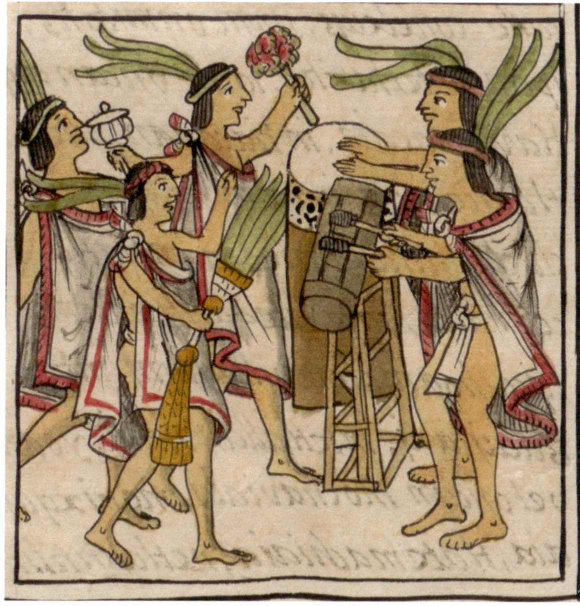

Fig. 5. Florentine Codex, book 4, chapter 7, dances on the day 1 Flower. Mexico, c. 1575. Ink and pigment on paper. Biblioteca Medicea Laurenziana, Florence, vol. 1, book 4, fol. 19v.

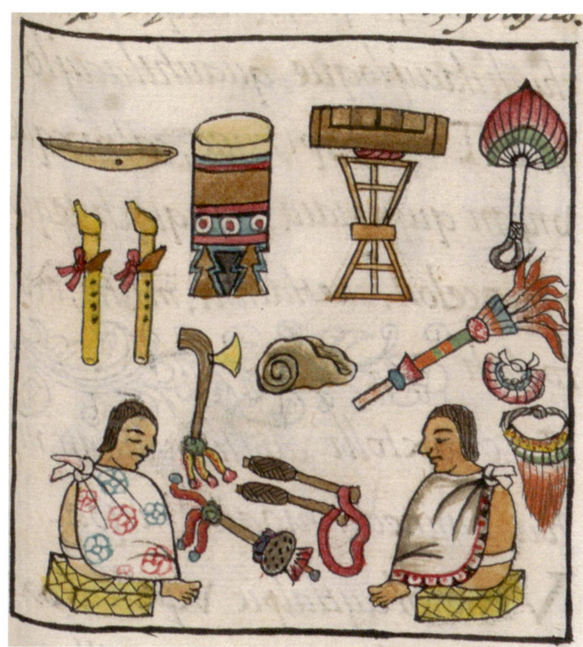

Fig. 6. Florentine Codex, book 8, chapter 14, the paraphernalia of the dances. Mexico, c. 1575. Ink and pigment on paper. Biblioteca Medicea Laurenziana, Florence, vol. 2, book 8, fol. 30r.

out of quetzal feathers. But more prevalent in the images is a smaller fan fashioned in an upside-down heart shape; when the artists depicted the paraphernalia used in the dance, they included this fan at the top right of the image (fig. 6), and other feathered ornaments fill its right side. Because of the distinctive reddish-pink feathers of the fan, it is likely to be a *tlauhquecholiecacehoaztli*, a red spoonbill feather fan. Such ovate fans had clear military associations; made of gray feathers, they were carried by the *tequihua*, or seasoned warriors, who were among those entrusted to be "ambassadors and guides" by the *huei tlatoani*, or supreme Mexica ruler in the pre-Hispanic period.[21] When made of feathers from the roseate spoonbill, the *tlauhquecholiecacehoaztli*, which is specifically identified as dance paraphernalia, was one of the gifts that the Mexica *huei tlatoani* gave to other rulers in the Valley when he assembled them to watch gladiatorial sacrifices on the successful completion of a war.[22] Thus, the distinctive feather fans pictured in these dances served as emblems of military victory and examples of royal Mexica largess.

Another accompaniment of the dances depicted in the codex consists of a large flower and leaf, seen carried in figures 2 and 4, looking something like a calla lily. This is a *huacalxochitl*, represented at large scale, a plant carried by dancers and rulers alike. Its erect spadix was linked to the ruler's sexual potency; palace ladies would pleasure themselves with it, presumably when the ruler was away or enjoying himself in someone else's bed.[23]

Performances

In the preceding discussion we've encountered a number of the features of pre-Hispanic performances, features that distinguished them from the mundane and unmarked events of daily life. The events that the Nahua knew before the Conquest as *netotiliztli* and *macehualiztli* were bracketed temporally, spatially, iconographically, aurally, and kinesthetically. They were performed in special liminal periods for a set amount of time, as in the wake of one ruler's death and before the consecration of the next, when they were danced for four days. Some of the sources discuss them as having happened especially at night, another liminal period, and the dance training of young warriors, specifically, was carried into the night. Most pre-Hispanic dances happened in enclosed plazas of the *cuicacalli* or the palace itself; the forced dances performed by the defeated are described as happening in front of temples. Since we know that the Templo Mayor of Tenochtitlan sat within a large plaza defined by the *coatepantli*, or "serpent wall," the dances carried out by defeated foreign warriors happened also in defined plazas. Sometimes, special costumes marked the dancers, like the red net-diamond pattern of the *cuicacalli* dancers, and shared among them are feathered bouquets and the distinctive pointed feather fans. We know less about the aural and kinesthetic dimensions of the dance, but the loud and low beat of the hollow drums would have signaled the presence of dances well beyond the boundaries of visibility, and the existence of named songs that were danced tells us of recognized and repeated musical forms. The regular movements shown in the Florentine depictions, with arms and legs raised in unison or opposition, suggest that the basic vocabulary of the dance was a fairly limited one. Colonial observers, as well, commented on the "stately" nature of the movements.

All these features set off the performances as separate from the mundane. Anthropologists have long recognized that dances can have special social functions, and among these functionalist roles that anthropologists have observed in other cultures, one among them is education, as cultural norms are transmitted through dance from one generation to the next. Pre-Hispanic dance took on such a role in the night dances of the *cuicacalli*, as the older priest-instructors kept their young charges awake with spirited dancing. Other dances that have been analyzed by anthropologists are competitive ones, in which social boundaries within groups are articulated and negotiated. Paul Spencer makes the point that "dance is a highly appropriate idiom [of confrontation] because it can display precisely the power, initiative, and coordinated discipline that gives strength in the event of an encounter; it can be overbearing."[24] Such a function may have been in play when the Mexica lords called in their neighboring rivals to dance for four days in the coronation rituals; a ruler's skill in the dance and his endurance may have been among the ways that he proved himself ready to rule within a competitive gathering of peers.

Dances, as we've also seen, were part of Mexica ritual performances, like the feast day of 1 Flower or the *pochteca* ceremony in honor of Huitzilopochtli, constituted as such by spaces, costumes, utterances, songs, and movements appropriate to the event. The presence of named dances and associated songs, which may have had lyrics, added a representational level to specific dances; that is, the *chichimecayotl* or the *atequil-izcuicatl* may have been *about* the Chichimec, or about baptisms, in the same way that the dance of *Moros y cristianos* performed in modern Mexico is about an episode in Spanish history. In fact, the dances might also have been commemorative reenactments, like the Catholic Mass's restaging of Jesus's Last Supper, where the original event provided an essential kernel of meaning for viewers.[25] Unfortunately, in the case of the indigenous dances, while we have an idea of when, why, who, and where, we have little idea of *what* was being danced, if anything. If they were commemorative, did they reenact a military victory or defeat, as the ethnic names applied to them suggest? Or did they reenact sacred events, serving to bring the past into the present? Or did they have no representational quality at all, serving instead like incense or musical ornament to mark the sacrality or importance of another event?

If we return to the descriptions in the ethnohistorical sources discussed above, we can see two qualities ascribed to the pre-Hispanic dance context that suggest both function and representation. Dances were used to display the power of the Mexica ruler before his peers in other Nahua polities, and probably used by other Nahua polities in the same way. The naming of dances after military orders, their connection to military defeats, suggests that dances had a specifically commemorative role. And while we may never be able to recover all the particular meanings that they once carried for an interpretive community made of pre-Hispanic indigenous viewers and performers, one extraordinary native manuscript, the Codex Tlatelolco, reveals that many pre-Hispanic meanings were carried over into the colonial period.

Mitotes after the Spanish Conquest

Despite the connections ceremonial dances had with both Mexica militarism and the rituals that transformed a Mexica princeling into a semidivine ruler, they continued to be performed after the Spanish Conquest. Their enduring presence in Mexico City, as Tenochtitlan was renamed after the Conquest, is worth examining, given that Mexico City became the seat of the viceregal court after the appointment of Antonio de Mendoza in 1535, and thus the stage for increasingly elaborate Habsburg festival culture. Key agents in the acceptance of the dances were the Franciscans, who were first in charge of evangelizing Mexico City's large indigenous population. From the time of their arrival in 1524, they sought benign forms of indigenous ritual to use as vehicles in the introduction of orthodox Catholic practices. And while they moved to ban rituals like the sacrifices of animals and humans, they welcomed dances to the festive sphere, since in and of themselves dances were not seen to have any fixed idolatrous associations, nor was the recondite iconography of their feathered accouterments problematic. Eager to capitalize on the rich ceremonial life of their native charges, the Franciscans quickly created sanitized versions of once-pagan songs for Christian ritual use, but left the form and some of the accouterments of their accompanying dances unchanged.[26] Most Franciscans held that such performances could quickly drop their earlier idolatrous meanings once they were carried out in the sacralized space of the church patios, their words translated into ones praising God, the Virgin, and the saints, rather than, say, Huitzilopochtli.[27]

While Franciscan chroniclers often describe with great pride the huge numbers of indigenous neophytes who came together in massive dances in newly built monasteries in Mexico City, their words reveal the continuities between the pre-Hispanic and the early colonial periods in the music and the movement of the dances, the times when they were performed, and dancers' accouterments, particularly feather fans and bouquets. Writing in the late sixteenth century, Mendieta praised the order and the beauty of the dances, which could involve thousands of people. He tells us how the ordered mass moved in time to the beat of two drums, the *huehuetl* and the *teponaztli*. Although the steps that he describes are simple ones, he still noted that dancing was a prized skill.[28] The Franciscan Motolinia reveals the indigenous tendency to perform the dances at night, as they had been performed in the *cuicacalli*: "The songs are graceful and harmonious. In many places the dancing and singing begin at midnight and numerous lights illumine the patios."[29] Mendieta witnessed that

> at times they brought to the dance plaza cones of roses and of other flowers, or bouquets to carry in their hands, and garlands that they put on their heads, in addition to the costumes that they used in the dance, rich cloaks and feather costumes, and others carried in their hands small beautiful feathers instead of bouquets.[30]

And the Florentine Codex reveals that the demand for objects made out of feathers, among them paraphernalia to be used in dances, was still keeping the featherworkers busy as late as the 1570s, when the manuscript was composed. The Spanish text of the manuscript incidentally reveals the continued presence of featherworkers in Mexico City as it declines to include a description of contemporary featherwork to match the prolix Nahuatl description, declaring, "whoever wants to see and learn the names [of the tools used by featherworkers], will be able to learn and see with his own eyes the featherworkers themselves." As we shall see, once they were sanctioned by Franciscans in charge of indigenous evangelization in Mexico City, indigenous dances and their distinctive paraphernalia migrated into the festival culture developing around the city's viceregal court, in which both indigenes and Spaniards participated.

Mitotes in a Sixteenth-Century Political Context

In "sanitizing" native dances for religious use, the Franciscans seem to have been mostly concerned with recasting the temporal and spatial elements and some of the utterances. They moved dances out of the *cuicacalli* and the *coatepantli*-defined plaza and into the church *atrio*; they called for them to be performed on major feasts of the Catholic Church; they set new words in praise of saints and the Virgin to the traditional metered rhythms, and soon dances became a fundamental feature of Catholic celebrations in Mexico City and across New Spain. At the beginning of the seventeenth century, the chronicler Domingo Francisco de San Antón Muñón Chimalpahin Cuauhtlehuanitzin wrote about the *maceuhque* (dancers) performing at Corpus Christi, an important occasion for indigenous-inflected celebrations.[31] Though there is not much comment from earlier sources, by his era indigenous dances were firmly established as part of celebrations in the political sphere, and he reports that people all around came into Mexico City—"*macehuaco mitotico*" (there they danced, and danced)—for Viceroy Juan de Mendoza y Luna in 1604.[32]

This passage into the political sphere offers us another opportunity to look at the iconography of the dance and parse its attendant meanings, given an extraordinary image that appears in the Tlatelolco Codex, produced sometime around 1560 (fig. 7). It represents one of the most important of all royal ceremonies (and, given the longevity of Charles V and Philip II, the two Habsburg rulers of New Spain in the sixteenth century, one of the rarest): the *jura*. This oath of allegiance was taken by all royal officials upon the accession of a new monarch, and in New Spain, its celebration included a *mitote*. News of the ascent of Philip II reached Mexico in 1557, and the official *jura* was held in Mexico City on June 6 of that year. It was celebrated with exceptional pomp, and in Mexico City, all sectors of the city, including its indigenous residents and their leaders, participated. Their presence is known to us not only because alphabetic texts of the period discuss it, but also because the Tlatelolco Codex, created in the northern part of Mexico City, an area that had been an independent polity before being defeated by and absorbed into Tenochtitlan in 1473, devoted an extensive visual description to the event.[33]

The codex is an annals style history, offering a timeline of events beginning in 1542 and ending in 1560. Vertical red lines divide the codex year by year; the year that concerns us, 1557, is elaborately rendered, and while it forms part of a longer strip, its artist, or artists, composed this section as a single integral unit. It shows a collection of events arranged into four horizontal registers. At top left, in the uppermost register, is the figure of don Cristóbal de Guzmán Cecetzin (Cecepatic; r. 1557–1562). He was a descendant of the Mexica ruling family of Tenochtitlan, and he had been chosen to be the indigenous governor of Mexico City in 1557. Below his figure the toponym of Tenochtitlan appears as a small cactus growing from a rock; behind his head, his name is rendered hieroglyphically. While this image may pertain to his seating as governor, the center of the page is devoted to the events of the *jura* for Philip II, which happened in June. Here, in the second, third, and fourth registers, we see indigenous and royal governments brought together to take the oath to the newly anointed king.

The second register of this page is dominated by a raised platform, called a *cadalso*, measuring about ten meters long and five wide, that was erected for the occasion on the Plaza Mayor outside the cathedral's west door and opposite the royal palace, which sat to the west of the plaza at that time (it would move to the east in 1562 to the space it still occupies today). This was constructed by indigenous laborers who brought the adobe bricks.[34] On it, the highest ranking Spanish officials of the royal government and the Catholic Church are seated, including don Luis de Velasco, the viceroy (center left), and Archbishop Alonso de Montúfar, dressed in his red cape and archbishop's miter (center right). The book in his hands, the open Gospel, will be the site of the most important moment of this ritual. Upon it, those gathered will swear an oath of allegiance to the new king, whose presence is signaled by the banner, an eagle bearing his coat of arms, held aloft by an unnamed standard bearer standing at left.[35] To the immediate left of the banner is don Alonso de Zorita, then president of the Audiencia or royal court, and at the far right end of the *cadalso* is Diego López de Montealegre, another royal judge and member of the Audiencia, seated facing left. Taken as a whole, this image is clearly a shorthand and highly edited version of what actually happened on the Plaza Mayor in 1557. A textual account of the same event written by a Spanish scribe and entered in the official notes of the Mexico City council depicts the event somewhat differently, recording throngs of crowds on the plaza as witnesses. In addition, it tells us of participation of the city's Spanish *cabildo*, or town council, whose members also took the oath. In contrast, the indigenous painter of the Tlatelolco Codex omits this local Spanish city government, with which the indigenous community in the city and its governors were frequently at odds.

But most notable is the bottom half of the page (registers three and four), which is dominated by

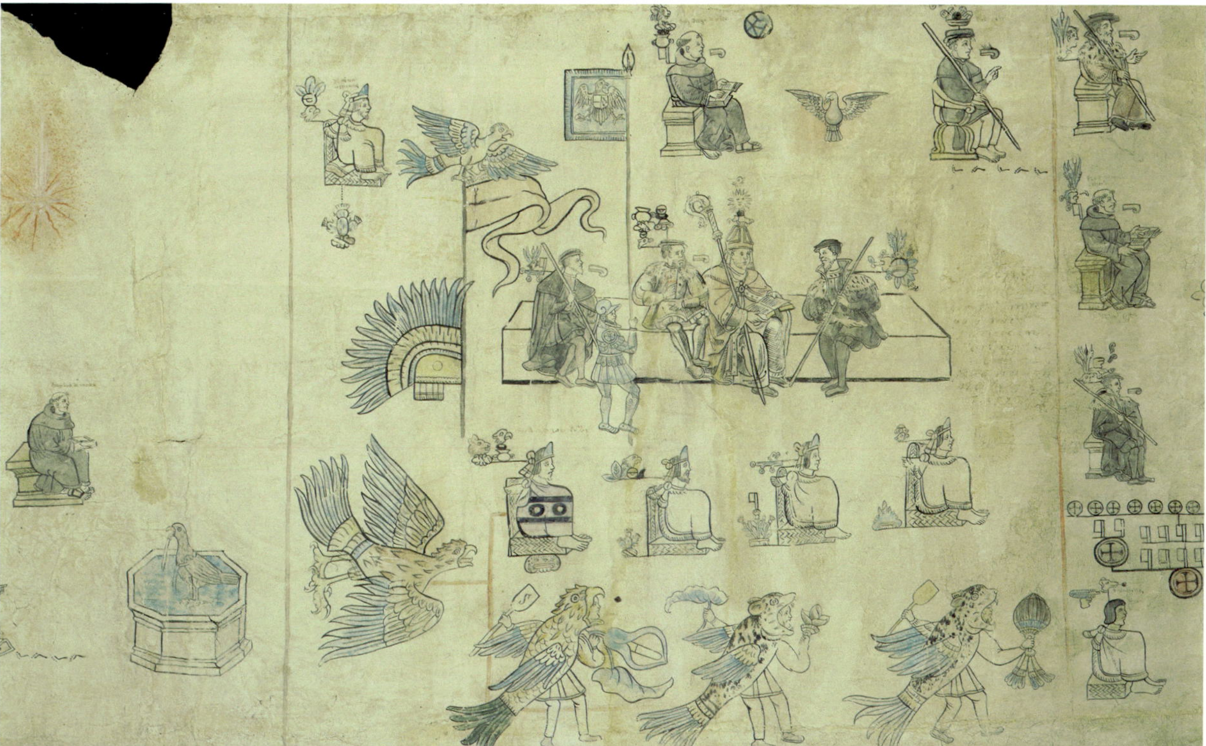

Fig. 7. Tlatelolco Codex, part 8. Mexico, c. 1560. Ink and pigment on paper. Biblioteca Nacional de Antropología e Historia, Mexico City. CONACULTA-INAH-MEX. Reproduction authorized by the Instituto Nacional de Antropología e Historia.

a depiction of a joyous indigenous celebration of the *jura* (fig. 8). The third register shows a gathering of indigenous lords whose cities had once been leaders in the Aztec empire, their forebears ruling the land in the pre-Hispanic period. Joining them is the ruler of Tlatelolco, whose independence from Tenochtitlan had been reestablished, likely by Viceroy Mendoza; this lord had been seated as ruler in 1549.[36] These four leaders offer an indigenous counterpart to the royal government seated above. The third register begins on the left with the ruler of Tlatelolco, don Diego de Mendoza Imauhyantzin; next to him to the right is the ruler of Tenochtitlan, don Cristóbal de Guzmán Cecetzin (again); then follows the ruler of Tlacopan (bastardized as Tacuba today), don Antonio Cortés Totoquihuaztli; and finally, at the far right is the ruler of Texcoco, don Hernando de Pimentel.[37] Glyphs that render their names, or parts of their names, are attached to their heads. And as in other manuscripts, they are seated on the traditional seat of authority, the *tepotzoicpalli*, with the glyphic toponyms of their polities connected to the bases of their seats. The artist renders these indigenous lords conservatively, in static profile, in contrast to the dynamic and unsettled postures of the figures seated above, a visual choice made in other native manuscripts of the period.

Although we know that the celebration of the *jura* took place on the Plaza Mayor, and standard protocol would have given preeminence to the indigenous leader of Tenochtitlan, don Cristóbal de Guzmán Cecetzin, this manuscript from rival Tlatelolco shows the scene differently. Don Diego de Mendoza, the ruler of that polity, is shown in a position of greatest prominence: his *tepotzoicpalli* is slightly larger than those of this three companions, and he wears a *tilmatli* (cloak) that carries a band of bold black ring shapes framed by two black bands, the same pattern that indigenous buildings of authority carried on their façades. Since don Diego was the most likely patron of this manuscript, his status here may have been enhanced at his request, a visual record of the jockeying for power that Valley elites engaged in both before and after the Conquest.

In this image on the page of the Codex Tlatelolco we can read the political subjugation of indigenous lords to their new Spanish masters seated above. But of course, the event was about *everyone's* subjugation to the newly anointed king. Notwithstanding, the fourth register at the bottom of the page makes it clear that this is a Nahua-inflected celebration, translated into indigenous terms, just as the oath of loyalty to the Spanish king that these seated lords took was translated into Nahuatl. Here we find a rare visual record of the *netotiliztli/macehualiztli* being performed (fig. 8). Just as in the pre-Hispanic period (recall Durán's description of the four days of dances that accompanied the investitures of rulers), indigenous dance marked the ruler investiture of the *jura*. Not only did the performance allow a display of political relationships and hierarchies, but it marked a politically liminal period; dances were also performed during the *entrada* of the viceroy.[38]

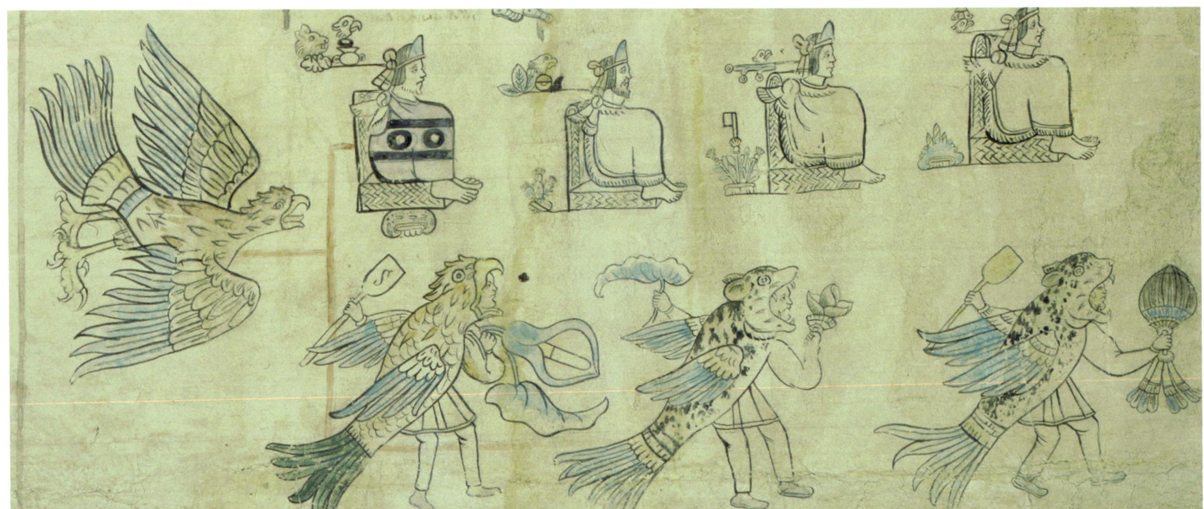

Fig. 8. Detail of fig. 7.

As presented in this scene, the *netotiliztli/macehualiztli* registers a number of changes that may be colonial-era introductions. To begin, it is not the lords themselves who are shown dancing, but unnamed young men below. And the performance includes not just them but also an enormous eagle. Indeed, this is no ordinary eagle. Its wing and tail feathers are blue-green, the same color as the feathers above in what appears to be a quetzal feather headdress or a *quetzalpatzactli*, a quetzal feather back device, repurposed as a standard, attached to the pole holding the pennant that flies above the scene.[39] The body of this enormous "eagle" is red, the upper part of his wings and tail yellow. What we are witnessing seems to be not any real bird, but an elaborate bird costume. It is very similar to the bird costume worn by the dancing figure on the left of the fourth register, an indigenous man wearing a Spanish-style tunic over pants as well as closed shoes, whose face appears out of the beak of the costume. In front of him are two other costumed figures, both dressed as winged ocelots. All three carry objects in their outstretched hands: the outermost figures carry paddle-shaped objects, one of which is marked with an "S," while the bird figure also carries an oversized blossom and leaf of the *huacalxochitl* flower, and the center figure just its leaf. Moreover, the figure on the right carries an ovate feather fan, albeit made with gray feathers, not pink ones. Thus in this scene we can recognize the conventional paraphernalia of sacred dances, particularly the objects carried by warriors. The Florentine Codex lists some of the elements of dance costumes still being made in the 1570s, the decade after this manuscript was painted, particularly the kinds of feathered ornaments worn on the body or carried in the hand:

> Insignia borne on the back are made, with which there may be dancing; and all the dance array, gear, and ornaments: the quetzal feathers, head ornaments, bracelets for the upper arm with precious feathers, gold bands for the upper arm; fans—fans of heron, of red spoonbill, of troupial, of crested guan, of quetzal feathers; and hand banners, quetzal feather hand banners with troupial feathers in alternating bands, heron feather banners, gold banners tufted with quetzal feathers at the tips.[40]

Not mentioned in the Florentine Codex list are full-body costumes made out of feathers like those we see in the Tlatelolco Codex; indeed the bird and ocelot costumes shown here on the bodies of the three dancers are unprecedented additions to the dances: the Florentine Codex illustrations show us pre-Hispanic dancers in loincloths and conventional cloaks (*tilmatli*) or short stoles, not animal costumes. And the colonial observers cited above mention cloaks, but not full-body costumes. Where could these extraordinary costumes have originated? And what did they signify when worn here?

Heritage Costumes

If we turn to the Codex Mendoza, a manuscript made in the 1540s to document pre-Hispanic tribute paid to the Mexica in Tenochtitlan, we can find the probable source of the ocelot costumes (fig. 9). War costumes appear in the center of folio page 20r, complete with helmet-masks; at the bottom right, one of them is an ocelot costume, its black spots set against a background of yellow. Such yellow ocelot suits appear on other pages as well (fols. 21v, 23v, and 31r), as well as white ones (fol. 25r) and blue ones (fols. 29r, 37r, 51r) and red ones (fol. 54r). They, and everything else on this page, were items of tribute demanded by the Triple Alliance of conquered regions, to be delivered three times a year. This page documents the tribute to be delivered by the province of Petlacalco, whose name glyph appears at the upper left of the page. Here, we see it was responsible for delivering one of these precious suits three times a year, along with three suits of other patterns, suits that were made not from ocelot skin, but from *feathers*, carefully sewn into cotton backing, rachis by rachis, thousands of feathers, crafted to resemble the spotted pelt. These elaborate, extraordinary suits were destined to be given to the highest ranking of the Mexica military elite, as reward and public sign of their prowess in battle. They were also to be worn by these elite Mexica warriors into the next round of conquest battles, which in turn would bring more territory and more such tribute to Tenochtitlan; thus they were intimately associated with the relentless cycle of Mexica military expansion.[41]

While the Florentine Codex of c. 1570 tells us

that featherworkers were kept busy making dance costumes, in its inventory of items being produced in the later sixteenth century it does not mention anything like the feather ocelot suit pictured in the Codex Tlatelolco. Instead, these were likely heritage costumes, and proof positive that the native lords in the city safeguarded old, if not heritage costumes, comes from a 1564 lawsuit; when accused of excesses in their ceremonies, the indigenous lords of Tenochtitlan, including the successor to don Cristóbal de Guzmán Cecetzin, who is pictured in the Tlatelolco Codex, attested that they had "kept some feather items in their community [that is, the palace of the indigenous government] for their enjoyment and public festivals, and have had them for more than 25 years."[42] We also know that feathered costumes were prized by indigenous elites in the colonial period and were among the items that were designated in wills, objects passed down from generation to generation; in her research on indigenous costume, Justyna Olka has identified a number of feather garments of different types named in wills.[43] This evidence makes it quite likely that these dancers of the c. 1560 Tlatelolco Codex wear heritage costumes, and the iconography of the Codex Mendoza attests that they were military ones.

However, the feathered garments worn by the Tlatelolco dancers are somewhat distinct from the ocelot suits pictured in the Codex Mendoza. The dance costumes are not full body suits, but are more like hooded (or headed) capes, draped over the shoulders. The armholes with sleeves that appear in the Mendoza are not visible here. It's worth recalling that these pre-Hispanic feather suits were among the few seamed garments created by the pre-Hispanic Nahua; in general, indigenous clothing was made of uncut cloth, because cutting and seaming fabric weakens its overall struture.[44] The arm seams would have been one of the most vulnerable parts of such a seamed garment, especially when used for vigorous arm movements in warfare. And by the 1560s, when the Codex Tlatelolco dancers put them on, the sleeves would have worn out. Feathers were expensive, and perfectly matching ones may have been hard to come by, given the competition for feathers that new forms of Spanish and ecclesiastical patronage triggered, or they may have been unavailable, given shifts in long-distance trading patterns effected by the Conquest. To replace the sleeves and cover the empty armholes, these dance costumes in the Codex Tlatelolco have feather "wings" attached to that part of the garment. Sewing together the leg panels—another seamed and vulnerable part of the garment—would have resulted in the fish-like tails that the Codex's artist represents here.

Because feathered ocelot costumes came from the Mexica past—indeed, they may have been either created for or garnered by specific military campaigns—the inclusion of them transforms this celebratory dance into a commemorative event reenacting Mexica militarism. In the Florentine Codex, written in the decade after the Tlatelolco Codex was completed, its writers tell us that certain feathers were first made available because of the conquests of Ahuitzotl (r. 1486–1502), thereby establishing these feathers as a signifier of this specific campaign of discovery and conquest.[45] The pairing of these dance costumes with the colored eagle costume is also highly significant in that eagle (*quauhtli*) and ocelot (*ocelotl*) knights were the two most elite castes of pre-Hispanic warriors, appearing on the *huehuetl* discussed above; the Florentine Codex tells of *in quauhtenamitl, in ocelotenamitl* being the army's avant garde.[46] The near-life-size pre-Hispanic ceramic sculptures found at the Casa de las Aguilas adjacent to the Templo Mayor are warriors in eagle costumes, the raptor's great beak overshadowing the human visage, as in the leftmost dancer in the Codex Tlatelolco. And the abundant ocelot costumes in the Codex Mendoza show us specific parallels to the outfits worn by these dancing performers.

Would indigenous audiences have understood the dance costumes used in the *jura* as battle gear of elite warriors; that is, would the commemorative role that I have ascribed to the costumes have obtained in the late sixteenth century? We simply do not have enough evidence to establish how this particular community interpreted the costume, but in early scenes of the Codex Tlatelolco, indigenous rulers of the 1540s are shown wearing feathered gear as they head off to battle; another indigenous manuscript painted in the 1560s, the Codex Osuna, shows indigenous soldiers setting off to conquer "la Florida," and they seem to be wearing feather skirts.[47] Thus, it

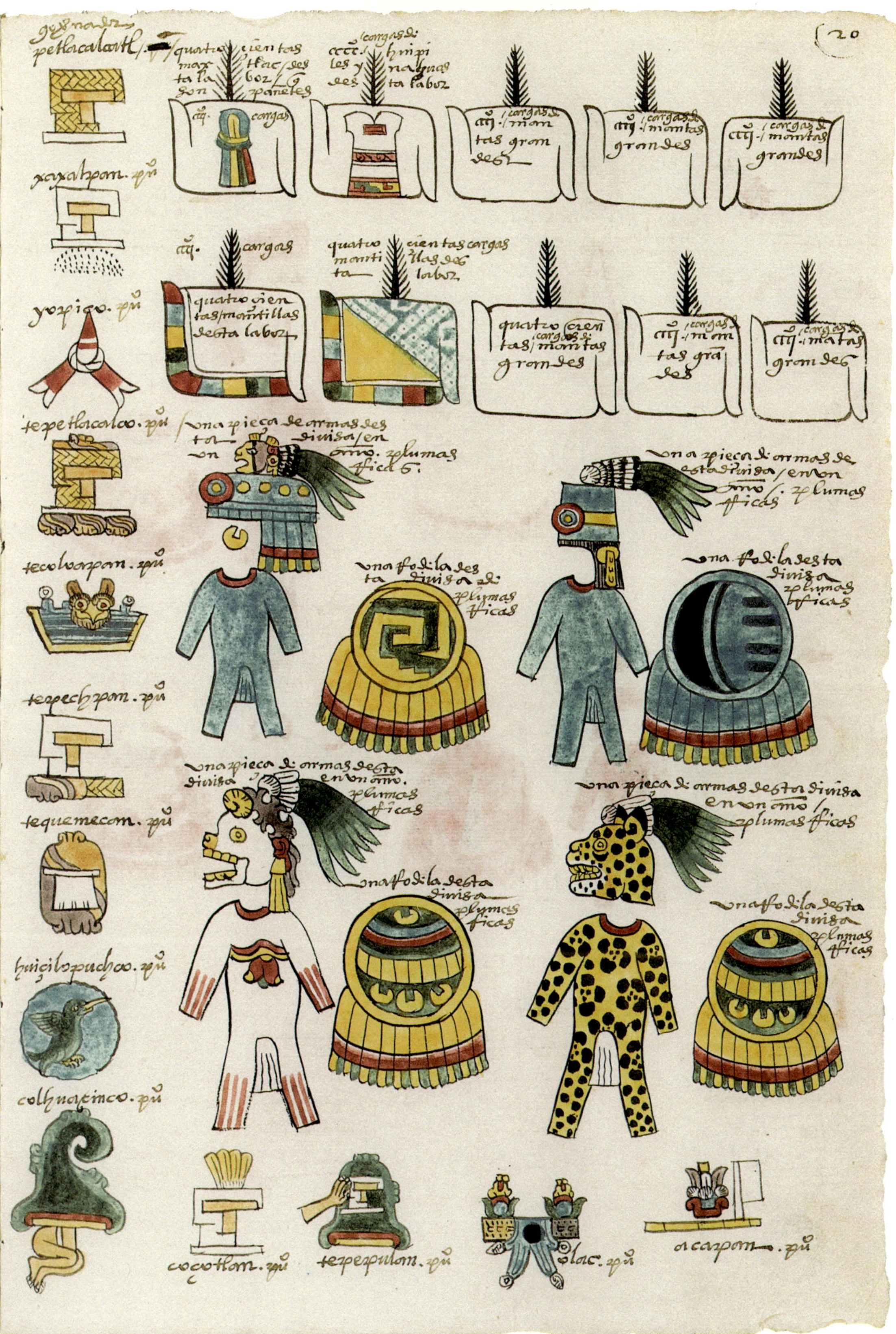

Fig. 9. Codex Mendoza, fol. 20r, tribute from Petlacalco. Mexico, c. 1542. Ink and pigment on paper. The Bodleian Libraries, The University of Oxford, MS. Arch. Selden A. 1.

is a clear possibility that when indigenous viewers in Mexico City saw dancers of the *netotiliztli/macehualiztli* at the *jura* of Philip II, they understood in these feathered heritage costumes a very particular commemorative purpose of marking indigenous military prowess, both past and present. Such an understanding is quite different from the one Spanish and Creole viewers would bring to similar "scenes in which Indians perform ritualized expressions of loyalty to the crown" in the art of the seventeenth century, which, as Michael Schreffler has argued, "emphasiz[ed] the idea that Spain's victory in Middle America was so complete that conquered peoples voluntarily and ritually swore their obedience to their new sovereign."

The importance of these costumes to the native elite is underscored by the red line that runs from the large image of the colored eagle, connecting it to the Tlatelolco ruler, don Diego de Mendoza, and the first two dancers. The rarity of the costumes, as well as the skill of the dancers, made the *netotiliztli/macehualiztli* special events, and this symbolic capital was marshaled by indigenous lords within the Valley, who were the patrons of the dances as well as owners of dance costumes. Don Diego de Mendoza Imauhyantzin, pictured here, was a ruler of somewhat dubious legitimacy, and this picture, as well as many others created by his family into the seventeenth century, served to underscore his authority.[48] The red line that connects him to the colorful eagle costume shows him in the position of patron of the dances, and possibly also as the supplier of these valuable heritage costumes.

This scene in the Codex Tlatelolco, then, offers us valuable insight into the hybrid performance culture of Mexico City. On the surface, it renders the *jura* celebration with the pairing of two visually equivalent orders: above on the second register, Habsburg officials are seated on the raised platform, as they swear on the open book held by the archbishop, with turquoise speech scrolls marking the oaths emerging from their mouths; below on the third register, the indigenous governors are seated on their individual *tepotzoicpalli*, but they are not shown taking the translated oath in Nahuatl, because no speech scrolls emerge from their mouths. Instead, they are linked to the performers of the ceremonial dances that appear below in the fourth register. But here the conceptual alignment between the Spanish celebration and the indigenous one is pulled off axis by the associations of the dance. The dances and the costumes used in them were ways of performing indigenous rulership itself—on this particular occasion, putting it on display for the gathered crowds in the Plaza Mayor of Mexico City, the great majority of whom, it should be noted, were the city's indigenous residents. The sonorous dances were meant to enchant the crowd; the steady and insistent beat of the drums carried across the city on the strong air currents of the early rainy season. Thus, while Spanish observers might have seen in the dances performed at the Habsburg *jura* a sign of general indigenous joyousness, the iconography of these particular dances also underscored the near-magical potency of indigenous rulers and their historical claims to military prowess.

Mitotes and *concheros*

If the seventeenth-century *biombo* that launched this inquiry has led us back in time to the fifteenth- and sixteenth-century origins of the dances, it also points forward, to the present (fig. 1). Today, two of the spectacles it displays—dancers and *voladores*—will be familiar to anyone visiting Mexico City's main tourist attractions, where they have come to figure as signs of that city's exotic "Indianness," revealing modern Mexico's enduring connection to its Aztec or pre-Hispanic past. *Voladores* have a permanent metal pole set up steps away from the entrance to the Museo Nacional de Antropología, which features the country's greatest collection of pre-Hispanic artworks and is one of the highlights of the city for tourists. These performers are costumed as Totonacs, an ethnic group from the northeast of Mexico, and can be regularly seen spinning down from the sky to delight museum visitors, particularly foreign ones. Only three kilometers away is Mexico City's Zócalo, as the Plaza Mayor is now known, one of the largest urban plazas in the world and another must-see for Mexican visitor and foreign tourist alike. The area in front of the Museo del Templo Mayor, a museum showcasing Aztec art from the century before the Conquest (c. 1450–1520), is frequently occupied by throngs of dancers dressed in fanciful

"Aztec" garb. While women are often clothed in long dresses, the bare-chested men are the most riveting spectacle, often sporting fantastical feather headdresses, short kilt-like skirts of leather or printed animal-skin fabric, beaded belts, breastplates, and armbands, along with elaborate leg rattles (fig. 10). These rattles are made from shells and have given the dancers their contemporary name: *concheros*, from the Spanish *concha*, or shell. When the *concheros* congregate, and they may number anywhere from a dozen to a thousand, they fill the area around them with the relentless beat of their skin-covered drums and join together in a simple dance of shuffling steps, moving in lines and circles.

Although the history of *concheros* has its roots earlier in the twentieth century, these contemporary spectacles are a relatively recent phenomenon in the Zócalo, where they have gained force in the last three decades. *Concheros* today are part New Age religionists, part tourist spectacle. Unlike the *voladores*, who perform almost exclusively for tourists, who marvel at their physical daring, the *concheros* have a wider intellectual and spiritual appeal. Their membership comprises Mexicans who are on "a conscious search for a social identity grounded in a largely invented Mexica past";[49] a recent celebration in 2008 of the anniversary of the founding of Tenochtitlan brought thousands together on the Zócalo, some seasoned dancers and others eager novices drawn in by the spectacle. Their links to the Aztec past are recently forged ones, as attested by the banners they carry, which bear images of Aztec divinities known from facsimiles of pre-Hispanic sacred manuscripts published in the twentieth century. And at the edges of the dance, the modern-day shamans who often accompany the *concheros* offer spiritual cleansings with incense and incantations, for a fee. As they do so, crowds of surrounding tourists drawn to the nearby Museo del Templo Mayor and adjacent Catedral Metropolitana snap pictures of the spectacle, and of themselves and the dancers. Uploaded to Flickr or Picasa, or put into a digital album at home, these pictures form both public and private souvenirs of an exotic, tropical journey.

While it would be easy to dismiss the contemporary phenomenon of the *concheros* as merely an invented tradition handed down from a fabricated past, or a simple ploy to feed touristic appetites for an exotic "Indian Mexico," I think they are helpful in understanding earlier spectacles of dancing Indians, like the one we have seen in the late seventeenth-century *biombo* and in the earlier Tlatelolco Codex (figs. 1, 7, and 8).[50] Like the modern *concheros*, who are widely known because the colorful spectacle they perform has been captured by local and international tourists and carried outward in albums or on the Internet, so too were our seventeenth-century dancers. Since many *biombos* are known from European collections, we understand them as having been souvenirs from a New World voyage or tour of duty, brought back from Mexico City by viceregal elites. Sofia Sanabrais finds an early record of such a *biombo* in an inventory of the goods of Luis de Velasco II, who served as viceroy of New Spain; upon his death in Spain his estate included *biombos*, including one "from the Indies."[51] Likewise, Gustavo Curiel's investigation into inventories

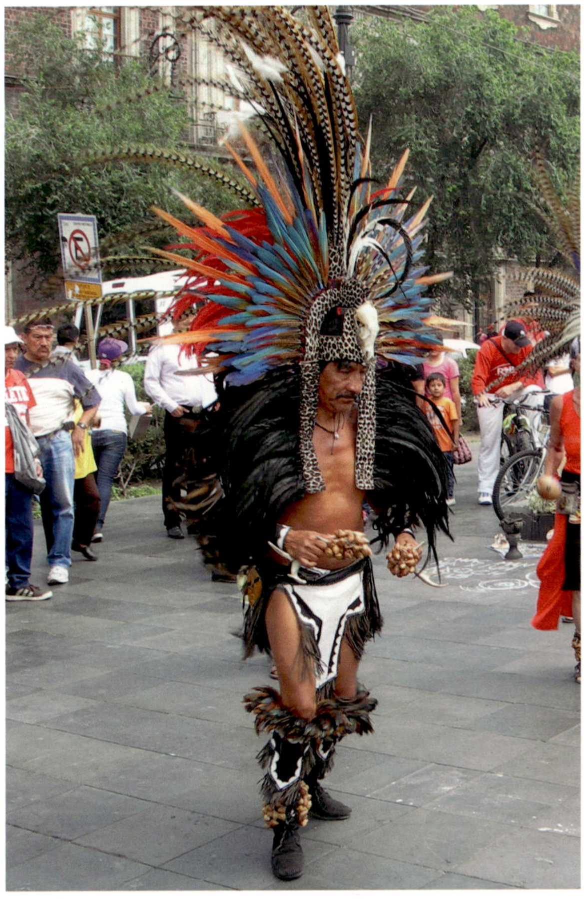

Fig. 10. *Conchero* dancer on Mexico City's Zócalo. Mexico, 2013. Photo: Byron Hamann.

has revealed how *biombos* were prized among high elites in New Spain and Spain.[52] Given that many of them include imagery specific to Mexico City's history or contemporary culture, we can easily imagine them proudly displayed in salons from Madrid to Seville as proof of an American encounter. In this context, their imagery—particularly *voladores* and dancing figures costumed as Indians—is a token of the strangeness of these transatlantic American cities under Habsburg rule, as well as a souvenir of a journey made possible by the extension of Habsburg power across the globe.

Some of this near-touristic detachment is encouraged by the format of this *biombo* (fig. 1). When we view it, our visual position is that of an omniscient spectator. While figures in the lower left seem, like us, to be nonparticipant observers of the scene, thus giving us an imaginative foothold into the pictorial space, our viewpoint is not coincident with theirs. Instead, we float somewhat above the scene, so that we see all the figures arranged across the pictorial field; such viewpoints, as Michael Schreffler has written in dealing with another set of *biombos*, "served a ... symbolic function, representing the city as subject to the [Habsburg] King's gaze and control."[53]

These implied audiences, and the detached role of viewer, in turn, help us read the particular imagery of this *biombo* in its seventeenth-century context. At the time the *biombo* was painted, the scenes collated on its space—the wedding, the *voladores*, the *mitote*—were understood by Spanish and Creole viewers as signs of successful Indian acculturation, despite their somewhat exotic appearance. These painted Indians had abandoned pre-Hispanic polygamy and embraced Catholic-sanctioned marriages; their pagan festivals had taken on new meaning, particularly the *mitote*, which was used to celebrate Corpus Christi and their successful evangelization.[54]

Contemporary dances also give us insight into the indigenous dances in their earlier sixteenth-century context by offering something of the urban, public experience of the dances themselves, an experience that the static painted image or the manuscript page largely denies us. Today, the *concheros* perform in the same spaces as did sixteenth-century indigenous dancers, where they are a riveting but also disruptive presence in the center of the modern city. Their ebullient costume, particularly the male undress, sets them off from other urban Mexicans who observe them, because conventional urban dress in Mexico, particularly male dress, is quite conservative. Also setting them off is the *concheros'* fixedness in the urban square; all around them, people move rapidly from one place to another, their attention on their destinations, while the *concheros* are relatively static, occupying one part of a plaza, with their attention turned inward on themselves and each other, on the repetitive and synchronized movements of circular dances. Most remarkable is their extended and largely invisible presence in the urban square: the scent of sage incense used in the curing rituals permeates the surrounding air; the persistent beating of skin-covered drums announces their presence for blocks around them. Despite their rather tenuous historical connections to the sixteenth-century native dances of Mexico City, the presence of today's *concheros* allows us imaginative purchase onto the past phenomenon, as a lived experience within the urban sphere.

While sixteenth-century Spanish and Creole viewers may have seen indigenous dancers with their feather costumes as an exotic presence in the public square, one successfully corralled to celebrate Habsburg kings, to indigenous viewers they were well-known markers of important political events, particularly liminal states and transitions. The loud beating of drums that accompanied them, as well as songs set to these traditional rhythms, carried the presence of the dancers well beyond the main plaza into the streets of the surrounding city, more than the traditional brass instruments sponsored by Spanish citizens. The feather costumes the dancers wore—again, an exotic spectacle to Spanish and Creole viewers—were likely well known by the city's indigenous players to be expensive heirloom garb and a vestige of triumphant Mexica militarism. Thus, in considering the multifaceted character of festivals in Spanish America, as this volume does, it is important to remember the contributions that the New World's indigenous peoples made to those distinct cultures, and how much participation by indigenous elites inflected and sustained Habsburg festival culture in the region known as the Indies.

Notes

[1] The author thanks the Mayer Center at the Denver Art Museum for sponsoring the conference where this paper was first presented, and Julie Wilson and especially Donna Pierce for spearheading the publication. I am also indebted to Lauren Toole, whose work on dance and performance in an undergraduate tutorial in the spring of 2011 helped me in thinking about *mitotes*.

[2] My thanks to Eric Bianchi for helping in instrument identification.

[3] For a foundational work on Habsburg ceremonial culture in Mexico City, see Linda Ann Curcio-Nagy, *The Great Festivals of Colonial Mexico City: Performing Power and Identity* (Albuquerque: University of New Mexico Press, 2004).

[4] R. Joe Campbell, *Florentine Codex Vocabulary* (1997), available at http://www2.potsdam.edu/schwaljf/Nahuatl/florent.txt; Frances Karttunen, *An Analytical Dictionary of Nahuatl* (Austin: University of Texas Press, 1983), allows for *i'totiliztli* "a dance," but the attested forms in both Molina and Sahagún are another nominative form, *mototiliztli*. See Alonso de Molina, *Vocabulario en lengua castillana y mexicana y mexicana y castellana* (Mexico City: Editorial Porrúa, 1977) and Campbell, *Florentine Codex Vocabulary.*

[5] Luis Reyes García, ed. and trans., *¿Cómo te confundes? ¿Acaso no somos conquistados? Anales de Juan Bautista* (Mexico City: Biblioteca Lorenzo Boturini, Insigne y Nacional Basílica de Guadalupe, Centro de Investigaciones y Estudios Superiores en Antropología Social, 2001), 196–197. Karttunen, *An Analytical Dictionary,* 232, points out that the verb *tequia* is often associated with baptism.

[6] Bernardino de Sahagún, *Florentine Codex: General History of the Things of New Spain,* 12 vols., trans. Arthur J. O. Anderson and Charles E. Dibble (Santa Fe: School of American Research and University of Utah, 1950–1963), bk. 8, ch. 14, par. 7, 25–26. The Spanish version is Bernardino de Sahagún, *Historia General de las Cosas de Nueva España,* 2nd ed., 2 vols., ed. Alfredo López Austin and Josefina García Quintana (Mexico City: Consejo General para la Cultura y las Artes y Editorial Patria, 1989), 2:521.

[7] Diego Durán, *The History of the Indies of New Spain,* trans. and ed. Doris Heyden (Norman: University of Oklahoma Press, 1993), 166, 170, and 473, tells us of military captives dancing.

[8] "*Una de las cosas principales que en toda esta tierra habia, eran los cantos y bailes, así para solemnizar las fiestas de sus demonio que por dioses honraban.*" Gerónimo de Mendieta, *Historia eclesiástica indiana,* 2nd ed., ed. Joaquín García Icazbalceta (Mexico City: Editorial Porrúa, 1993), bk. 2, ch. 31, 140.

[9] Karttunen, *An Analytical Dictionary,* 130, notes that the connection is ambiguous because it is not known whether *macehua*, "to dance," has an internal glottal stop, nor are the vowel lengths clear.

[10] Sahagún, *Historia General de las Cosas de Nueva España,* 1:53; Sahagún, *Florentine Codex,* bk. 1, ch. 16.

[11] Sahagún, *Florentine Codex,* bk. 8, ch. 14, par. 7; Sahagún, *Historia General de las Cosas de Nueva España,* 2:521. On music, see Miguel León Portilla, "La música en el universo de la cultura náhuatl," *Estudios de cultura náhuatl* 38 (January 2007): 129–163.

[12] Dances are depicted in Sahagún, *Florentine Codex,* bk. 4, ch. 7, in a description of the festivities on the feast day 1 Flower; the second and third times in bk. 8, ch. 14, par. 4 and bk. 8, ch. 17, where they accompany description of training in the *cuicacalli* and *telpochcalli*; and a fourth, bk. 9, ch. 8, devoted to the *pochteca* celebrations. It is not the specific terms *netotiliztli* and *macehualiztli* that create the couplet, but other variations from their root words.

[13] Sahagún, *Florentine Codex,* bk. 8, ch. 14, par. 4.

[14] Durán, *The History of the Indies,* 306–307.

[15] Durán, *The History of the Indies,* 321–322 and 405–406.

[16] Richard Townsend, "Coronation at Tenochtitlan," in *The Aztec Templo Mayor,* ed. Elizabeth Hill Boone (Washington, DC: Dumbarton Oaks, 1987), 371– 409. Some of the archeological work carried out has been summarized in María Teresa García García, "El Señorío de Acolhuacan," *Arqueología mexicana* 10, no. 58 (November–December 2002): 46–51, and Saul Alcántara Onofre, "El jardín de Nezahualcóyotl en el cerro de Tetzcotzinco," *Arqueología mexicana* 10, no. 58 (November–December 2002): 52–53.

[17] Karttunen, *An Analytical Dictionary,* 15, gives *āyacachtli* as "rattle."

[18] Donald McVicker, "Notched Human Bones from Mesoamerica," *Mesoamerican Voices* 2 (2005), 1–31.

[19] The Malinalco *huehuetl* is currently in the Museo de Arqueología e Historia del Estado de México, in Tenango del Valle; the *atl-tlachinolli* symbols are also featured in a *teponaztli* now at the American Museum of Natural History in New York.

[20] Sahagún, *Florentine Codex,* bk. 9, ch. 20, 91. "They made that which was the dance array of Moctezuma, in which a dance was danced. When a feast day came, they displayed for him, they made attractive to him, whatsoever one he might want, in which to dance" (*iehoatl quichioaia, in tlein imâcehoallatqui motecuçoma in ipan macehoaia, mitotiaia: in icoac ilhuitl quiçaia, quitlatlattitia, quitlanenectiaia, in çaço catlehoatl queleuiz in ipan mitotiz...*).

[21] Codex Mendoza, fol. 67v; the fans are illustrated on fols. 66r, 67r, and 68r. Frances F. Berdan and Patricia Rieff Anawalt, eds., *The Codex Mendoza,* vol. 3 (Berkeley: University of California Press, 1992).

[22] Sahagún, *Florentine Codex,* bk. 9, ch. 20, 92.

[23] Jeanette Favrot Peterson, *The Paradise Garden Murals of Malinalco: Utopia and Empire in Sixteenth-century Mexico* (Austin: University of Texas Press, 1993), 93. Sahagún, *Florentine Codex,* bk. 11, ch. 7, par. 10, 208.

[24] Paul Spencer, *Society and the Dance: The Social Anthropology of Process and Performance* (Cambridge: Cambridge University Press, 1985), 22.

[25] See the classic study by Maurice Halbwachs, *On Collective Memory*, ed. and trans. Lewis A. Coser (Chicago: University of Chicago Press, 1992).

[26] Arthur J. O. Anderson, trans., *Bernardino de Sahagún's* Psalmodia Christiana (Christian Psalmody) (Salt Lake City: University of Utah Press, 1993), xvii–xxv.

[27] Franciscans were likely influenced by the writings of Pope Gregory the Great, who argued for the expedience of such substitutions in pagan conversions. One of the earliest Franciscan chroniclers, Motolinía, underscores the change in meaning because of the changing of the texts of the songs: "Attired in white shirts and mantles and bedecked in

feathers and with a bouquet of roses in their hands, the Indian lords and chiefs perform a dance and sing in their language the songs that solemnize the feast which they are celebrating. The friars have translated these songs for them and the Indian masters have put them into the meter to which the Indians are accustomed." Motolinía, or Toribio de Benavente, *Motolinia's History of the Indians of New Spain,* ed. and trans. Francis B. Steck (Washington, DC: American Academy of Franciscan History, 1960), 141.

[28] Mendieta, *Historia eclesiástica indiana,* bk. 2, ch. 32, 140–142.

[29] Motolinía, *Motolinia's History of the Indians of New Spain,* 141.

[30] Mendieta, *Historia eclesiástica indiana,* bk. 2, ch. 32, 143.

[31] Domingo Francisco de San Antón Muñón Chimalpahin Cuauhtlehuanitzin, *Annals of His Time,* ed. and trans. James Lockhart, Susan Schroeder, and Doris Namala (Stanford, CA: Stanford University Press, 2006), 44–45. Emily Umberger discussed the associations with Corpus Christi in her important article on a *biombo* now in the Museo de América, "Monarchía Indiana in Seventeenth-Century New Spain," in *Converging Cultures: Art and Identity in Spanish America,* ed. Diana Fane (Brooklyn, NY: The Brooklyn Museum and Harry Abrams, 1996), 46–58; Carolyn Dean has explored the importance of indigenous celebrations of Corpus in Cuzco in *Inka Bodies and the Body of Christ: Corpus Christi in Colonial Cuzco, Peru* (Durham: Duke University Press, 1999).

[32] Chimalpahin, *Annals of His Time,* 78–79; note how he uses both root terms (*i'totia* and *macehua*) for dancing.

[33] A brief textual account appears in the city's *Actas de Cabildo.* Ignacio Bejarano, ed., *Actas de cabildo de la ciudad de México* (Mexico City: Aguilar e hijos, 1889). Perla Valle, "La Lámina VIII del Códice de Tlatelolco. Una propuesta de lectura," *Dimensión Antropológica* 2 (1994), http://www.dimension-antropológica.inah.gob.mx/?p=1556.

[34] Measurement recorded in Luis Chávez Orozco, ed., *Códice Osuna: Reproducción facsimilar de la obra* (Mexico City: Ediciones del Instituto Indigenista Interamericano, 1947), 137.

[35] Xavier Noguez and Perla Valle, *Códice de Tlatelolco* (Mexico City: Secretaría de Relaciones Exteriores, 1989).

[36] María Castañeda de la Paz, "Filología de un 'Corpus' pintado (siglos xvi–xviii): De Códices, Techiloyan, Pinturas y Escudos de Armas," *Anales del Museo de América* 17 (2009): 79.

[37] The presence of Tlacopan's ruler at the *jura* was evidence of his loyalty to the crown, later invoked in a request to the crown for exemption from tribute. AGI Justicia, leg. 1029, no. 10, discussed in Amos Megged, "Cuauhtémoc´s Heirs," *Estudios de cultura náhuatl* 38 (January 2007): 363–364. The presence of these same four rulers also appears in Bejarano, ed., *Actas de cabildo de la ciudad de México,* June 4, 1557.

[38] See Curcio-Nagy, *The Great Festivals of Colonial Mexico City.* Michael J. Schreffler, *The Art of Allegiance: Visual Culture and Imperial Power in Baroque New Spain* (College Park: Pennsylvania State University Press, 2007), 88–89.

[39] The base element of the Tlatelolco Codex looks like a headpiece, and many pages of the Codex Mendoza show similar feather ensembles as if headdresses (see for instance, fol. 24r, 26r, 28r, 30r, 32r, 34r, 37r, 40r, 43r, 45r, 49r, 52r, and 54r), but fol. 23r and 65r show them as back elements, and the Florentine Codex also suggests that the *quetzalpatzactli* was worn on the back; Sahagún, *Florentine Codex,* bk. 8, ch. 12, 33–35. See the recent discussion of the famous feather "penacho of Moteuczoma" in Sabine Haag, et al., *El Penacho del México Antiguo* (Altenstadt, Germany, Vienna, Austria, and Mexico City: ZKF Publishers, Kunsthistorisches Museum, and Instituto Nacional de Antropología e Historia, 2012).

[40] Sahagún, *Florentine Codex,* bk. 9, ch. 20, 92, "… ihuitica motzacoa mopepechoa in icoac monequi: auh mochioa in tlamamalli in ipan mâcehoalo, ioan in isquich mâcehoallatquitl, in netotiloni, in nechichioaloni in quetzalli, in icpacxochitl, in machōcotl, in matemacatl in êcacehoaztli, aztaecacehoaztli, quauhquecholecacehoaztli, çaquanecacehoaztli, coxolêcacehoaztli quetzalecacehoaztli, ioan macpanitl, quetzalmacpanitl çaquantica tlatlapanqui, uiuiltecqui aztapanitl, teucuitlapanitl, quetzaltzontecomaio …."

[41] Durán, *History,* describes the elaborate feather costumes that elite warriors carried into the field of battle, "clothed head to foot with all the richness conceivable," 184.

[42] Luis Chávez Orozco, ed., *Códice Osuna: Reproducción facsimilar de la obra* (Mexico City: Ediciones del Instituto Indigenista Interamericano, 1947), 36.

[43] Justyna Olko, *Turquoise Diadems and Staffs of Office: Elite Costume and Insignia of Power in Aztec and Early Colonial Mexico* (Warsaw: Polish Society for Latin American Studies and Centre for Studies on the Classical Tradition, University of Warsaw, 2005).

[44] Patricia Rieff Anawalt, *Indian Clothing before Cortés* (Norman: University of Oklahoma Press, 1981).

[45] Sahagún, *Florentine Codex,* bk. 9, ch. 19, 90.

[46] Sahagún, *Florentine Codex,* bk. 9, ch. 2, 6.

[47] Vicenta Cortés Alonso, ed. and trans., *Pintura del gobernador, alcaldes y regidores de México: Códice Osuna* (Madrid: Ministerio de Educación y Ciencia, 1973), fol. 8r.

[48] Castañeda de la Paz, "Filología de un 'Corpus' pintado (siglos xvi–xviii)," 78–97.

[49] Susanna Rostas, "The Concheros of Mexico: A Search for Ethnic Identity," *Dance Research: The Journal for the Society for Dance Research* 9, no. 2 (Autumn, 1991): 3–17, quotation on p. 15.

[50] Susanna Rostas, *Carrying the Word: The Concheros Dance in Mexico City* (Boulder: University Press of Colorado, 2009) is a recent ethnography. For observations of *concheros* from the 1940s, see Martha Stone, *At the Sign of Midnight: The Concheros Dance Cult of Mexico* (Tucson: University of Arizona Press, 1975).

[51] Sofia Sanabrais, "The Biombo or Folding Screen: Examining the Impact of Japan on Artistic Production and the Globalization of Taste in Seventeenth-Century New Spain" (Ph.D. diss., New York University, 2005), 216–217.

[52] Gustavo Curiel, "Los biombos novohispanos: escenografías de poder y transculturación en el ámbito doméstico," in *Viento detenido. Mitologías e historias en el arte del biombo: Colección de biombos de los siglos XVII al XIX del Museo Soumaya* (Mexico City: Asociación Carso, 1999), 9–32.

[53] Schreffler, *Art of Allegiance,* 27.

[54] Barbara E. Mundy, "Moteuczoma Reborn: Biombo Paintings and Collective Memory in Colonial Mexico City," *Winterthur Portfolio* 45, no. 2/3 (Summer/Autumn 2011): 161–176.

Mourning Rites, Processions, and Funerary Monument

The Mexico City Inquisition and Funerary Observances for the Death of King Philip IV (1666)

Gustavo Curiel

"Philip IV 'the Great' is dead."
News Reaches the Viceroy's Palace; Proclamations Are Made; the City Puts on Mourning

News regarding daily events in Spain arrived in the Viceroyalty of New Spain after a substantial delay. The overseas realms lived several steps behind the inexorable succession of events in the metropolis, and vice versa; news of whatever was happening this side of the Atlantic was slow to arrive in Madrid. The Spanish monarchy comprised a dual reality with its different parts geared to different rhythms, though forming part of the same machinery. Sooner or later, repercussions of everything that happened in Spain would be felt in the distant society of the viceroyalty, above all if the news involved the dominant spheres of royal power or religion.

Isidro de Sariñana records in his printed account of the funeral observations the arrival in Veracruz of the sad news of the death of Philip IV (fig. 1).[1] The king had died almost eight months before, on September 17, 1665. A small ship, with a lateen sail and a single mast at the fore, docked at the fort of San Juan de Ulúa. Sariñana relates:

> The tartane arrived with the news of the death of His Majesty … on Wednesday the twelfth of May of this year of sixteen hundred and sixty six; the Royal Officials … dispatched the mail with the letter [for] His Excellency the Viceroy the Marqués de Manzera, advising him of the sad news …. The mail reached the Royal Palace of this City [of Mexico] on Saturday the fifteenth, at seven o'clock in the evening.[2]

Antonio de Robles also records, in his *Diario de sucesos notables*, the belated arrival of the news. In his entry for Sunday May 16, 1666, he makes the following comment: "Chests: Sunday 16, at ten o'clock … the [mail] chests were delivered: they brought the news of the death of our King Philip IV on September 17 last year '65."[3] Robles adds more information regarding the king's death and data regarding his public life. He states that the king died "aged sixty years, five months and

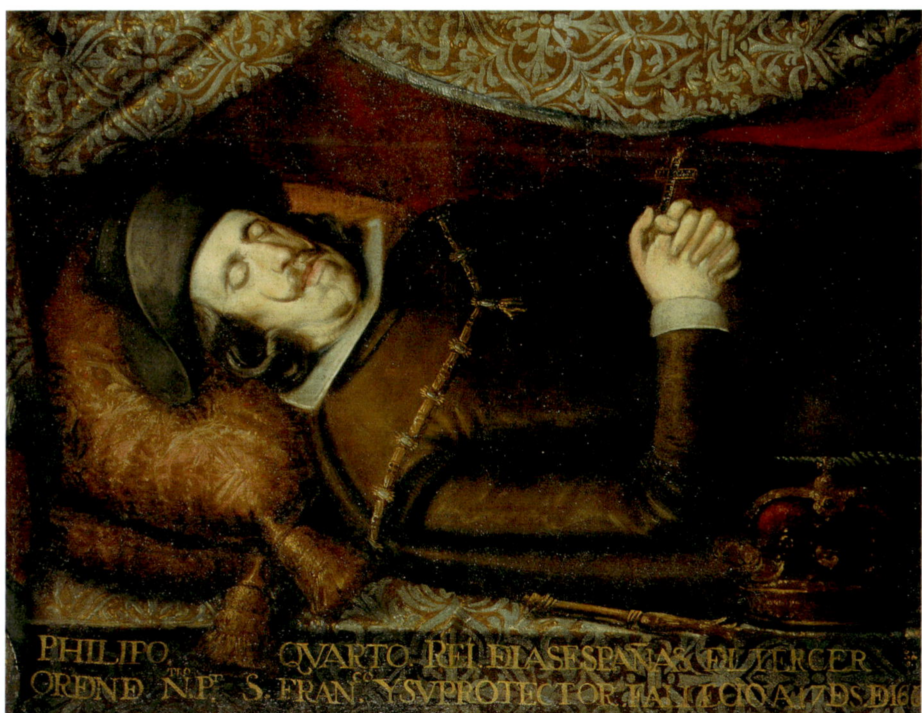

Fig. 1. Anonymous, *Mortuary Portrait of Philip IV*. Spain, circa 1665. Real Academia de la Historia, Madrid, Spain.

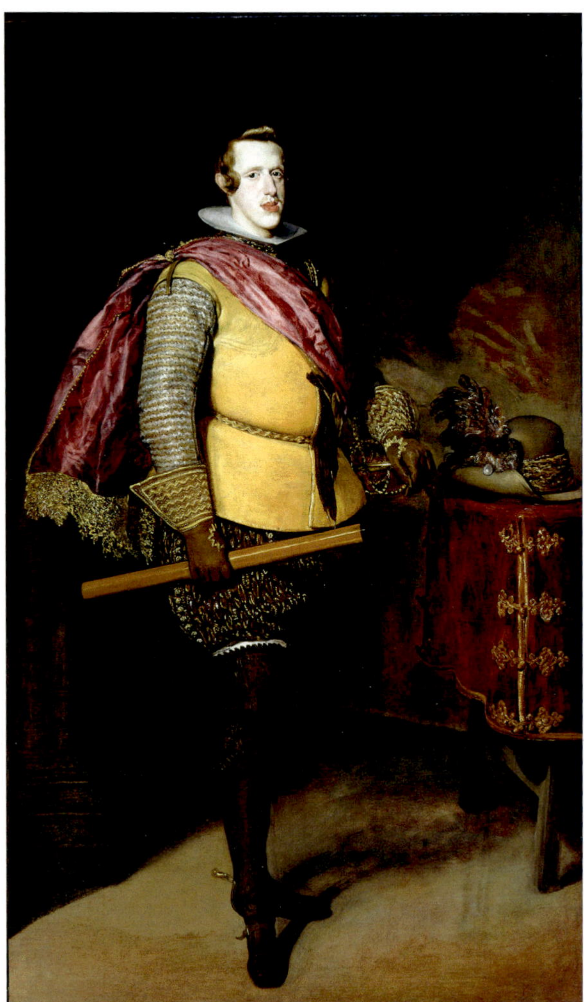

Fig. 2. Diego Rodríguez de Silva Velázquez, *Felipe IV*. Spain, circa 1625. John and Mable Ringling Museum of Art, Sarasota, Florida, USA.

nine days, and had reigned forty-four years, five months and seventeen days" (figs. 2–4). He had been born in the city of Valladolid, on Good Friday, the eighth of April, 1605. He took the oath as heir to the throne in the church of San Jerónimo in Madrid, on Sunday, October 13, 1608, when he was little over three years old. Philip IV was married for the first time to Doña Isabel de Borbón, daughter of the king of France (fig. 5). After her death he contracted marriage for the second time with her niece the archduchess Doña Mariana of Austria, on October 7, 1649 (fig. 6).

The information offered by Robles was peppered with morbid details, including medical minutiae regarding the death of the representative of the House of Austria:

> Having been afflicted by a palsy for some years, which prevented the use of his right arm ..., on Wednesday the twelfth of May of this year of sixteen hundred and sixty six, he suffered deterioration of his urinary system and distemper of the liver. On opening the body for embalming, half of his right kidney was found to be shriveled up and beside it was a stone like a chestnut, full of fleshy protuberances in the form of thorns.[4]

News of the deaths of members of the royal families of Spain was habitually received with diverse acts of mourning throughout the Spanish dominions. The Viceroyalty of New Spain was no exception—the political, the religious, the social, and the artistic being all intermingled in the acts.

The mail chests also contained a *Real Cédula*—or royal letters patent—issued by the widowed queen (fig. 6) in Madrid on October 18, 1665. In this dispatch, she, as acting head of state (*reina gobernadora*), ordered her vassals to perform the customary public demonstrations and to dress in rigorous mourning fashion; they were to perform the funeral services and honors with solemnity, and Viceroy Antonio Sebastián de Toledo, Marqués de Mancera (fig. 7), was to take particular care in supervising the acts that were to take place.[5]

Immediately, the viceroy issued instructions—in a letter of May 21—for the entire Realm of

New Spain to perform the customary demonstrations with due decorum, decency, and solemnity.[6] This instruction reached the Court of the Holy Inquisition the following day;[7] it ordered the ministers of that tribunal to come out onto the street in mourning after the signal of the first tolling of bells and to make manifest their pain and their commiseration at such a great loss.[8]

Although part of the population was already dressed in black, it was not until May 26 that Mancera made public and official the news of the king's death; he also decreed the rigorous use of mourning.[9] The first official proclamation was made by crier. At eleven o'clock in the morning, the mayor (*corregidor*), the city councilmen (*alcaldes ordinarios*), the chief of police (*alguacil mayor*), the chief prosecutor (*procurador mayor*) with his secretary (*escribano*), and all the bailiffs (*alguaciles*) and ministers on horseback departed from the *Ayuntamiento* building, or seat of municipal government, in the direction of the viceroy's palace (fig. 8). They were preceded by drummers and trumpeters, and their horses were draped in black to the ground, "their persons all with long black mourning gowns (*lutos largos*) and hooded cloaks (*capuces*) over them, and the drums and trumpets muted."[10]

Once the first proclamation had been made on the paved area in front of the viceroy's palace, they met with Mancera, and a sign was given with a kerchief to the verger of the cathedral to begin tolling the bells. The great bell opened the lamentation with two hundred tolls, the rhythmic sound of mourning, and was then joined by the bells of the seventy-seven churches of the city, that is to say, the parish churches, those of the friaries and convents, the hospital and university chapels, and the hermitages and churches of the poorer quarters outside the city bounds (*arrabales*). The first tolling lasted from eleven o'clock to three in the afternoon. Then the cathedral bells gave seven clamors. That day, the bells, with their voices of death, rang out until eight o'clock at night; the metallic tones continued throughout the following days.[11]

The contingent that had left the *Ayuntamiento* continued disseminating the sad news, making the second announcement in front of the archbishop's palace, and repeated the act in front of the palace of the Inquisition and in the street of

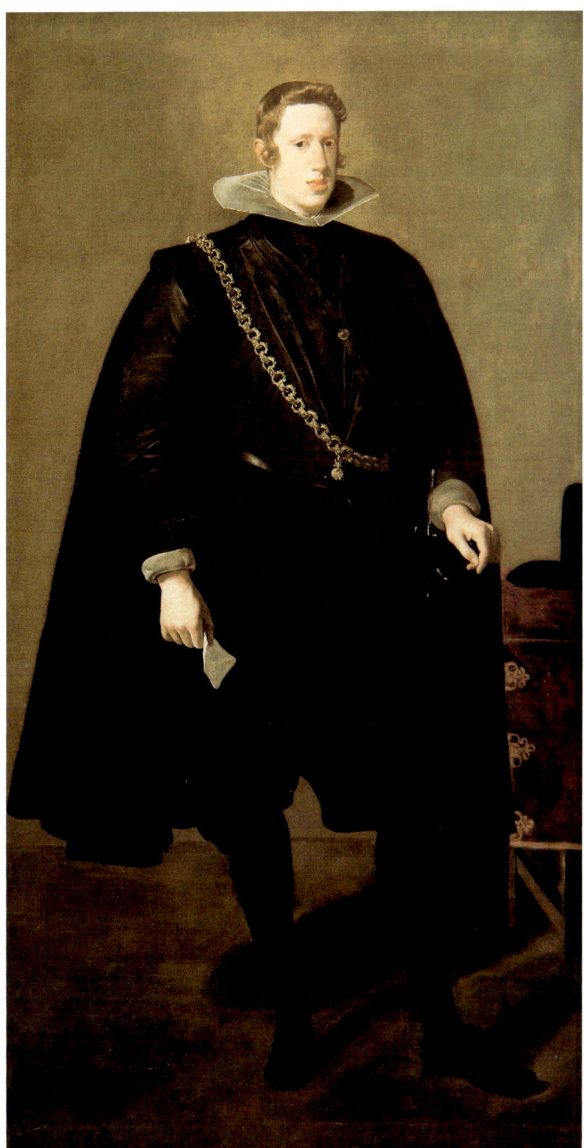

Fig. 3. Diego Rodríguez de Silva Velázquez, *Felipe IV*. Spain, circa 1624. Bequest of Benjamin Altman, Metropolitan Museum of Art, New York, USA.

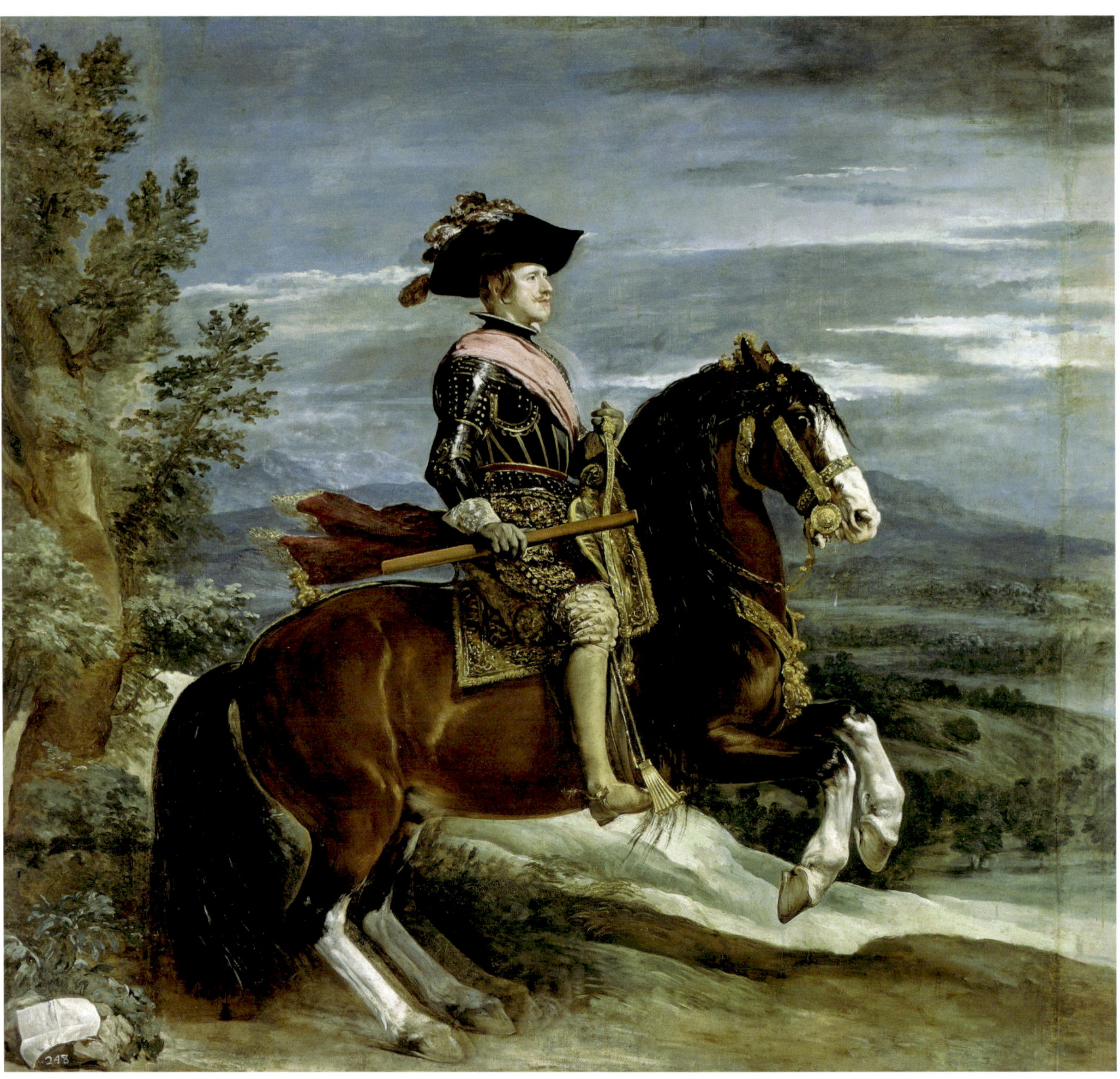

Fig. 4. Diego Rodríguez de Silva Velázquez, *Philip IV on Horseback,* painted for the Salón de los Reinos of Buen Retiro Palace, 1631–1636. Museo del Prado, Madrid.

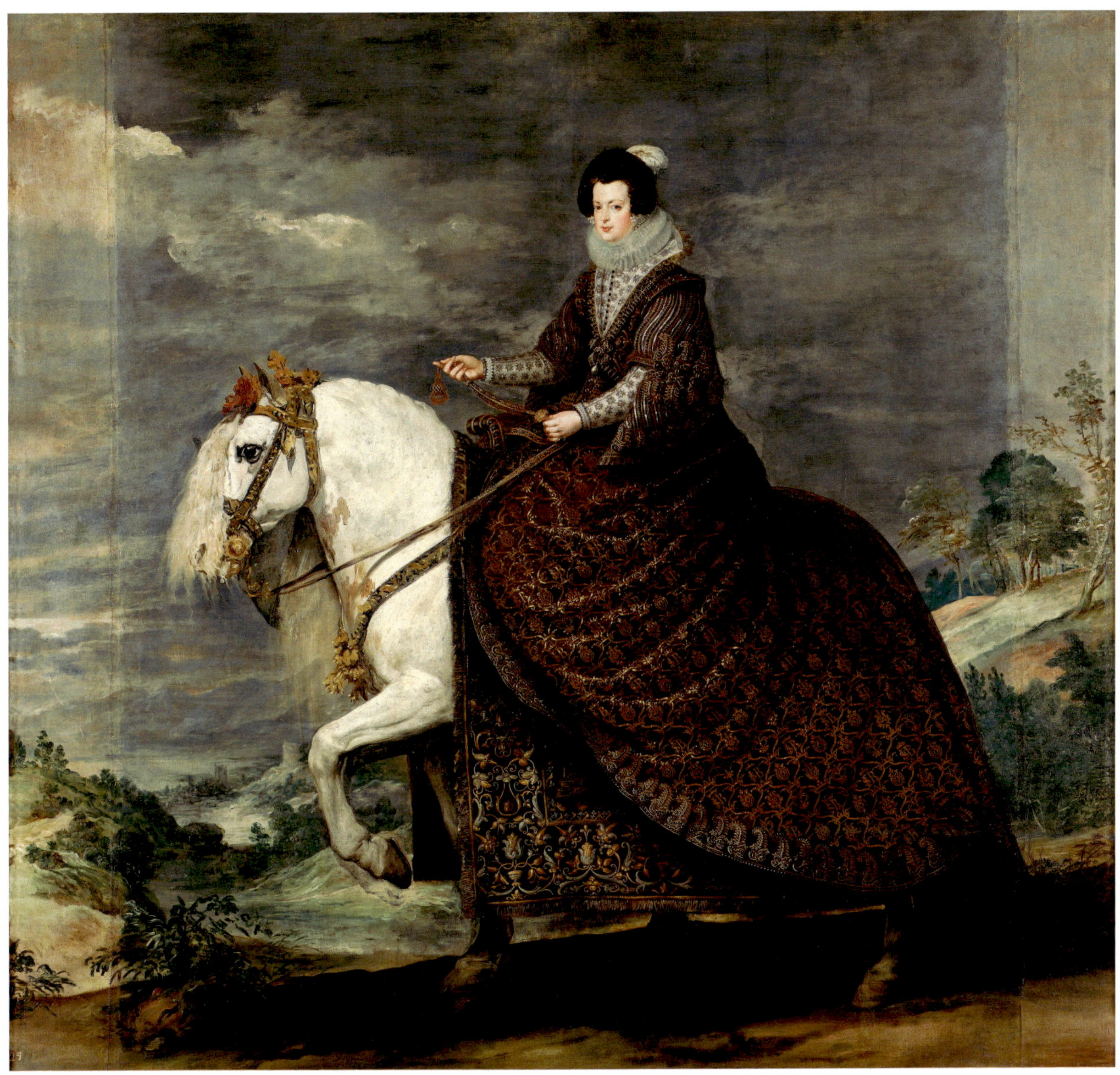

Fig. 5. Diego Rodríguez de Silva Velázquez, *Portrait of Queen Isabel of France on Horseback*, painted for the Salón de los Reinos of Buen Retiro Palace, 1635–1636. Museo del Prado, Madrid.

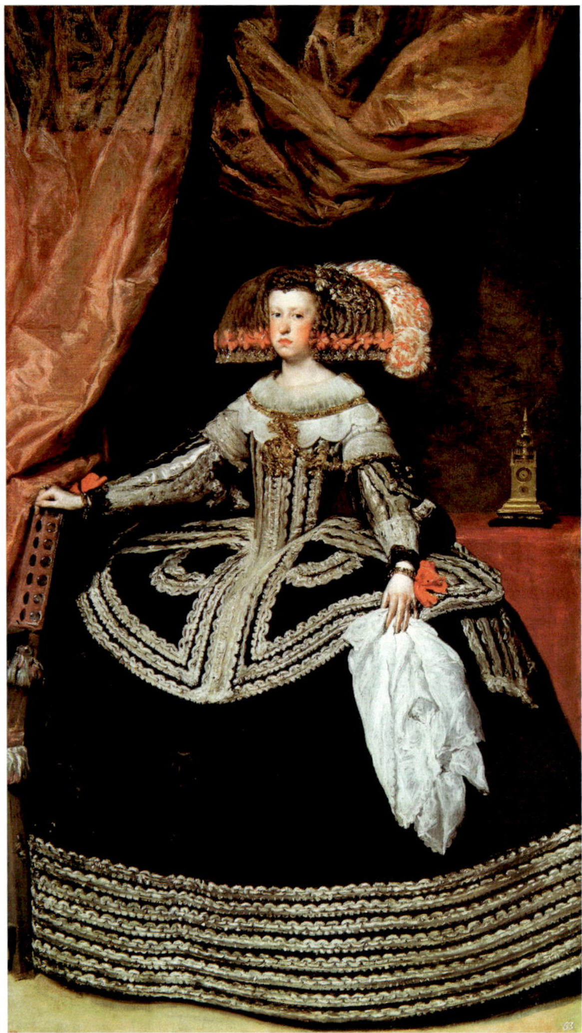

Fig. 6. Diego Rodríguez de Silva Velázquez, *Portrait of Queen Mariana de Austria*. Spain, circa 1652. Museo del Prado, Madrid.

San Francisco; the final proclamation took place before the *Ayuntamiento*. The corporation's notary, or *escribano mayor*, gave legal witness to the events taking place that morning and registered them in the books of the *cabildo* or city council.[12] As for the sanctions contemplated for those who failed to dress in black, there would be a fifty-*peso* fine for Spaniards, and for the rest of the population one of twenty *pesos*. Indians and paupers would be exempt from the use of such dress. Nevertheless, Sariñana relates that the impact of the news on the indigenous community (the so-called *República de indios*) was so great that all, from the Indian nobility to the most downtrodden members of the community, united publicly in the expression of their feelings "and so [the Indians without resources] dyed black the only meager garments they possessed, condemning themselves [thereby] to many more years of mourning."[13] Little by little, assembly rooms, daises (*estrados*), windows, and balconies were covered with a multitude of black drapes; the spaces of power were all in mourning.

The Court of the Inquisition Renders Its Condolences to Viceroy Mancera

As was to be expected, the news gave rise to considerable movement in the Inquisition, which—as supreme court overseeing the defense of the Christian faith—had been very much favored by Philip IV. It was necessary to have mourning garments made and distributed among the members of the corporation and to give official condolences to the viceroy and his consort. There was an enormous mass of paperwork concerning the vestments. Both custom and regulations stipulated that mourning clothes were not to be given to those absent or sick; that if both father and son served the Inquisition, such clothing would be given to only one of them; those in retirement did, however, qualify; if a member of the Inquisition belonged to some other guild, the clothing would have to be awarded there and not by the Inquisition; of the institution's physicians only the oldest would be eligible.[14]

The Inquisition resolved, in a hearing of May 18, to give to the visiting inquisitor, Don Pedro de Medina Rico (who, as it happens, was very ill), to the inquisitor Don Juan de Ortega y Montañés, and to the *fiscal*, Don Nicolás de las Infantas y

Venegas, each fourteen *varas*, or some 13 yards (the *vara* was a measure equivalent to 0.84 meters, a few inches less than a yard) of fine black imported twenty-four-thread-count woolen cloth from Segovia (Spain) for the fabric of their mourning garments. Sixty *varas*, or 55 yards, of so-called Castilian *bayeta* (actually Mexican-produced flannel) were allowed for the dress of their chaplains and servants, and the drapes of their carriages. An additional thirty *pesos* were granted for the make-up of the clothing and the hats. The cascades of cloth also reached the secretaries, Marcos Alonso de Huidrobo, Diego Martínez Hidalgo, Martín López de Ochandiano, and Pedro de Arteta, who were distinguished with ten and-a-half *varas* of fine cloth from Segovia and 12 *pesos* each for the making up, plus the hats and caps. The same was allotted to the receiver (*receptor*), the *licenciado*, Francisco López Sánz, and the notary for sequestrations (*notario de secuestros*), Don Juan de la Serna de Haro. The Inquisition's physician, Dr. Pedro de los Arcos Monroy, was given the same length of cloth, but four *pesos* less for the making up. Other members of the Inquisition, namely, the keeper of the secret prisons, his assistant, the official messenger or *nuncio*, the regular jailer, and the doorkeeper all received ten-and-a half *varas* of local "Castilian" flannel, plus eight *pesos* for the making up and the hats. The fabrics they were allotted were of lesser quality than the imported ones.[15]

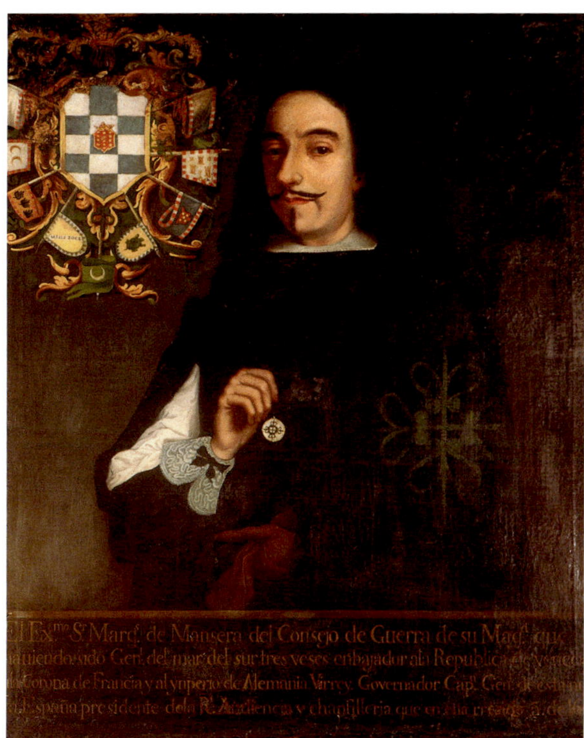

Fig. 7. Anonymous, *Portrait of Don Antonio Sebastián de Toledo, Marqués de Mancera, Viceroy of New Spain*. Mexico, circa 1666. Gallery of the Viceroys of the Ayuntamiento of Mexico City.

The inquisitors also arranged for the principal chamber of the Inquisitional Tribunal, its seat of honor, and the main table to be draped in "Castilian" flannel, "within the bar," while for the floor and the benches closest to the seat of honor, local textiles would be used. For the same chamber the inquisitors assigned to the corporation's secretary and receiver the job of buying the black drapes and everything else necessary for the funereal stage setting.[16] The Inquisition had now done all it could until the moment when the viceroy of New Spain would put on black attire, indicating the start of public mourning.

Condolences in the Viceroy's Palace

One of the acts of courtly fidelity through which the Realm of New Spain reaffirmed its allegiance to the Spanish Crown was the offering of condolences by the various authorities and corporations of the city to the viceroy and his consort, as the Crown's representatives, in the viceregal palace; the act was attended by a multitude. Mancera decided to receive official condolences on June 4 at ten o'clock in the morning in the general assembly room. Following standard protocol, he would begin with the Court of Appeals, or *Real Audiencia*. Immediately after, he would receive the members of the Tribunal of the Inquisition or *Santo Oficio*, to continue then with the long queue of other governmental bodies of the viceroyalty: the Court of Audit (*Tribunal de Cuentas*), the City Council, the Municipal Regiment, the Royal University (*Real Universidad*), the Chamber of Commerce or *Consulado de Mercaderes*, the Court of the Holy Crusade (*Tribunal de la Santa Cruzada*), and the College of Physicians or *Protomedicato*. In the afternoon the cathedral chapter and the city's eight religious orders offered their condolences to the governors.[17]

So that the members of the Court of the Inquisition could prepare themselves decently for the function, they were informed by the palace that they would have the use of the first room next to the main staircase of the building; then Inquisitor Ortega and the *fiscal*, Don Nicolás de las Infantas, would go to offer their condolences to the viceroy and his consort, observing the protocol normal to such acts of gravity.[18]

The time appointed for setting out from the building of the Holy Office *(Santo Oficio)* for the offering of condolences was nine o'clock in the morning. From there, the members of the Inquisitorial Tribunal would depart in an orderly procession of carriages, arranged by hierarchy, in the direction of the viceregal palace. Since the offering of condolences was an act of great importance, it was decided that the *fiscal* would write up an account of everything that took place. The members of the Tribunal of the Faith (*Tribunal de la Fe*) appeared dressed in black from head to toe in typical mourning garb, consisting of long capes known as *lobas* and another hooded cape known as a *capuz* over the top, all "made of flannel with their skirts very long, and all of them wearing their [normal religious] habits closely fitted beneath the *lobas*."[19] The officials wore the badge of the Inquisition to distinguish themselves from the "ministers," or members of the tribunal; the latter wore, besides the *lobas*, a type of cap known as a *gorrilla* on their heads, beneath the hoods of the *capuces*. Both Inquisitor Ortega and the *fiscal* wore, over the flannel soutanes (*sotanas de bayeta*), open *lobas* of imported woolen cloth, the sleeves and the collar closed in front, with very long skirts, and the hooded *capuz* (also of imported cloth) over their shoulders but not covering their heads, on account of their status as churchmen. The inquisitor also wore a cap (*bonete*) and on top of his apostolic hat. *Fiscal* Don Nicolás had covered his head with a tasseled hat. Having gone out into the street with great dignity they got into the sixteen carriages that were to take them to the palace. The coaches of the ministers and that of the tribunal were themselves cloaked in mourning, as were the coachmen and the horses. The bulkiness of the vestments, however, meant there was a problem of space within the vehicles; as a result, more than one of the party had to make his way on foot. The file of carriages was completed by a coach in which the chaplains and priests of the inquisitors traveled.[20]

Once at the palace doors, the defenders of the faith were received by a private secretary (*secretario de cámara*) who told Ortega, on behalf of the judge (*oidor*) of longest standing, that as soon as the *Real Audiencia* came out they would be received. The representatives of the Inquisition went to the upper story of the building by the main staircase, their skirts loosened to facilitate the ascent. Immediately afterwards, two of the viceroy's gentlemen-in-waiting showed them to the room that had been set aside for them, where they remained seated. While this was going on, inside the general assembly room, where Mancera was, a dispute was being settled: differences (relates Don Nicolás de las Infantas) among the court reporters (*relatores*), the notaries (*escribanos de Cámara*), and the Royal University. This delayed the audience.[21] Once the *Real Audiencia* had given its condolences to Mancera and his consort, Doña Leonora María del Carretto (who was giving audience in another room) Ortega and the *fiscal* went in to speak to the viceroy; before entering they left their hats and took their bonnets. The viceroy was standing, next to a seat adjacent to the door. Mancera received from Inquisitor Ortega—who spoke in the name of the court—the words of condolence, which the viceroy accepted, expressing his gratitude.[22]

According to Sariñana, the general assembly room impressed with the bareness of its walls; the windows let in very little light; black curtains were hung over the doors, and even the floors wore funeral drapes.[23] The baldachin, the daises, and the chairs of the chamber had also been covered with black baize (*bayeta*). The whole precinct was a dismal refuge of pain, a cheerless theater of sadness. "His Excellency's seat was beneath the baldachin, and at the sides arranged in wings, [were] the sufficient number [of chairs] for those who were to be seated."[24] Behind Mancera were the Count of Santiago, Don Fernando Altamirano de Castilla, and two secretaries, the private secretary and the secretary of state and war.[25]

Circulation in the palace had been planned so that the *Real Audiencia* and the *Santo Oficio* would not collide with each other nor fill the royal spaces to congestion. Once the *Real Audiencia* had left the audience with the viceroy's consort, the inquisitor entered the room where Doña Leonora was waiting to receive the official condolences, just as had taken place a few moments before with the viceroy. The chambers of the viceroy's consort were naked of all adornment, with the daises and cushions all covered with black baize.[26]

Once the condolences had been given, the whole body of inquisitors went downstairs, entered their carriages once again, and returned to the courtroom whence they had departed that morning. Once back in the "Houses of the Inquisition," Ortega thanked his ministers and told them to be prepared with the necessary mourning paraphernalia by Wednesday, August 25—the day when the performance of vigil and the funeral exequies would begin in the church of Santo Domingo, adjacent to the palace of the Inquisition.[27] The Inquisition was preparing other acts of demonstration of mourning, namely the procession to the Dominican church, the eulogy or *Laudatio Funebris*, the panegyric sermon, the vespers, the prayers for the dead, the burial, the unveiling of the funerary monument or catafalque (*túmulo*), and the printed book that would be sent to Spain as an incontrovertible proof of what New Spain's Inquisition had done in Mexico City.

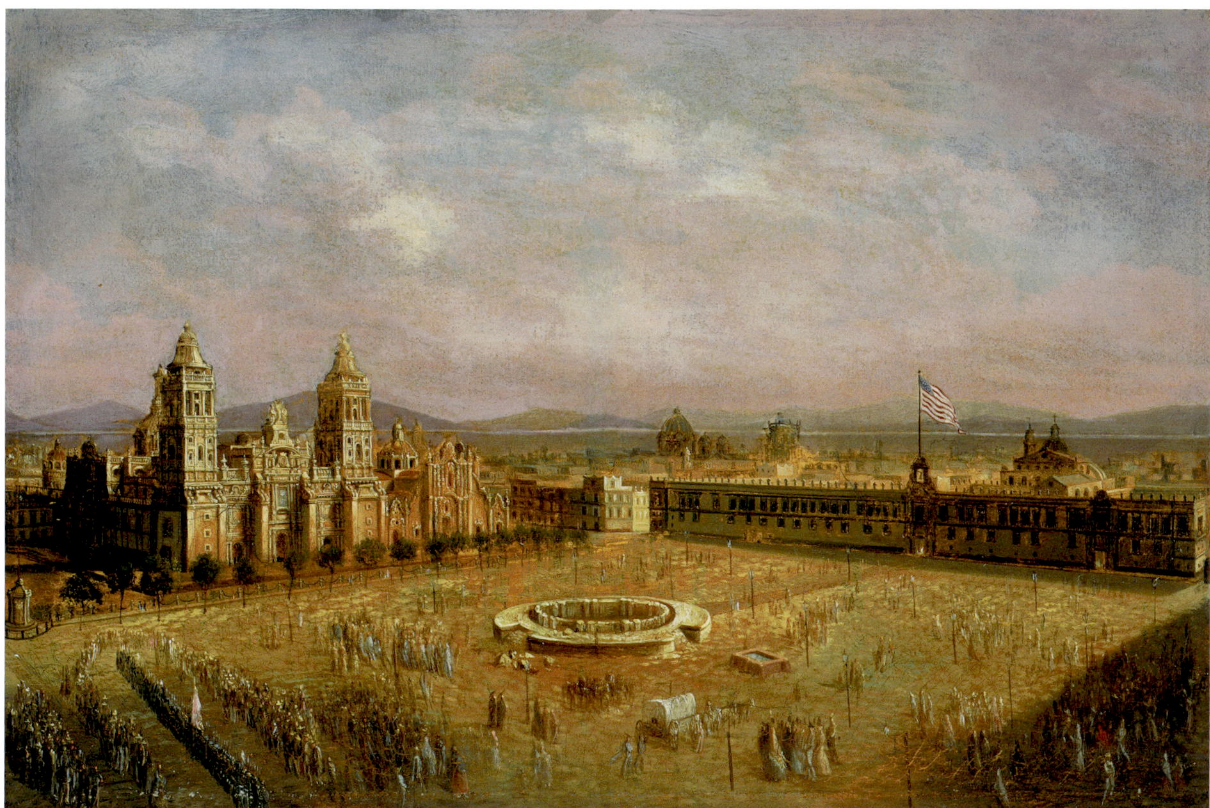

Fig. 8. Pedro Gualdi, *Plaza of Mexico City (Cathedral on left, Palace of the Viceroys on right)*. Mexico, 1847. Oil and gouache on paper, 9½ x 14½ in. Denver Art Museum; Gift of Mrs. Frederic H. Douglas, 1956.72.

Ephemeral Celebrations in the Church of Santo Domingo: The Procession and the Catafalque

The First Day

At midday on Wednesday, August 25, the Royal Monastery (*Real Convento*) of Santo Domingo began the tolling that was to continue the whole day. Once again all the bells of the city echoed the signal of mourning. As soon as the acts programmed for the courtroom of the adjacent Inquisition building had finished, a procession, or *pompa fúnebre,* made its way round the whole *plazuela* of Santo Domingo towards the doors of the Dominican church (figs. 9–11). The procession bore the royal insignia to deposit them on the grandiose monument—an astounding work of ephemeral art that the Inquisition had paid for.

Between two and four o'clock in the afternoon, the contingents of the different religious orders arrived at the building of the Holy Inquisition; each of them recited special prayers for the dead in the principal hall of the *Audiencia* (courtroom), which was draped in mourning from floor to ceiling.[28] In the center of this room, upon a raised bier covered by a rich pall of black velvet, the royal insignia were placed: namely, the crown, the scepter, and the sword, symbols of King Philip IV's majesty.[29] They were surrounded by twelve candles on tall candle-holders (*blandones*) and torch stands, which scarcely illuminated the doleful precinct. Lights and shadows moved at a rhythm in tune with the baroque ephemeral artifice, conferring on the funereal space the required seriousness and gravity. The religious orders were received by chaplains and ministers of the Inquisition, who handed them candles of different sizes, according to each member's place in the hierarchy. Once the communities of friars had sung the prayers before the royal symbols, they passed into the patios and corridors of the building in order to wait for the procession to begin, in which they were to participate. The cathedral's cross was also brought to the Inquisition's building, accompanied by numerous clergy of the capital's principal church, who also took part in the processional act.[30]

Before the services were finished in the main judgment-hall of the Inquisition, Visiting Inquisitor Don Pedro de Medina Rico, who had finally joined in the acts, making light for a moment of the illness that afflicted him, took his place at the right-hand head of the bier, beside Ortega and the *fiscal,* Don Nicolás de las Infantas, as supreme authorities of the Court of the Holy Inquisition (*Tribunal del Santo Oficio*).[31] It was then that the cathedral choir and orchestra, under the direction of its Kapellmeister, intoned a response, while the hall was filled with incense and canticles.[32] By this time, outside thousands of people had filled the *plazuela* of Santo Domingo, overflowing into the neighboring streets and crowding the windows and roofs of nearby buildings, jostling for the best positions to view the solemn procession.

The viceroy—accompanied by Doña Leonora and their daughter—was inside the Inquisition's building. In their honor the convent of San Jerónimo—where Sor Juana Inés de la Cruz was to take up residence shortly after—had been commissioned to produce four magnificent trays of sweetmeats and two of pastry lozenges, which were offered at a break in the formalities when the viceroy and his family "took chocolate." The viceroy had expressed his wish to see "from on high" (*desde las alturas*) "the accompaniment made by the ministers of the *Santo Oficio* at the Tribunal." After drinking chocolate, the viceroy's family attended the services in the church of Santo Domingo.[33]

Finally, at half-past-four in the afternoon, the silent procession went out into the square; its members walked slowly along a walkway with a handrail and a fence that had been made to prevent their feet being muddied were it to chance to rain, and in order to avoid physical contact with the common people. They walked thus upon an ephemeral catwalk at a height of about sixteen inches (half a *vara*). The viceroy's guard of halberdiers and other individuals took care of the flow and the safety of the procession. The plan was that they should make a complete circuit of the *plazuela* until reaching the doors of the church.[34] Although August in Mexico is prone to torrential rains, the weather on that occasion was temperate, mild, and fresh: the sky was covered by benign clouds "that—without the threat of rain—gave shade and calmed the afternoon."[35]

The procession was opened by three or four *cofradías* (lay brotherhoods); immediately following were the religious orders—not divided by the antiquity of their foundation, as was usual, but mixed. The third group of the procession was that of the cathedral, with the cross that the clergymen had brought with them to the Inquisition. In this contingent went the visiting inquisitor, Dr. Medina Rico, who headed the cathedral contingent. The fourth body was made up of the members of the Inquisition, who accompanied the royal insignia.[36] These symbols were carried by three recognized familiars of the Inquisition with the rank of captains. The insignia were deposited on shining silver trays and covered with transparent black veils.[37] Once the royal symbols had passed, the standard of the faith came into view, with the sword of justice and the olive of mercy (symbols of the Inquisition). *Fiscal* Don Nicolás de las Infantas, who was the custodian of the standard, had brought it out from the main door of the Inquisition, where he handed it over to the provincial of the Dominicans, who held it aloft during the course of the procession.[38] Two other provincials—of the Mercedarians and of the Jesuits—held the cord of the standard's tassels. More representatives of the Inquisition accompanied them. Ortega and *Fiscal* Don Nicolás closed the procession with another large group of representatives of the tribunal.[39]

In silence, and with complete mourning dress, they passed around three sides of the square on the raised walkway until they arrived at the Calle del Águila; at this point they met a group of Dominican friars who had come out to receive them and accompany them to the interior of their church. The friars of Santo Domingo carried a tall cross in an act of welcome to the cathedral cross, Inquisitors Medina and Ortega, the *fiscal*, the royal insignia, and the body of the members of the Tribunal.[40] Both crosses were of silver and were accompanied by candlesticks of the same metal.

Once they had entered the church, the most important persons took their seats, while the standard of the faith was set firmly on a gilded pedestal in the form of a lion. The viceroy and his consort were seated in the first chapel on the right-hand side, protected by latticework screens.[41]

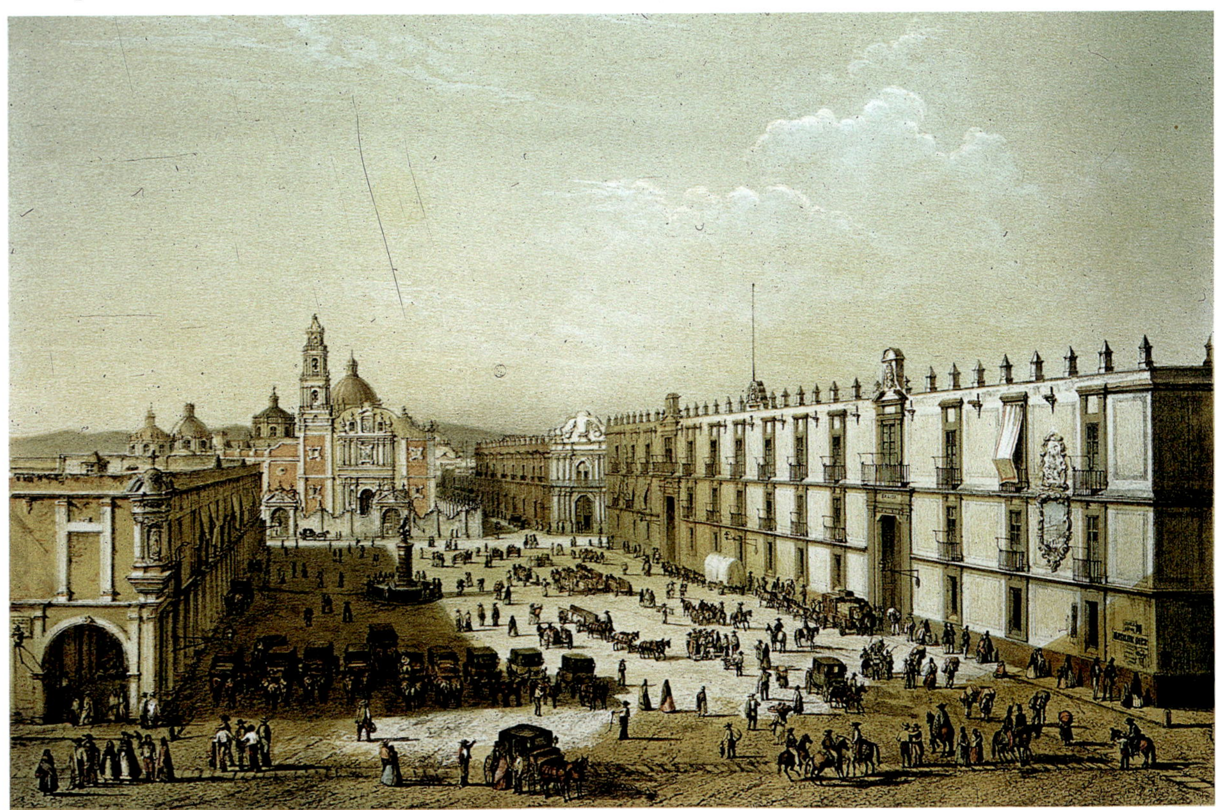

Fig. 9. Pedro Gualdi, *Plaza of Santo Domingo de México.* Mexico, circa 1840. Oil on canvas. Private collection. Photo: Instituto de Investigaciones Estéticas, UNAM. Photo: Marisela González Cruz. Santo Domingo is center left; Palace of the Inquisition is center right.

A multitude of important persons occupied the seats distributed the whole length and breadth of the nave and the side chapels; for this purpose benches were brought in from different religious houses, since those of Santo Domingo were insufficient. Then the cathedral minstrels began to play, and new compositions were performed, written especially for this solemn occasion by the Kapellmeister; the choir sang the regular vespers, plus antiphons, psalms, and lessons.[42]

The great catafalque, or funerary monument, was covered with candles that burned from the base of the monument to the statue of faith at the top, the figure that crowned the symbolic pyre and even surmounted the apotheosis of Philip IV, whose figure also embodied allegorically that of Numa Pompilius, king of the Romans. The wax that had been chosen for the occasion was of the finest quality, selected to burn without smoke. To mitigate the stifling heat, it was necessary to open the clerestory and other windows of the church.[43] As a precaution against a possible fire, tubs of water and buckets were taken up onto the church roof.[44] Everything was ready to begin the funeral oration, read in Latin by Fray Antonio de Monroy, rector of the Dominican college of *Porta Coeli*. Once the *Laudatio Funebris* was finished, now after nightfall, the people dispersed and all the participants returned to their institutions of origin. The Inquisition went back to its own premises by the boarded walkway, while the members of the religious communities, who carried lighted candles, tried to find the way back through the darkness to their respective churches.

The Second Day

Each religious order was assigned a chapel where its members observed the vigil and performed sung masses. The members of the different communities began to arrive in the church from six o'clock in the morning of Thursday, August 26; they brought from their own places of worship a multitude of luxurious ornaments and everything necessary to celebrate those services.[45] In all the chapels and altars of Santo Domingo the candles flickered and crackled—as many as 2,400 in total, counting those upon the catafalque, the high altar, and the chapels.[46] Each group of friars finished

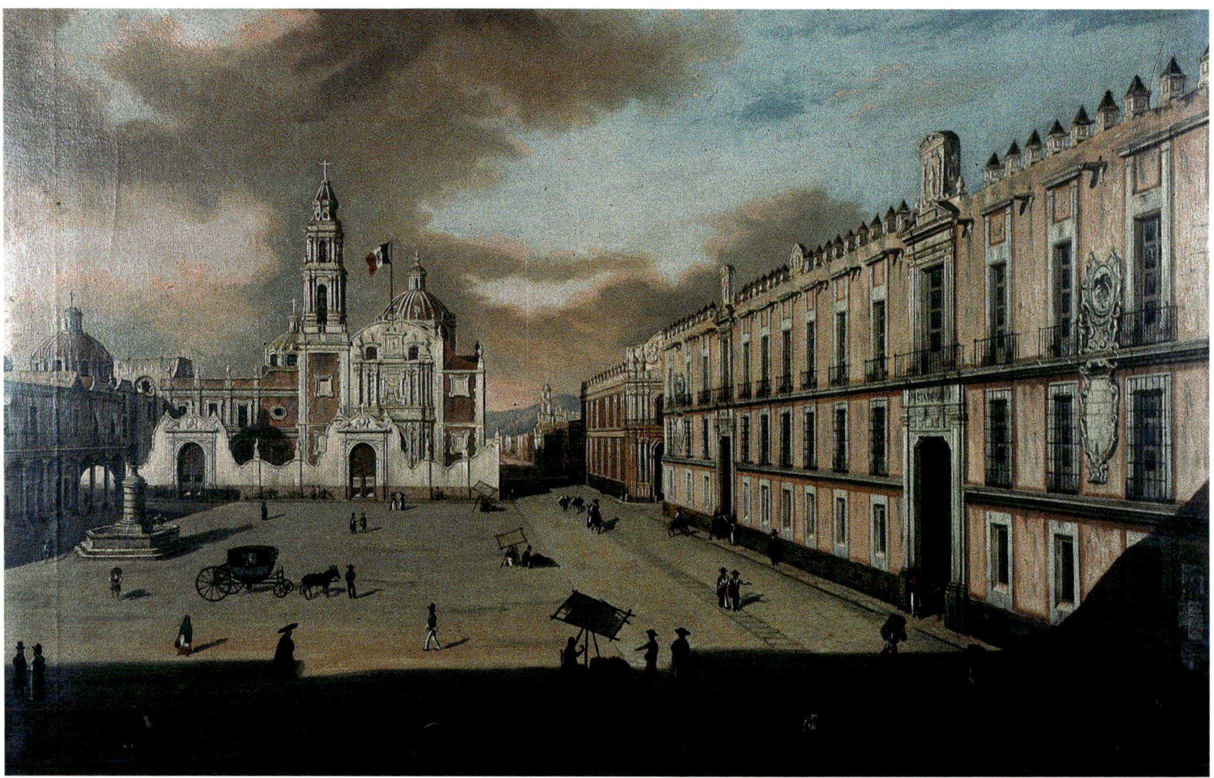

Fig. 10. John Phillips, *Plaza de Santo Domingo de México*. Mexico, 19th century. Lithograph from *México Ilustrado* (Mexico: Imprenta Litográfica Day & Son, n.d.). Santo Domingo is center left; Palace of the Inquisition is center right.

its mass with a prayer for the deceased spoken at the foot of the catafalque. By nine o'clock in the morning this stage of the proceedings was over. Around ten, the inquisitors and the *fiscal* arrived, accompanied by ministers, officials, and familiars of the Holy Office; they performed prayers and, seated, followed the mass officiated by the visiting inquisitor, Medina Rico.[47] The cathedral choir and musicians gave extra luster to this act, and more prayers for the dead were performed; then the inquisitorial authorities ascended to the first level of the catafalque to listen to the panegyric sermon, which had been entrusted to Fray Alonso de la Barrera, rector of the Royal University. Five further prayers for the deceased, and music performed by the choir and instrumentalists, closed the act. At two o'clock the defenders of the faith returned to the Inquisition building with the same accompaniment with which they had left it. The catafalque was on view to the public for a week.

The Catafalque or Imperial "Mausoleum"

Sixty days before, on June 26, the celebrated "master of the art of carving and sculpting" (*entallador y escultor*) Pedro Ramírez (the elder) had been legally commissioned by the Inquisition to construct the funerary catafalque that was to be raised in the crossing of the church of Santo Domingo.[48] The same artist, of Sevillian origin, had also been commissioned to erect the catafalque paid for by the *Real Audiencia* for the funeral honors in the cathedral of Mexico City on July 23 and 24. Although an engraving of the Mexico cathedral catafalque survives published in the book *Llanto del Occidente* (figs. 12–16), one of the Santo Domingo monument does not. However, since the latter was made by reusing portions of the former, it is possible to obtain an idea of its composition by comparing written descriptions with the engraving of the cathedral catafalque. The work at Santo Domingo followed a general design and full-scale details stipulated in the contract (*Condiciones*), although subsequently the structure and symbolism of this imperial "pyre" or "mausoleum" varied from the original plan. Its complex symbolic message was the product of the erudite minds of the Jesuits Francisco de Uribe and Antonio Núñez de Miranda, who worked in collaboration with Pedro

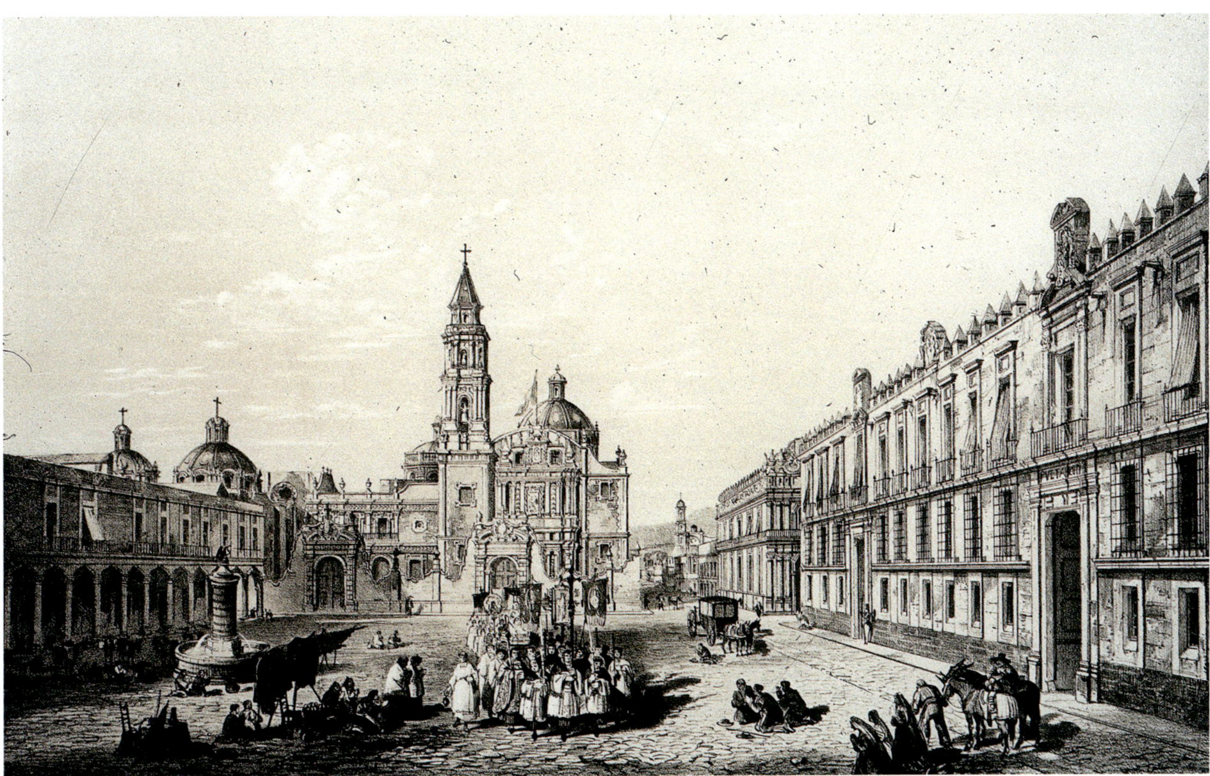

Fig. 11. Casimiro Castro Campillo, *Plaza de Santo Domingo de México*. Mexico, 1855–1856. Lithograph from *México y sus alrededores* (Mexico: Editorial Decaen, 1855–1856). Santo Domingo is center left; Palace of the Inquisition is center right.

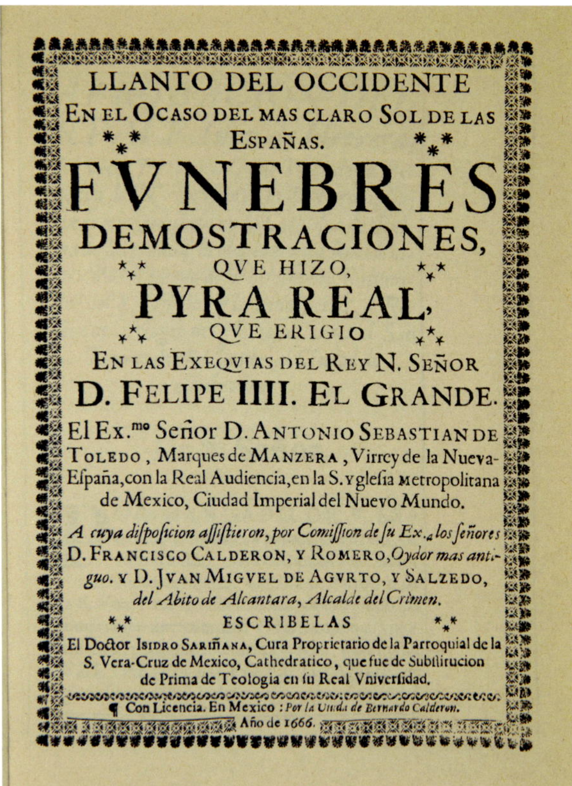

LLANTO DEL OCCIDENTE
EN EL OCASO DEL MAS CLARO SOL DE LAS
ESPAÑAS.
FVNEBRES
DEMOSTRACIONES,
QVE HIZO,
PYRA REAL,
QVE ERIGIO
EN LAS EXEQVIAS DEL REY N. SEÑOR
D. FELIPE IIII. EL GRANDE.
El Ex.mo Señor D. ANTONIO SEBASTIAN DE
TOLEDO, Marques de MANZERA, Virrey de la Nueva-
España, con la Real Audiencia, en la S. yglesia Metropolitana
de Mexico, Ciudad Imperial del Nuevo Mundo.
A cuya disposicion assistieron, por Comission de su Ex.a los señores
D. FRANCISCO CALDERON, Y ROMERO, *Oydor mas anti-guo.* Y D. JVAN MIGVEL DE AGVRTO, Y SALZEDO,
del Abito de Alcantara, Alcalde del Crimen.
ESCRIBELAS
El Doctor ISIDRO SARIÑANA, Cura Proprietario de la Parroquial de la
S. Vera-Cruz de Mexico, Cathedratico, que fue de Substitucion
de Prima de Teologia en su Real Vniversidad.
¶ Con Licencia. En Mexico: *Por la Viuda de Bernardo Calderon.*
Año de 1666.

Fig. 12. Title page of *Llanto del Occidente en el ocaso del más claro sol de las Españas ...*, published by the widow of Bernardo Calderón. México, 1666. Bibliófilos Mexicanos, A. C.

Ramírez.[49] It is worth appreciating the scale of what Ramírez had undertaken to perform in the contract, or *Concierto de obra*:

> The undertaking [to which I am bound] is to make a base (*planta*) with eight painted canvases based on the "hieroglyphics" that they have asked for. With four levels (*gradas*) that descend like cascades on each of the four sides. And upon this base, I have to seat twelve columns with their pedestals and cornice. And this first stage is to bear eight sculpted statues of the subjects of their choice. And in the center of it I have to make an urn in the form of a pedestal, where the tomb is to be seated. On the second stage four columns, pedestals, and a cornice are to be raised. And in the center of it a statue of Our King Philip the Fourth. And at both sides another two, such as they may request. And on the upper part a hemispherical dome with its pedestals, whereupon is the [statue of] Faith. To all of which work I must give its due finish with every perfection and art. And the paintings ..., [execute them] with much variety of marbling.[50]

Ramírez's preliminary cost estimate was one thousand five hundred *pesos*; he requested one thousand *pesos* in advance and the remaining five hundred when the work was finished and placed in the church. He also specified that once the exequies were finished at Santo Domingo he would retain ownership of the catafalque (the same stipulation had been made of the cathedral monument). Immediately the Inquisition adjusted the payments to Ramírez to two equal parts. He would receive 750 *pesos* as an advance; the rest would be paid when the work was finished. Ramírez would certainly have made use of the same team of 150 workers who had built the cathedral catafalque a month earlier; for ease of operation the Santo Domingo monument was made behind locked doors in the innermost patio of the convent building.[51]

By August 7 the work was well under way. Ramírez—who was by his own avowal both a master sculptor and an architect—sent a letter to the work's patrons in which he asked for an adjustment of the agreed price, since

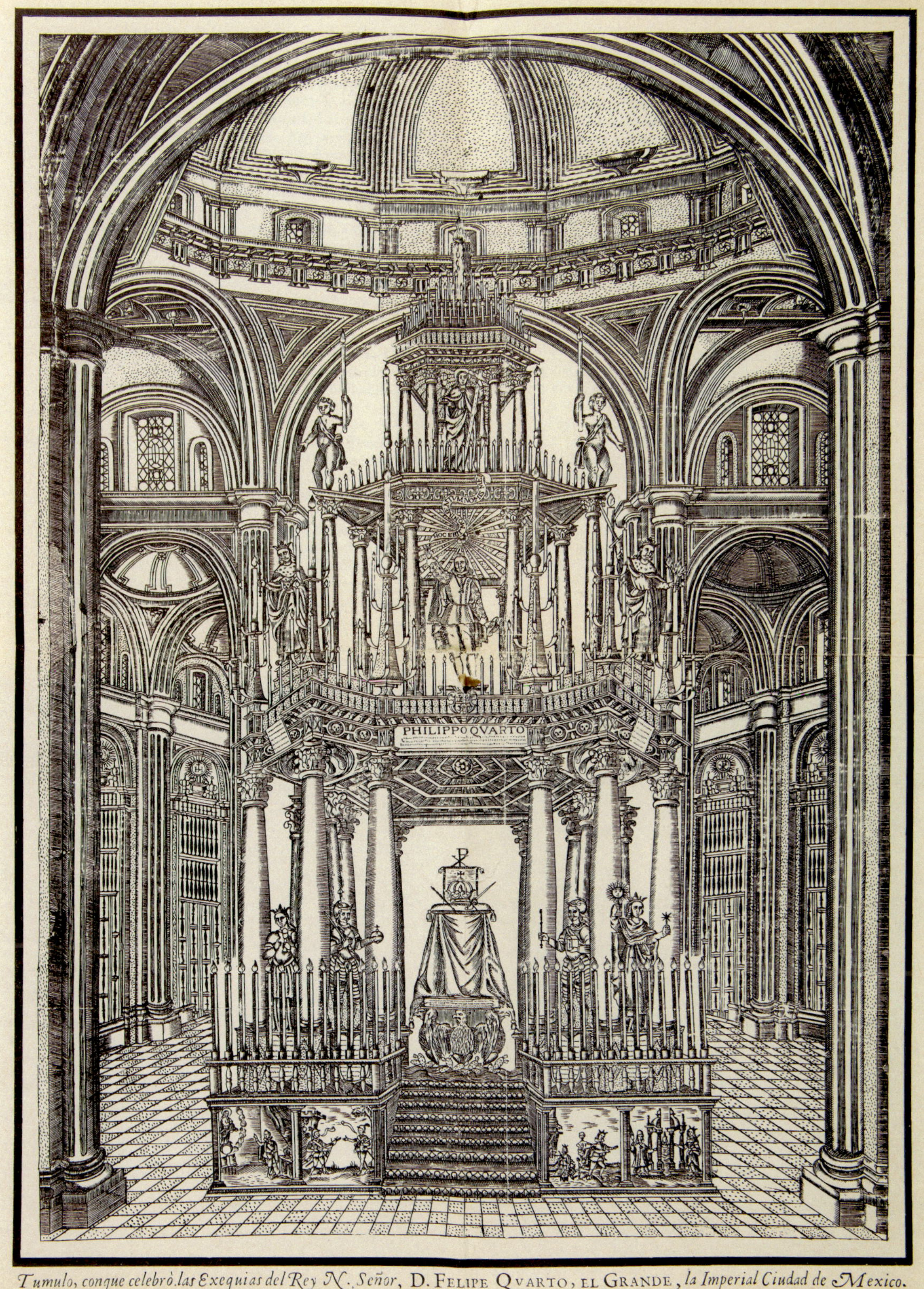

Fig. 13. Engraving of the catafalque of Philip IV in the Cathedral of Mexico. Overview. From *Llanto de Occidente …*, published by the widow of Bernardo Calderón. México, 1666. Bibliófilos Mexicanos, A. C. Portions of it were reused in the Santo Domingo catafalque.

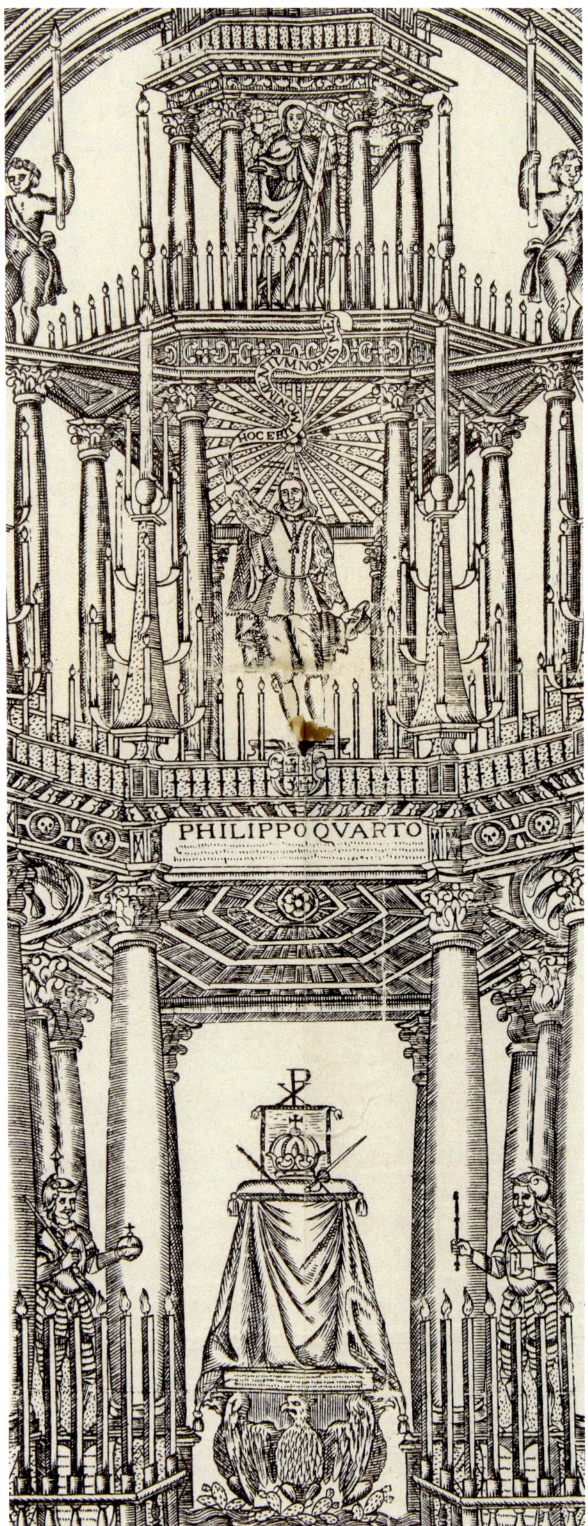

Fig. 14. Detail of fig. 13.

> it is not possible to cover the work that is being done with [even] three thousand *pesos*, on account of the things that have been added, such as the eight pinnacles, the candleholders, and statues that have been renovated as well as other new ones, and many inscriptions, along with many other things.

Ramírez asked the Inquisition for a "help towards the cost" (*ayuda de costa*) or a "financial bonus"—in an appeal to the munificence of the monarchy, the royal will—in addition to the 750 *pesos* that were due to him. On August 9, the Inquisition postponed for a later date the question of the "help towards the cost," but agreed to pay the remaining 750 *pesos*, although the work was not completely finished.

Afterwards, on September 2, Ramírez presented the inquisitors with a report in which he detailed the changes he had made and the extent to which he had been able to reuse material from the catafalque made for the cathedral, showing that while he had indeed made some new use of the previous work, the changes were of a thoroughgoing nature. Ramírez informed his clients that he had added eight pinnacles equipped with candlesticks with rims to catch the wax and with pedestals. Ten pedestals were made anew for the ten statues, and eight ornamental brackets (*repisas*) were added "for greater beauty of the fabric." The colors of the eight canvases that were already done were altered to tone down the colors, and they were perfected (fig. 15). Eight hundred tin candlesticks were supplied (400 were new, and 400 came from the previous catafalque, but had to be reduced in size).

Over the boarded floor of the crossing, Ramírez constructed a kind of bridge in order to distribute the weight of the catafalque, adding large planks "in two parts."[52] As for the inscriptions, the artist explained, so much had been added that he himself had had to pay an extra twenty *pesos* to the *bachiller* (scribe) who transferred the Jesuits' texts to the catafalque. Regarding the substantial changes he made to the original monument from the cathedral, Ramírez explained that the first stage was altered from a triangular to a square plan and that four lengths of new cornices were made and painted. On the cornice fourteen "hieroglyphics" or emblems were painted (fig. 16). Furthermore, he had "cut and taken to pieces the large catafalque from the Holy Cathedral Church; which proved of no benefit to me since I had to adjust it all to the taste of your lordship."[53]

In order to solve the problem of the extra items and the structural modifications, both the Inquisition and Ramírez agreed that experts be appointed to inspect and value the work. The Inquisition had recourse to the opinion of its chief inspector of works (*maestro mayor de obras*), the architect Rodrigo Bernal, who estimated that the additional work was worth five hundred *pesos*. After various petitions Ramírez was awarded 300 *pesos*, since many of the items claimed by the artist as new were said by the Inquisition to have been contemplated in the initial contract.[54] In the end the Inquisition paid him a total of 1,800 *pesos*.

With this majestic catafalque of twenty-four *varas* (some 20 meters or 66 feet) in height, eleven *varas* in width, and thirty-three in "circumference"—a work brimming with exquisite humanist wisdom—the Inquisition sought to legitimate the existence of the Spanish monarchy in American lands, and also to justify the role of the inquisitorial court in its struggle against the enemies of the Church. The figures in it represented Philip IV (disguised as the Roman Emperor Numa Pompilius), the Eucharistic Lamb, the Ship of Faith, the Immaculate Conception, the Virtues of Good Government, the nymph Ægeria, the goddess Pallas Tritoneia, the Graces, the nymphs of Parnassus, Vesta and her court of virgins, etc.[55] Posted within an ephemeral fortress, crowned by the figure of Faith, they defended the interests of the Crown, while resisting the "hurricanes of the plague of heresy and idolatry." Together with them were four kings of Rome and four Catholic kings, Tatius and the Sabines, the sun and the planets of the fourth heaven, and a zodiac, as well as emblems such as eagles, the wellspring, the star, the lion, white lilies (*azucenas*), a ship, a clock, a scythe, a phoenix, etc.[56] Quotations from Plutarch, Dionysius of Halicarnassus, Virgil, Nonius Marcellus, Ovid, and Pausanias gave the didactic message solidity. Three hundred and forty-six years ago, under the skies of Mexico City, the Crown and the Cross united in a single symbol, under the protection of the sword and the olive of justice and mercy; Philip IV could rest in peace.

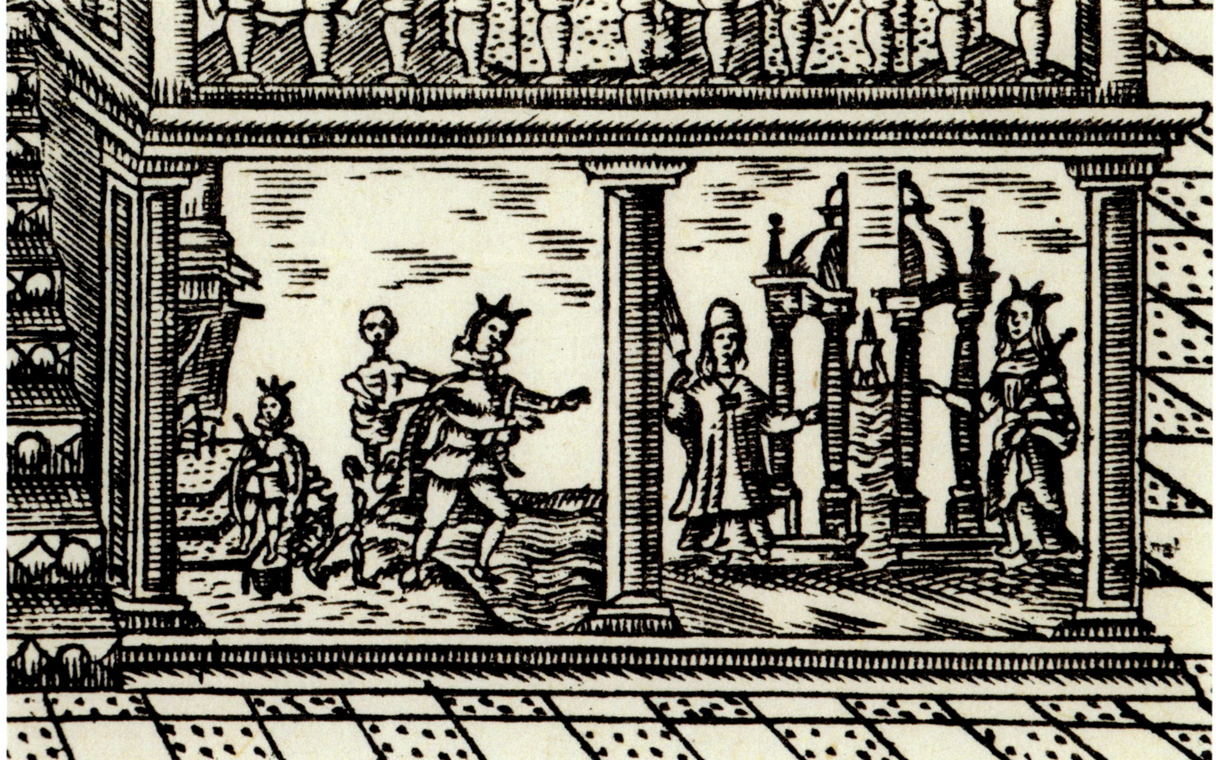

Fig. 15. Detail of fig. 13.

Artists and Expenditures

There is some interesting information about the participation of individuals who contributed to the various components of these ephemeral celebrations. The Inquisition's records (*Autos*) include the names of participating artists, the accounts, details of expenditures, disputes regarding items of mourning dress, and the quotations offered for the adjudication of claims, as well as orders of payment and adjustments regarding original quotations.[57]

The master tailor Jacinto de Saravia was commissioned to sew up and hang the drapes in the main courtroom; for this purpose he made use of six journeymen from his workshop who worked on May 27 from two o'clock in the afternoon until eleven o'clock at night. Master tailors Alonso de Peñalúa and Phelipe Campos gave their opinion on Saravia's work, for which he was requesting twenty-four *pesos*. Finally, on June 10, the Inquisition conceded him an order of payment for eighteen *pesos*.

The inquisitors commissioned the Dominican friar Alonso de la Barrera, who was an assessor (*calificador*) of the *Santo Oficio*, a judge (*juez ordinario)* of the Bishopric of Yucatan, and rector of the University of Mexico, to write the panegyric sermon. The funeral oration (*Laudatio Fvnebris* or *Oratio finus*) delivered at the *vigilia*, or eve of the principal mass, was read by his fellow Dominican Fray Antonio de Monroy, at the time secretary to the provincial of the Order of Santo Domingo and rector of the Dominican college of *Porta Coeli*. This prayer was written and delivered in Latin. There is no record in the *Autos* of any payment having been made to either friar. Both texts were included in the printed text published by the widow of the famous printer Bernardo Calderón (figs. 17–19).

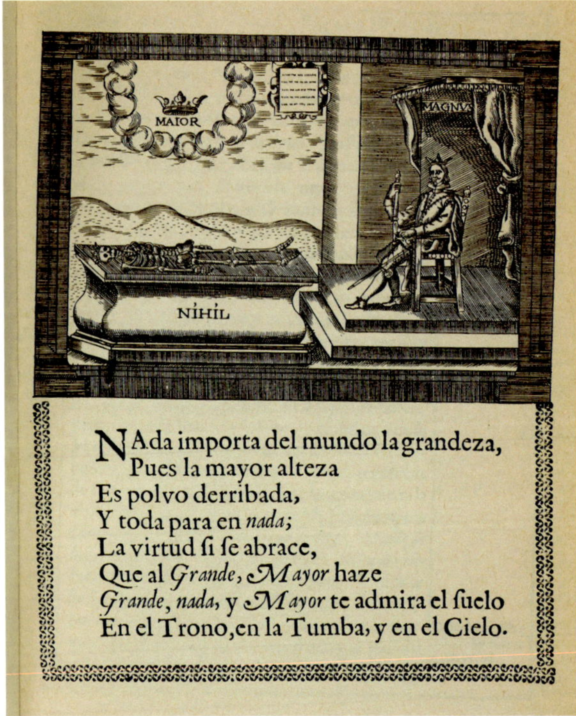

Fig. 16. *Hieroglyphic of Phillip IV*. Engraving from *Llanto del Occidente* . . ., published by the widow of Bernardo Calderón. México, 1666. Bibliófilos Mexicanos, A. C.

Both the Baroque symbolism of the complex iconographic program of the sarcophagus and the subject matter of its intricate emblems, hieroglyphics, sculptures, poems, and paintings were the product of the personalities of the moment: the Jesuits Francisco de Uribe and Antonio Núñez de Miranda, who were assessors (*calificadores*) of the *Santo Oficio* and professors (*catedráticos de prima*) at the Colegio de San Pedro y San Pablo in Mexico City. It is worth remembering that Father Núñez de Miranda was the confessor of the poetess Sor Juana Inés de la Cruz, dubbed the "Tenth Muse," and also of Catharina de San Juan, better known as the "China Poblana."[58] Both Jesuits worked closely with the sculptor and joiner Pedro Ramírez in order to work out the intricate messages that the symbolic pyre was intended to express. According to the published account, a scale drawing plus full-scale details of the monument were presented to the inquisitors for their approval. The name of the *bachiller* who transferred the Jesuits' Latin texts to the architecture of the sarcophagus is unknown; it is stated only that Ramírez paid him the sum of twenty *pesos* for his work.

On May 18, the inquisitorial authorities resolved to search around the city for the fabrics that were to clothe in black the members of the tribunal and the courtroom itself. The materials came in three degrees of quality: fine imported cloth from Segovia of twenty-four thread count; the local flannel known as *bayeta de Castilla*; and a poorer-quality local flannel or baize (*bayeta "de la Tierra"*). The cost of the fabrics came to the fabulous total of 2,108 *pesos* and 1 *real*. For comparison, at the time a young male slave cost around

400 to 500 *pesos* and the annual rent on a house of good quality was approximately 100 *pesos*.

The breakdown of the purchases consisted of 115.5 *varas* of black cloth from Segovia, the very finest; 232.5 *varas* of "Castilian flannel" (*bayeta de Castilla*), as well as 70 *varas* of the same material which were used to drape the courtroom; and more than 33 *varas* of local flannel or baize to cover the benches. Three ounces of silk were used to fix the drapes of the hall; gilded tacks and ribbons were also purchased to secure those of the mortuary stage setting. Captain Martín Ibáñez de Ochandiano, Inquisition secretary (*secretario del Secreto del Santo Oficio)*, and *licenciado* Francisco López Sanz, receiver and notary (*notario ayudante del Secreto)*, were entrusted with the purchase of the cloth from Juan de Santa Ibáñez, Captain Joseph Rodríguez de Medina's cashier, and from one Juan López. The Indians who carried the black fabrics to the Inquisition building received three-and-a-half *reales*. The *Autos* record a charge of 114 *pesos* for the make-up of the mourning clothes given to the inquisitors, the *fiscal*, the *secretarios de visita* and the *secretarios del Secreto* (secretaries of the court), the *regidor* (councilman), the accountant, the *notario de secuestros*, the jailer and his assistant, and the messenger, who also filled the role of doorman. It is known that, by express request, an extra set of mourning dress was given to the Inquisition's accountant, Don Florián Rey de Alarcón; its cost was 12 *pesos*, and ten-and-a-half *varas* were used in the making up of this clothing. On July 5, the Inquisition released the payment of 2,108 *pesos* and 1 *real*. Andrés de Fuentes placed other drapes on the pillars of the church, pews of the familiars of the *Santo Oficio*, and the floor in front of the sarcophagus. The drapes were removed officially on Saturday, November 6.[59]

Another of the heavy costs defrayed by the Inquisition was that of the wax that was burned during the exequies, conferring upon the monument the appearance of a veritable pyre. There were candles lit in the courtroom, on the sarcophagus, on the church's altars, and in its incorporated chapels, as well as those distributed among the religious communities. In a hearing the inquisitors accepted the quotation offered by the master candlemaker, Captain Sebastián Guerra. The cost per *arroba* (25 lbs.) of the finest wax (*cera bujía*,

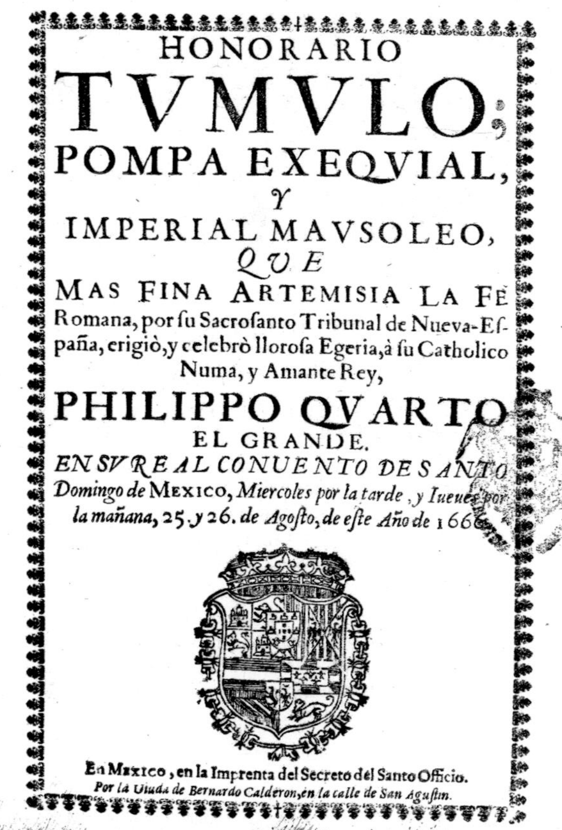
HONORARIO
TVMVLO;
POMPA EXEQVIAL,
Y
IMPERIAL MAVSOLEO,
QVE
MAS FINA ARTEMISIA LA FE
Romana, por ſu Sacroſanto Tribunal de Nueva-Eſpaña, erigiò, y celebrò lloroſa Egeria, à ſu Catholico Numa, y Amante Rey,
PHILIPPO QVARTO
EL GRANDE.
EN SV REAL CONUENTO DE SANTO Domingo de MEXICO, *Miercoles por la tarde, y Iueues por la mañana,* 25. *y* 26. *de Agoſto, de eſte Año de* 1666.

En MEXICO, en la Imprenta del Secreto del Santo Officio.
Por la Uiuda de Bernardo Calderon, en la calle de San Auguſtin.

Fig. 17. Title page of *Honorario Tvmvlo, pompa exequial ...*, published for the Holy Office of the Inquisition by the widow of Bernardo Calderón. México, 1666.

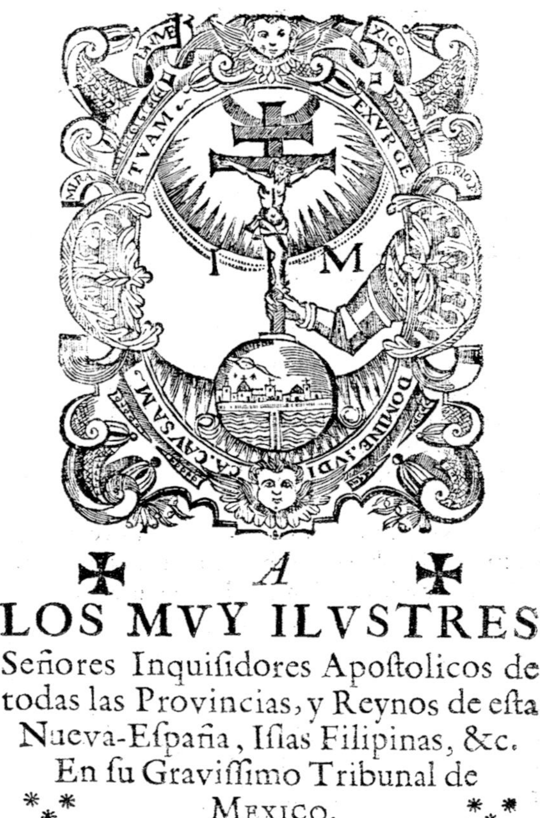

Fig. 18. Shield of the Inquisition of Mexico, engraving in *Honorario Tvmvlo, pompa exequial . . .*, published for the Holy Office of the Inquisition by the widow of Bernardo Calderón, México, 1666.

PHILIPPO MAGNO
DOMINICO, VICTORI A CRVCE,
Potentiſſimo HISP. & INDIARVM REGI IV.
NVMÆ ſuo, vere Romano; Catholico, Orthodoxo, Pontificio; Pro ſpirante Religionis templo, in ſe ipſa ſibi ipſi erecto, ſarcto, Tectoque, dum viveret: Mortuo, Orbis vtriusque deſiderio: ſepulto Militantis Eccleſię planctu: ęquo ſed Triumphantis Gaudio, feſtoque.

SACRUM FIDEI TRIBVNAL MEXICANVM, Optimo Parenti parentans, DOMINICAM PYRAM *gratitudinis igne à corde accenſam, debitæ iuxtà, ac ſolutæ Patrono Maximo* FIDEI, *Supremum pignus.*

P. D. C. Q.

Fig. 19. Latin inscription from the catafalque of Philip IV in the Church of Santo Domingo of México, published in *Honorario Tvmvlo, pompa exequial . . .*, published for the Holy Office of the Inquisition by the widow of Bernardo Calderón, México, 1666.

probably pure beeswax) was 21 *pesos*, while that of "ordinary wax" was 18 *pesos*.

In the *Autos*, there are various documents that refer to aspects of the purchase, weight, and uses of the wax, as well as that which was returned unburned. This visual resource played a fundamental role in giving the Baroque festival the desired luminous splendor; the extravagant use of this material was also an indication of economic power. Andrés de Fuentes received from Captain Guerra the necessary wax for the adornment of the sarcophagus and the church (on the high altar alone one hundred candles of two pounds each); the *nuncio* Gerónimo del Castillo was responsible for obtaining the wax for distribution to the religious communities. The wax took the form of candles (denominated *bujías*, *hachas*, *cirios*, and *velas*) of different weights and qualities. The candles on the sarcophagus burned from August 25 and throughout the following days; it was thus necessary to replace constantly what was consumed. The bill for the wax reached something over 5,528 *pesos*, the cost of 217 *arrobas*. This sum was, however, reduced by 3,792 *pesos*, 2 *reales*, and 3 *tomines*, for the wax that was left over, which was carefully weighed. In the end, Captain Guerra Escudero received 1,737 *pesos*, 4 *tomines*, and 5 *granos*.

On August 3, the master cutler Juan de Robles testified that he had made the gilded sword that would be used in the burial of the king, which, according to the swordsmith, was worth 16 *pesos*. The inquisitors cut him down a *peso* in the haggling over the accounts.

At its morning session on August 5 the tribunal agreed to have made what was called a "*valla y palenque*" (as the description of the works seems to suggest, a fenced walkway), for, as has already been mentioned, it was the rainy season. For the greater dignity of the procession, the Inquisition desired that the boarded walkway and the palisade should surround the whole *plazuela* of Santo Domingo (and part of the convent cloister). This was a large-scale item of carpentry work. The *Autos* state that the walkway (*valla*)

> is to be made all the way round the *plazuela* . . ., with bridging timbers and cross pieces for the said walkway, and posts and poles (*morillos*) for the palisade, peltry strips [for lashing

the timbers], and stain for the said poles; and for the [payment of] carters for fetching and carrying the said timber, and the rental of the carts, and wages of the craftsmen to assemble it. For each section has to be [made up with] three bridging timbers so that the said cross pieces shall not tremble.[60]

The above information appears in the quotation submitted, on August 3, by Rodrigo Bernal de Ortega, chief inspector (*maestro mayor*) of the Inquisition's works, who requested, in the first instance, 240 *pesos* for his work.

Now, for the procession that had been made from the palace to the cathedral in connection with the sarcophagus raised by the *Real Audiencia*, a similar walkway had been constructed at a cost of 540 *pesos*, since—it was stated—that circuit was of considerable length. The Inquisition considered Rodrigo Bernal's quotation for the Santo Domingo walkway to be excessive, and so decided to call for a second estimate from the carpenters who had built the walkway between the cathedral and the viceroy's palace. The call for bids was answered by Antonio Baptista Solano and Antonio de Moya, master carpenters, who at first asked for 300 *pesos*, more than the price estimated by Bernal. Afterwards, they came down to 200 *pesos*. Bernal then equaled the second bid, reducing his quote to 200 *pesos* and including in it the cost for the miniature catafalque (*tumbilla*) and tiered benches for the courtroom. Finally, on August 14, an agreement was reached in acceptance of Bernal's estimate. The *valla* or walkway would need to have a breadth of four-and-a-half *varas*, and a height of half a *vara*, so that surface water could pass underneath. The timber for carrying out the work was hired. Bernal undertook to repair all the holes he would have to make in the paved areas in order to seat the structure. There was an adjustment of 10 *pesos* in favor of Bernal in view of the fact that apparently the work had to have a continuation within the main patio of the Dominican convent.

Another payment was made to Nicolás de Lora, commissioned to hang the drapes in the Tribunal's principal courtroom; since it was discovered that the fabric purchased was insufficient, he obtained more. This payment also included the cost of distributing the wax required by the eight religious orders; the total paid out was 18 *pesos* and was made on September 2.

Gerónimo del Castillo presented a very curious account (*Memoria y Razón*). This refers to an expenditure made for delivering to Santo Domingo benches, candlesticks, and other articles loaned by various churches and religious houses in the city. The convent of Santa Clara lent twenty pews. Ten more were brought from the convent of La Concepción, six from that of San Lorenzo, another ten from La Encarnación. Six bronze candlesticks were obtained from the Casa Profesa, two sculptures of lions from the same source, four candlesticks from the Merced, four more from La Trinidad, and others—an unspecified quantity—from the Colegio de San Pedro y San Pablo. Four candlesticks came from San Francisco, two altar frontals from the same church, and a luxurious black cloth from the house of the Marshal of Castile (*Mariscal de Castilla*). The chairs used by the viceroy and his consort when they visited the *De Profundis* room of the Dominican convent were also brought into the church. Nails, tacks, and pins were also obtained for hanging the drapes in the hall of the Audiencia. A staging and screen were erected for the viceroy and his consort when they attended the services in the church. The cathedral contributed chairs and carpets for the use of its prebendaries and canons. Even the cathedral altar boys contributed to the effort by carrying a lectern to the Dominican church. The account presented by Gerónimo del Castillo amounted to 43 *pesos*, 7 *tomines*. The Inquisition paid Castillo's account without questioning it.

For his part, master carpenter Simón de los Santos requested payment of 32 *pesos*, on account of having taken down a gilded railing, that of the nave of the church, so that the catafalque could be seen in all its splendor. The railing had to be put back and thus needed repairs using gold leaf, plus timber, nails, sand, and lime, and tradesmen to do the work of reinstallation. After some argument he was paid twenty *pesos*.

Andrés de Fuentes included in his bill the cost of breakfasts, lunches, and suppers, as well as hot chocolate, that were given to the ten men who worked on the catafalque and kept vigil throughout the week that it was on view to the public. He himself had been responsible for hanging the drapes on the pillars of the church, on the pews of the familiars of the Inquisition who attended the services in the church, and on the floor before the catafalque. Fuentes arranged for the making of the scepter of gilded wood (which cost six *pesos*) and the tin candle snuffers, and also provided the ropes and buckets for lifting the candles onto the catafalque and for providing the necessary water in case of fire. He was paid 146 *pesos* on October 2.[61]

Licenciado Francisco López Sánz, receiver of the Court of the *Santo Oficio*, was in charge of buying the luxurious transparent "mantle of glory" that covered the royal crown, scepter, and sword, at a cost of 12 *pesos*. It was a delicate fabric of imported silk. The symbolic objects were placed upon fine cushions.

Francisco López Capilla, the Mexico City cathedral's Kapellmeister, took part, along with the entire staff of singers and minstrels, in all the exequies: vespers, sung mass, and the sung prayers for the dead of the second day. One hundred *pesos* were paid for him, his instrumentalists, and the choristers.

The *Autos* include a payment dated October 11 in favor of the Jesuits Francisco de Uribe and Antonio Núñez de Miranda for their work in the composition and design of the catafalque, and their writing of "sonnets and epigrams" (fig. 19). But the payment, which amounted to 100 *pesos*, was not actually released until December 23, 1667, by which time Uribe had died. Núñez de Miranda expressed his wish that the sum be used to pay for the manufacture of a chalice, a salver, and cruets, which were being made for the feast of the Immaculate Conception, or Virgen de la Purísima, of the confraternity of the same name, based at the college of San Pedro y San Pablo, at which Núñez was a prefect.

The Inquisition's receiver, Francisco López Sánz, was in charge of buying, from the convent of San Jerónimo, the four trays of luxury sweetmeats and two trays of pastry lozenges that were offered when the Marqués de Mancera and his family "took the chocolate" in the House of the Inquisition. The six trays cost 57 *pesos*, 4 *reales*.

One of the last procedures mentioned in the *Autos* is the information presented on June 15, 1666 by Paula de Benavides, widow of the famous printer Bernardo Calderón. Doña Paula was the Inquisition's printer, and she had been commissioned to print the book describing in full detail the obsequies organized by the Inquisition (figs. 17–19). Calderón's widow also printed the book *Llanto de Occidente* recording the funeral honors performed for Philip IV in the Mexico City cathedral, which included engravings of that catafalque (figs. 12–16). Both works are full of valuable information regarding art, daily life, and the history of the printing press in Mexico. The Inquisition publication—praised and commented on in parts by Guillermo Tovar de Teresa in his extremely useful *Bibliografía novohispana de arte*—includes the complex baroque texts of Uribe and Núñez de Miranda, as well as the funeral oration and the panegyric sermon.[62]

Doña Paula informed the Inquisition that the book consisted of 21 signatures or gatherings, for which 134 quires of clean, undamaged paper were necessary. The 150 copies were parchment bound, and twelve of them were also provided with ribbons. The widow asked for payment of 236 *pesos*. Immediately the Inquisition called on the equally famous printers Juan Ruiz and Francisco Lupercio to value Doña Paula's work; their judgment was that the widow should lower her overall price to 202 *pesos*, 2 *reales*. This is what was finally paid, against the judgment of the *fiscal* of the *Santo Oficio*, who for unexplained reasons recommended that the payment should be even further reduced to 180 *pesos*.

On April 22, 1667, 24 copies of the book were sent to Madrid with a letter addressed to the inquisitor general of Spain. On October 19 of the same year, more than a year after the celebration of the funeral rites in Mexico City, the Spanish tribunal of inquisitors replied somewhat laconically: "the Inquisitor General being present, it has pleased him to thank you, sirs, for the attention and pomp with which you have celebrated those honors. May the Lord bless you and keep you."[63]

Notes

Translated by Christopher Follett. I am grateful to Michael Brown, Mayer Fellow at the Denver Art Museum, and to María José Esparza Liberal of the Instituto de Investigaciones Estéticas at the Universidad Nacional Autónoma de Mexico, for assistance with locating images.

[1] Isidro de Sariñana, *Llanto de Occidente en el ocaso del más claro sol de las Españas y Noticia breve de la deseada, última dedicación del templo metropolitano de México*, facsimile of the editions of 1666 and 1668, including a monograph on Isidro de Sariñana y Cuenca by Guillermo Tovar de Teresa (Mexico City: Bibliófilos Mexicanos, 1977).

[2] Ibid., 3r. The tartane is a type of small boat for coastal use; in Veracruz a boat of that kind was customarily used to carry the crates or chests containing the mail to the fortress.

[3] Antonio de Robles, *Diario de sucesos notables (1665–1703)*, ed. Antonio Castro Real (Mexico City: Porrúa, Colección de Escritores Mexicanos 1946), 1:18.

[4] Ibid.

[5] Isidro de Sariñana, *Llanto de Occidente*, 4r–4v.

[6] *Autos en razón de las honras, túmulo, lutos, y gastos que se hicieron por la muerte del Rey Nuestro Señor don Felipe quarto, que está en Gloria; pésame que se dio al virrey, y lo demás concerniente a ella.* Archivo General de la Nación, México, Inquisición, vol. 33-1508, exp. 5, fs. 1r–80r. Lote Riva Palacio. Hereafter cited as *Autos*.

[7] As regards the three inquisitors who were in office at that time, it is worth recording the following. Don Pedro de Medina Rico was born in Lucena, Spain. He was a *colegial mayor* of Santa María de Jesús at the University of Seville, as well as holding a chair there (*catedrático de decreto*). He was *abogado de fábrica* and *juez de testamentos* to the Archbishopric of Seville. He was also a visiting inquisitor (*inquisidor visitador*) at Cartagena de Indias (Colombia). He was *inquisidor fiscal* at Zaragoza, Spain. In June 1654 he arrived in New Spain, where he also served as *inquisidor visitador*. He died in Veracruz on May 30, 1669, just as he was intending to return to Spain.

Inquisitor Don Juan de Ortega y Montañés was born in the village of Siles, Jaén, June 23, 1627, the son of Diego de Ortega Montañés—president of the *Real Consejo* of Castile—and of Doña María Patiño. His family included numerous knights of different orders. He studied law at the University of Alcalá de Henares, 1649–1653, obtaining the degree of doctor of jurisprudence. He arrived in New Spain and was elected bishop of Durango. He was acting bishop (*obispo efectivo*) of Guatemala. Later, he went to the diocese of Michoacán, where he remained until 1700, when he was appointed archbishop of Mexico. He was twice interim viceroy: for ten months the first time (1696) and the second, for a year (1701–1702). He died in Mexico City in 1708. Other data and the inventory of his fabulous collection of paintings can be consulted in Juana Gil Bermejo, "El expolio de un obispo – México 1708," in *Anuario de Estudios Americanos*, vol. 27 (Seville: Escuela de Estudios Hispanoamericanos, 1970).

Inquisidor fiscal Don Nicolás de las Infantas y Venegas was born in Lima around 1638, son of Andrés de las Infantas y Mendoza (who was born in Córdoba, Spain) and Doña Ana de Villegas, a native of Lima. He had two brothers, Francisco and Bernardo Antonio de las Infantas, both knights of the Order of Santiago, as were his father and he himself. His uncle Luis de las Infantas was *oidor* (civil magistrate) of Guatemala. Nicolás de las Infantas was a familiar of the Inquisition in Lima and also served as president of the Audiencia (court of appeal) of Quito (1674). My thanks are due to Dr. Javier Sanchiz Ruiz of the Instituto de Investigaciones Históricas de la Universidad Nacional Autónoma de México for having kindly provided me with biographical data on the inquisitors.

[8] *Autos.*

[9] Isidro de Sariñana, *Llanto de Occidente*, 6r.

[10] Ibid., 7r.

[11] Ibid., 9r–9v.

[12] Isidro de Sariñana, *Llanto de Occidente*, 7r.–7v.

[13] Ibid., 10r.

[14] Ibid.

[15] Ibid.

[16] Ibid.

[17] See, in the *Autos*, the description given by *Fiscal* Don Nicolás de las Infantas y Venegas. Sariñana also offers detailed information regarding the *pésame* given to the viceroy and his consort. Cf. 18r. ff. This includes the names of all those who attended the palace and their positions.

[18] *Autos.*

[19] Ibid. *Lobas* are soutanes or cassocks; *capuces* are long hooded capes worn over the soutane or other items of dress specifically for mourning (*tr.*).

[20] Ibid.

[21] Ibid.

[22] Ibid.

[23] Isidro de Sariñana, *Llanto de Occidente*, 22r. ff. In the *Autos* there is also information to this effect.

[24] Ibid.

[25] Ibid.

[26] Ibid.

[27] *Autos.*

[28] *Honorario Tvmvlo, Pompa Exequial, y Imperial Mavsoleo, que Mas Fina Artemisia La Fe Romana, por su Sacrosanto Tribunal de Nueva-España, erigió, y celebró llorosa Egeria, a su Catholico Numa, y Amante Rey, Philippo Qvarto El Grande. En sv Real Convento de Santo Domingo de Mexico, Miércoles por la tarde, y jueues por la mañana, 25 y 26. de Agosto, de este Año de 1666* (Mexico City, "en la Imprenta del Secreto del Santo Officio. Por la Viuda de Bernardo Calderón, en la calle de San Agustin"). Hereafter *Honorario Tvmvlo*. Two copies are known of this work. One is in the Biblioteca Nacional de México and another in the Biblioteca Pública del Estado in Orihuela, Spain, which was the one consulted for this paper. Cf. Biblioteca Virtual del Patrimonio Bibliográfico: http://bvpb.mcu.es/es catalogo_imagenes.

[29] Ibid.

[30] Both the *Autos* and the *Honorario Tvmvlo* include important information about the procession. See also Clara García Ayluardo, "El privilegio de pertenecer. Las comunidades de fieles y la crisis de la monarquía católica," in *Cuerpo político y pluralidad de derechos. Los privilegios de las corporaciones novohispanas*, ed. Beatriz Rojas (Mexico City: Centro de Investigación y Docencia Económica, Instituto Mora, 2007), 85–128.

[31] Ibid.
[32] The cathedral Kapellmeister was Francisco López Capilla.
[33] *Autos*. As regards the different buildings that made up the Palace of the Inquisition, see Francisco Santos Zertuche, *Señorío, dinero, y arquitectura. El palacio de la Inquisición de México, 1571–1820* (Mexico City: El Colegio de México, Universidad Autónoma Metropolitana-Azcapotzalco, 2000); and Francisco de la Maza, *El palacio de la Inquisición (Escuela Nacional de Medicina)* (Mexico City: Universidad Nacional Autónoma de México, Instituto de Investigaciones Estéticas, 1951).
[34] The *Autos* state: "And the said fence (*valla*) and walkway (*palenque*) has to lead from the main door of this Santo Oficio until the crossing that leads to the Convent of the Incarnation (*Convento de la Encarnación*). And has to turn after the pedestal of the cross that is in the said *plazuela* [of Santo Domingo] and beside the portal, as far as the door of the Church of Santo Domingo. And from the said door of Santo Domingo to the fence of the door of this Holy Office the same walkway has to be made for the return of your lordship, after the interment and mass of the following day."
[35] *Honorario Tvmvlo*.
[36] Ibid.
[37] See below, the purchase of "a mantle of glory."
[38] *Honorario Tvmvlo*.
[39] Ibid.
[40] Ibid.
[41] Ibid.
[42] There is information regarding the music both in the *Honorario Tvmvlo* and in the *Autos*.
[43] *Honorario Tvmvlo*.
[44] Ibid.
[45] Ibid.
[46] Ibid.
[47] Ibid.
[48] *Autos*. As regards the family of artists surnamed Ramírez see Efraín Castro Morales, "Los Ramírez, una familia de artistas novohispanos del siglo XVII," *Boletín de Monumentos Históricos*, no. 8: 5–36.
[49] Regarding the symbolism of the Inquisition's catafalque, see Víctor Mínguez Cornelles, *Los reyes distantes. Imágenes del poder en el México virreinal* (Castelló de la Plana: Universidad Jaime I, 1995); the same author's *Los reyes solares. Iconografía astral de la monarquía hispánica* (Castelló de la Plana: Universidad Jaime I, 2001); and, likewise, "La muerte del príncipe: reales exequias de los últimos austrias en México," *Cuadernos de Arte Colonial*, no. 6 (mayo 1990): 5–31. For the procession staged by the municipal government (*ayuntamiento*) on the occasion of the death of Philip IV at San Luis Potosí, Mexico, see Alfonso Martínez Rosales, "Reales exequias en San Luis Potosí," in *Juegos de ingenio y agudeza. La pintura emblemática de la Nueva España* (Mexico City: Museo Nacional de Arte, 1994), 170–177. Another relevant work is Alicia Bazarte Martínez and Miguel Ángel Priego Gómez, *El gran teatro de la muerte: las piras funerarias en Zacatecas* (Zacatecas: Fondo Estatal para la Cultura y las Artes de Zacatecas, 1998).
[50] *Autos*. The descriptions by Ramírez that appear next were taken from the *Autos*.
[51] *Honorario Tvmvlo*.
[52] There is information on the reinforcement of the boarded floor of the church in the *Autos*, and likewise in the *Honorario Tvmvlo*. In the latter we read: "se fortificó todo el plan de la Capilla mayor con una planta de vigas gruesas, encadenada y trabada con cortes, encajes y empalmes, pies derechos y tornapuntas; en que se levantaba a recebir el telar que subía a la altura del pavimento del zócalo." The text is rather obscure but seems to describe a strong jointed base made of thick beams, with a triangulated framework erected upon it, to receive the plinth upon which the rest of the monument was constructed; the text continues to state that, in this manner, "without any ugliness its beautiful contrivance was made firm."
[53] *Autos*.
[54] Guillermo Tovar de Teresa includes in his *Bibliografía novohispana de arte* the complete description of the catafalque that appears in the printed account. He is the first author to have made known in detail the disposition and symbolism of the work executed by Pedro Ramírez at Santo Domingo. Cf. by this author, *Bibliografía novohispana de Arte. Impresos mexicanos relativos al arte de los siglos XVI, XVII*, with foreword by José Pascual Buxó, 2 vols. (Mexico City: Fondo de Cultura Económica, 1988), 1:195–200.
[55] *Honorario Tvmvlo*.
[56] *Ibid*.
[57] Unless stated otherwise, the information presented here was taken from the *Autos*.
[58] María Dolores Bravo Arriaga, "Signos religiosos y géneros literarios en el discurso del poder," in *Sor Juana y su mundo. Una mirada actual* (Mexico City: Universidad del Claustro de Sor Juana, 1995), 116. See also, by the same author, *El discurso de la espiritualidad dirigida. Antonio Núñez de Miranda, confesor de Sor Juana* (Mexico City: Universidad Nacional Autónoma de México, 2001). Also, "Algunos poemas del túmulo a Felipe IV de Antonio Nuñez de Miranda y Francisco de Uribe," *Calíope: Journal of the Society for Renaissance and Baroque Hispanic Poetry* 4, no. 2 (1984): 29–37.
[59] Antonio de Robles, *Diario de sucesos notables*, 1:25.
[60] The passage is rather imprecise and open to interpretation. The original states that the *valla* (interpreted as meaning a walkway) "se ha de hacer en la plazuela …, toda en contorno …, así de puentes como de tendidos para dicha valla, y pies derechos, y morillos para el palenque, colambre para [amarrarlos], y tinta para dar a dichos morillos, y acarreos de carros de traída y llevada de dicha madera, y alquileres de ella, y gente para armarla. Que ha de tener cada tramo a tres puentes porque no tiemblen dichos tendidos." There is also information in the printed document regarding the "*valla y palenque*," as well as the passage that was made from the palace to the cathedral.
[61] The extra sum he was awarded for his work is not specified.
[62] See note 54 above.
[63] "[P]resente el inquisidor general, ha parecido agradeceros señores, la atención y lucimiento con que celebrasteis dichas honras. Dios os guarde."

Between Monarchic and Local Identity

An Ephemeral Facade for Charles IV's Proclamation Ceremony in Mexico (1789)

Beatriz Berndt L. M.

Images of governors have been consumed, from Imperial Rome to our present, as media to spread and promote causes, doctrines, policies, or ideas. In this essay, I focus on a ceremony that took place cyclically in Mexico, the capital of the Viceroyalty of New Spain, when a Spanish king died and political order had to be reestablished. In order to show how images helped to express notions or values concerning the Hispanic monarchy and its sovereign at the end of the eighteenth century, I refer to iconic and written testimonies and to the creative process of a local architect, explaining basic political concepts that were represented in the ornamental program of a temporary facade that was designed to cover for a few weeks the principal facade of the city hall of Mexico City, an ephemeral architecture made of wood and canvas of which we still have memory in a print.

While the French Revolution was being consolidated, on December 27, 1789, inhabitants of the capital of New Spain celebrated the solemn festivities of inauguration of a new monarch. Nine months before, on March 13, there arrived at the city hall of Mexico City a *real cedula* (royal order) in which Charles IV of Bourbon reported that his father Charles III had died and ordered his subjects to wear mourning clothes and carry out obsequies to indicate grief over his death. Moreover, since a rite of succession was necessary, the heir to the throne ordered the viceroyalty to organize formalities and public events appropriate to the inauguration of the next reign.[1] Five weeks later, the city council took the first measures relating to the proclamation ceremony, such as designating deputies to contact a clarinetist and a kettledrummer, and to arrange the minting of coins and medals. Among other points, its members also agreed by a majority of votes to the nomination of six commissioners responsible for the ephemeral facades that, for some weeks, were to cover the principal (external) frontages of the viceregal palace of Mexico, the city hall, and the archbishop's palace. To oversee the design and manufacture of the first, the council designated Chief Constable Joaquín Romero de Caamaño and Antonio Rodríguez de Velasco; for the second, Don Francisco María Herrera and José Mariano de Mimiaga; while the third was to be supervised by Alejandro Manuel Acevedo de Estrada Cosío y Guerra, Marquis of Uluapa, and Felipe Antonio Teruel. According to what was set down in the council records, José Ángel de Cuevas Aguirre y Avendaño and Don Antonio Méndez Prieto were not only to organize bullfights, tournaments, and fireworks, but also to make all the necessary arrangements to illuminate the temporary facades at night.[2] Meanwhile, Captain Don Manuel de Monroy Guerrero y Luyando and Ignacio Beye Cisneros took responsibility for decorating the city hall, where important ceremonies were to take place including the hand-over of the pennant to the royal standard bearer and the final act of acclamation and obedience to the monarch, with a gala ball to be held in the grand hall.

The land surveyor and master architect Ignacio de Castera (1750?–1811) submitted a project dated June 12, 1789 to the council members.[3] De Castera detailed the ephemeral architectural works and monuments he proposed as a gift to the monarch, an estimation of their costs, their nighttime illumination, and the firework displays that would be lit in front of each, together with the distribution of costs between the city council and the city's guilds. He proposed to carry out the enthronement ceremony in the first few days of November, when the rainy season was over, so we can deduce that in his view, the preparations would take a little over four months. While he presented written descriptions of a number of objects—mentioning decorative issues, the production of two mounted statues, and an allegorical carriage—he also appended to the text eight drawings. These include the designs for five temporary facades, two triumphal arches, and an obelisk, most of which present Classical formal elements. De Castera went on to emphasize that the monetary cost of the architectural works and monuments would be minimal in comparison with their effect, however, if it were necessary to adhere strictly to an estimated budget, he proposed eliminating one triumphal arch and the allegorical carriage, in order not to sacrifice better-quality or more pertinent work. Meanwhile, although he accepted the need to comply with council decisions on time and budget, and to await a decision on the design proposals to which he would later give their final form, in the last paragraph of the manuscript he indicated that he would reject any amendments made to the drafts, since he had created them "with intensive study"—a condition that would be difficult to meet by the council, given that De Castera was only offering his services.

Though all the images were appealing, for the council members the proposal for the facade to cover the city hall frontage would be of particular interest, not only because they had to pay for these works, but because they were the promoters of the royal celebrations in the city. For the occasion, De Castera drew the elevation of a building with a portico projecting from the facade (fig. 1).[4] In the central section of the first story he set an elliptical arch with bosses on the archivolt and on the exterior surface of the jamb, and placed two cherubim on the keystone, holding a coat of arms. To either side he drew two semicircular arches with garlands suspended among the central voussoirs and adornments on the spandrels. He also included two niches at either end of the arcade, above which oval medallions sat with a woven band of leaves. To support this part of the work, he designed six pilasters with projecting blocks to the rear.

For the upper volume, he drew a kind of triumphal arch with single and paired Corinthian columns, and on the entablature placed war trophies, together with four cherubim, two of which bear pennants. The draughtsman embellished the tympanum of the pediment with a sketch of the royal coat of arms with draped garlands, while the acroterion, supported by twin pilasters, was enhanced by a radiant aureole and a pair of trophies with weapons and military attire and insignia. Four straight arches extended the length of the gallery on the first story of the facade. For the pilasters that formed the entrance span, the master architect designed a projecting embossment and a pedestal with a shaft in the form of an inverted obelisk, which included a space for inscriptions. Here, he also delineated an escutcheon to display

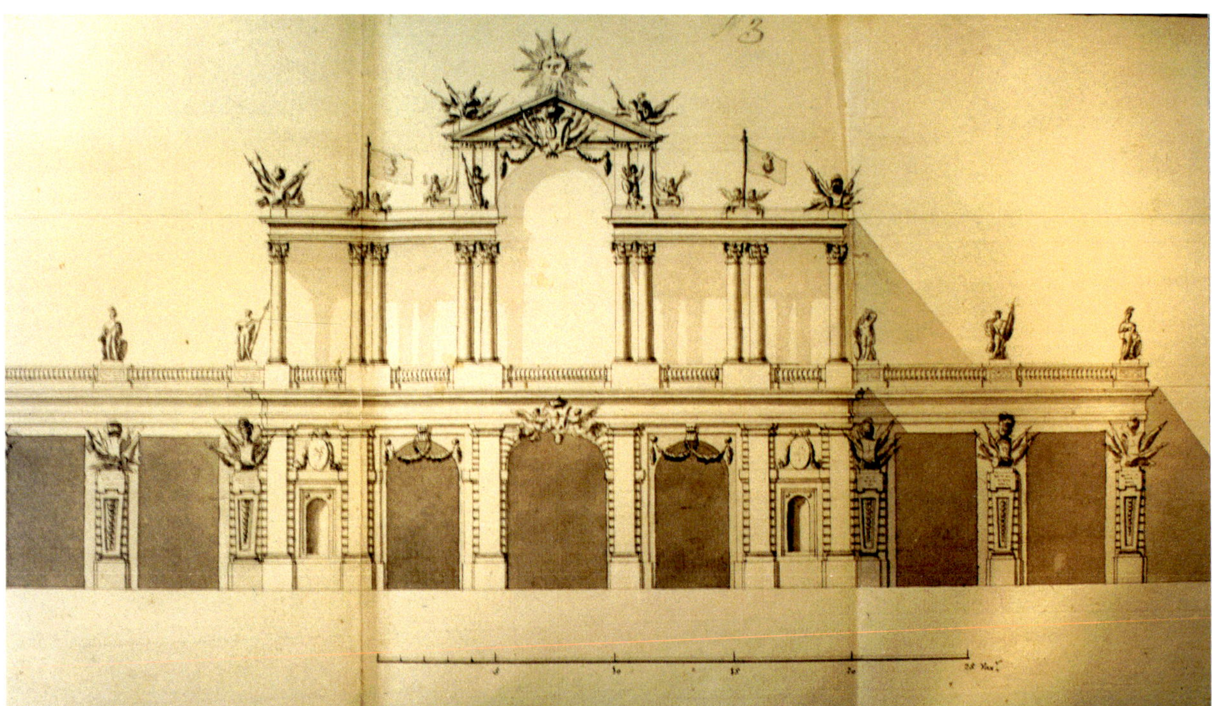

Fig. 1. Ignacio de Castera, *Design of an Ephemeral Facade for the City Hall of Mexico for Charles IV's Proclamation Ceremony*. Mexico, 1789. Drawing, 11½ x 22¼ in. (29 x 56.5 cm). Archivo Histórico del Distrito Federal "Carlos de Sigüenza y Góngora," Fondo Ayuntamiento de México-Gob. D.F., *Historia. Jura y funerales de reyes*, vol. 2282, file 21, project no. 3.

a coat of arms or similar ornamental element, to be framed by pennants and a morion helmet. To endow the work with greater splendor, De Castera designed an attic story with balustrades for the entablature of this arcade, with six figures of gods from Classical antiquity set on pedestals with inscriptions on the dados.

In this and the other drawings, De Castera successfully designed a politically symbolic decorative program in which he included coats of arms, war trophies, woven laurel leaves, gods and heroes from Classical mythology, and royal portraits. These would help to circulate the image of the new sovereign among his subjects for the first time, while emphasizing values and virtues that transmitted an idea of the occupant of the throne and the form of government. From the outset, De Castera was evidently aware that the role of the architectural and decorative work was to reinforce a triumphant discourse of the political system, a notion that would also be manifested in the symbolic language of the proclamation ceremony.

It bears mentioning that De Castera held the position of master builder of the city from October 1781. Given that the city council ratified his work by vote every year, it is clear that in March or April 1789 the council members must have commissioned him to create and design the ephemeral work. At the time he took on the project, Mexico's master architect and city planner was restoring two residences belonging to the convent of St. Bernard and inspecting deterioration to the arches of the Chapultepec aqueduct.[5] He completed the documentation, calculations, and drawings in the month of June in order to present the council members with an idea of the appearance, location, purpose, and cost of the ceremonial architecture. Some weeks later, at the request of Governor-Intendant Bernardo de Bonavia y Zapata, the commissioners of the celebrations were summoned to a regular and extraordinary session of the council on the morning of August 17, where they had to report progress in their tasks. Antonio Rodríguez de Velasco, Francisco María de Herrera, and Felipe Antonio Teruel stated they would soon be in possession of representations of the ephemeral architecture, so we can deduce that De Castera was at that point completing the first drawings approved by the council.[6]

De Castera may have delivered an account of the decorative figures during this period, as the initial project states that he would present "an inventory of the statues and paintings for use with the citations mentioned, indicating whether they are *décimas*, quatrains, sonnets, etc., and their distribution in each of the blank spaces left in the drawings."[7] Fortunately, a handwritten document has been preserved that, though it lacks his signature, enumerates the decorations for the principal facade of the viceregal palace, the council chambers, and the archbishop's palace (fig. 2).[8] This source gives documentary evidence about themes and locations of the paintings and sculptural work, but does not give details of the prose and verse inscriptions. Despite De Castera's refusal to accept external amendments, the text also informs that changes were made to the ornament of some facades, as well as significant alterations of an architectural or decorative order. It is enough to check the initial drawings for the city hall against this summary to see that the architect maintained the garlands, royal coats of arms, solar motif, medallions, and military trophies. At the same time, however, new elements were incorporated—whether on De Castera's own initiative or at the request of the city council—such as the portraits of Charles IV and his consort, a family tree, a dynastic series with monarchs from the Houses of Habsburg and Bourbon, coats of arms from towns and cities, and geographical personifications of Europe, America, Madrid, and Mexico City, the capital of New Spain. Documentary evidence also shows that the radiant aureole was transformed into a victory figure of Apollo in his horse-drawn chariot.

This second decorative program coincides entirely with that of a commemorative print made by José Joaquín Fabregat (1748–1807), which recorded the temporary facade as seen by those attending the ceremony of the pledge of allegiance in 1789 (fig. 3). Thanks to this print we know that, though he does not describe them in writing, De Castera made substantial modifications to the architectural design of the facade for the city hall. The composition is described further on, but at this point it is worth mentioning that the city's master architect retained the idea of the facade as a portico, together with the intention to maintain order,

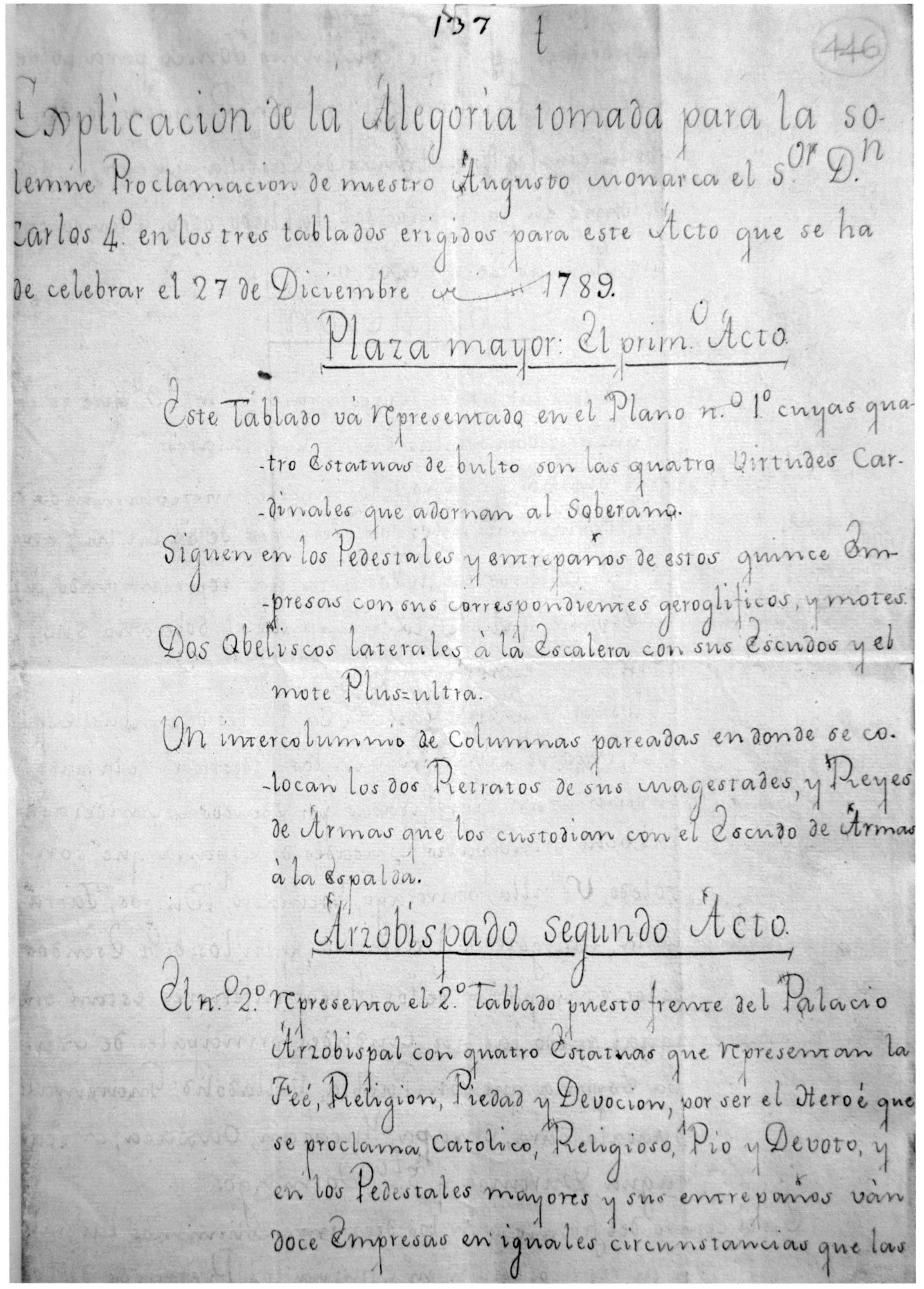

137

446

Explicacion de la Alegoria tomada para la solemne Proclamacion de nuestro Augusto monarca el S.or D.n Carlos 4.o en los tres tablados erigidos para este Acto que se ha de celebrar el 27 de Diciembre de 1789.

Plaza mayor: el prim.o Acto.

Este Tablado và representado en el Plano n.o 1.o cuyas quatro Estatuas de bulto son las quatro Virtudes Cardinales que adornan al Soberano.

Siguen en los Pedestales y entrepaños de estos quince Empresas con sus correspondientes geroglificos, y motes.

Dos Obeliscos laterales à la Escalera con sus Escudos y el mote Plus=ultra.

Un intercolumnio de Columnas pareadas en donde se colocan los dos Retratos de sus magestades, y Reyes de Armas que los custodian con el Escudo de Armas à la espalda.

Arzobispado segundo Acto.

El n.o 2.o representa el 2.o Tablado puesto frente del Palacio Arzobispal con quatro Estatuas que representan la Feé, Religion, Piedad y Devocion, por ser el Heroè que se proclama Catolico, Religioso, Pio y Devoto, y en los Pedestales mayores y sus entrepaños vàn doce Empresas en iguales circunstancias que las

Fig. 2. "Explicación de la alegoría tomada para la solemne proclamación de nuestro augusto monarca el s[eñ]or d[o]n Carlos 4º en los tres tablados erigidos para este acto que se ha de celebrar el 27 de diciembre de 1789," S.l. [México], undated [1789], Archivo de la Antigua Academia de San Carlos, Biblioteca Lino Picaseño, Facultad de Arquitectura, UNAM, shelf 4, document 446, no folio number. Photo permission: Dirección General de Patrimonio Universitario, UNAM.

anteriores, y un intercolumnio Jonico para colocar el Docél, ò Pavellon en que van los Retratos de S.S. M.M.: Por la espalda las Armas de Castilla y Leon, y por delante en lo inferior del Tablado otro Escudo con las Armas de Mexico.

Diputacion

La Fachada de este Tablado se representa en el nº 3º que es con la que se adornaron las Casas Capitulares.

En el Cuerpo Superior y centro de los quatro intercolumnios que resaltan, vàn los dos Retratos de S.S. M.M., en los inmediatos estan dos Estatuas representando à la España y America tributando al Soberano sus Armas y Tesoros.

A los que siguen están las Capitales de ambas Españas, Madrid y Mexico; y en los Pedestales de la parte superior están significadas por Escudos y Vanderas las ocho principales Ciudades de España que son Toledo, Sevilla, Santiago, Granada, Burgos, Tarragona, Zaragoza y Valencia, y en los diez Escudos de los entrepaños de los Arcos inferiores estan en igual modo las diez Ciudades principales de Nueva España que son Puebla, Valladolid, Guatemala, Guadalaxara, Chiapa, Yucatán, Oaxaca, Nicaragua, Durango y Sto Domingo.

En el centro del frontis y en los diez intercolumnios laterales à su resalto están en Estatua los Retratos de los once Soberanos de España que ha tenido la América, en memoria de su fiel reconocimiento.

En el primer Cuerpo inferior del resalto del centro, vá el Árbol Genealógico de nuestros Soberanos, y à los lados el primero, y ultimo Virrey, el uno con los Yndios antiguos vencidos en señal de triunfo, y el otro con los Yndios presentes que perseveran bajo su Dominio en señal de su lealtad.

Bajo el bacon del centro donde está el R.[l] Pendón está colocado el Escudo de Armas de Mexico, y en la parte Superior en el frontis vá el de las Armas de España, y por remate el Sol, que es la principal alegoria con que se significa al Soberano benefico à todos sus Dominios.

En las Pilastras, Zoclos, Sobrepuertas y demàs hai varias Empresas alusivas al asunto.

harmony, and proportionality in the structure and ornamentation alike. On the other hand, he chose to increase the number of arches in the first story, while conferring greater importance on the upper level, designing a gallery and a larger-scale portico.

As we have no drawings or prints to reveal the appearance of the viceregal palace and archbishop's palace during the ceremonies, the handwritten document may come closest to the form taken by the ephemeral architecture built for the festivities. The city's master architect went into detail only with regard to the council chambers, whether because that proposal was the furthest advanced or because he thought it would carry greater weight before the council. However, in the brief lines of the text, the author managed to give a general idea of the ornamentation of the facades that for a period covered the seats of viceregal power and the archbishop's curia.

From the first project, signed in June 1789, De Castera was aware that his drawings might be converted into prints, not only to immortalize the appearance of the buildings, but also because the record of their magnificence would perpetuate the feelings of loyalty and respect fixed in the hearts of the viewers. Indeed, De Castera encouraged the production of prints, something that, it seemed to him, would have a greater purpose than building ceremonial apparatus of which no trace would remain.[9] Though the architect may also have used it to put his own talents on display, Fabregat's loose-leaf print may have been produced for the city council to send to Spain to accompany a written confirmation of the pledge of allegiance ceremony held in the capital of New Spain;[10] the iconic discourse—the view of the city hall adorned with its symbolic decorative program—would have been corroborative evidence that the city had carried out the ceremony and thereby accepted its legal and political implications.

It is probable that Fabregat's print is only a modest echo of the eleven illustrations included in the luxury publication *Description of the public ornaments with which the Royal Court of Madrid has joyfully proclaimed the ascension to the throne of our sovereigns King Charles IV and Doña María*

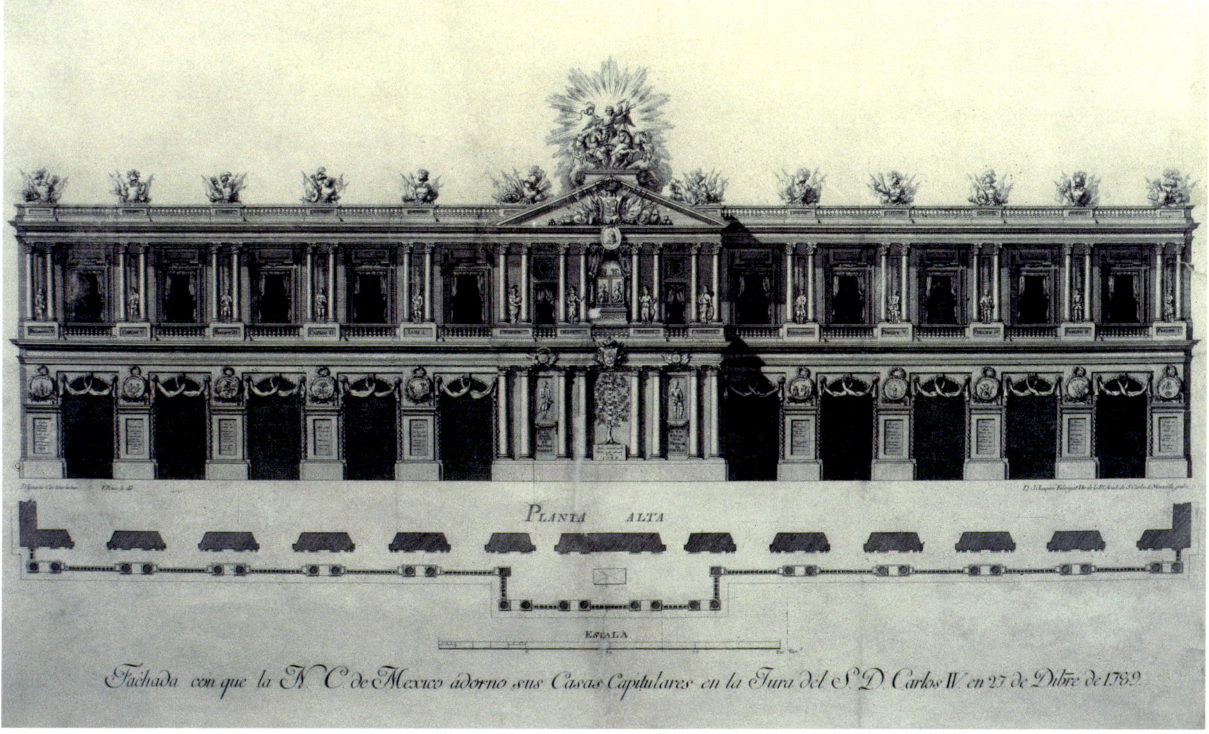

Fig. 3. Ignacio de Castera, Francisco Reyes, and José Joaquín Fabregat, *Fachada con que la n[obilísima] c[iudad] de Mexico adorno sus casas capitulares en la jura del s[eñor] D[on] Carlos IV en 27 de di[ciem]bre de 1789*. Mexico, 1789–1790. Print, 10½ x 21½ in. (27 x 54.5 cm). Instituto de Investigaciones Estéticas, Universidad Nacional Autónoma de México. Photo permission: Dirección General de Patrimonio Universitario, UNAM.

Luisa…, prepared at the request of the Royal Academy of Fine Arts of San Fernando under royal license, promoted by the Count of Floridablanca, and available to the public by the end of 1789.[11] Artists connected to the life of the Madrid academy, such as Juan Pedro Arnal (1735–1805), Ventura Rodríguez (1717–1785), Francisco de Goya (1747–1828), and Luis Paret (1746–1799), were involved in the design and decoration of the temporary constructions for the royal ceremonies in Madrid. Their efforts were followed by the production of eleven prints that recorded both the beauty of certain temporary facades and monuments and the exact Classical principles according to which they were manufactured. It is possible that the set of plans and elevations, most of which were produced by Francisco de Paula Martí (1762–1827), served as a model for an edition printed the following year at the expense of the town council of Seville.[12] This latter work came to light together with three prints showing the "ornaments" that hid the exterior of Seville's town hall during the celebrations for the new reign, along both its right-hand side and gallery and its principal facade (fig. 4). Despite the overelaborate style of certain decorative elements, Martí's print of the facade presents an architectural project with Classical tendencies that occupies the greater part of the composition. Beneath it, inscriptions can be read detailing the authorship, the scale in rods, and the title of the image.

Although the view of a noble building with the facade adorned for the occasion of a royal birth or marriage was a well-known theme in Spanish printmaking in the final decade of the eighteenth century, the compositional layout and landscape format of the illustrations for the enthronement celebrations in Madrid and Seville bear special

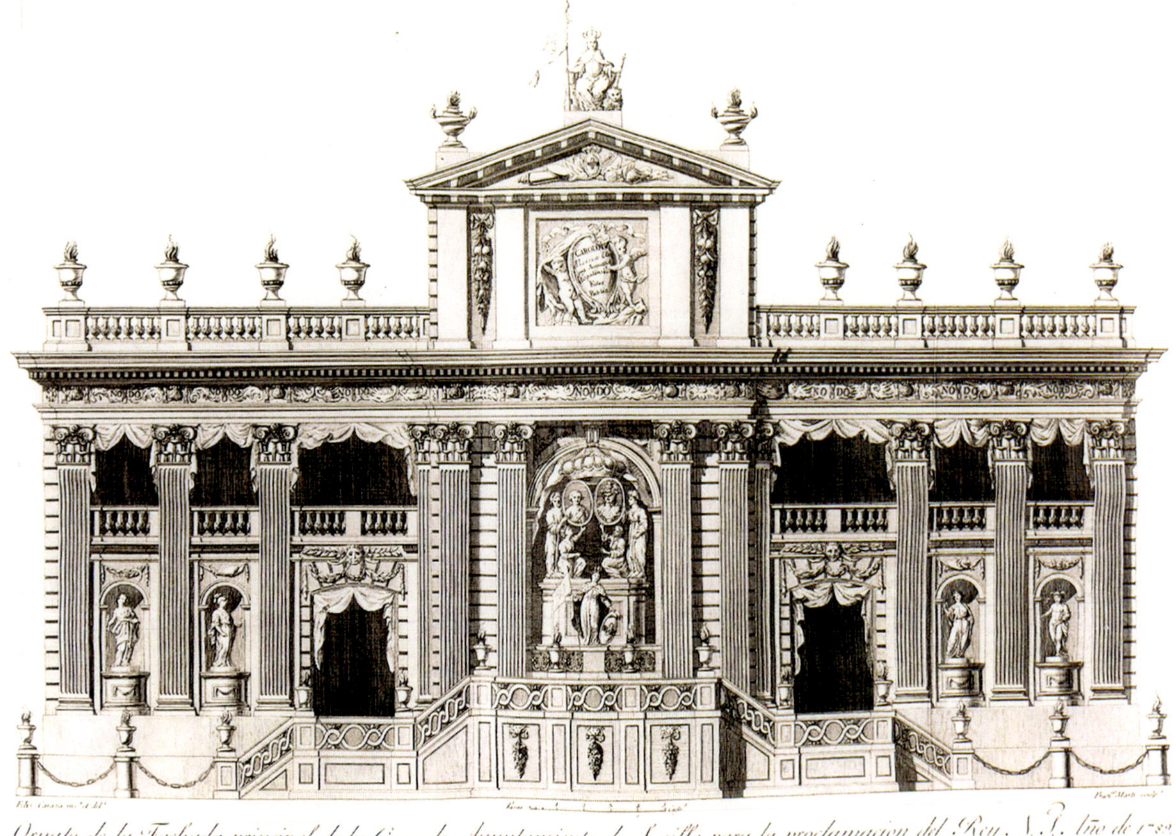

Fig. 4. Félix Caraza and Francisco de Paula Martí, *Ornato de la Fachada principal de la Casa de Ayuntamiento de Sevilla para la proclamación del Rey N.S Año de 1789.* In Gil, C. R. M. P. Manuel, *Relacion de la proclamacion del rey nuestro señor Don Carlos IIII, y fiestas con que la celebró la muy noble y muy leal ciudad de Sevilla, de cuya orden se da á luz […].* Madrid, Imprenta de la viuda de don Joaquín de Ibarra, 1790. Print, $13\frac{1}{3}$ x $22\frac{1}{2}$ in. (34 x 57 cm). © Biblioteca Nacional de España.

relation to the print Fabregat made in Mexico. Born in Valencia, Fabregat had been appointed as a supernumerary academician at the Royal Academy of San Fernando (1774) in Madrid, where he worked on significant publishing projects including prints of plans and elevations for the 1787 Spanish edition of the treatise of Vitruvius,[13] together with other commissions in which prints were used to reproduce paintings and drawings. As a skilled draughtsman and printmaker who held the position of Master of Drawing at the Royal Academy of San Carlos in Mexico City, he was a natural choice to record the architectural designs of Ignacio de Castera while at the same time disseminating academic principles and ideas.

Once the final design for the architectural ornamentation that was to cover the city hall was determined, it was set down on paper by De Castera's draughtsman, Francisco Reyes (*fl.* 1787–1805) and then delivered to Fabregat for intaglio printmaking. The images of the external facade and the upper floor occupy the larger part of the image transferred to the paper; beneath the elevation inscriptions identify those involved in producing the print, while the title appears below the horizontal section: *Fachada con que la n[obilísima] c[iudad] de Mexico adorno sus casas capitulares en la jura del s[eñor] D[on] Carlos IV en 27 de di[ciem]bre de 1789* ("Facade with which the most noble city of Mexico adorns its city chambers for the pledge of allegiance to Don Carlos IV on December 27, 1789") (fig. 3).

The design of this plan view allows us to understand the shape of the second level, the number of supports (twenty-eight columns and two pillars), the number, distribution, and rhythm of the openings, and the arrangement of the two outer ends, which held firm the wooden scaffold supporting the facade. The elevation shows the exterior of a Classical-style building on two floors, with a portico projecting from the center of the facade. This prominent section was blind on the first story and open on the second, indicating that its function was more decorative than for providing access or shelter. The front elevation also shows the ornamental details, some of which had symbolic connotations.

For the lower body (fig. 5), De Castera set out ten semicircular arches with foliage detailing on

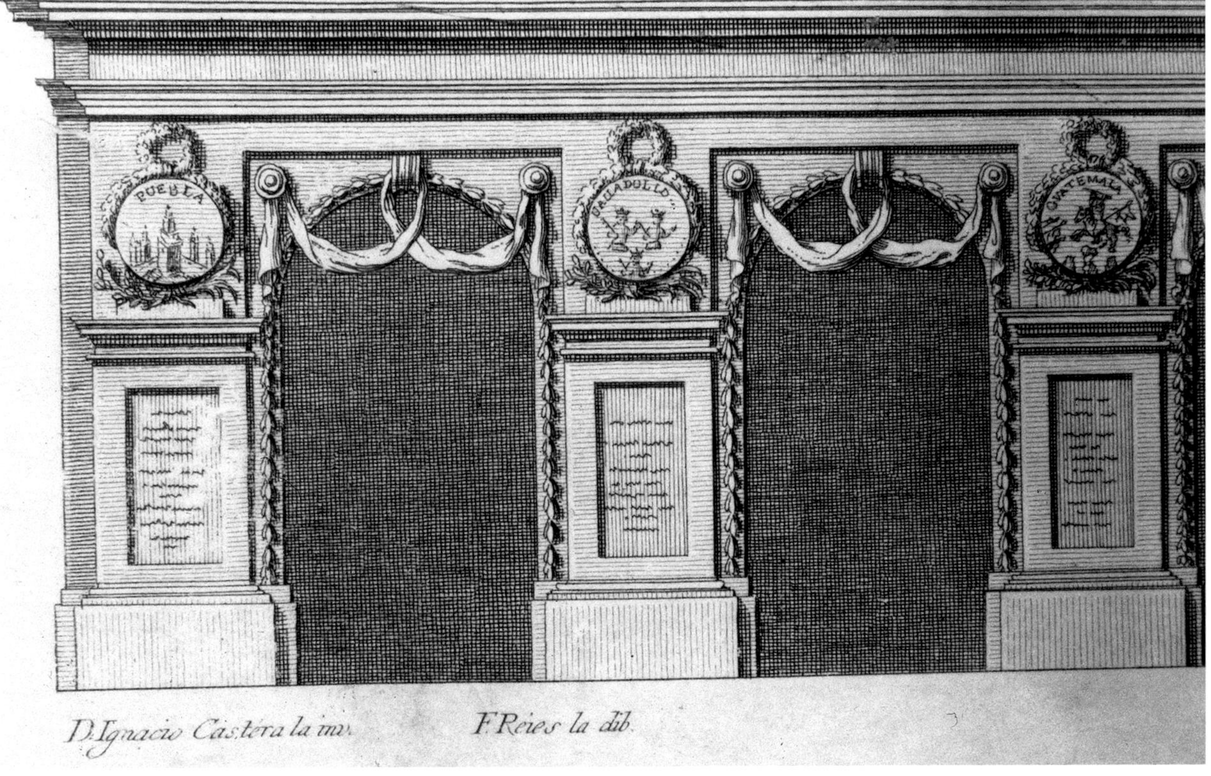

Fig. 5. Detail of fig. 3. Bottom, left.

the archivolt and the outer surface of the jamb, as well as cloth swags that hung between the keystones and the circular adornments attached to the spandrels. According to the print, above each arch there was a lintel on which the straight entablature of the lower story rested, supported by ten pilasters. These latter were decorated with medallions painted with the coats of arms of ten cities of New Spain, Puebla, Valladolid, Guatemala, Guadalajara, Ghalapa [*sic*], Yucatán, Oaxaca, Nicaragua, Durango, and Santo Domingo,[14] which were surrounded by palm leaves and woven strips of laurel leaves, while prose and verse inscriptions by Bruno José de Larrañaga, treasurer of the viceregal capital, were inscribed on the dados of the plinths.[15]

The upper body was formed by a gallery composed of paired Corinthian columns, with sculptural effigies of Spanish sovereigns (ten in all) between each pair, resting on low pedestals on which the name of each was inscribed (fig. 6).[16] Each pair of columns was flanked by a Corinthian balustrade, behind which there rose a straight arch with funiculus or spiral moldings on the jambs and a kind of embossment on the frieze, and to the sides and bottom of which hung denticles together with vegetation in the form of garlands and clusters. On the straight entablature, De Castera designed an attic story with Corinthian balustrades and a dozen war trophies comprising mail coats, helmets, morions, lances, quivers with arrows, cannons, drums, and military insignia—standards and pennants—for carrying onto the field of battle (fig. 7). All these elements were set on small bases on which might be read the names of the "principal cities of Spain, namely Toledo, Sevilla, Santiago, Granada, Burgos, Tarragona, Zaragoza and Valencia."[17]

The portico projecting from the facade was of two stories with a pediment and acroterion, which maintained proportion and balance with regard to the whole group of structural and decorative elements (fig. 8). Paired Ionic columns were placed on the ground floor with the figures—seemingly sculptures—of Hernán Cortés (right) and the

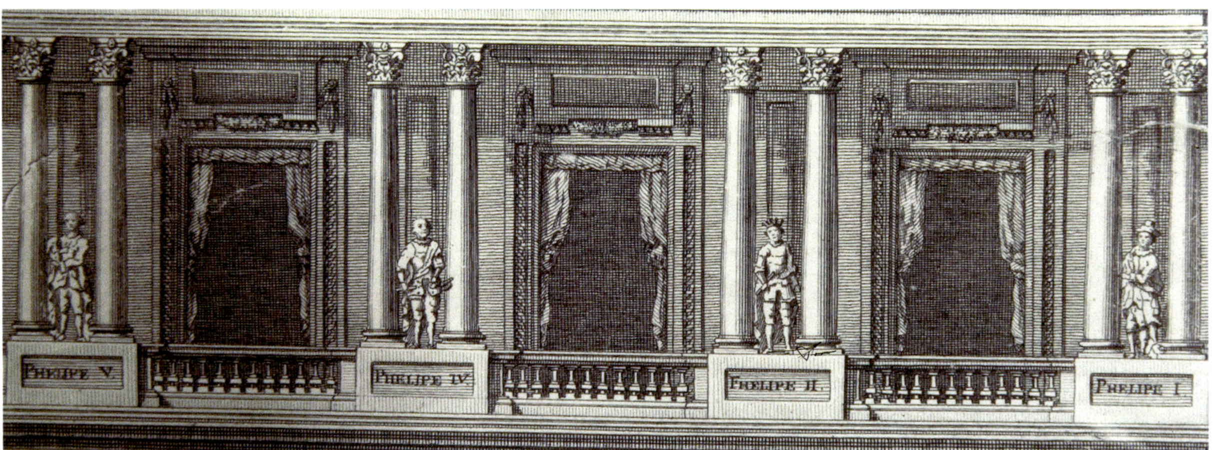

Fig. 6. Detail of fig. 3. Upper, right.

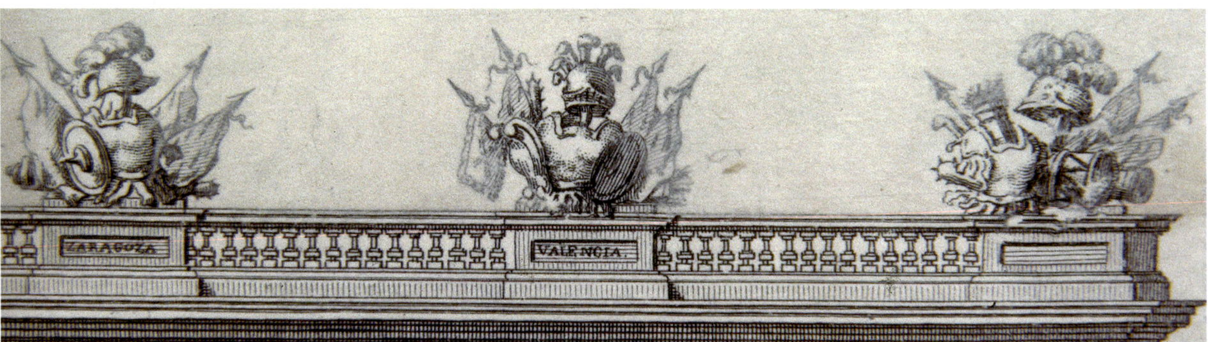

Fig. 7. Detail of fig. 3. Top, right.

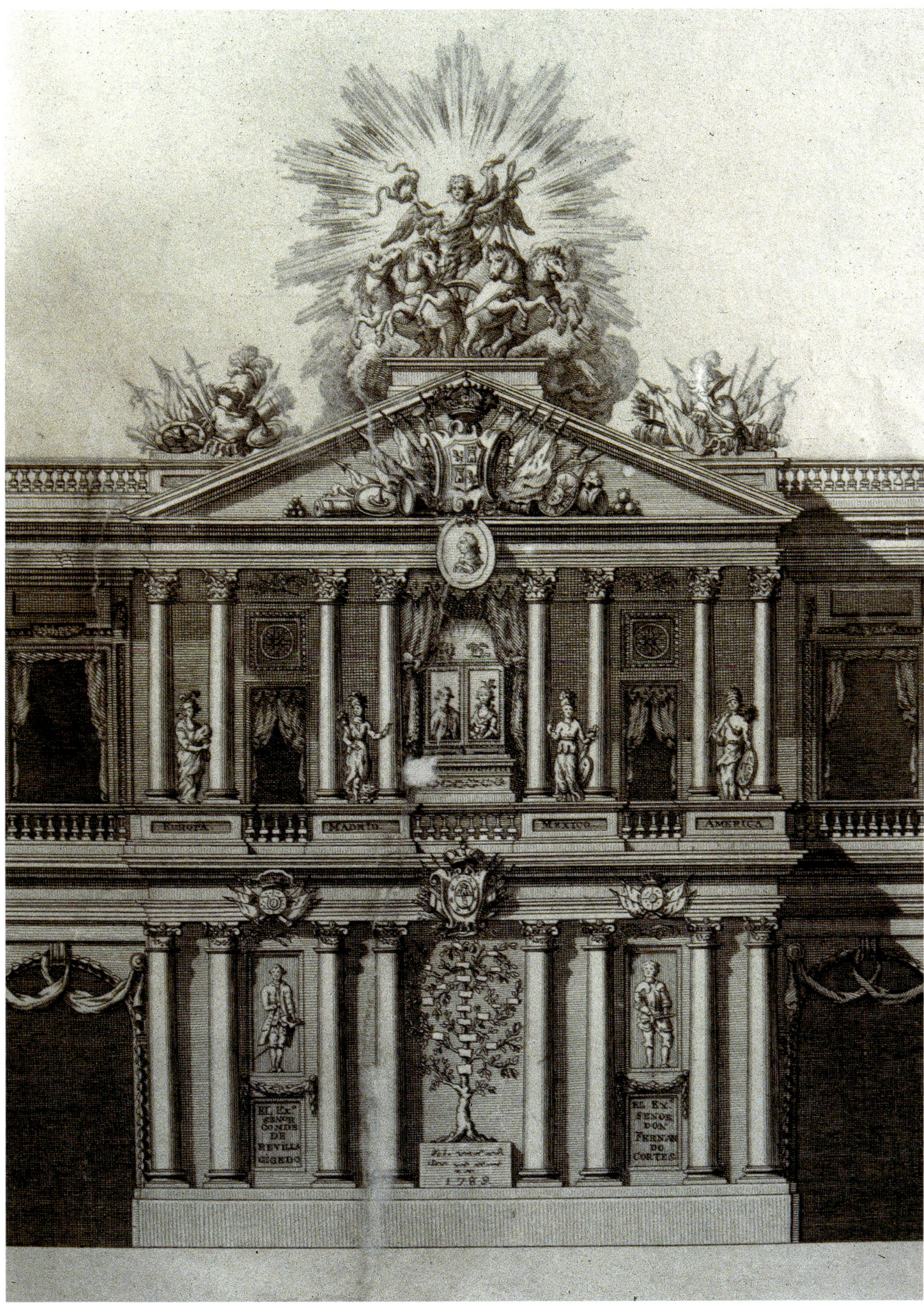

Fig. 8. Detail of fig. 3. Portico, center.

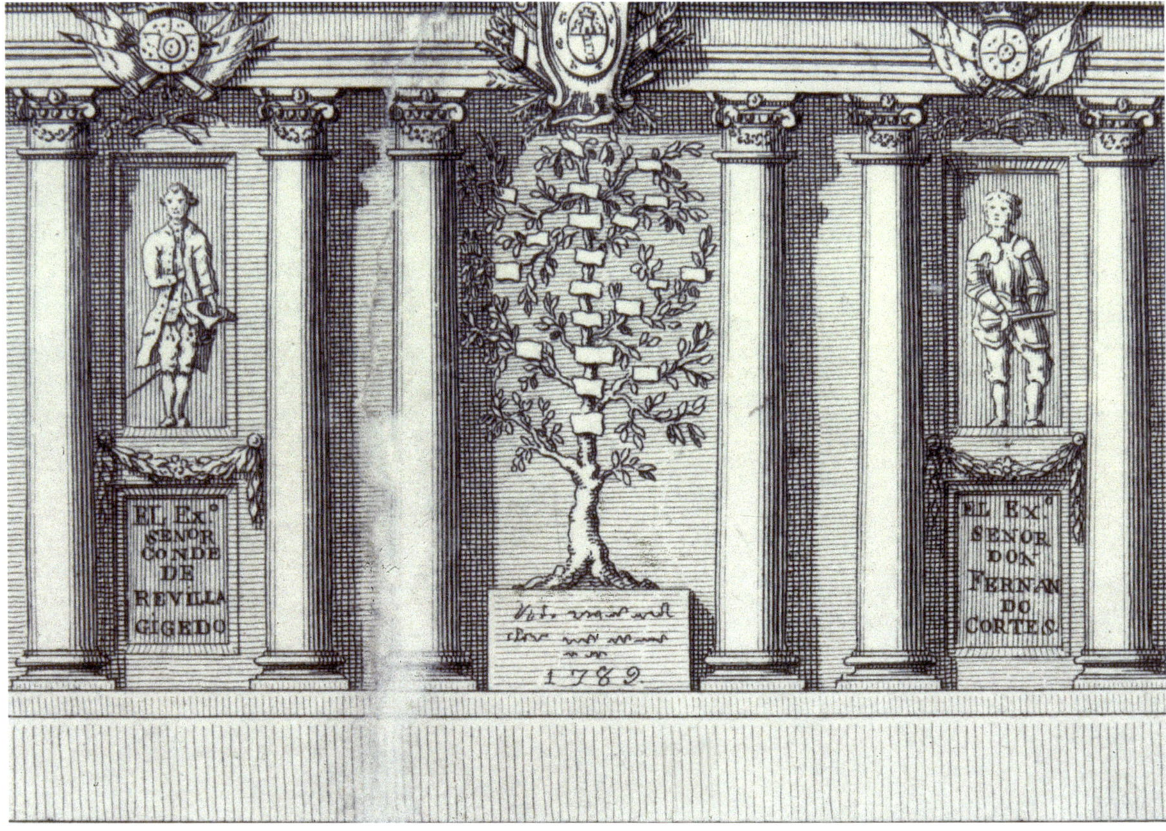

Fig. 9. Detail of fig. 3. Portico, lower center.

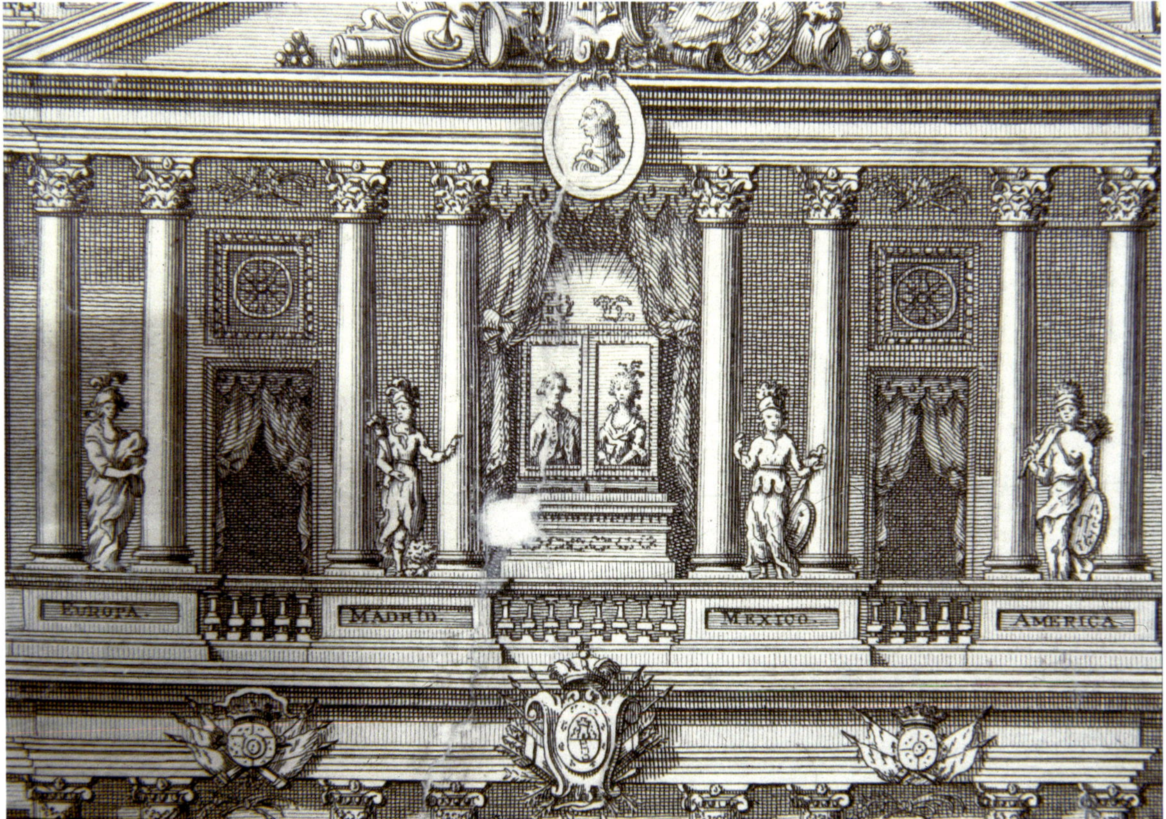

Fig. 10. Detail of fig. 3. Portico, upper center.

current viceroy, the Second Count of Revillagigedo (left) set into the two flanking bays, "one with the old Indians defeated in indication of triumph, and the other with the present-day Indians who persist beneath his rule in indication of loyalty."[18] Beneath each of these effigies hung a garland over a panel with the names, respectively, of the first governor of the territory and the holder of the title of viceroy at the time of the proclamation ceremony (fig. 9). The central bay was decorated with a family tree of the Spanish monarchy, set on a plinth that contained an explanatory text and recorded the year of the celebrations. Among the branches of the tree, a series of small scrolls indicated the family kinships between members of the royal house. Along the cornice the coats of arms of the conqueror and the second Count of Revillagigedo were placed to emphasize their lineage, while the coat of arms of the capital of the viceroyalty, set upon a crowned escutcheon and flanked by quivers and arrows, acquired greater prominence thanks to its size and central position.

The second story of the portico was supported by smooth-shafted, paired Corinthian columns, in order to maintain the visual rhythm of the rest of the upper level. To preserve unity in the project, De Castera repeated the combination of Corinthian-order balustrades set between horizontal plinths, to the rear of which straight arches with drapery could be seen, though smaller here than in the wings and crowned by a decorative motif of a rosette surrounded by a molding with pearls (fig. 10). De Castera also embellished the interstices in each set of paired columns with four geographical personifications. Their attributes and the descriptions on the plinths below tell us that two of these represented Europe and America "paying tribute to the sovereign with their arms and treasure,"[19] while the second pair embodied Madrid and Mexico, one as the residence of the king and his court, and the other as head of the viceroyalty and the foremost city in Spanish America. These four geographical personifications flanked the draped canopy safeguarding the portraits of King Charles IV and his queen consort, María Luisa of Parma. The print shows the paintings on display, indicating that the view was taken after the pledge of allegiance ceremony and the *sparsio*, or distribution of commemorative coins.

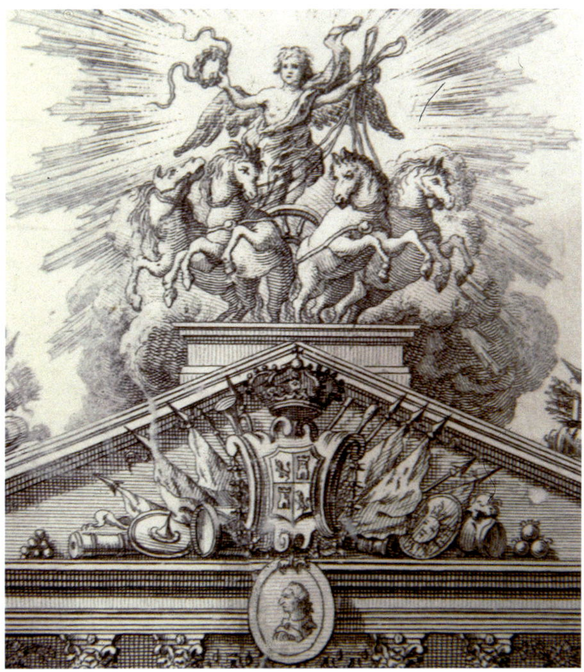

Fig. 11. Detail of fig. 3. Portico, top center.

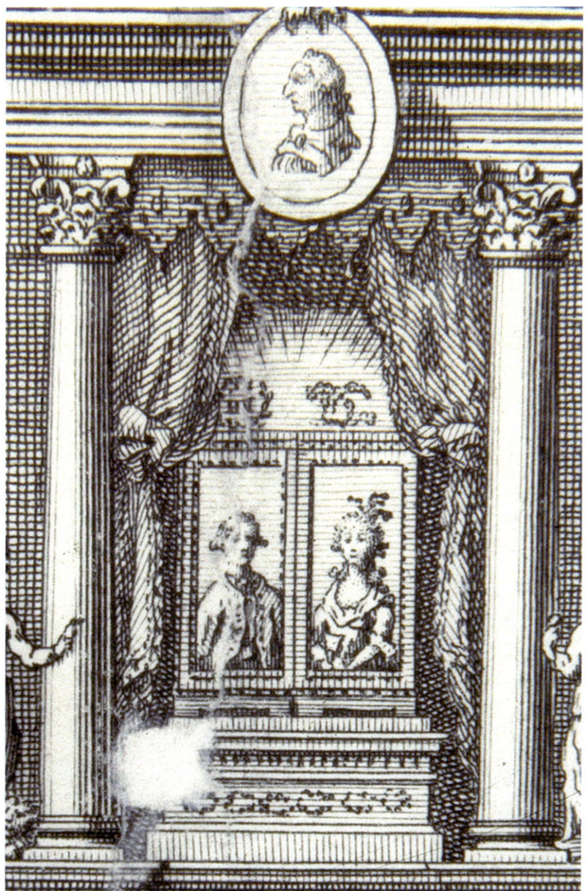

Fig. 12. Detail of fig. 3. Portico, center.

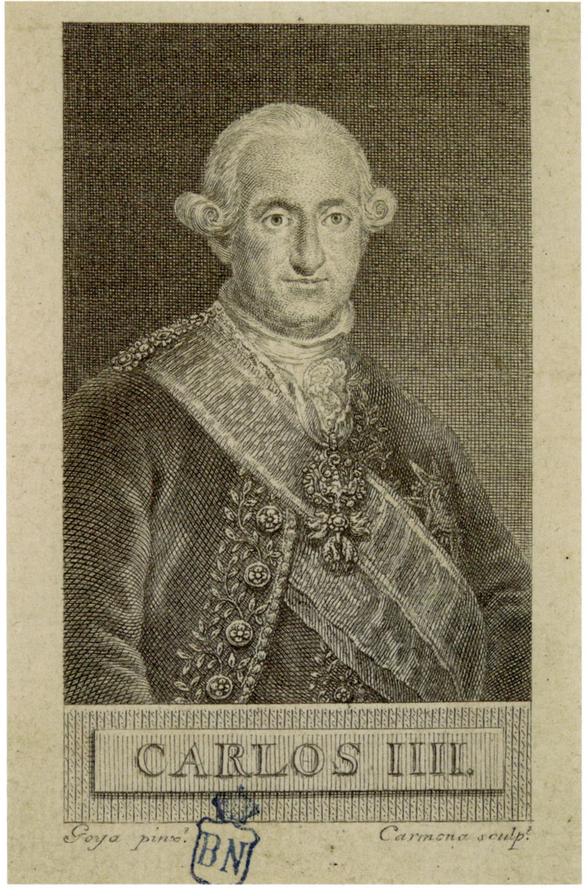

Fig. 13. Manuel Salvador Carmona after Francisco de Goya, *Portrait of Charles IV*. Madrid, 1789. Print, 5 x $3^{1}/_{3}$ in. (12.5 x 8.6 cm). © Biblioteca Nacional de España.

The frieze of the entablature above the painted effigies of the monarchs included an oval bearing the profile image of the deceased Charles III. The tympanum of the triangular pediment was adorned with the coat of arms of Castile and León, displayed on an escutcheon with the royal crown and enhanced with various trophies of war grouped on either side and to the rear, which included pennants, lances, cannons with cannonballs, drums, trumpets, helmets, and bucklers (fig. 11). Above this pediment rose the figure of Apollo driving his chariot pulled by four spirited horses, with a radiant aureole and clouds gathered behind; the representation of the Olympic god was triumphant in character, as he raised a laurel crown in his right hand.[20]

As the above description indicates, some of the ornamental elements are linked to the representation of individuals, while others embody ideas or values about the unity, permanence, and legitimacy of the Spanish monarchy, as well as about the relationship between the viceroyalty and the Crown. Recall that from the outset of the project De Castera was aware that the ephemeral facades would play a decisive role in conjuring feelings of respect and veneration among the king's subjects.[21]

Consider, for example, the half-length portraits of King Charles IV and his queen consort, María Luisa of Parma (fig. 12). These were placed on the principal balcony beneath a crimson awning embroidered in gold thread. Though it is frequently stated that most such works were of poor quality because they were produced in haste, a certain physiognomic resemblance had to be apparent, likely afforded by a printed or painted model. The monarch's effigy in Fabregat's composition is not detailed, though it bears some relationship with the official portrait painted by Francisco de Goya y Lucientes (1746–1828) at the beginning of 1789, engraved afterwards by Manuel Salvador Carmona (1734–1820), Printmaking Director of the Royal Academy of San Fernando and of outstanding projects at the Royal Calcography. In Carmona's engraving after Goya, Charles IV was wearing court dress and powdered wig, and bearing the Order of the Golden Fleece together with the cross and sash of the Order of Charles III and the sashes of Saint Januarius and Saint Esprit (fig. 13).[22] Due to his meritorious work in copperplate etching and engraving, Mariano Brandi (*fl.* 1776–1824) produced that same year a print after a portrait of the king by Rafael Ximeno y Planes (1759–1825) with almost the same posture, wig, and insignia (fig. 14). Along with the possible influence of both printed models, it is also important to note that Fabregat was acquainted with the features of the sovereign because years before he had produced an allegorical full-length effigy of Charles of Bourbon as heir to the throne as well as a half-length portrait of the prince after Anton Raphael Mengs (1728–1779).

Although attributes such as the crown, royal mantle, and scepter cannot be distinguished in Fabregat's print of 1789, it is certain that the reproduction of a royal portrait in Mexico, and its subsequent public exhibition, was a means for the king to "preside"—at a symbolic level—over the solemnities, not only because he was the principal object of the ceremony of the pledge of allegiance, but also in order to reinforce the notion that he was in some sense present in spite of the geographic distance. Thus, when the curtain was opened, the painted image of the occupant of the throne was revealed to public view for his subjects to see him for the first time.[23]

Since the sixteenth century the figure of Apollo had frequently served to exalt the beneficent authority and legislation of a Spanish monarch and to indicate his patronage of the arts and sciences, together with the peace and harmony of his reign. But in 1789 contemplation of the god in his solar carriage was especially fitting to remind subjects not only that a king sees all things, like the sun in its daily passage, but also that following the death of a king—the "nightfall" of a sovereign—would come the hereditary prince, as surely as the sun returns to illuminate the new day. That is, monarchical succession should occur in an orderly and natural manner, without interruptions such as those that the first branch of the House of Bourbon was going through in France.[24]

Dynastic series served to transmit ideas about power, position, and a right to rule that was passed on in cyclical and successive fashion, thanks to direct descendancy and continuity of the monarchy. Painted or sculptural series of kings were fundamental elements found in representative buildings

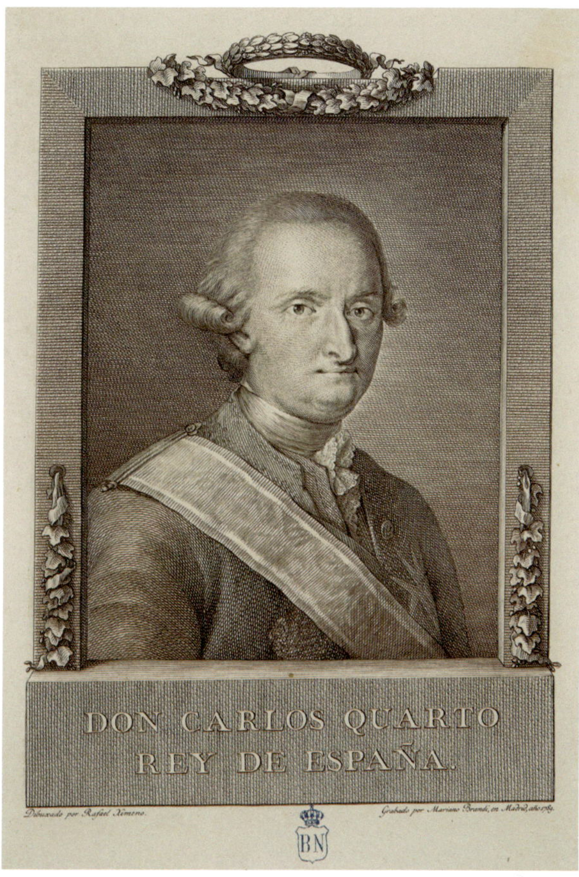

Fig. 14. Mariano Brandi after Rafael Ximeno y Planes, *Portrait of Charles IV.* Madrid, 1789. Print, $8\frac{5}{8}$ x $6\frac{1}{4}$ in. (21.9 x 15.9 cm). © Biblioteca Nacional de España.

connected to the monarchy, and served not only to portray their protagonists, but also to endorse their dynastic rights and express recognition of their ancestry and lineage. As a visual strategy, such series were much used in the sixteenth and seventeenth centuries, and even in the eighteenth, as witnessed by the sculpture gallery of Spanish sovereigns created by the Benedictine friar Martín Sarmiento for the Royal Palace of Madrid.[25]

This visual formula was taken up again in Mexico due to its symbolic effectiveness; the images of Charles IV's predecessors expressed notions about the legitimacy and permanence of the political system, though the oval effigy of Charles III was placed in a more prominent position because the memory of his death was still recent. Placing the deceased king in full view encouraged loyalty towards the hereditary prince and also functioned as a prelude to the discourse of dynastic continuity.

Ever since the Houses of Trastámara (1369–1516) and of Habsburg (1516–1700), family trees and scrolls with series of vignettes of monarchs had enjoyed popularity in the Iberian peninsula as a useful means of demonstrating dynastic legitimacy. Connected by branches or lines that spread from a single trunk, the effigies of the ancestors of a king succeeded each other until they reached his own portrait together with those of his family. The continuity of successive generations in a straight line preserved the purity of blood or nobility of a royal house that sought to retain power. Consequently, genuine and unquestionable lineage secured the family's earthly right to rule.

To reinforce this last idea, the city hall's decorative program also expressed an historical justification: flanking the family tree were full-length portraits of the conqueror Hernán Cortés and the current viceroy, the second Count of Revillagigedo. These figures allude to the permanence of New Spain as a territory of the Spanish Crown, following the military conquest and two hundred sixty-eight years of continuous, legitimate viceregal government and Spanish rule.

On the other hand, the geographical personifications of Europe and America did not hold aloft terrestrial globes or symbols of abundance; rather, in delivering up their arms and treasures to the king in sign of homage and fealty, they declared that Charles IV held possessions in both portions of the earth, together with the power and authority to govern them. Thus the iconographic program made clear the political unity between both continents which, despite separation by the ocean, formed part of a single order overseen by the occupant of the throne—visually recalling the motto *Utraque unum* ("Both are one") used by Charles III of Bourbon.

Geographical personifications of the "capitals of the two Spains"—Madrid and Mexico City—symbolized the heads of state in Europe and America, as well as the seats of the courts of the sovereign and the viceroy. Since these and other cities represented in the facade formed part of the body politic, its inhabitants had to yield to the power, authority, and control of the Spanish Crown. In order to practice unlimited, absolute sovereignty and to centralize his rule, years before Charles III of Bourbon had made significant administrative, military, judicial, and economic reforms. Among other affairs, commercial monopolies were banned, professional militias were established, and new boundaries between jurisdictions were created. In fact, a motif in Fabregat's print reveals that absolutist policies were in force and accepted by Mexico's council in 1789. De Castera indicated that coats of arms in the lower body of the facade only corresponded to ten important viceregal cities, however, they also represented heads of new jurisdictions known as *Intendencias*. This motif promoted the idea of political unity, because some inhabitants of New Spain had resisted this governmental system since its complete establishment in 1786. Members of the council chambers must have been aware of the symbolic significance of accepting a single order, considering that the capital of the viceroyalty was itself head of the *Intendencia* of Mexico.[26]

With the approval of the city council, De Castera constructed an extraordinary design of ephemeral architecture that can be traced in its entirety, from the process of preparing the iconographic program through the subsequent architectural transformation. It is plausible that the council used influence on the city's master architect: in June 1789 the symbolic decorative program was only a triumphant discourse of government, while in December a more concrete vision of the absolutist system was represented. According to iconic and written testimonies, any viewer who contemplated the temporary facade of the city hall during the proclamation ceremony observed not only the royal portraits of Charles IV and his consort, but a range of images that expressed ideas and values concerning the continuity of the political system, the legitimacy of the new monarch, the jurisdiction he held over his possessions, and the political unity of the state under his title. With compelling arguments expressed in an abbreviated fashion, the city council of Mexico City approved the dissemination of a discourse on the identity, intent, and justification of Bourbon rule, as well as on the status of New Spain as its subject. From this perspective, Fabregat's loose-leaf print not only corroborates that the proclamation ceremony took place in Mexico and that the city council accepted the legal and political implications of the pledge of allegiance: it is also a local defense in favor of a Bourbon king and the absolutist monarchy, expressed while in France the National Assembly accomplished reforms for the Constitutional Revolution.

Notes

Concepts and information in this essay are examined in depth in my study "Las fiestas de proclamación de Carlos IV en la ciudad de México (1789 y 1790): sus programas artísticos y su significación política" (Ph.D. dissertation, Universidad Nacional Autónoma de México, to be submitted in 2015).

I owe special thanks to Dr. Donna Pierce, who graciously invited me to participate in the 2010 Mayer Center Symposium as a guest scholar, and in 2012 as a lecturer.

[1] "[Royal seal] A la ciudad de México, participandola averse muerto el s[eñ]or rey Carlos Tercero, y ordenandola que alce pendones en el r[ea]l nombre del, con el de d[o]n Carlos Quarto," Madrid, December 24, 1788, Archivo Histórico del Distrito Federal "Carlos de Sigüenza y Góngora" (henceforth AHDF), Fondo Ayuntamiento de México-Gob. D.F., *Historia. Jura y funerales de reyes*, vol. 2282, file 15, f. 161r.– v.

[2] Copy of the council records with the first measures approved to undertake the celebrations for the proclamation of Charles IV, Mexico, April 20, 1789, AHDF, *Historia. Jura y funerales de reyes,* vol. 2282, file 15, ff. 159r. –160r.

[3] "Los m[aes]tros mayores de arquitectura [*sic*] presentando planos ó dibujos de los tablados p[ar]a la proclamacíon de n[uestro] c[atólico] m[onarca]," Mexico, June 12, 1789, AHDF, *Historia. Jura y funerales de reyes,* vol. 2282, file 21, ff. 193r. –199r.

[4] *Ibid.*, drawing no. 3, f. 202r. This brief essay gives priority to analyzing the facade of the council chambers, since this is the only design whose development can be traced in its entirety from preparing the iconographic program through subsequent architectural transformation.

[5] Information on his title and activities is taken from Regina Hernández Franyuti, *Ignacio de Castera: arquitecto y urbanista de la ciudad de Mexico (1771–1811)* (Mexico, Instituto de Investigaciones Históricas Dr. José María Luis Mora, 1997), 24–26 and 172–174. This source also indicates that he was designated the master-in-chief of the royal drainage channel (1783), an academician of merit at the Royal Academy of San Carlos (1791), and master-in-chief of the viceregal palace of Mexico (1794).

[6] Copy of the council records in which those commissioned to create the ephemeral architecture give an account of their progress. AHDF, *Historia. Jura y funerales de reyes*, vol. 2282, file 17, f. 167r. Interestingly, the council members refer to the plan and elevation drawings as "maps."

[7] "Los m[aes]tros mayores de arquitectura," f. 194v.

[8] "Explicacion de la alegoria tomada para la solemne proclamacion de nuestro augusto monarca el s[eñ]or d[o]n Carlos 4º en los tres tablados erigidos para este acto que se ha de celebrar el 27 de diciembre de 1789," S.l. [Mexico], undated [1789], Archivo de la Antigua Academia de San Carlos, Biblioteca Lino Picaseño, Facultad de Arquitectura, UNAM (henceforth AASC), shelf 4, document 446, no folio number. *Apud* Justino Fernández, *Guía del Archivo de la Antigua Academia de San Carlos (1781–1800)*, supplement 3 of no. 37 of the *Anales* of the Institute for Aesthetics Research (Mexico, UNAM, Instituto de Investigaciones Estéticas, 1968), 51. The document may have been preserved in this archive since 1789, when various plans belonging to the chief architect of the city were sent to the Royal Academy of San Carlos to be inspected by Antonio González Velázquez and Miguel Costansó. *Apud Guía del Archivo*, 58–59 (summary of docs. 504 to 516).

[9] "Los m[aes]tros mayores de arquitectura," f. 195v.

[10] Many reports can be read in the Archivo General de las Indias in Seville, sent from different parts of the Americas to Domingo Antonio Porlier, secretary of state for grace and justice of Castile and the Indies. It bears noting that *relaciones*, or published accounts of events, not only described details of the proclamation ceremonies but demonstrated the publication sponsors' loyalty to the new monarch.

[11] Joseph Moreno, *Descripción de los ornatos públicos con que la corte de Madrid ha solemnizado la feliz exáltacion al trono de los reyes nuestros señores Don Carlos IIII y Doña Luisa de Borbón y la jura del serenisimo señor Don Fernando, Principe de Asturias* (Madrid: Imprenta Real de Madrid, 1789). On the circumstances in which this work came to light, see Javier Fernández Delgado, "Política y memoria del buen gusto. Las fiestas reales de 1789," *Goya. Revista de Arte* (Madrid, Fundación Lázaro Galdiano), nos. 181–182 (July–October 1984): 63–67. Unfortunately, a second project developed by the Royal Academy of History was never published.

[12] P. Manuel Gil, C. R. M., *Relacion de la proclamacion del rey nuestro señor Don Carlos IIII, y fiestas con que la celebró la muy noble y muy leal ciudad de Sevilla, de cuya orden se da á luz...* (Madrid: Imprenta de la viuda de don Joaquín de Ibarra, 1790).

[13] Marco Pollion Vitruvio, *Los Diez Libros de Arquitectura de M. Vitruvio Polión. Traducidos del latín y comentados por don Joseph Ortíz y Sanz, presbítero* (Madrid: Imprenta Real, 1787).

See Carmen Blanco Sánchez, "La edición vitruviana de la Imprenta Real," *Goya. Revista de Arte* (Madrid, Fundación Lázaro Galdiano), nos. 181–182 (July–October 1984): 68–74.

[14] "Explicacion de la alegoria." Although the document in the archive gives the term "Chiapa," in the corresponding position on the print "Ghalapa" [Jalapa] can be read.

[15] Juan Francisco de Azcárate gave this information in a dictum on a literary work by Larrañaga involving the placing of a bronze equestrian statue of Charles IV. See Bruno José de Larrañaga, *Poema heroico en celebridad de la colocación de la estatua colosal de bronce de nuestro católico monarca el señor don Carlos Cuarto, rey de España y emperador de la Indias* (Mexico City: Oficina de don Mariano de Zúñiga y Ontiveros, 1804), dictum of Juan Fco. de Azcárate, 2. The information also appears in Clara Bargellini, "La lealtad americana: el significado de la estatua ecuestre de Carlos IV," in *Iconología y Sociedad: Arte Colonial Hispanoamericano. XLIV Congreso Internacional de Americanistas*, Estudios de Arte y Estética, no. 26 (Mexico City: UNAM, Instituto de Investigaciones Estéticas, 1987), 212.

[16] On the print, from left to right: Fernando V (of Castile and II of Aragón, "the Catholic"), Carlos V, Felipe III, Carlos II, Luis I, Fernando VI, Felipe V, Felipe IV, Felipe II, and Felipe I.

[17] "Explicacion de la alegoria."

[18] *Ibid.*

[19] *Ibid.* In this handwritten document, the geographical personification is described as Spain and not Europe.

[20] In its triumphant character and frontal composition, this figure brings to mind the gouache *Allégorie de Louis XIV en Apollon dans le char du Soleil précédé par l'Aurore et accompagné par les Heures*, painted towards 1662–1667 by Joseph Werner (1637–1710), which belongs to the collection of the Musée National du Château de Versailles et de Trianon.

[21] "Los m[aes]tros mayores de arquitectura," f. 196v. At the same time, he indicated that equestrian statues may exalt a monarch, perpetuate his memory, or present him as an example to his successors.

[22] See Clemente Barrena, Javier Blas, Juan Carrete, and José Miguel Medrano, *Calcografía Nacional: catálogo general* (Madrid: Real Academia de Bellas Artes de San Fernando, Calcografía Nacional, 2004), I: 196. The authors indicate that, from 1790 to 1798, this printed picture illustrated *Calendario manual y guía de forasteros en Madrid*; naturally, the copperplate had to be retouched on different occasions (as an example, 2,500 prints were produced in 1789 and 17,500 more the year after).

[23] The effigy of a new sovereign was reproduced in painting, sculpture, prints, and coins so multiple images could be seen during and after proclamation celebrations.

[24] It is peculiar that the figure of Apollo is the only element of the iconographic program mentioned in detail by other commentators. See Francisco de la Maza, *La mitología clásica en el arte colonial de México*, Estudios y Fuentes del Arte en México, 24 (Mexico City: UNAM, Instituto de Investigaciones Estéticas, 1968); José Miguel Morales Folguera, *Cultura simbólica y arte efímero en Nueva España* (Seville: Junta de Andalucía, Consejería de Cultura y Medio Ambiente, Asesoría Quinto Centenario, 1991); and Víctor Mínguez, *Los reyes solares: iconografía astral de la monarquía hispánica*. Col•lecció Humanitats 7 (Castellón de la Plana: Publicacions de la Universitat Jaume I, 2000). On solar iconography as a symbolic expression of the Spanish monarchy from the Renaissance to the beginning of the nineteenth century, and in particular when used in royal obsequies, see the study by Víctor Mínguez.

[25] See Sara Muniain Ederra, *El programa escultórico del Palacio Real de Madrid y la Ilustración española*, Colección *Tesis Cum Laude*, Serie Arte, 7 (Madrid: Fundación Universitaria Española, 2000). On images depicting descent and dynastic legitimacy before the eighteenth century, see the articles by Miguel Falomir Faus, "Imágenes y textos para una monarquía compleja," in *El linaje del emperador*, Exhibition catalogue, Iglesia de la Preciosa Sangre, Centro de Exposiciones San Jorge, October 24, 2000–January 7, 2001 (Madrid: Ediciones El Viso, S.A., 2000), 61–77; Javier Portús, "El retrato cortesano en la época de los primeros Austrias: historia, propaganda, identidad," in *El linaje del emperador*, 17–39; and José Manuel Matilla, "El grabado y la casa de Austria: la imagen del rey, la difusión de la idea dinástica y la memoria de los hechos imperiales," in *El linaje del emperador*, 79–97.

[26] For fundamental studies of this topic, see Áurea Commons, *Las intendencias de la Nueva España*, Espacio y Tiempo, 4 (Mexico City: UNAM, Instituto de Investigaciones Históricas, 1993), and Horst Pietschmann, *Las reformas borbónicas y el sistema de intendencias en Nueva España: un estudio político administrativo* (Mexico City: Fondo de Cultura Económica [Sección de Obras de Historia], 1996).

Celebrating the Patriarch(s) of Puebla

The Municipal Council and the Cult of Saint Joseph

Frances L. Ramos

In November 1778, the Council of the Indies confirmed the permission first granted by Rome's Congregation of Rites for American cities to crown statues of Saint Joseph. Ten years later, Puebla de los Ángeles, New Spain's "second city" in prestige and importance, finally crowned its most revered image of the Patriarch in an elaborate ceremony that spanned three days. The statue, which had been held temporarily in Puebla's cathedral for a novena, processed from the heart of the city to the parish of Saint Joseph, at the northernmost limits of the urban sprawl (fig. 1).[1]

People from the city's six parishes and numerous barrios gathered along the processional route and blanketed the effigy with flowers. As Saint Joseph crossed into the atrium of the church, organizers released doves into the air, each decorated with a tiny piece of tinsel, as well as a banner and shield bearing the insignia of one of the city's barrios. According to the priest of Puebla's parish of Saint Joseph and the panegyrist in charge of the commemorative sermon, the Patriarch brought Puebla's ethnically disparate barrios together and united people of all social stations so that "the great man did not scorn the small man, nor did the small man have to envy the great one." He emphasized that the enormous turnout made "manifest with evidence" that "this entire city

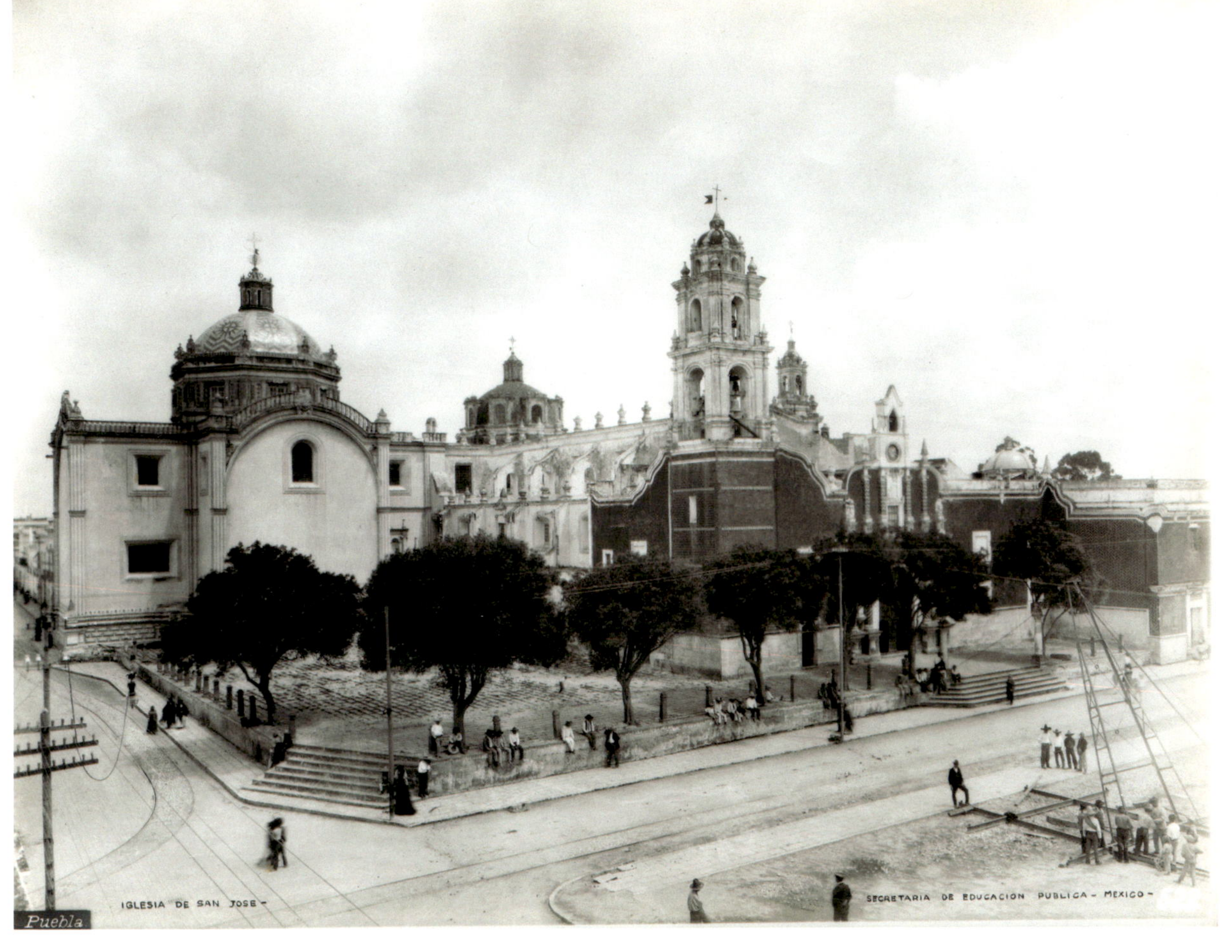

Fig. 1. Guillermo Kahlo, *La Parroquia de San José, en Puebla de los Ángeles*. Mexico, c. 1910. D. R. © Fototeca Antica, A.C. / Colección Jorge Carretero Madrid.

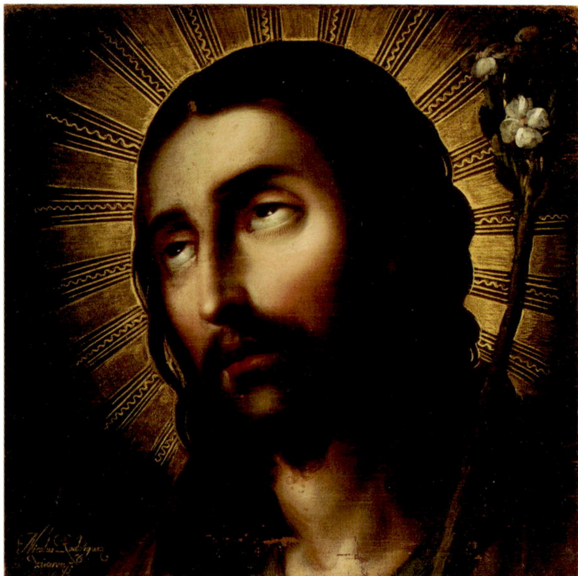

Fig. 2. Nicolás Rodríguez Juárez (1667–1734), *Saint Joseph*. Mexico, c. 1700. Oil on canvas, 13¼ x 13¼ in. Denver Art Museum; Gift of Robert J. Stroessner, 1991.1158.

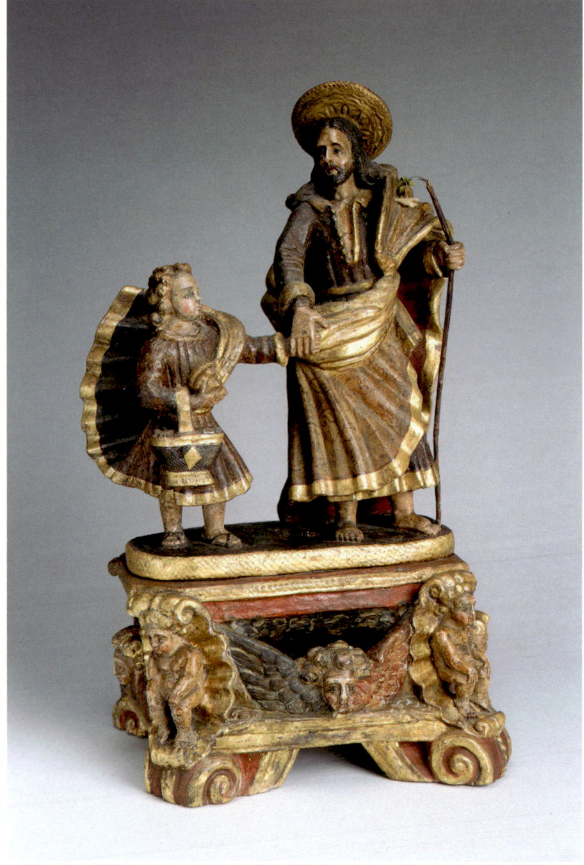

Fig. 3. *Saint Joseph with Jesus*. Mexico, 18th century. Paint and gold leaf on *tecali* (Mexican alabaster), 18 x 10½ x 7¾ in. Denver Art Museum; Frederick and Jan Mayer Collection, 9.2000.

of the Angels recognizes you [Saint Joseph] as its Lord."[2] As the titular saint of Puebla's second largest parish, the patron saint of one of its most important confraternities, the patron saint of the municipal council and city as a whole, and finally, the patron saint of the Spanish Empire, the Patriarch commanded a large following.

By 1773, Puebla de los Ángeles enjoyed the advocacy of sixteen patron saints, but out of all of these Joseph proved the most popular, reflecting a broader colonial trend.[3] As Charlene Villaseñor-Black has shown, New Spain preceded the mother country in its enthusiasm for the Patriarch. Whereas Saint Joseph's cult grew substantially in importance in Spain during the early seventeenth century, by 1555 the First Mexican Provincial Council had already proclaimed Joseph patron saint of the conversion in New Spain and made his feast day obligatory. Given that missionaries quickly came to regard the native people as perpetual children, the choice of the Patriarch made symbolic sense. Mentioned only eight times in the Gospels, the medieval Saint Joseph, most often depicted as a fragile old man in the background of paintings, enjoyed only minor status. But starting in the fifteenth century, Joseph's cult began to grow, and following the Council of Trent, he transformed into a symbol of masculine authority. When the cult of the Holy Family developed in the seventeenth century, Joseph gradually came to be depicted often as a virile young man and nurturing father, especially in the New World.[4] In late seventeenth- and eighteenth-century devotional paintings of Saint Joseph, he is often painted serene, with his eyes cast upwards, and, of course, young, as in one painting by the famed Mexican artist Nicolás Rodríguez Juárez (fig. 2). While Joseph began to figure prominently in images of the Holy Family in the early seventeenth century, by the late seventeenth and eighteenth centuries, images of a nurturing Saint Joseph proved ubiquitous in a variety of artistic media, and not necessarily in the company of Mary.[5] He proved a popular subject for sculptures of ivory figurines from the Philippines and is even depicted holding the Christ Child by the hand in a rare eighteenth-century example of a sculpture made of *tecali*, or alabaster, from central Mexico (its main source was not far from Puebla) (fig. 3).

The election of Saint Joseph as a patron saint made sense within the context of the colonial Spanish-American city, which contemporaries typically understood as an extended family. In Puebla, the municipal council, or *cabildo*, grasped the political utility of the Patriarch, making him patron saint in 1555 and eventually committing itself to what, by the late seventeenth century, would be four elaborate public rituals. As this paper illustrates, Puebla's councilmen (or *regidores*) saw themselves as patriarchs of the republic and conflated their authority with that of Saint Joseph as a way of showcasing their power. Although Saint Michael the Archangel is Puebla de los Ángeles's foundational saint, by the mid-seventeenth century Joseph surpassed all of Puebla's other patron saints in importance.[6] By the year of the coronation ceremony in 1788, Saint Joseph had arguably become the city's most popular saint, and this, I contend, was not only the result of the increasing popularity of Joseph throughout the empire; Puebla's councilmen deliberately nurtured his cult through the promotion of elaborate public ceremonies.

In the early modern Spanish world, people sought the aid of Saint Joseph for a variety of material problems, but in New Spain he became a popular advocate in particular against violent storms, lightning strikes, and associated fires. Early missionaries also may have associated Saint Joseph with Tlaloc, the ancient god of rain, as a way of facilitating the indigenous peoples' acceptance of Catholicism. Native people may have made this connection with little prompting; both feast days fell within the month of March, and Joseph, often depicted holding a flowered staff, may have resembled a god of fertility.[7]

Recently, scholars have started to examine the political implications of the cult of the saints, arguing that municipal councilmen not only elected saints to deal with the vagaries of nature, but also relied on saints as agents of social and political control and as embodiments of interrelated corporate identities. In cities throughout the empire,

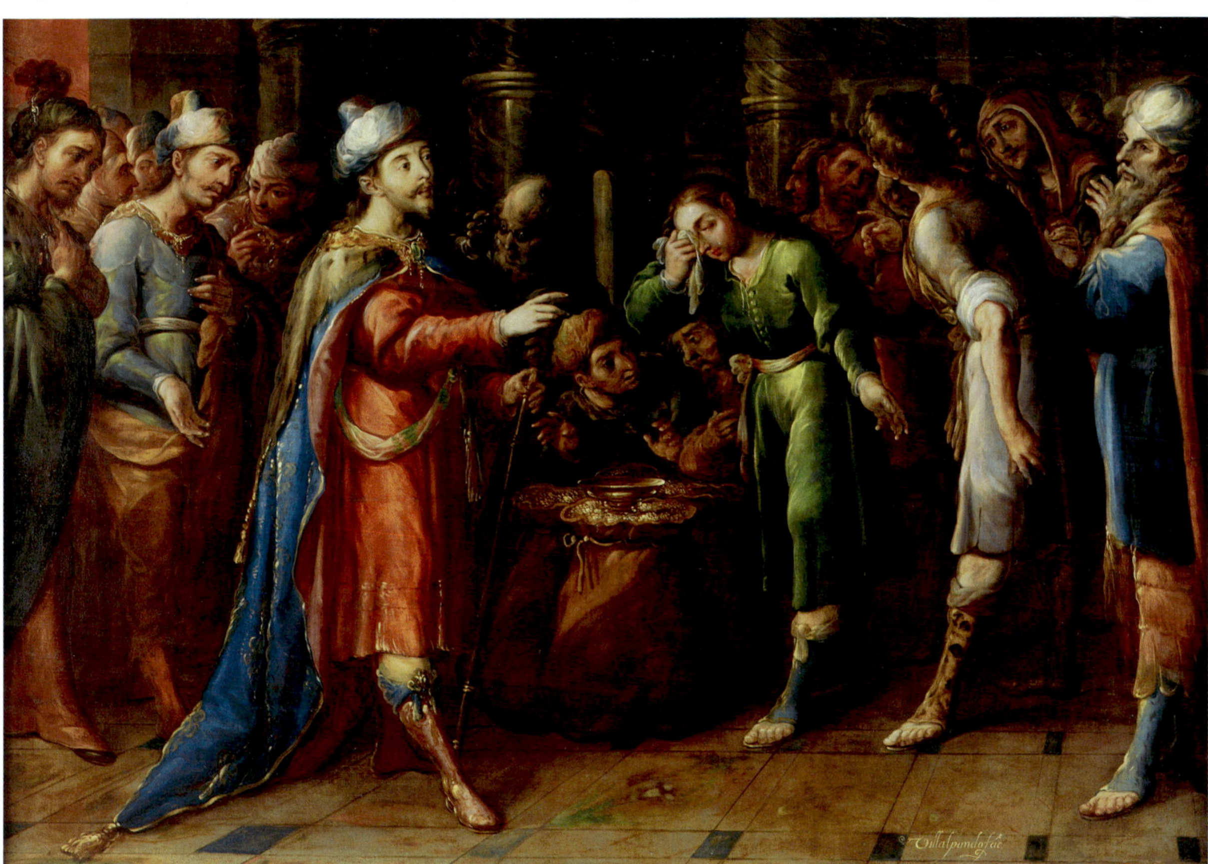

Fig. 4. Cristóbal de Villalpando (c. 1649–1714), *Joseph Claims Benjamin as His Slave*. Mexico, 1700–1714. Oil on canvas, 59⅞ x 82⅝ in. Denver Art Museum; Gift of Frederick and Jan Mayer, 2009.761.

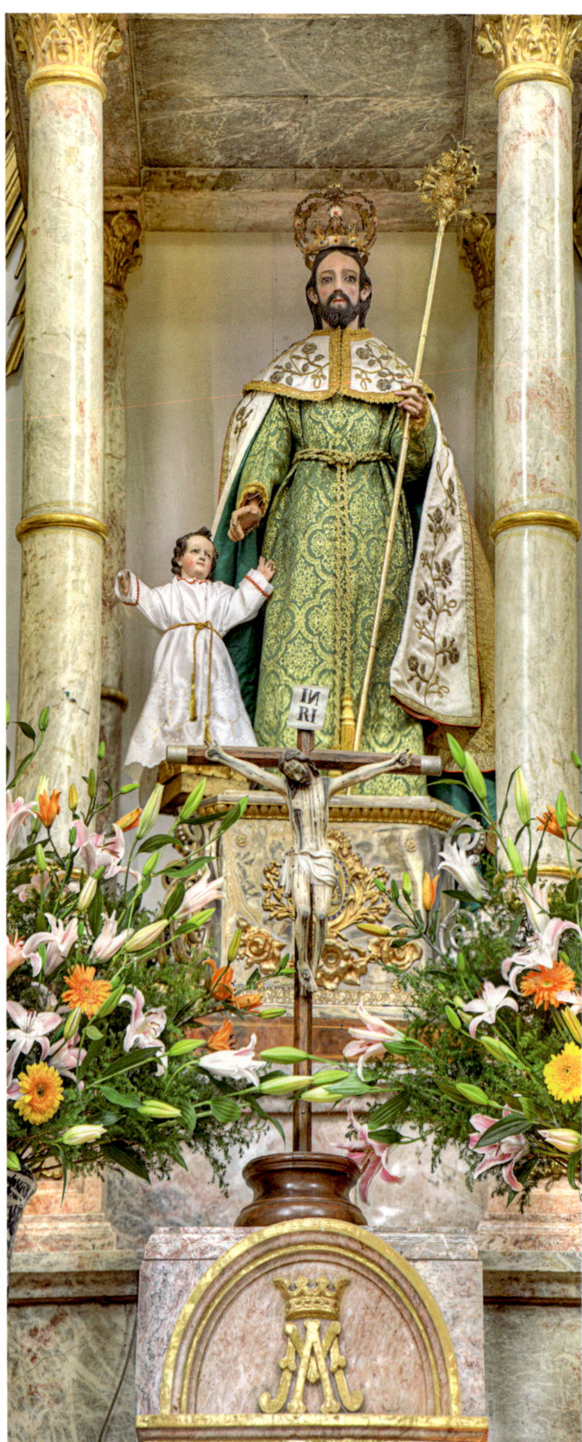

Fig. 5. Andrés Fernández de Sandrea, *Saint Joseph with Christ Child*. Parish of San José, Puebla, Mexico, late 16th–early 17th century. Oficina de Turismo de la Ciudad de Puebla/José Pérez Torrealba.

saints served as centripetal forces. Often, Crown officials, high-level clergy, and municipal leaders co-opted popular cults capable of uniting disparate groups.[8]

In New Spain, Saint Joseph served as a powerful symbol of unity and political authority. Art historians Jaime Cuadriello and Villaseñor-Black have focused in particular on the exegetical and iconographic evolution of Saint Joseph from a marginal figure to a consummate authority figure.[9] As both adeptly show, Saint Joseph came to be associated with royal authority and, by extension, with colonial ministers. Panegyrists associated Saint Joseph the Patriarch with Joseph of Egypt, son of Jacob and vizier, or assistant, to the pharaoh. In New Spain, Joseph of Egypt represented good government, and visual depictions of the vizier became popular. Famed painter Cristobál de Villalpando, for example, produced a large series depicting scenes from the life of Joseph, including *Joseph Claims Benjamin as His Slave,* where the vizier is represented at the height of his power, elegantly dressed in his palace and holding the telltale staff of office (fig. 4).[10] Many panegyrists, including those in Puebla, argued that Joseph of Egypt prefigured Joseph the Patriarch much as John the Baptist prefigured Christ. Some panegyrists took to describing Joseph of Egypt as "viceroy," thereby conflating the trope of Patriarch with that of vizier. The Josephs would both come to represent good government.

Saint Joseph in the City of Angels

Puebla's councilmen first elected Joseph the Patriarch as a patron saint in 1555, only fourteen years after the city's foundation. Later, Puebla's cathedral chapter would institute a separate novena in honor of the saint, and, seizing on the political utility of Joseph, Charles II named him patron of the empire in 1679. But the councilmen, who had long embraced the Patriarch, would eventually come to sponsor between three and four different annual celebrations in his honor, not including March 19, his feast day, an occasion in which councilmen also played an important participatory role. Although Saint Joseph was a popular advocate for *poblanos* (citizens of Puebla) in general, *regidores* treated him as a projection of their own authority.

Puebla's municipal council took an active

interest in the cult of Saint Joseph within the first few decades of the city's foundation. According to Puebla's origin myth, in 1531 the first bishop of Tlaxcala and a group of Franciscans reportedly discovered the site of the would-be city of Puebla on the feast day of Saint Michael, who soon became Puebla's first patron saint. In 1555, the same year that the First Mexican Provincial Council named Joseph patron saint and advocate of the Church in Mexico, Puebla's *regidores* elected Joseph the city's second patron saint.[11] One year later, the dean of the cathedral chapter, the *cabildo*'s *alcaldes ordinarios* (annually elected constables), its *alcalde mayor* (senior constable), two *regidores*, and another prominent citizen accompanied the bishop, dean, and chanter of Puebla's cathedral chapter to select the physical site of the future parish of Saint Joseph. Five of the gentlemen who composed the selection committee had been original founders of the city and likely had participated in various conquest expeditions before settling down in Puebla. It is likely, therefore, that as founders not only of Puebla, but of the viceroyalty, committee members appreciated the symbolic implications of naming the new parish after the recently elected patron saint of the Church in New Spain. In choosing the site of the parish, the committee considered future expansion and rightly foresaw that it would become "one of the principal parishes of said city." In approving the site during the council meeting that followed, the *cabildo* made its devotion abundantly clear. Councilmen agreed that it would be the "first and principal parish of this city" and specified that it would have "preeminence in all things and processions" and that it would be "preferred to the other parishes that are and will be in this city and its barrios."[12]

The parish eventually acquired a sculpture of Saint Joseph to which devotees would soon attribute miraculous powers (figs. 5 and 6). Writing in the eighteenth century, Mariano Fernández de Veytia y Echeverría recounted the popular tale of the effigy's origin. In just one afternoon, six rays of lightning reportedly struck a thick tree in the plaza in front of the Patriarch's church, and an artist then crafted the image from the remains of its trunk. Attributed to the sculptor Andrés Fernández de Sandrea and standing approximately three-and-a-half-feet tall, the statue of Joseph

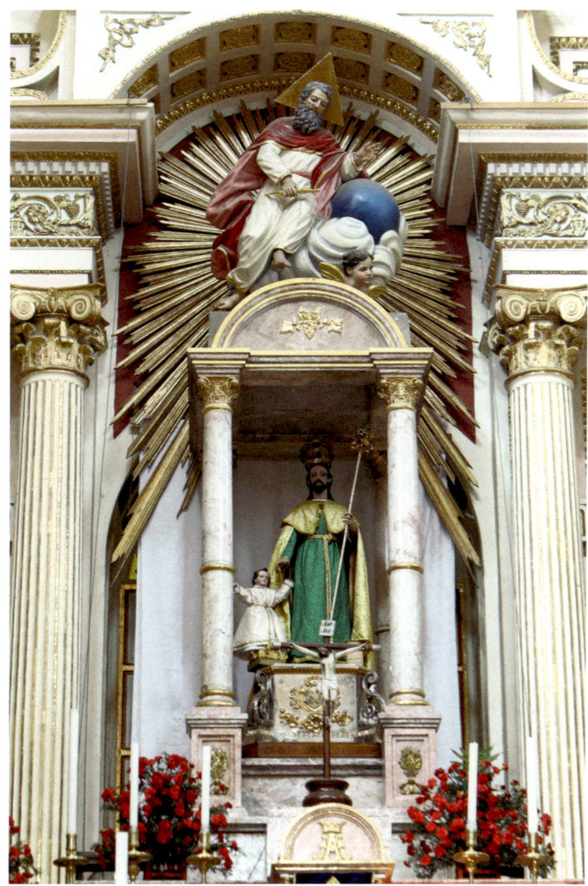

Fig. 6. Main altar of the Parish of San José, Puebla, Mexico. Oficina de Turismo de la Ciudad de Puebla/Fabián Valdivia Pérez.

carried his iconic staff in one hand and held the infant Jesus in the other. Eventually, Joseph would become the patron saint of the confraternity of carpenters housed in the parish church. Members saw to his daily maintenance, dressing him in French embroidered silk on special occasions and adorning him with pearls and other jewels donated by devotees. In 1776, the confraternity had the sculpture retouched by the most famous *poblano* sculptor of his time, José Villegas Cora. According to Fernández Echeverría y Veytia, this mainly consisted of flattening his hair, retouching his face, and adding glass eyes, but as art historian Franziskca Neff has observed, it seems that Cora also changed the composition of the sculpture, from Joseph holding the Christ Child to Joseph guiding an independent statue of Jesus at his side.[13]

The confraternity, therefore, played an important role in promoting Saint Joseph's cult, but the *cabildo* also played a key role, if not the most crucial one. After having named Joseph patron of Puebla in 1555, in 1611 the *cabildo* renewed its vow and elevated the Patriarch to a position on par with Saint Michael. Alarmed by recent storms and fatal lightning strikes, the *cabildo* held a raffle for a new advocate. As was the custom, councilmen wrote names of candidates on slips of paper and placed them inside a vessel. A young boy then drew out three slips of paper, and Saint Joseph twice came out the winner. The destruction must have been significant, given that the *cabildo* also decided to use municipal funds to pay a priest to say weekly masses of appeasement in honor of Saint Joseph; thenceforward, the chaplain elected annually by the *cabildo* to say mass before council meetings also had the responsibility of seeing to these masses of appeasement.[14] According to chronicler Juan Villa Sánchez, by the mid-eighteenth century *poblanos* had come to credit the weekly masses for the subsiding of storms in number and intensity.[15]

The nomination of Saint Joseph in 1611 raises questions regarding the *cabildo*'s previous commitment to the cult. The fact that the council chose to nominate an already elected patron saint suggests that observance had become lax, and the *cabildo* minutes even indicate as much.[16] The election also suggests strengthening ties to the city's recently established Convent of San Joseph, which would eventually be renamed the Convent of Santa Teresa. Officially founded in 1604, the convent had begun as the Recogimiento (house of reclusion) de San Joseph in Vera Cruz. Soon after its establishment, the wealthy founders adopted the Patriarch as their special advocate, and possibly seeing this as a sign, a Franciscan lent the women the writings of Saint Theresa, the most famous devotee of the Patriarch and the founder of the Discalced Carmelite order. Inspired, the women then decided to found the first Discalced Carmelite convent in New Spain, which they did in the more temperate city of Puebla. According to some contemporary observers, the city's governing elite and leading citizens attended the mass commemorating the foundation of the Convent of San Joseph.[17] This foundation, along with the fatal lightning strikes seven years later, may have inspired Puebla's councilmen to recommit to the cult. Significantly, on March 19, the annual feast day of Saint Joseph, when the *cabildo* and cathedral chapter participated in a joint procession of palms from the cathedral to the parish, they stopped in two locations: the Church of Santa Clara and the Church of Santa Teresa.[18]

After councilmen reelected Saint Joseph in 1611, they continued to participate in a joint procession of palms with the cathedral chapter on March 19, but started sponsoring an elaborate annual ceremony on the octave, or eighth day following his feast day, which also included the celebration of vespers the evening before. From then on, *regidores* vowed to pay for a sung mass featuring a choir of musicians, and to pay for bullfights, fireworks, and mock jousts to mark his patronage. In all, the festivities took on a grandeur paralleled only by the feast day for Saint Michael, the feast of the Immaculate Conception (which the municipal council celebrated for only a limited number of years), and Corpus Christi.

Municipal leaders soon committed themselves to even more commemorations in honor of Saint Joseph. In 1638, the cathedral chapter named Joseph patron saint of the diocese against storms and lighting and began celebrating an annual novena for Joseph in September to mark the end of the rainy season, and the *cabildo* assumed responsibility for hosting the events of the last

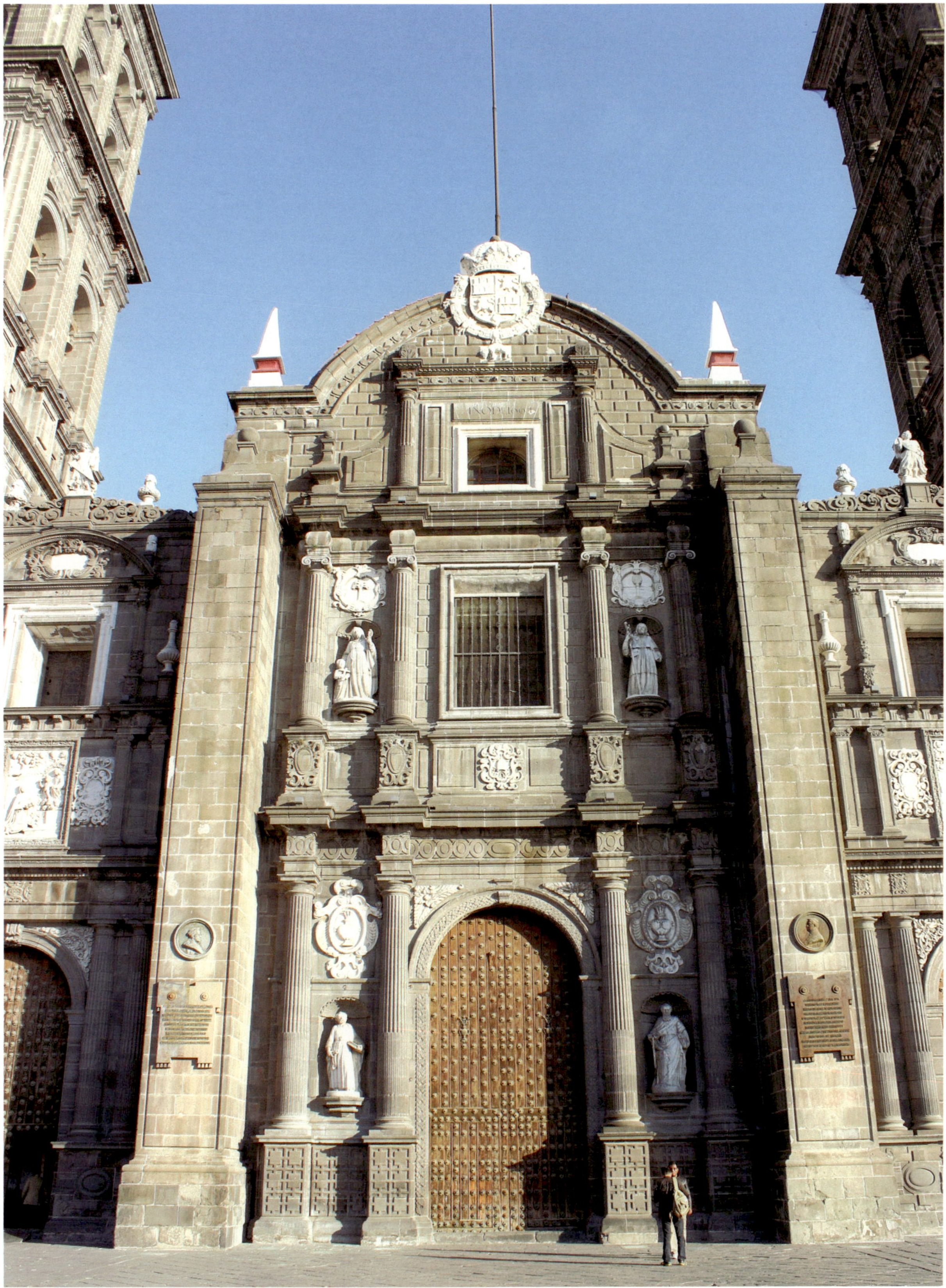

Fig. 7. Main entrance of the Cathedral of Puebla, ornamentation under the direction of Vicencio Varrocio Escayola. Completed 1664. Oficina de Turismo de la Ciudad de Puebla/Fabián Valdivia Pérez.

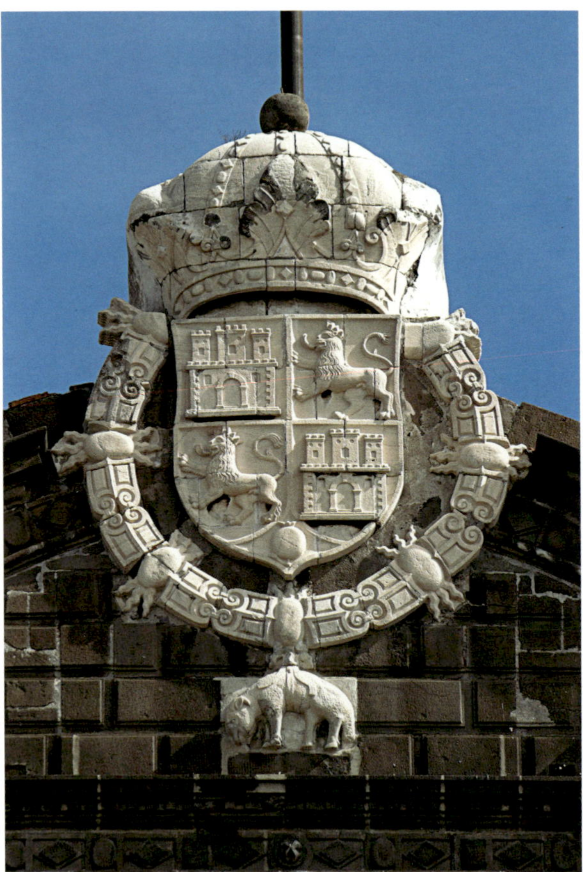

Fig. 8. Coat of arms of Charles V, main entrance of the Cathedral of Puebla, Mexico. Oficina de Turismo de la Ciudad de Puebla/Fabián Valdivia Pérez.

day.[19] Then, in 1680, the municipal council received a royal decree naming Joseph patron of the Spanish Empire, with a papal brief awarding a plenary indulgence to all who visited a church devoted to Joseph on his feast day. The *cabildo*, in turn, vowed to celebrate and partially subsidize a special celebration for Joseph, distinguished from other commemorations as the "*patrocinio,*" or patronage of Joseph over Spanish America. It would involve a novena, or nine days of prayers of thanksgiving in honor of the saint. The *cabildo* helped to subsidize the event, but continued to hold its own celebration on the octave of his feast day. [20]

Eight years later, the *cabildo* moved its own special commemoration of Joseph to the last day of the novena.[21] Given that councilmen understood their role partially as advisory to the king and believed that the *cabildo*, at least to some extent, served as an extension of royal authority, they likely chose to associate their festival with the *patrocinio* as some sort of proclamation regarding legitimacy and political rule. By 1688, the *cabildo* had cemented all of its ritual obligations to Saint Joseph. On his feast day, it participated in a public blessing of candles, bread, and palms, and a procession featuring the miraculous effigy of Saint Joseph as its centerpiece. It celebrated Joseph's patronage over the Spanish empire with a novena beginning on the Sunday following Easter, and on the last day of the novena marked his special role as Puebla's patron saint against storms and lighting. It also thanked Joseph on the last day of an annual novena held every September for his protection during the rainy season. These ceremonial obligations would remain the same until 1751, when the cathedral chapter asked the *cabildo* to move the customary joint procession of palms from March 19 to the week after Easter, also coinciding with the novena acknowledging Joseph as patron of the Spanish Empire. The *cabildo* agreed, but continued to attend mass on the Patriarch's feast day in the cathedral, where, with a special dispensation from the pope, a priest blessed a large number of candles to serve as protection from storms and lightning.[22]

The *cabildo* never wavered in its devotion to the Patriarch, even when faced with serious fiscal challenges at the turn of the eighteenth century.

The municipal council had long enjoyed the privilege of collecting the royal sales tax for the Crown, but lax collection practices and corruption had resulted in the *cabildo*'s struggling to make payments. By 1694, councilmen voted to lower every councilman's and employee's salary and suspended the weekly masses in honor of Saint Joseph. Also, by this time, the *cabildo* had stopped holding jousts and bullfights in honor of Joseph, though it continued to mark his advocacy for Puebla with a sung mass, sermon, flowers, candles, and fireworks.[23] To put these modifications into perspective, fiscal challenges had forced councilmen to stop holding bullfights in honor of the feast day of Saint Michael as well, and this occasion also marked the anniversary of the foundation of the city. Mock jousts, anyway, were falling out of fashion, with Puebla's 1696 viceregal entrance featuring the last mock joust sponsored by Puebla's *cabildo*.[24] Twenty-three years after suspending the masses in honor of the Patriarch, the *cabildo* had not forgotten about its obligation; having "recuperated" from its terrible debt, in 1717 the council reinstated the masses of appeasement.[25]

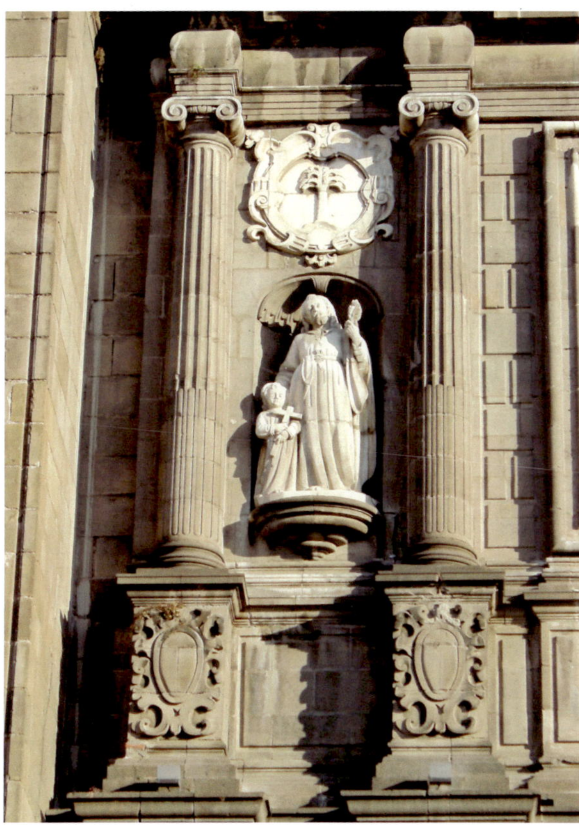

Fig. 9. Sculpture of Saint Joseph and Christ on the facade of the main entrance of the Cathedral of Puebla, Mexico. Oficina de Turismo de la Ciudad de Puebla/José Pérez Torrealba.

The *cabildo* continued to prioritize Saint Joseph in an increasingly crowded ceremonial arena. By the turn of the century, the council had elected many more patron saints to each of whom it owed 25 *pesos* a year to help defray feast-day expenses, but it continued to spend the most money on commemorations devoted to Saint Joseph, with the feast day of Saint Michael in second place. In 1741, for example, the *cabildo* spent 335 *pesos* on its celebrations for Saint Joseph, 181 *pesos* on the feast of Saint Michael, and a combined amount of 250 *pesos* for all of its other patron saints.[26] By the eighteenth century, Saint Joseph arguably surpassed Saint Michael in importance, at least in measurable terms of time and money spent on his cult.

Joseph would have a strong iconographic presence in the city of Puebla, and in a telling indication of the saint's political importance, the main entrance of Puebla's cathedral incorporated a statue of the Patriarch (fig. 7). Its placement on the main entrance underneath the coat of arms of Holy Roman Emperor Charles V highlights Joseph the Patriarch's association with political authority (figs. 8 and 9). The entire facade is a testament to

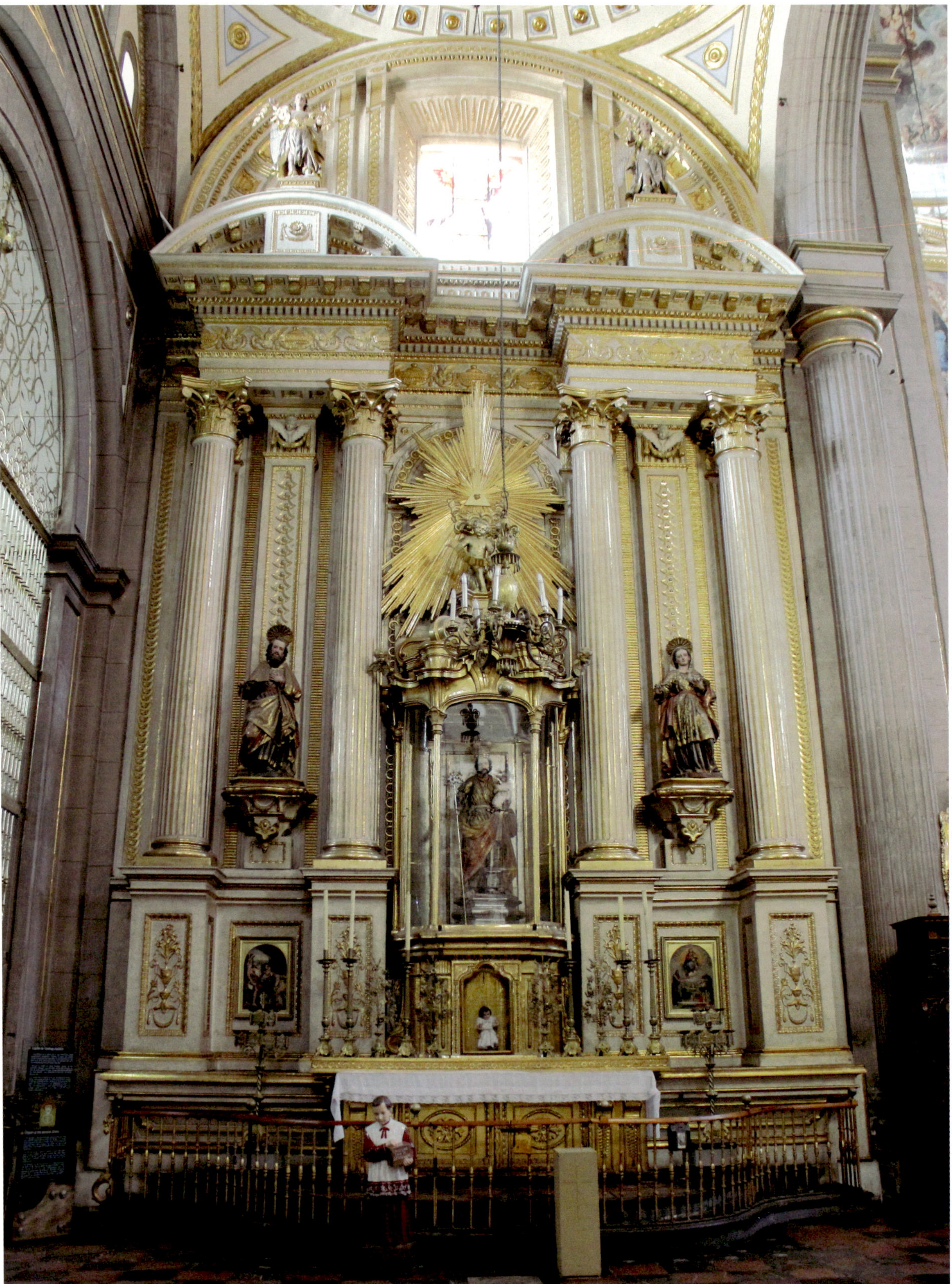

Fig. 10. Altar of San José in the Cathedral of Puebla, Mexico. Late 18th century. Oficina de Turismo de la Ciudad de Puebla/ Fabián Valdivia Pérez.

the *patronato real*, the Spanish monarch's patronage of the Church in America. It resembles a triumphal arch, and at the base, or the first of its three tiers, stand two sculptures: Peter to the right and Paul to the left, the "pillars" of the Church. In the second tier, Saint Joseph stands to the left side, directly opposite a sculpture of Saint James (or Santiago), the patron saint of Spain. Interestingly, the facade's ornamentation, under the direction of master sculptor Vicencio Varrocio Escayola, was completed in 1664, long before Charles II named Joseph patron saint of the Spanish Empire.[27] Still, it indicates a pervasive understanding of Saint Joseph as representative of political authority more generally and as intimately tied to the Spanish Crown more specifically.

Inside the cathedral, Joseph has his own altar next to the Altar of the Kings at the far end of the cathedral (fig. 10). His placement next to the Altar of the Kings is not incidental, and not only because the latter celebrates the Spanish Crown and the *patronato real*. On the other side of the Altar of the Kings, symmetrical with Saint Joseph's altar, stands the altar to Saint Michael, Puebla's other primary patron saint. Saint Joseph's altar features a fine sculpture of the Patriarch attributed to Cora or his workshop (fig. 11). Yet it did not take the place of the miraculous sculpture of Saint Joseph housed in his titular parish. The cathedral chapter continued to move Saint Joseph the Patriarch from his parish church to the cathedral for its novena every September.

Actions taken by the city's political elite worked to increase directly the visibility of the Patriarch. At the beginning of the eighteenth century, Puebla's traditional oligarchy came under attack; a reformist *alcalde mayor* drove many *regidores* out of the municipal council, and in 1714 he appointed honorary *regidores* to fill the seats left by the perpetual *regidores*, who had purchased their positions for life. These honorary councilmen were affiliated with important commercial families whose members would continue to serve intermittently as honorary *regidores* for decades to come.[28] By the 1760s, the parish of Santo Ángel Custodio had an altar dedicated to Saint Joseph. A wealthy Spaniard helped to establish a confraternity in the Patriarch's honor, and according to chronicler Fernández Echeverria y Veytia, it

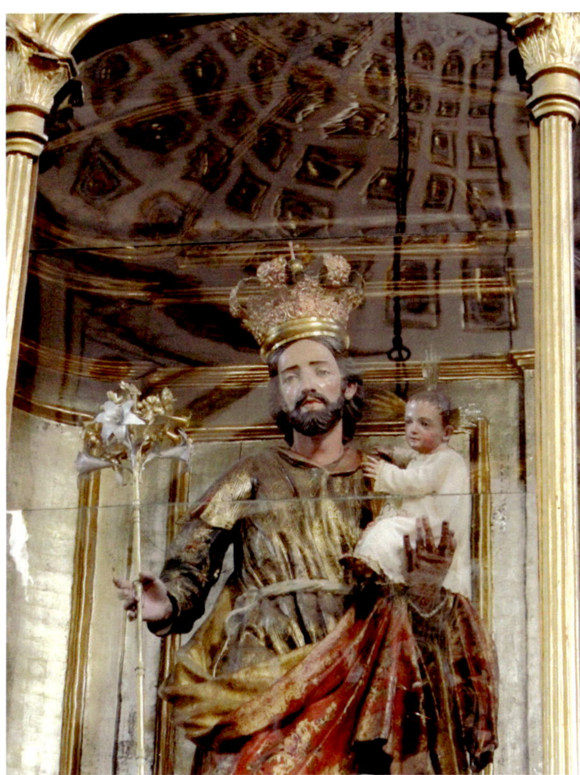

Fig. 11. José Villegas Cora or his workshop, sculpture of San José in the Cathedral of Puebla, Mexico. Late 18th century. Oficina de Turismo de la Ciudad de Puebla/Fabián Valdivia Pérez.

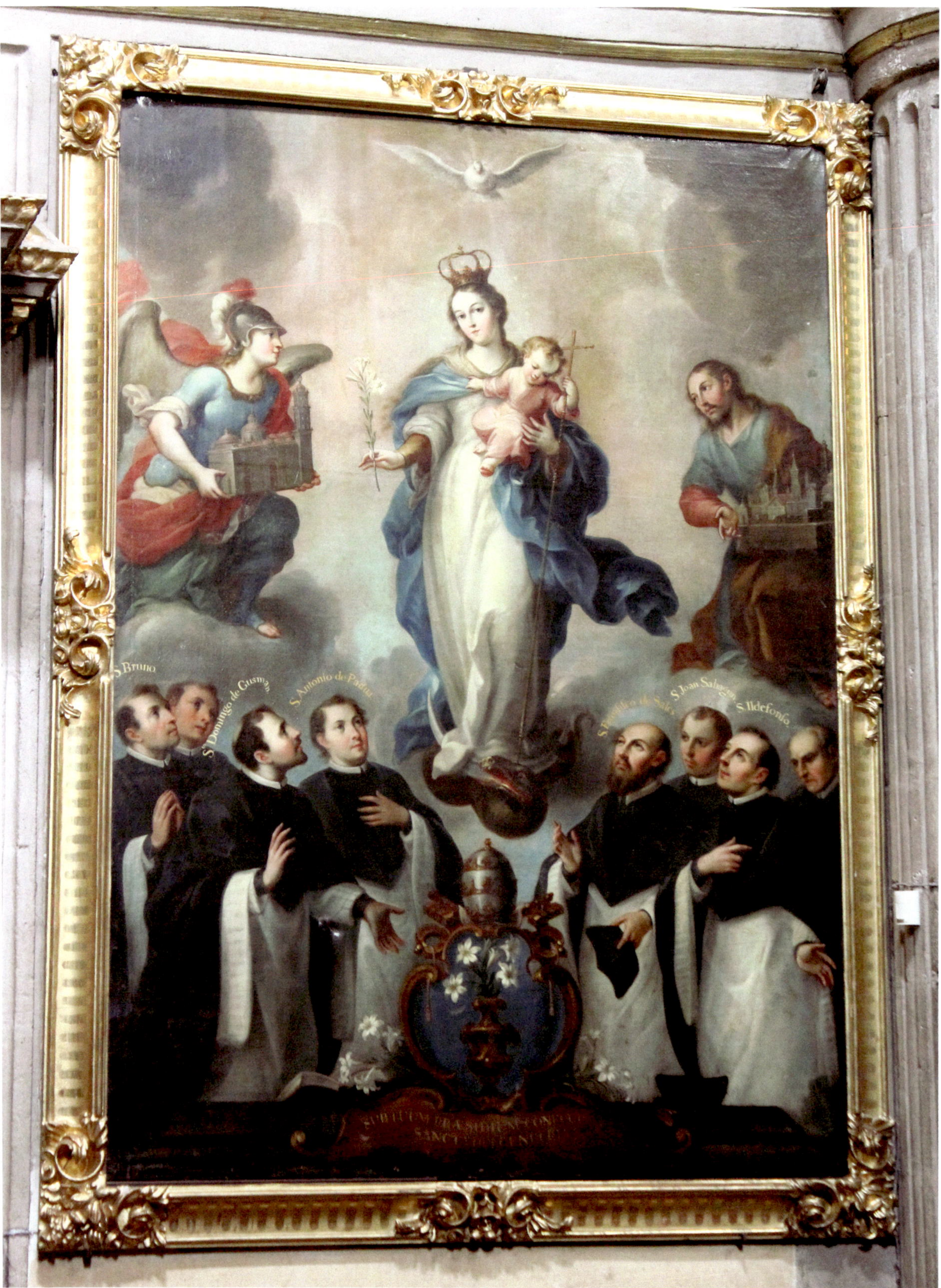

Fig. 12. . José de Ibarra (1685–1756), *Inmaculada Concepción, San Miguel Arcángel, y San José con canónigos*. Mexico, 1732. Oficina de Turismo de la Ciudad de Puebla/Fabián Valdivia Pérez.

attracted members from the highest strata of society. Colonel of the militias, wealthy merchant, and ex-honorary *regidor* Eugenio González Maldonado served as the confraternity's first *mayordomo*, or president, indicating that Puebla's ascending political elite recognized the saint as a useful symbol; by supporting the Patriarch's cult, the merchants may have sought to cast themselves as patriarchs of Puebla, much as the city's perpetual councilmen enjoyed strong ties to the parish of Saint Joseph.[29]

As both the Church and different segments within the political elite embraced the cult of Saint Joseph, he slowly came to stand for the city as a whole. A painting by renowned artist José de Ibarra illustrates the intimate connection between the Patriarch and Puebla (fig. 12). Commissioned in 1732 for a side of the entrance to the cathedral's choir stall, it features the Immaculate Conception, patroness of the cathedral, hovering over members of Puebla's cathedral chapter "disguised" partially as a group of saints who had all been members of religious orders.[30] She is flanked by the city of Puebla's two most important patron saints. To her right is Saint Michael, titular saint of Puebla, holding the cathedral, and to her left is Saint Joseph, holding up the entire city of Puebla. The painting visually places Saint Joseph on equal footing with Saint Michael the Archangel, but by choosing to have him (instead of Saint Michael) cradle the city in his hands, Ibarra and his patrons acknowledged Joseph's central role as caretaker of the *poblano* community.

Pageantry, Political Authority, and Popular Memory

Clearly, the cult of Saint Joseph lent itself to co-optation, as ambitious elites, cathedral chapter members, New Spain's archdiocese, and even the Crown all staked claims to the Patriarch's cult. But within the city of Puebla, the municipal council staked the strongest claim to the cult by either funding or simply participating in elaborate ceremonies. Councilmen likely understood the political importance of making frequent appearances in full regalia within the parish of Saint Joseph. Since its foundation, the parish had grown notably in size and importance, indicating that the *cabildo*'s early predictions regarding the parish were not off the mark, at least not entirely. While the *Sagrario Metropolitano*—the parish attached to the cathedral—remained the most important and densely populated, the parish of Saint Joseph consistently came in second.[31] This diverse but overwhelmingly Spanish and *mestizo* parish served as the headquarters of some of the city's most lucrative businesses. Partially controlling the cult of Puebla's second largest and most racially diverse parish likely proved useful to councilmen, who, when participating in feast-day processions from the municipal palace to the parish or from the parish to the cathedral, traversed the important *Calle de los Mercaderes*, or Street of the Merchants.

Feast-day commemorations required councilmen to participate *en cuerpo de ciudad* or as the "body," or embodiment, of the city. Councilmen processed to the church that hosted the event with two pages carrying the council's ceremonial maces. These bore the city's coat of arms and made clear that councilmen were attending not as individuals, but as the *Nobilísima Ciudad*, or "Most Noble City," a title awarded by Holy Roman Emperor Charles V. In the early modern Spanish world, seating mattered as a reflection of status, and councilmen sat together during mass on the right side of the nave, a symbolic place of honor.[32] Colonial law specified that when *cabildo* members attended a function *en cuerpo de ciudad*, they should have benches reserved exclusively for their use. While many attendees sat on the floor or were forced to remain standing during religious services, councilmen sat in relative comfort elevated above the rest. Anyone who sat there uninvited could be fined up to 100 *pesos*.[33] When religious leaders asked the *cabildo* to attend specific ceremonies, they always specified that they do so *en cuerpo de ciudad*, believing that this would help to "authorize" the event and set a good example for the populace.[34]

Rules of etiquette further underscored the privileged position of councilmen and helped to broadcast their authority. Puebla's aldermen enjoyed a variety of ceremonial prerogatives that they jealously guarded as distinguishing markers of status. These privileges mirrored those of other corporations farther up the scale of power; that is, *cabildo* members enjoyed modified versions of the same privileges enjoyed by the king, viceroys, and members of the *audiencia* (the highest royal tribunal of New Spain). These, in turn, helped define councilmen as representatives of the royal person. In Mexico City, officiating prelates always blessed the archbishop and then the viceroy and *audiencia* judges with holy water when they entered a church for a religious function. Similarly, in Puebla, when councilmen attended a function *en cuerpo de ciudad*, a priest would first sprinkle holy water over the bishop and proceed then to bless the *alcalde mayor* and *cabildo*.[35] The *Recopilación de leyes de los reinos de Indias* (the seventeenth-century compilation of Spanish American law) specified that ceremonies involving the king should be echoed with his viceroys in Peru and Mexico. For example, when the king attended high mass and received the "peace"—a sacred image—he knelt before the officiating prelate and kissed the vessel, or *portapaz*, which held the object. Likewise, Book 3, Title 15, Law 10 of the *Recopilación* specified that viceroys should kneel before the officiating prelate when receiving the peace. Local leaders, in turn, complied with the dictates of court ceremonial. As advisors to the king, Puebla's *regidores* and *alcaldes mayores* also received the peace during feast-day ceremonies and did so kneeling, underscoring the reverence of the monarch for the Catholic faith.[36]

Ceremonial distinctions such as these telegraphed the *cabildo*'s importance to the city's overwhelmingly illiterate population. On the feast days of Puebla's patron saints, the officiating priest always bowed his head in deference to the *cabildo* as he walked down the aisle toward the main altar. Priests had an obligation to welcome the *cabildo* at the beginning of each sermon, and failure to do so could provoke scandal.[37] Councilmen, moreover, figured prominently in the procession of the city's patron saints, with specific councilmen even carrying the poles of the ceremonial *palio*, or canopy used to cover the sacred images.[38]

While the feast days of all of Puebla's patron saints worked to the benefit of city leaders, councilmen identified most closely with the Patriarch, and the ceremonies in honor of Saint Joseph communicated the importance of the cult while also underscoring the authority of councilmen. According to a manual for *regidores* housed in Puebla's municipal archive, councilmen were "fathers of the Republic" and were to be recognized publicly as such.[39] Through 1751, the procession on Saint Joseph's feast day embarked from the cathedral to the parish, and after the mass and sermon, the councilmen and cathedral chapter prelates participated in a blessing of bread and palms followed by a procession from the parish back to the cathedral. After 1751, the municipal council and cathedral chapter moved this aspect of the ceremonies to the day of the *patrocinio*. As Saint Joseph and his entourage moved through the parish streets, people waved palms in an obvious reference to Christ's triumphal entrance into Jerusalem. But since Puebla's *cabildo* and cathedral chapter acted as *pater familias*, when the effigy processed through the streets people celebrated both the triumph of the saint and the supremacy of municipal leaders—the patriarchs of their city—just as when waving palms upon Christ's triumphal entrance people celebrated the king of the Jews and the head of the eventual Church. The *cabildo* regarded this aspect of the ceremony as so important that it even paid for the palms and for a courier to bring them to the Patriarch's church.[40]

However solemn, most religious occasions incorporated festive elements that attracted people from outside the immediate parish and served socially integrative functions. Puebla's citizenry created communities most directly through confraternity involvement. Members attended to each other when ill, participated in the funerals of fellow members, and helped to organize elaborate festivities in honor of their patron saint. Confraternity members from many of Puebla's numerous brotherhoods would have participated in the feast-day procession in honor of Saint Joseph. While members of Spanish confraternities did not generally attend all the festivities to which they were invited, officials from the city's more popular confraternities usually did. In fact, at least two or three confraternities always attended a procession for a saint, and by the late seventeenth century, confraternities considered mutual support to be a "very ancient custom," and expected a donation of only two *reales* for showing up at the festivities of other sodalities.[41]

Feast-day spectacles with their accompanying processions provided important respites from everyday life. Some extraordinary processions, such as that held for the coronation of Saint Joseph

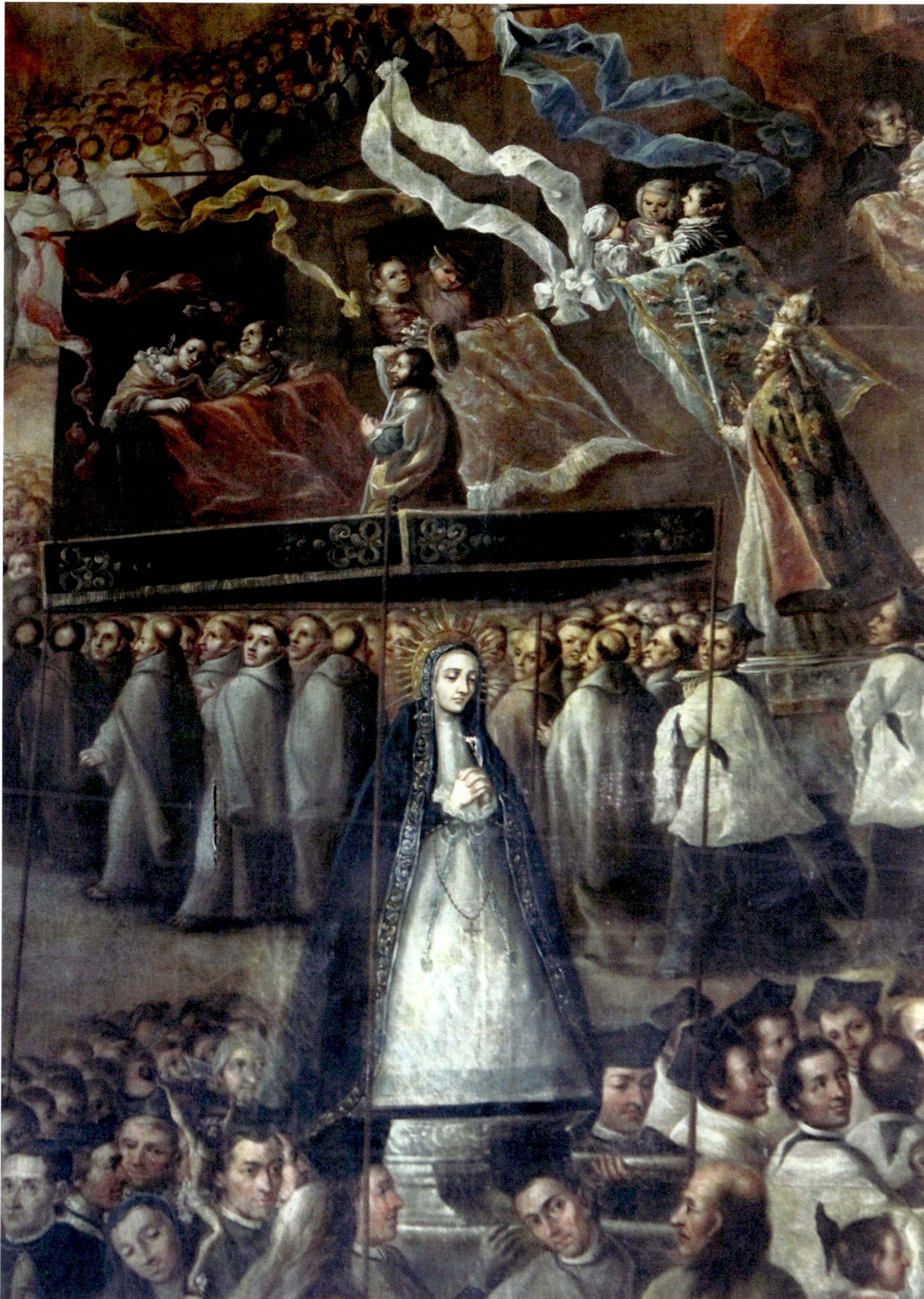

Fig. 13. (Detail) Pablo Joseph Talavera, *Procession of Our Lady of Solitude and Saint Joseph*. Mexico, 18th century. Oil on canvas. Housed in Puebla's Church of la Soledad. Oficina de Turismo de la Ciudad de Puebla/Fabián Valdivia Pérez.

in 1788, involved thousands of participants and onlookers. Wealthy *poblanos* enjoyed the pageantry from the comfort of their balconies, which were often adorned with richly embroidered tapestries, as illustrated by an eighteenth-century painting depicting a procession of Our Lady of Solitude and a sculpture of Saint Joseph (fig. 13). However, even cyclical feast days constituted festivals. Important occasions for revelry and sociability, patron saint festivities often ran over the course of eight days, and, well aware of the liturgical calendar, vendors from as far as Tlaxcala would descend upon Puebla's parishes at specific times throughout the year. They sold *pulque*, the traditional indigenous beverage made out of the maguey cactus, as well as food, and set up so many games and diversions that the feast day and its octave essentially constituted a fair. [42]

On Saint Joseph's feast day and its octave, vendors and entertainers likely set up in the Plazuela de San José directly in front of the main doors of the church. In 1634 Pope Urban VIII granted the rector of the Confraternity of the Glorious Patriarch [Our] Lord Saint Joseph the right to have palms, *panesitos* (or small breads), and other "decent things" blessed on his feast day so that the faithful could use these objects as a form of protection against storms and lighting.[43] The *cabildo* contributed to the festivities by paying for the palms that were blessed on the feast day and covering all costs associated with the last day of the octave, including musicians for the sung mass, candles, and elaborate firework displays. In addition to the blessed objects, *poblanos* would have left the festivities with other tangible reminders of Joseph the Patriarch's beneficence, as well as

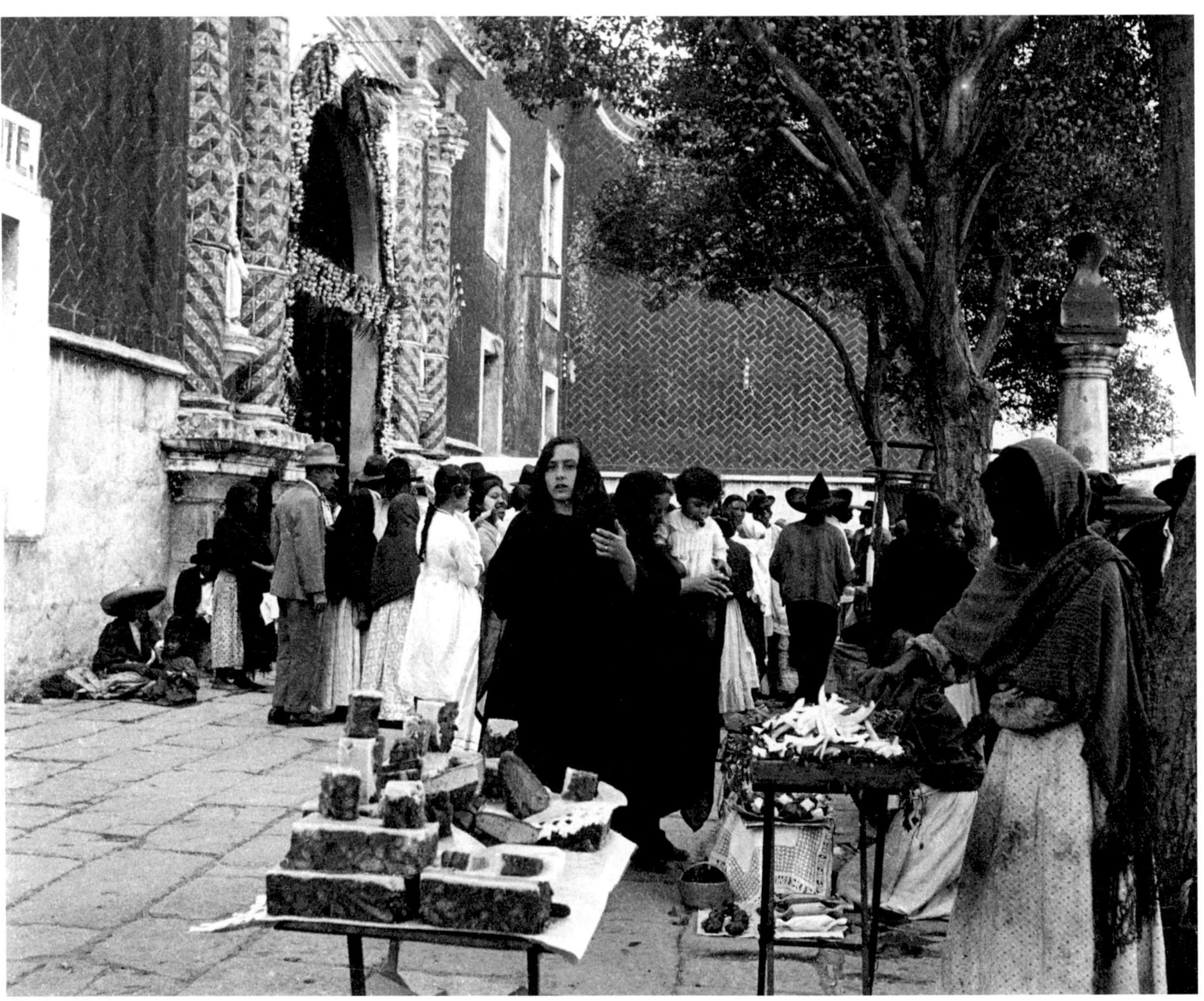

Fig. 14. Guillermo Robles Callejo, *La parroquia en las fiestas de San José*. Mexico, 1922. D. R. © Fototeca Antica, A.C. / Colección Jorge Carretero Madrid.

the beneficence of the patriarchs of the city. As was customary on most religious feast days, vendors likely sold engravings of the Patriarch that devotees could place on their home altars.

While we lack descriptions of the eighteenth-century festivities, we know that in the nineteenth century numerous vendors sold holy objects outside the church, and the confraternity helped raise money by selling blessed candles.[44] In the early twentieth century, the feast day attracted thousands of residents who not only bought holy objects, food, and drink, but also played games like the *palo encebado*, in which participants paid to attempt to climb up a greased pole in order to win a prize (figs. 14 and 15). It is likely that in the eighteenth century residents also indulged in similar diversions. In fact, feast day festivities could get quite raucous. In 1716, the Barrio del Carmen held bullfights on the feast day of the Immaculate Conception, and apparently the event precipitated so many "scandals" and "public sins" that the *cabildo* refused to grant the barrio a license to hold bullfights the following year.[45] But for authorized celebrations like those in honor of Saint Joseph, local leaders benefitted from the jovial atmosphere insofar as positive feelings generated by the festivities could then spill over to them as hosts.

On the day of the *patrocinio*, councilmen processed from the parish of Saint Joseph to the cathedral and sat together *en cuerpo de ciudad* during mass, but they reserved most effort and resources for the last day of the novena following the *patrocinio*; after 1688, this was the day on which councilmen acknowledged Saint Joseph's advocacy on behalf of Puebla. Councilmen participated in a procession returning Joseph, who

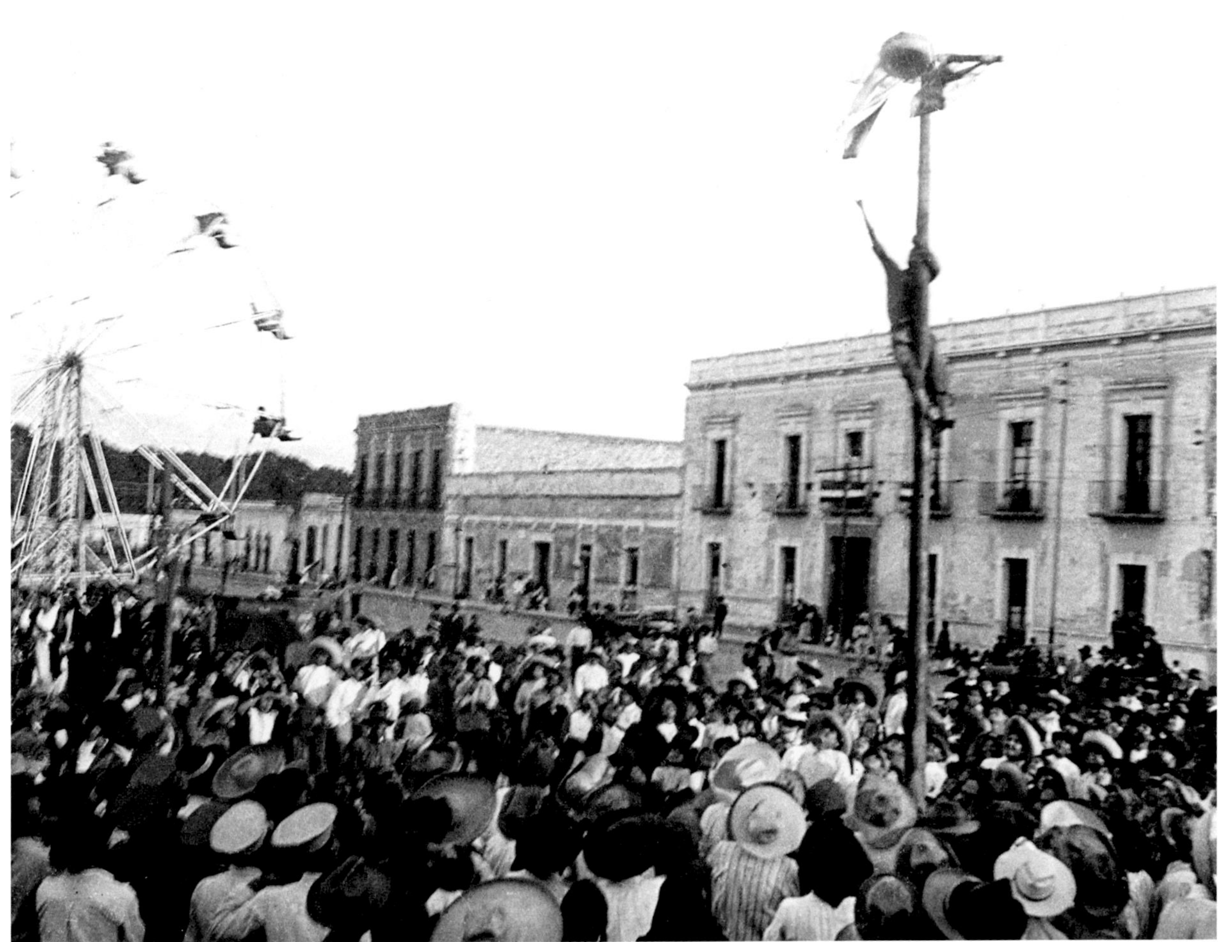

Fig. 15. Guillermo Robles Callejo, *Plaza de San José en las fiestas del Patriarca*. Mexico, 1922. D. R. © Fototeca Antica, A.C. / Colección Jorge Carretero Madrid.

had been held in the cathedral for the novena, to his parish. *Regidores* paid for roses to decorate the church, wood for bonfires, musicians to accompany the procession, and even an elegant lunch, which included wine and hot chocolate, for the officiating priest and other ecclesiastical leaders.[46] Councilmen usually spent the most money for the candles held during the procession, which later lit the inside of the parish of Saint Joseph. In 1741, for vespers on the eve of the ceremony and mass the following day, the *cabildo* spent over 233 *pesos* on candle wax alone.[47]

The festivities also included elaborate fireworks that quite literally highlighted the Patriarch and local ministers. In 1740, for example, a master of pyrotechnics ignited sparkling pinwheels during the procession and outside the church during mass; he set off dozens of single blast explosions, known as *cámaras*, at the onset of the Gloria, at the reading of the Gospels, and at the moment the priest lifted the Eucharist into the air. Significantly, the fireworks artisan also put a spotlight on the *cabildo*, setting off blasts when the councilmen entered and exited the church. The only other occasions that warranted such a use of fireworks were Corpus Christi and the feast day of Saint Michael.[48]

Councilmen also spent a great deal of money on the novena held every September, seeing it as another way to appease and honor their special patron. Also, by cosponsoring the event, councilmen reaffirmed proprietary rights over the cult, and the novena resonated with the populace, who saw it as a way of thanking Joseph for protecting the city throughout the rainy season. Most of the costs went toward lighting the cathedral, but the council also paid for fireworks. On the first day of the novena, councilmen made sure the streets were swept and well lit with luminaries, and they personally carried the Patriarch on their shoulders from his parish to the cathedral, where he would reside for the course of the novena. The *cabildo* also covered costs associated with the last day of the novena, and, together with the cathedral chapter prelates, accompanied the Patriarch on his return to his namesake church. Although fiscal records are far from perfect, it seems that the amount spent on September's novena fluctuated wildly; in 1737, the *cabildo* spent 75 *pesos*, while in 1741 it spent 229 *pesos*.[49]

Lighting, fireworks, seating, placement in processions, and all of the public distinctions and courtesies extended to the *cabildo* underscored its authority and legitimacy. But sermons and devotional manuals also worked to influence how people viewed Saint Joseph and, by extension, local leaders. Although councilmen had no direct role in shaping this literature, the genres reveal pervasive understandings regarding the political significance of the Patriarch, and at times highlight the *cabildo* as an enthusiastic promoter of his cult.

By the late seventeenth century, orators had become skilled at connecting Saint Joseph to political authority. In 1680, the ceremony inaugurating the *patrocinio* clearly intended to make the obvious connection between Saint Joseph and Charles II, who had just named Joseph patron saint of the Spanish Empire in 1679. Cathedral canon and famed panegyrist Diego de Victoria Salazár argued that Joseph of Egypt, favorite son of Jacob, prefigured the Patriarch, and stressed how he acted like a dedicated leader, seeing to the welfare of his own tribe but also that of his sons Ephraim and Manasseh. The sermon, therefore, highlighted Joseph's role as both a leader and a father and then compared Charles II's decision to elect Saint Joseph as patron saint of the empire to Jacob's decision to place Joseph of Egypt (whom the sermon essentially conflated with Joseph the Patriarch) in charge of two tribes. The panegyrist compared this to Charles II's dominion over both the Old World and the New, and on behalf of the monarchy, asked Joseph to watch over "not only two provinces, but instead two Kingdoms; not only two tribes, but instead two Worlds."[50]

Victoria Salazár then explained why Charles II chose to promote Joseph the Patriarch to patron saint of the empire. In order to reach the infant Jesus, the Magi needed to go through his parents, Mary and Joseph. He explained how in 1654, Philip IV had ordered churches to hold an annual mass for the Virgin to acknowledge her support for Spain, a ceremony that would be attended by the *cabildo* through Independence. Now, Victoria Salazár stressed, by promoting Joseph to patron saint of the empire, the Crown had assured the support of both of Christ's parents, who could not but influence their child to extend his support to Puebla.[51]

Significantly for the *cabildo*, Victoria Salazár remarked on how the municipal council had elected Joseph as a patron saint of the city long ago. He acknowledged that the Archangel Michael had acted as the first "protector" of the city, but that even he looked to Joseph as Puebla's primary guardian. He argued that Joseph surpassed the Archangel Michael in stature because archangels understood that they needed to defer to Joseph's authority. As evidence for this, he cited how the Archangel Gabriel stopped acting as the custodian of Mary when she married Joseph.[52] Saint Joseph, therefore, acted as the consummate example of a good custodian and served as Puebla's rightful principal saint. Victoria Salazár stressed how Joseph cared for Mary and helped Jesus escape the murderous designs of King Herod.[53] By painting such an idealized picture of patriarchal authority, Victoria Salazár invited comparisons to monarch Charles II. However, by mentioning the *cabildo*, he also associated the Patriarch with the patriarchs of Puebla.

By this time, councilmen had come to identify strongly with the Patriarch. In 1687, senior constable and *regidor* Miguel Raboso de Guevara paid for the printing of a sermon honoring the feast day of Saint Joseph in Puebla's Jesuit Church of the Espíritu Santo. Panegyrist Juan de Robles emphasized Joseph's compassion and his role as protector of Mary and Jesus, and placed him firmly as second only to Christ and the Virgin Mary.[54] One year later, Nicolás Carrasco Moscoso gave a sermon commemorating Saint Joseph's patronage of Puebla and the *cabildo*'s decision to move the city's commemoration to the last day of the *patrocinio*. Carrasco Moscoso expressed admiration for how the *cabildo* promoted the cult. He recounted how the *cabildo* first elected Joseph in the sixteenth century and surmised that, because of "ingratitude and neglect," Joseph "lifted up the hand of his patronage" and allowed lightning to threaten the city once again. He then compared the ratification of the oath in 1611 to the vow made by Jacob to honor God, as Jacob reaffirmed the original oath taken by his father Abraham.[55] As Robles had done a year earlier, Carrasco Moscoso described Joseph as second only to Christ and the Virgin Mary and, interestingly, characterized the saint as a consummate authority figure, noting that he is always depicted holding a staff, a classic symbol of authority. Through his staff, Joseph bestowed his protection, and many members of the audience would have also associated staffs with the authority invested in the municipal council. Upon their election, *alcaldes ordinarios* (constables), for example, were awarded staffs of office. The priest ended the sermon by praising the city's cathedral chapter, its religious orders, and most especially, its *cabildo*.[56]

Joseph continued to play an important spiritual and political role in Puebla throughout the eighteenth century. Writing in the late eighteenth century, chronicler Mariano Fernández Echeverría y Veytia stated that "Whenever there is some affliction or public necessity like war, pestilence, scarcity of water or the like, the City [the municipal council] or the venerable *cabildo* [the cathedral chapter] brings this Holy Image to the cathedral and makes a novena for it, with the certainty of obtaining the benefit that is desired from the mercy of the most holy Patriarch." According to the chronicler, experience had proven that Saint Joseph would answer the prayers of the city's parishioners. He singled out the English occupation of Havana on August 12, 1762, during the Seven Years War, and how after the parish's miraculous sculpture of Saint Joseph arrived in the cathedral the following month for the annual novena, Bishop Domingo Pantaleón Álvarez y Abreu ordered that it remain in the cathedral until the conclusion of the war. When an "unexpected" peace was achieved seven months later, he saw this as the result of the intercession of Saint Joseph. The city then commemorated the peace by returning the Patriarch to his home church with a solemn procession.[57]

When Puebla celebrated the coronation ceremony for Joseph in 1788, Father Díaz y Tirado used the ceremony to emphasize the importance of Joseph to the city as a whole. At key moments during the sermon, the panegyrist made note of the *cabildo*'s decision to make Joseph a principal patron of the city. But he also emphasized how Saint Joseph had worked to "unite the spirits of discord" that had traditionally fractured the city. During certain feast days, members of competing barrios had taken to gathering into squadrons to wage war with rocks, sticks, and small arms, and many people reportedly died or suffered serious injuries during these feast-day battles.[58] During the coronation, Díaz y Tirado cryptically described these *guerras* as the "original sin" of the barrios. Puebla's indigenous residents represented a variety of different ethnicities, and people generally tended to settle in the same barrio with members from their own ethnic group. The "wars" may have been shaped, at least initially, by ethnic rivalries that predated the Conquest, but, according to the panegyrist, devotion to Saint Joseph helped people overcome their historical disdain. As if to symbolize this newfound unity, Puebla's wealthier citizens donated jewels to adorn his crown, which, in the end, contained 417 precious stones, including diamonds and emeralds.[59] After declaiming on about Joseph's obedience, his commitment to Mary and Jesus, and the pain that he suffered during his life, Díaz y Tirado concluded the sermon by asking Saint Joseph to protect the city and by reminding him that the "*Nobilísima Ciudad* swears and has sworn to always be under your PATRONAGE."[60]

However much he symbolized *poblano* identity, the city's residents also continued to recognize Saint Joseph as an advocate for the Spanish Empire; in 1794, while Spain fought against revolutionary France, the parish of Saint Joseph organized a novena to ask for the Patriarch's support. Puebla's parishioners donated money for the event, covering the cost of candles, music, luminaries, and masses, and on the last day of the novena, Díaz y Tirado again gave the sermon. The *cabildo* of course attended with its maces of authority, as did the cathedral chapter and representatives from the city's religious orders and schools. After mass, distinguished guests and parishioners all participated in a procession around half of the expansive Plazuela de San José.[61]

In the first part of the sermon, Díaz y Tirado juxtaposed the disobedient Adam with the obedient Joseph, who, despite the shame placed on his honor, believed the Archangel Gabriel that Mary carried the son of God. He obeyed the will of God and protected Mary and the baby Jesus, thereby

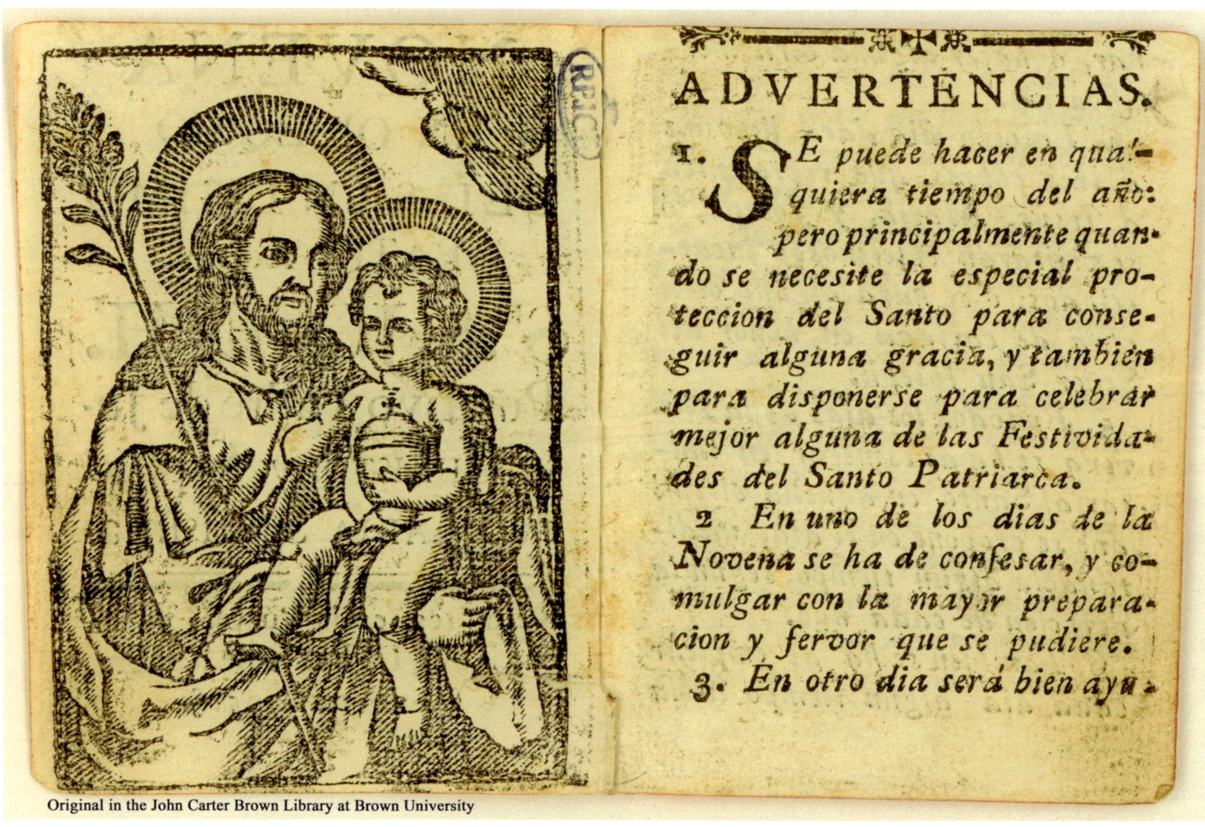

ADVERTENCIAS.

1. *SE puede hacer en qualquiera tiempo del año: pero principalmente quando se necesite la especial proteccion del Santo para conseguir alguna gracia, y tambien para disponerse para celebrar mejor alguna de las Festividades del Santo Patriarca.*

2 *En uno de los dias de la Novena se ha de confesar, y comulgar con la mayor preparacion y fervor que se pudiere.*

3. *En otro dia será bien ayu-*

Fig. 16. Engraving of Saint Joseph. From *Novena en obsequio del Santísimo Patriarca Sr. S. Joseph. Putativo padre de Jesucristo, y esposo de María Santísima* (Puebla: Oficina de Don Pedro de la Rosa, 1795). Courtesy of the John Carter Brown Library at Brown University.

helping to "compensate in great part [for] the evils caused by the disobedience of Adam."[62] In the second part of the sermon, he stated that "Well expressed is the Divine Commandment to honor our Parents, and by this it is understood all the Elders," and extended this commandment to all superiors, such as kings, legislators, and judges.[63] To obey the king, then, is to obey your father. To commit patricide, as the French did with the execution of Louis XVI, is to go against natural law. Díaz y Tirado emphasized that respect for secular authority is tantamount to faith in God, citing the exchange in Matthew when two spies asked Jesus whether Jews should pay taxes, and Jesus eventually advised them to "Render therefore unto Caesar the things which are Caesar's; and unto God the things that are God's." Toward the end of the sermon, Díaz y Tirado railed against the influx of French décor and the declining popularity of decorating interiors with sacred images. He feared that these "profane" customs "are similar to Jacobinism."[64] The entire sermon acted as a cautionary tale intended to prevent the spread of such dangerous proclivities and emphasized the importance of respect for the king, as well as for the authority invested in all of his ministers. The councilmen in attendance were no doubt pleased by the content.

Feast days and special commemorations surely had the capacity to instill respect for authority and shape popular memory regarding the role of Saint Joseph in the history of New Spain and, even more specifically, Puebla. However, the extent to which parishioners carried messages home with them is difficult to gauge. Nevertheless, while practicing individual devotions in honor of Saint Joseph at home, people likely remained cognizant of his importance to New Spain and Puebla, both spiritually and politically. For Puebla's literate minority, devotional manuals facilitated this connection. In the eighteenth century, Puebla saw a proliferation of miniature devotional manuals directed toward guiding people through prayer either on the nineteenth day of each month or throughout the course of a novena. The former devotion arose in the eighteenth century in remembrance of the Patriarch's feast day on March 19. According to one manual, the innovation, which had presumably begun in a small number of churches, had been so well received that many churches had started to emulate the practice and, consequently, attracted a large number of people to hear mass and take communion. The anonymous author stressed the historical importance of the Patriarch for New Spain, noting that after the conquest of the New World, the early missionaries encouraged devotion to Saint Joseph; he reminded readers that the First Provincial Council elected the saint as the patron of the recently established Church and then elaborated on how the Third Mexican Provincial Council confirmed the election. He stated that devotion to the Patriarch extended into the home, as mothers "affectionately invoke his protection." According to the author, Joseph was the quintessential patriarchal figure, as Mary obeyed him as her husband and Christ as his son. Significantly, the preamble to the manual also emphasized that since the city of Puebla started venerating Saint Joseph as its "special patron," it had stopped being "infected by malignant tempests," which had "plagued" it in the past.[65] Devotional manuals capitalized on Saint Joseph's paternal qualities, and at least two manuals published in Puebla featured the same engraving of Joseph tenderly holding the Christ Child (fig. 16).[66]

The devotional manuals for novenas also stressed the political importance of the Patriarch and his special advocacy for New Spain. In 1789, Puebla's carpenters' guild sponsored the publication of a manual, probably as a way of commemorating the coronation in 1788. The author, José Francisco Valdés, recommended demonstrating gratitude to God for all of the many benefits he had bestowed on the "Americans," adding that "one of the major ones is having given us as Patron and Protector the Most Holy Patriarch [and] Lord Saint Joseph." According to Valdés, God inspired the priests who took part in the First Provincial Council to elect Joseph as patron of everything that had until that time been conquered and everything that would be conquered in the future. He argued that the exercises and nine days of prayer laid out in the manual were ideally suited to begin the third Sunday after Easter, or just one week after the conclusion of the *patrocinio.* However, the author also claimed that they could be done at any other time. One can imagine devotees using the manual in their observance of the *patrocinio* and the novena in honor of Saint Joseph in September. On October 21, 1806, Bishop of Puebla Manuel Ignacio González del Campillo awarded forty days of indulgences for every prayer included in the manual.[67]

Conclusion

Although the origin myth of Puebla de los Ángeles maintains that the city was founded on the feast day of Saint Michael the Archangel, by the eighteenth century Saint Joseph the Patriarch had arguably become Puebla's most revered saint—with a little help from the municipal council. As many orators made clear, Joseph represented the consummate authority figure, as God entrusted him with both Mary and Jesus, and many conflated him with his "precursor" Joseph of Egypt, the "viceroy." Appreciating the symbolic resonance of Joseph, Puebla's councilmen elected him as the city's second patron saint in 1555, the same year that Mexico's First Provincial Council named him patron of New Spain. After recommitting to his cult in 1611, councilmen began participating actively in his feast-day celebration and began holding their own special commemoration honoring Joseph eight days later. By the mid-eighteenth century, the *cabildo* sponsored three elaborate ceremonies in honor of the Patriarch and participated in four distinct commemorations.

The *cabildo*'s devotion to Saint Joseph helped to shape Puebla's religious culture and to elevate the Patriarch's standing among *poblanos*. Ubiquitous representations of Joseph testify to his importance, and some, like José de Ibarra's painting of the Immaculate Conception, illustrate his superior standing within Puebla's large pantheon of patron saints. Sermons and devotional manuals reminded *poblanos* of the *cabildo*'s crucial role in winning the Patriarch's support and the importance of Joseph to the collective history of New Spain and, more importantly, to Puebla. By the late eighteenth century, Saint Joseph had long transformed into a symbol of *poblano* identity. This, however, would not have been possible without the active support of the patriarchs of Puebla.

Notes

Several people and institutions helped me see this piece to fruition. Art historians Franziska Neff, Patricia Díaz Cayeros, and Beatriz Berndt León Mariscal recommended sources and offered helpful suggestions. I am particularly grateful to Franziska for generously sharing two of her forthcoming articles with me. Jorge Carretero Madrid, Director of the Fototeca Antica, took the time to locate the magnificent black and white photos I have included in this paper, and the Denver Art Museum and the John Carter Brown Library granted me the right to reproduce crucial images. Finally, I extend my deepest thanks to the Oficina de Turismo de la Ciudad de Puebla and its Chief of Publicity, Fabián Valdivia Pérez, for sending me many of the images included in this paper. Fabián, moreover, took most of the photos himself. I am in his debt.

[1] Joseph Atanasio Díaz y Tirado, *Sermón panegírico que en la plausible y festiva imperial coronación del santísimo patriarca Señor San Joseph, celebrada el día veinte y seis de Septiembre del año de mil setecientos ochenta y ocho en la ciudad de la Puebla de los Ángeles, predicó en la Iglesia Parroquial del Mismo santísimo Patriarca el Dr. D. Joseph Atanasio Díaz y Tirado* (Puebla: Oficina del Real Seminario Palafoxiano, 1789), not paginated.

[2] Ibid.

[3] At some point during the mid-1770s, Bourbon administrators ordered the *cabildo* to stop sponsoring commemorations for six specific saints, arguing that councilmen had never officially inducted them into the city's pantheon. See Libro que comprende específicas noticias de los patronatos jurados por votivos, 1773, Archivo Histórico Municipal de Puebla (hereafter AHMP), Libros Varios (hereafter LV) 9. For a broader discussion of Puebla's pantheon of patron saints, see Frances L. Ramos, *Identity, Ritual, and Power in Colonial Puebla* (Tucson: University of Arizona Press, 2012), especially chapter 4.

[4] See Charlene Villaseñor-Black, *Creating the Cult of Saint Joseph: Art and Liturgy in the Spanish Empire* (Princeton: Princeton University Press, 2006).

[5] Ibid., 62–64.

[6] According to Puebla's often-repeated origin myth, angels appeared to Bishop Julián Garcés on the eve of the feast day of Saint Michael and pinpointed for him the site of the future city. On the following day, the bishop set out with a group of Franciscans and discovered the site of which he had dreamt. The archangel's feast day (September 29) served as the anniversary of the city's foundation through Independence. For a good discussion of the development of the origin myth, see Antonio Rubial García, "Los ángeles de Puebla. La larga construcción de una identidad patria," in *Poder civil y catolicismo en México, siglos XVI al XIX*, ed. Francisco Javier Cervantes Bello, Alicia Tecuanhuey Sandoval, and María de Pilar Martínez López-Cano, 103–128 (Puebla: Instituto de Ciencias Sociales y Humanidades, BUAP, 2008). For the importance of the cult to the development of a distinctly *poblano* identity, see Frances L. Ramos, "Myth, Ritual, and Pride in the City of the Angels," in *Emotions and Daily Life in Colonial Mexico*, ed. Javier Villa-Flores and Sonya Lipsett-Rivera (Albuquerque: University of New Mexico Press, 2014).

[7] Villaseñor-Black, *Creating the Cult of St. Joseph*, 30.

[8] See Frances L. Ramos, "Saints, Shrines, and Feast Days in Colonial Spanish America," in *Cambridge History of Latin American Religions*, ed. Virginia Garrard-Burnett and Paul Freston (Cambridge: Cambridge University Press, forthcoming); Óscar Mazín Gómez, "Culto y devociones en la catedral de Valladolid de Michoacán, 1586–1780," in *Tradición e identidad en la cultura mexicana*, ed. Agustín Jacinto Zavala and Álvaro Ochoa Serrano (Morelia: Colegio de Michoacán, 1995), 306–343.

[9] Jaime Genaro Cuadriello Aguilar, "San José en tierra de gentiles: ministro de Egipto y virrey de las Indias," *Memoria del Museo Nacional de Arte* 1 (Fall-Winter) 1989: 5–33; Villaseñor-Black, *Creating the Cult of Saint Joseph*.

[10] Donna Pierce, Rogelio Ruiz Gomar, and Clara Bargellini, *Painting a New World: Mexican Art and Life, 1521–1821* (Denver: Denver Art Museum, 2004), 179–180.

[11] In his late-eighteenth-century chronicle, Pedro López de Villaseñor states that it is unclear when the *cabildo* elected Saint Joseph, but that minutes from 1556 already refer to him as a patron saint. However, in a sermon given in 1680, cathedral canon Diego de Victoria Salazár stated that Joseph had been first elected by the *cabildo* in 1555. See *Cartilla vieja de la Nobilísima ciudad de Puebla deducida de los papeles auténticos y libros antiguos, 1781* (Puebla: Secretaría de Cultura, 2001), 267 and Diego de Victoria Salazár, *Sermón que predicó en la Catedral de Puebla al nuevo patrocinio del Señor San José* (Puebla: n.p., 1680), B1v.

[12] López de Villaseñor, *Cartilla vieja de la Nobilísima ciudad*, 267–269.

[13] Mariano Fernández de Echeverría y Veytia, *Historia de la fundación de la ciudad de la Puebla de los Ángeles en la Nueva España, su descripción y presente estado* (Puebla: Ediciones Altiplano, 1962), 2:208–209; Franziska Neff, "Patronos de la ciudad de Puebla: noticias de Señor San José, su escultura principal, fiesta, y cofradía," *Encrucijada* 3 (forthcoming).

[14] Mariano Encisco y Texada, *Ordenanzas que debe guardar la Muy Noble y Leal ciudad de la Puebla de los Ángeles* (Puebla: Oficina de Don Pedro de la Rosa, 1787), 64–65; Libro que contiene los patronatos, 1769, AHMP, LV 20, 39r–39v.

[15] Juan Villa Sánchez and Francisco Javier de la Peña, *Puebla sagrada y profana: informe dado a su muy ilustre ayuntamiento el año de 1746 (Facsímile)* (1835; Puebla: Benemérita Universidad Autónoma de Puebla, 1997), 34.

[16] See the transcriptions from the *cabildo* meeting in Libro que contiene los patronatos, 1769, AHMP, LV 20, 31v–32v.

[17] See José Gómez de la Parra, *Fundación y primer siglo del muy religioso convento de Sr. S. Joseph de Religiosas Carmelitas Descalzas de la ciudad de la Puebla de los Ángeles, en la Nueva España, el primero que se fundó en la América Septentrional, en 27. de diciembre de 1604* (Puebla: Viuda de Miguel de Ortega, 1731), especially 1–55.

[18] See Franziska Neff, "El ritual de la palabra hablada. Esbozos de la sonoridad en las fiestas josefinas de la Angelópolis virreinal," in *Rituales sonoros en una ciudad episcopal* (Puebla: Benemérita Universidad Autónoma de Puebla, forthcoming).

[19] Patronatos jurados en esta N.C. de Puebla, 1773, AHMP, LV 9, 358r–359r.

[20] Libro que contiene los patronatos, 1769, AHMP, LV 20, 37v–38r.

[21] Fernández de Echeverría y Veytia, *Historia de la fundación de la ciudad de la Puebla*, 2:209. Also see the inaugural sermon commemorating the cabildo's decision to switch it to the last day of the *patrocinio*: Nicolás Carrasco Moscoso, *Sermón del patrocinio que contra los rayos y tempestades goza dichosa la ciudad de la Puebla en el esclarecido Patriarca San Joseph* (Puebla: Imprenta de Diego Fernández de León, 1688).

[22] Libro que contiene los patronatos, 1769, AHMP, LV 20, 126v–128r; Fernández de Echeverría y Veytia, *Historia de la fundación de la ciudad de la Puebla*, 2:209.

[23] Fernández de Echeverría y Veytia, *Historia de la fundación de la ciudad de la Puebla*, 2:209.

[24] *Actas*, 19 October 1696, Archivo Histórico Municipal de Puebla, microfilm of the *Actas* available in Biblioteca Nacional de Antropología e Historia (hereafter AHMP-BNAH, Actas de Cabildo (hereafter AC) 34, 115v–116r.

[25] Libro que contiene los patronatos, 1769, AHMP, LV 20, 39r–39v.

[26] Cuentas de propios, 1741, AHMP, Libros de Cuentas (hereafter LC), 253r–261r.

[27] Eduardo Merlo Juárez, Miguel Pavón Rivero, and José Antonio Quintana Fernández, *La basílica catedral de la Puebla de los Ángeles* (Puebla: Litografía Alai), 136–137, 140.

[28] For more on the disruptions within the *cabildo* and the introduction of honorary *regidores*, see Gustavo Rafael Alfaro Ramírez, "Administración y poder oligárquica en la Puebla Borbónica, 1690–1786" (PhD diss., Universidad Nacional Autónoma de México, 2006) and Frances L. Ramos, *Identity, Ritual, and Power in Colonial Puebla* (Tucson: University of Arizona Press, 2012), xxiii–xxiv.

[29] Fernández de Echeverría y Veytia, *Historia de la fundación*, 2:253–256.

[30] Paula Renata Mues Orts, "El pintor novohispano José de Ibarra: imágenes retóricas y discursos pintados (PhD diss., Universidad Nacional Autónoma de México, 2009), 161–162.

[31] Carlos Contreras Cruz and Claudia Patricia Pardo Hernández, "La cuenta de feligreses en Puebla de los Ángeles en 1777: población y estructura racial," in *El Obispado de Puebla: Españoles, indios, mestizos y castas en tiempo del virrey Bucareli, 1777*, ed. Carlos Contreras Cruz and Claudia Patricia Pardo Hernández (Puebla: Benemérita Universidad Autónoma de Puebla, 2007), 57–59.

[32] Alejandro Cañeque, "De sillas y almohadones o de la naturaleza ritual del poder en la Nueva España de los siglos XVI y XVII," *Revista de Indias* 64, no. 232 (2004): 609–634.

[33] *Recopilación de leyes de los reinos de las Indias* (Madrid: Julian de Paredes, 1681); Book 3, Title 15, Law 73.

[34] For references to how the *cabildo* "authorized" events, see for example *Actas*, 1 August 1742, AHMP-BNAH, AC 44, f. 445r; *Actas*, 17 June 1752, AHMP-BNAH, AC 47, 509r.

[35] *Recopilación de leyes de los reinos de las Indias*; Book 3, Title 15, Law 9; *Actas de Cabildo Eclesiástico*, 9 May 1769, Archivo de la Catedral de Puebla, Actas de Cabildo Eclesiástico, 37, 90v–103v.

[36] Book 3, Title 15, Law 21 of the *Recopilación de leyes de los reinos de las Indias* states that in Mexico City and Lima, if the *cabildo* attends a ceremony in which the viceroy and audiencia judges are not present, they should receive the peace as well. In Puebla and other New World cities, local leaders commonly received the peace. In Guatemala, for example, the *cabildo* established obligatory feast days with the condition

that officiating priests honor councilmen with a sprinkling of holy water and the ceremony of peace. Constantino Bayle, *Los cabildos seculares en la América española* (Madrid: Sapientia, 1952), 584–585.

[37] Libro que contiene los patronatos, 1769, AHMP, LV 20, 90r. In 1767, the Jesuit Order, shortly before its expulsion, held a celebratory mass to inaugurate its new church. The officiating priest failed to acknowledge the *cabildo*'s presence at the beginning of his sermon. Some *regidores* immediately complained, and the following day the priest apologized, claiming ignorance of proper protocol. He vowed to make sure that this never happened again and offered to make a public apology for his previous omission. See José del Castillo to the *cabildo*, Puebla, March 2, 1767, AHMP, Reales Cédulas 10, 497r.

[38] For a reference to this tradition, see *Actas*, January 2, 1726, AHMP-BNAH, AC 40, 474v.

[39] Curiosidades pertenecientes a la noticia de oficio de regidor, AHMP, Gobierno 1, 3r.

[40] Cuentas de propios, 1691, AHMP, LC 1, 12v; Cuentas de propios, 1704, AHMP, LC 1, 32v; Cuentas de propios, 1708, AHMP, LC 1, 60r.

[41] See El señor Inquisidor fiscal de este Santo Oficio contra D. Juan de Jáuregui y Barcena, canónigo doctoral de la Santa Iglesia de la Puebla y provisor, 1699, Archivo General de la Nación (hereafter AGN), Inquisición 711, Expediente 2, 108r–200r.

[42] Para que los puestos donde expende pulque en la ciudad de Puebla no se muden ni pasen a los barrios donde celebren fiestas, 1725, AGN, Inquisición 49, Expediente 213, 213v–215v. In fact, a directory for the ceremonies of the cathedral chapter refers specifically to the "fair" that accompanied the feast day.

[43] See Neff, "El ritual de la palabra hablada."

[44] Neff, "Patronos de la ciudad de Puebla."

[45] *Actas*, September 16, 1716, AHMP, AC 38, 328r; *Actas*, October 27, 1717, AHMP, AC 39, 66v.

[46] Memoria de los gastos para la celebridad del último día del novenario del Gloriosísimo Patriarca Señor San Joseph, 1724, AHMP, LC 2, 165r–165v.

[47] Gastos de la cera que se quemó para San Joseph, 1740, AHMP, LC 5, 97r.

[48] Para los fuegos del día de San Miguel y último día del novenario de San Joseph, 1740, AHMP LC 5, 106r–106v.

[49] Cuentas de propios, 1737, AHMP, LC 3, 376r–381v; Cuentas de propios, 1741, AHMP, LC 5, 253r–261r.

[50] Diego de Victoria Salazár, *Sermón que predicó en la Catedral de Puebla al nuevo patrocinio del Señor San José* (Mexico City: Juan de Ribera, 1680), 1v.

[51] Ibid., 3v–4v.

[52] Ibid., 5r–6r.

[53] Ibid., 6r–7v.

[54] Juan de Robles, *Sermón del gloriosísimo Patriarca, padre existimado [sic] del hijo unigénito de Dios. Esposo dignísimo de la madre del Eterno Verbo humanado. Nuestro Señor San Joseph* (Puebla: Viuda de Juan de Ribera, 1687).

[55] Genesis 28: 20–21.

[56] Nicolás Carrasco Moscoso, *Sermón del patrocinio que contra los rayos y tempestades goza dichosa la ciudad de la Puebla en el esclarecido Patriarca San Joseph* (Puebla: Imprenta de Diego Fernández de León, 1688), 1–3, 5, 9, and 13–14.

[57] Fernández de Echeverría y Veytia, *Historia de la fundación*, 2:209.

[58] Fernández de Echeverría y Veytia, *Historia de la fundación*, 1:xvii.

[59] Díaz y Tirado, *Sermón panegírico que en la plausible y festiva imperial coronación del Santísimo Patriarca Señor San Joseph*.

[60] Ibid.

[61] This is all described in the unpaginated preamble to Joseph Atanasio Díaz y Tirado, *Sermón panegírico—moral, que el veinte y ocho de octubre del año de mil setecientos noventa y cuarto, y último día del solemne novenario de desagravios, que con el motive de las actuales guerras contra los Franceses dedicaron los parroquianos de Sr. S. Joseph a su santísimo protector y patriarca* (Puebla: Oficina Palafoxiana, 1795).

[62] Ibid., 15.

[63] Ibid., 17.

[64] Ibid., 22.

[65] *Día diez y nueve, consagrado en honra, culto y reverencia del gloriosísimo Patriarca Sr. San Joseph, y devoción para celebrar su día, y en él implorar su admirable protección* (Puebla: Oficina de Don Pedro de la Rosa, 1784), not paginated.

[66] See *Día diez y nueve, consagrado en honra, culto y reverencia del gloriosísimo Patriarca and Novena en obsequio del Santísimo Patriarca Sr. S. Joseph. Putativo padre de Jesucristo, y esposo de María Santísima* (Puebla: Oficina de Don Pedro de la Rosa, 1795).

[67] See José Francisco Valdés, *Novena sagrada para implorar el patrocinio del Santísimo Patriarca Sr. S. Joseph, dispuesta por el R. P. Fr. Joseph Francisco Valdés, religioso de la Provincia de San Diego*, Reprinted at the expense of the Mayordomo de la Cofradía del Santísimo Patriarca, del Gremio de Carpinteros (1789; Puebla de los Angeles: Oficina de Don Pedro de la Rosa, 1806), not paginated.

La corte vestida de gala

The Royal Academy of San Carlos and the Spectacle of Colonial Life

Kelly Donahue-Wallace

In 1796, the sculpted equestrian portrait of Charles IV (fig. 1), better known by its tongue-in-cheek title, *El Caballito*, was installed in Mexico City.[1] The sculpture and its enclosure were commissioned by Viceroy Miguel de la Grúa Talamanca, the Marquis of Branciforte, and executed by Antonio González Velázquez and Manuel Tolsá of the Royal Academy of Three Noble Arts of San Carlos between 1794 and 1803. Although the sculpture was not yet finished, the viceroy held a festival to celebrate its installation on December 9, 1796, with a gilded wood surrogate in place of Tolsá's massive bronze sculpture (fig. 2) that would eventually, if briefly, stand in the middle of Mexico City's Zócalo.

A thorough account of the festivities appeared in the *Gazeta de México* newspaper. At 8:15 a.m. on December 9—the birthday of Spanish Queen María Luisa—a salvo of fifteen cannons sounded. The viceroy, his wife, and members of the court and the viceregal bureaucracy stepped onto the festooned balconies of the viceregal palace. They threw to the throngs below 3,000 silver medals engraved by academy founder Jerónimo Antonio Gil (fig. 3). Bells rang, music played, and the crowd spontaneously shouted patriotic declarations.[2] The viceroy and his court then processed to the cathedral for a mass of thanksgiving. Back at the palace, the viceroy sat beneath a canopy in the newly renovated *Salón del Besamanos* to

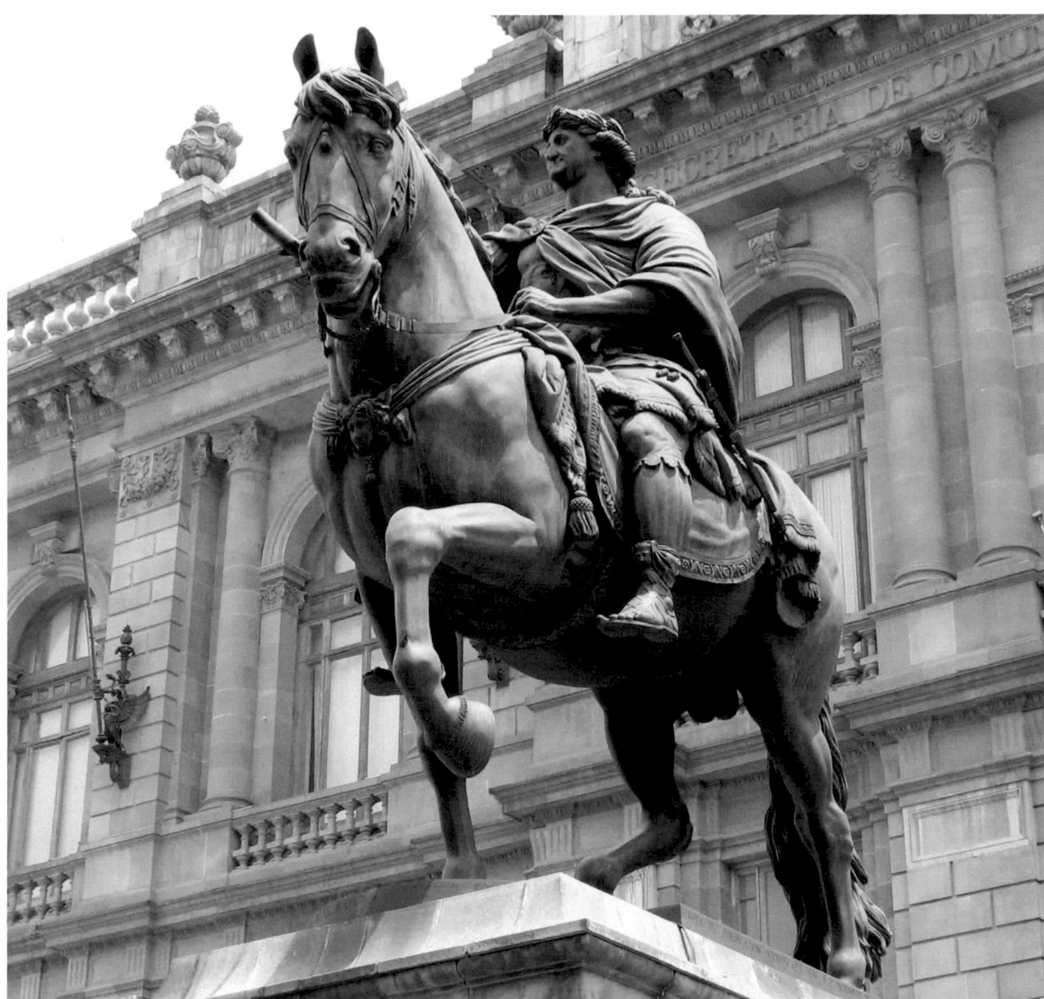

Fig. 1. Manuel Tolsá, *Equestrian Portrait of Charles IV*. Mexico, 1803. Bronze, 16 x 16½ ft. Photo: author

receive the ceremonial hand kissing from a hieratic procession of members of the civic and religious bureaucracy, local nobility, and visiting dignitaries. For three days, the elite—Mexico City's *nobles y ricos*—engaged in *paseos,* riding on finely outfitted horses and in elegant carriages through city streets. Onlookers enjoyed the spectacle of their finery as well as the nightly fireworks displays and the view of the city illuminated by candles, including 1,800 torches on one section of the palace facade alone. After a performance of the one-act play *The American Loyalty* at the Coliseo theater, the evening ended with a ball held at the viceregal palace.

This event, merging a celebration of the king, local fealty, and artistic achievement, would seem to fit the 1780 definition of a festival as established by the Royal Spanish Academy as a "public celebration done with popular participation so that the people achieve some respite from the fatigues of daily life."[3] The *Caballito* installation was also, thanks to the coincidence of the queen's birthday and the sculpture's subject, a *fiesta real,* specifically defined as "a celebration done to honor a royal person or in his presence."[4] The description similarly fits our modern understanding of a festival as a scheduled, planned, and scripted event, outside the normal routine of daily life, in which members of the community participate in prescribed and accepted roles that have the effect of reinforcing social and political hierarchies.[5]

The dedication of the interim sculpture was, however, not the only festival in which the Royal Academy of Three Noble Arts of San Carlos participated after its opening in the early 1780s. This first royal academy of any type in the Americas performed in myriad public celebrations; in most cases, the faculty and members of the governing councils played their scripted roles as members of the cadre of bureaucrats and dignitaries—broadly known as the court—participating in Mexico City's secular and sacred events.[6] On many occasions, academicians designed the ephemeral structures and figures for festivals, produced commemorative medals, and engraved the illustrations

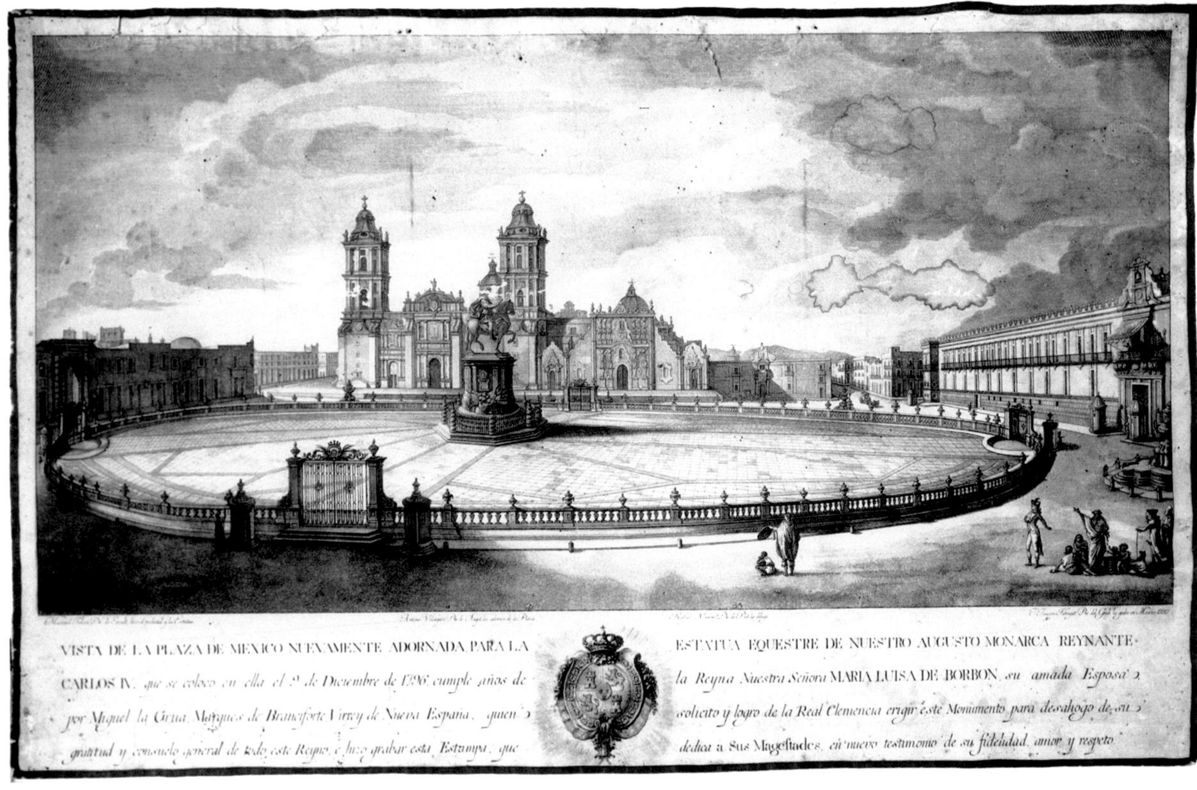

Fig. 2. José Joaquín Fabregat, *View of the Main Square of Mexico City.* Mexico, 1797. Engraving, 18 x 27 in. Nettie Lee Benson Latin American Collection, University of Texas, Austin, TX.

of the companion books, giving visual form and permanence to Mexican late colonial spectacle.[7]

This essay, however, focuses more narrowly on festivals specifically organized by or for the academy, arguing that these represented a campaign to insert this new institution into Mexican society. That is, the academy administration, specifically Jerónimo Antonio Gil, the founding director general, and the members of the institution's governing councils, employed a strategy specifically designed to introduce the academy and its purpose via Mexico City's festival life. Underpinning this argument is the understanding that, as in Europe, Mexican festivals operated as what has been called the "materialization of ideology."[8] That is, in this essay, I add myself to those scholars such as Linda Curcio-Nagy, Stephanie Merrim, William Beezley, and others who view festivals as illustrating social hierarchies and giving the state and the dominant classes "an opportunity to reiterate—for their own education and that of their subordinates—the moral values on which their authority rests."[9] This work also represents part of my larger study of Gil and his crusade to embody and promote the principles of the Spanish Enlightenment for those on American shores. Part of this campaign of insertion has already been revealed: the exploitation of the newspaper (fig. 4) to promote the academy's efforts, a point to which we will return later.[10] The use of this uniquely modern tool points to the broader—and seemingly contradictory—role of the academic festivals as embodying values of the Spanish Enlightenment, despite our understanding that the *ilustrados* (Enlightenment intellectuals) of the later eighteenth century placed little stock in the showy displays more commonly associated with the Baroque. On the contrary, I argue that the academy drew upon both Baroque spectacle and Enlightenment ideologies to guarantee the acceptance of this new, unfamiliar royal institution, whose significance for the Mexican nation went far beyond transforming its artistic taste.

Since the installation of the monumental royal portrait was a singular event in the history of the Mexican academy, let us consider the more common public festival at the Royal Academy of San Carlos: the *premio* event or academic award ceremony. These celebrations, which began even before the academy received royal approval in 1783, recognized the achievement of the institution's disciples. Academy statutes declared that prizes were to be awarded every three years, but the schedule was more flexible in reality. A public proclamation, published in the bi-weekly *Gazeta*

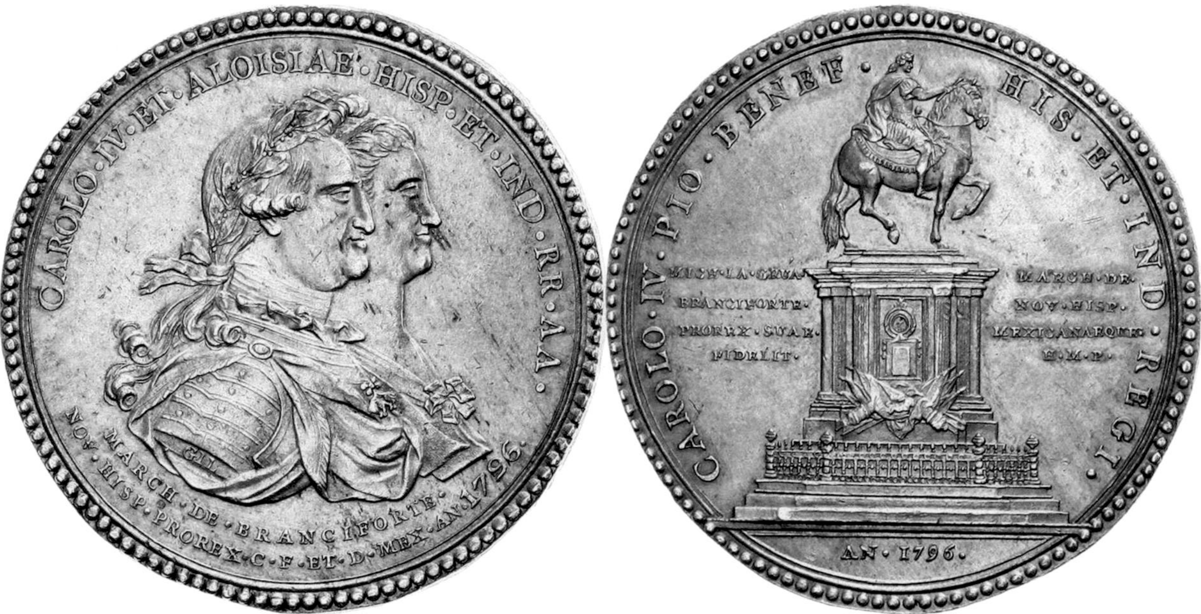

Fig. 3. Jerónimo Antonio Gil, *Medal Commemorating the Equestrian Portrait of Charles IV*. Mexico, 1796. Silver, $1^1/_3$ in. dia. Private collection.

de México, announced the upcoming competition, its date, and the thematic focus for each artistic medium. Entries were judged by the *Junta Pública*, a committee composed of academy faculty and distinguished persons from the community, and the winners were awarded medals of varying size and value.

In the June 30, 1784 issue of the *Gazeta de México*, an announcement declared that the Royal Academy of San Carlos designated November 4 of that year, "the day on which is celebrated our August Monarch's [saint's] day," for the distribution of academic prizes. Submissions would be honored "according to the merit of their respective competitors."[11] Unfortunately, Viceroy Matías de Gálvez (fig. 5) died on the evening of November 3, 1784, and the *premio* event was postponed for one year. By then, however, the ceremony had grown to include the academy's official inauguration and distribution of its newly approved statutes. The newspaper description of this long-awaited celebration reads,

> On the 4th day [of November], on which the Court, *vestida de Gala* (in ceremonial dress), celebrated the Saint's day of the [King] … and the most Serene Prince [of Asturias], the Most Excellent Viceroy [Bernardo de Gálvez, fig. 6], with the Royal *Audiencia* and Tribunals attended in the Metropolitan Cathedral the Mass of Thanksgiving, and once completed, his excellency returned to the Palace, and was visited according to custom in the *Salón del Besamanos* which, for being assigned for the celebration of the public opening of the Royal Academy of the Three Noble Arts of San Carlos of New Spain, showed on its walls all of the pieces honored by accord of its *Junta*.[12]

Attendees at the award ceremony listened to music and heard a lecture. After a summary of the academy's minutes, another speech, and still more music, the viceroy distributed the prizes, although Gil was still negotiating with the Crown on the exact appearance of the winners' medals, which were consequently not yet ready. In the meantime, five students worked live, producing works of painting, sculpture, architecture, and engraving, and delighting the witnesses with their performance of genius and industry. The event also included artillery salvos, a spectacularly outfitted *paseo* of well-dressed riders and carriages through the city streets, and abundant food. The evening ended with a trip to the Coliseo for a newly written production of the tragedy *Honorable Delinquent*.

The next *premio* event to be recorded in the *Gazeta de México* fell on August 25, 1787. As before,

> the Court *vestida de gala* commemorated the [saint's day] of our Most Serene Princess of Asturias, celebrating the Mass of Thanksgiving at the Metropolitan Cathedral, [attended by] the most Excellent Viceroy [the newly arrived Manuel Antonio Flores], Royal *Audiencia*, and Tribunals, who then celebrated with the corresponding Music and the rest, the distribution of Prizes awarded to the Students of the Royal Academy of the Three Noble Arts of San Carlos of this New Spain by this Illustrious body in the *Salón del Besamanos* of His Majesty in the Royal Palace.[13]

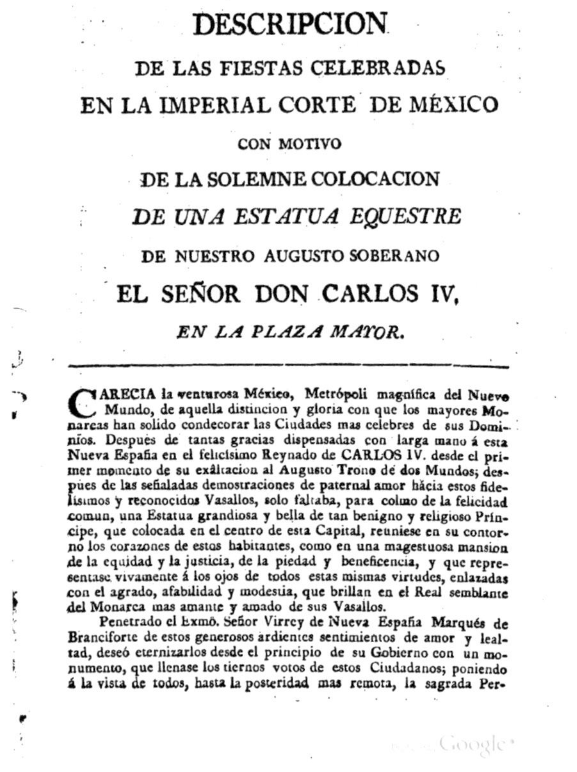

DESCRIPCION

DE LAS FIESTAS CELEBRADAS

EN LA IMPERIAL CORTE DE MÉXICO

CON MOTIVO

DE LA SOLEMNE COLOCACION

DE UNA ESTATUA EQUESTRE

DE NUESTRO AUGUSTO SOBERANO

EL SEÑOR DON CARLOS IV,

EN LA PLAZA MAYOR.

CARECIA la venturosa México, Metrópoli magnífica del Nuevo Mundo, de aquella distincion y gloria con que los mayores Monarcas han solido condecorar las Ciudades mas celebres de sus Dominíos. Despues de tantas gracias dispensadas con larga mano á esta Nueva España en el felicísimo Reynado de CARLOS IV. desde el primer momento de su exâltacion al Augusto Trono de dos Mundos; despues de las señaladas demostraciones de paternal amor hácia estos fidelísimos y reconocidos Vasallos, solo faltaba, para colmo de la felicidad comun, una Estatua grandiosa y bella de tan benigno y religioso Príncipe, que colocada en el centro de esta Capital, reuniese en su contorno los corazones de estos habitantes, como en una magestuosa mansion de la equidad y la justicia, de la piedad y beneficencia, y que representase vivamente á los ojos de todos estas mismas virtudes, enlazadas con el agrado, afabilidad y modestia, que brillan en el Real semblante del Monarca mas amante y amado de sus Vasallos.

Penetrado el Exmô. Señor Virrey de Nueva España Marqués de Branciforte de estos generosos ardientes sentimientos de amor y lealtad, deseó eternizarlos desde el principio de su Gobierno con un monumento, que llenase los tiernos votos de estos Ciudadanos; poniendo á la vista de todos, hasta la posteridad mas remota, la sagrada Per-

Fig. 4. Page from the *Gazeta de México*. Mexico, 1796. Ink on paper, 8¼ in. Photo collection of the author.

The prizes were again awarded by the viceroy, who encouraged the winners in their artistic progress. The evening ended with artillery salvos and a performance at the Coliseo, reached through brightly illuminated streets that were enjoyed by all of the city's residents.

The third example came just six months later, on January 20, 1788, when, once again, the court outfitted itself *de gala* to celebrate the king's birthday. A mass was followed by procession to the viceregal palace, the reception in the *Salón del Besamanos*, prize distribution and encouraging words from the viceroy, artillery salvos, and a collective trip to the Coliseo through the illuminated streets that were appreciated by all Mexicans.

Let us at this point pause to compare the Mexican award ceremonies to those held at the Royal Academy of San Fernando, effectively its parent institution in Madrid, and the model for so much of San Carlos's structure and administration.[14] Many of the elements of the Madrid prize distribution events were the same as in Mexico City, but several distinctions deserve note. Most significantly, Madrid's *premio* events had no mass, no procession, no *besamanos*, no *paseo*, no illumination of the square and city streets, and no trip to the Coliseo; its dates apparently held no political significance. The Madrid prize distributions were instead self-contained ceremonies, with poetry and music for attendees, and edifying lectures; an exhibition of the submitted work remained open for the following fortnight.[15] And although the ceremony was open to the public, and Madrid's citizens certainly attended the exhibitions in great numbers, Madrid award ceremonies lacked the festival atmosphere and the exploitation of the city, its spaces, its monuments, and its occupants as witnesses. In short, the Madrid award ceremonies may have been festive, but they were not festivals.

So why were the Mexican *premio* events, like the *Caballito* installation, conceived of as festivals? How are we to reconcile Madrid's sobriety with Mexico City's popular participation, masses, lighting displays, and processions through the festival location *par excellence*: the Zócalo?[16] Why did the American academy seek the ornamentation of people and spaces, as the court—understood as both a location and a population—became *vestida de gala*, with both elite bodies and the spaces they occupied decorated in sumptuous clothes, official uniforms, cloth swags and banners that hung from windows and balconies, and torches and candelabras that blazed in the night?

And—to pose my second central question for this essay—what explains what I consider to be the most significant aspect of the San Carlos *premio* events and the installation festival: the choice of queen's birthday, queen's saint's day, king's birthday, and king's saint's day? The pattern linking academy ceremony to the royal birthday or saint's day holds up for more than a decade beginning with the academy foundation and reaching its spectacular apogee with the *Caballito* 1796 installation (and reinstallation in 1803 when the sculpture was finally completed). In each case, the academy event was grafted onto the celebration of the royal day. In fact, the celebration of the award ceremony on a royal birthday was so important that in 1793, when the viceroy was indisposed and

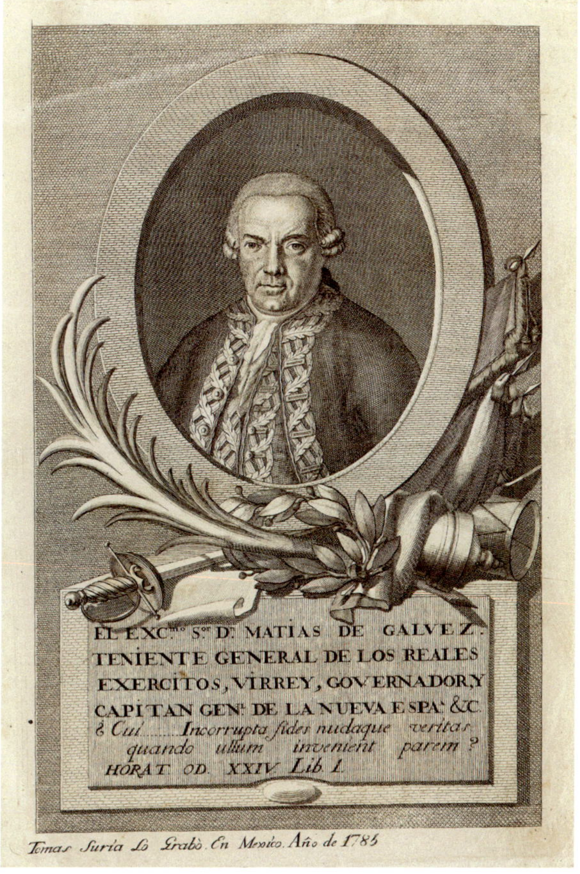

Fig. 5. Tomas Suría, *El Excmo. Sor. Dn. Matías de Gálvez.* Mexico, 1785. Engraving, 9½ x 6½ in. Denver Art Museum; Gift of the Frederick and Jan Mayer Collection, 2013.344.

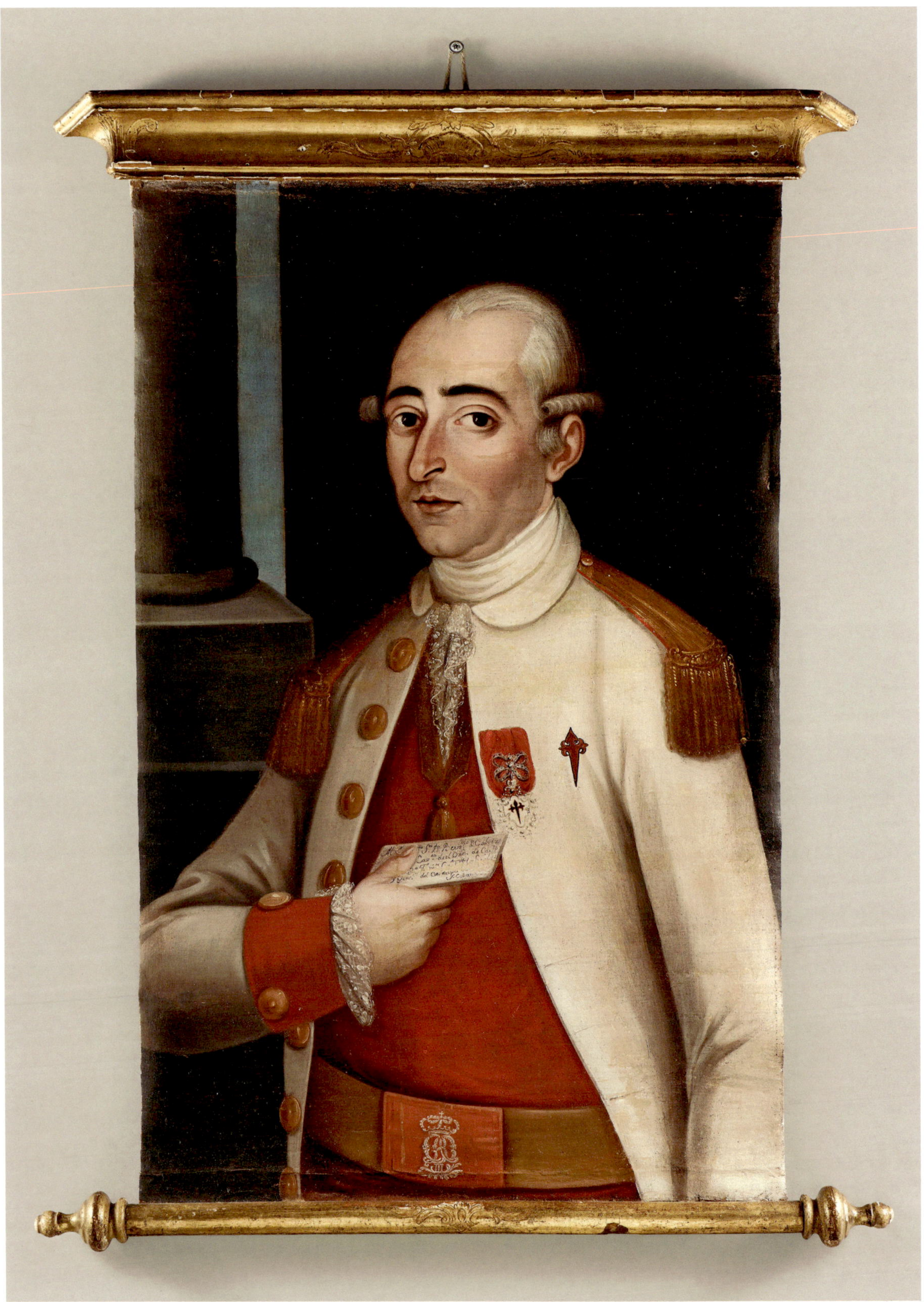

Fig. 6. *Portrait of Bernardo de Gálvez*. Mexico, 18th century. Oil on canvas with wood, 28¾ x 18½ in. Denver Art Museum; Gift of the Frederick and Jan Mayer Collection, 2013.327.

there were no rooms available in either the viceregal palace or the academy for the award ceremony, the Count of Revillagigedo issued a last-minute viceregal order that the prizes be nevertheless awarded on December 9, the queen's birthday, even if the ceremony was smaller and more private than normal, with just academy staff, students, and governing councilors in attendance.[17]

Why, of all of the significant days in the religious and political calendar, were the award ceremonies, the academy inauguration, and the *Caballito* installation attached to the birthdays and saints' days of the royal family? The Spanish academy of San Fernando did not schedule its award ceremonies on these days, nor was the date mandated in the San Carlos statutes. Hence, I am left to conclude that the shape of the event and its scheduling constituted local decisions, as the administrators and board of noble councilors of the Royal Academy of San Carlos in Mexico City, including the viceroy, who served as the institution's viceprotector, decided how and when to schedule their most significant and public events. Of course, the academy was named for King Charles III, its royal patron, so obsequious homage affected the choice.[18] But I believe there was more to it—and not just because the queen was not its patron and yet the events were held on her day as well; both the festival atmosphere and the connection to the birthday/saint's day were deployed as specific responses to the Mexican context.

To make this argument, let me return to the well-known history of the Academy of San Carlos.[19] Engraver Jerónimo Antonio Gil (fig. 7), academic of merit at the Royal Academy of Fine Arts of San Fernando, traveled at royal behest to Mexico City in 1778 to assume the position of Principal Engraver of the Royal Mint. His charge included establishing a drawing school not just to improve the quality of Mexican coin production, but to generally benefit Mexican industry and trades. Considering that roughly one-quarter of Mexico City's residents were engaged in artisanal activity at this time[20]—what we would call today manufacturing—and these people would benefit from this new form of instruction, Gil's mission to reform the practices and improve the training of this immense population takes on added weight.

The drawing school's success spurred Gil and mint administrator Fernando Mangino to promote the creation of a royal art academy in 1781, proposing this first to Viceroy Martín de Mayorga and then to King Charles III. At this point, the drawing classes became the so-called provisional school, with instruction provided by Gil and local Mexican artists; still, the focus was on more than just future fine artists, and disciples came from the ranks of virtually all trades, including those needing instruction in mathematics. As a 1783 report to Viceroy Matías de Gálvez would explain, "The skill and habit of drawing, which is the principal foundation of [these noble arts], influence at the same time nearly all arts that serve not just for greater comfort, but also the necessities of civic life to which we are accustomed."[21] Royal approval for the new academy came in 1783, thanks in no small part to compelling economic arguments like this and to the significant funding that had been secured from local institutions, communities, and individuals. Spanish academicians began arriving in 1786, while Gil, who served as the academy's director general and director of medal and coin engraving, continued in his post at the Royal Mint until his death in 1798.

The reasons for establishing an art academy in Mexico City are similarly well known. Although much has been said about the Bourbon desire to centralize power and to alter divergent colonial tastes, so much so that the Mexican academy has been called a *de facto* ministry of taste in an outdated narrative of the imposition of Neoclassicism over Baroque forms,[22] I would like to focus our attention away from fine arts to consider San Carlos's role in the immense Spanish eighteenth-century educational reform movement. The Bourbon monarchs and the *ilustrados* who populated their courts founded schools and academies with the principal goal of improving Spanish industry and promoting national progress.[23] By doing so, they sought to take the prerogative of education out of the hands of guilds and clergymen, whose methods were thought to have impeded Spanish progress via protectionist practices, conservative teaching methods and philosophies, jealousy, selfishness, and superstition.[24] Spanish youngsters were now to be educated in reading, mathematics, and trades in the light of day, away from the monasteries and closed private

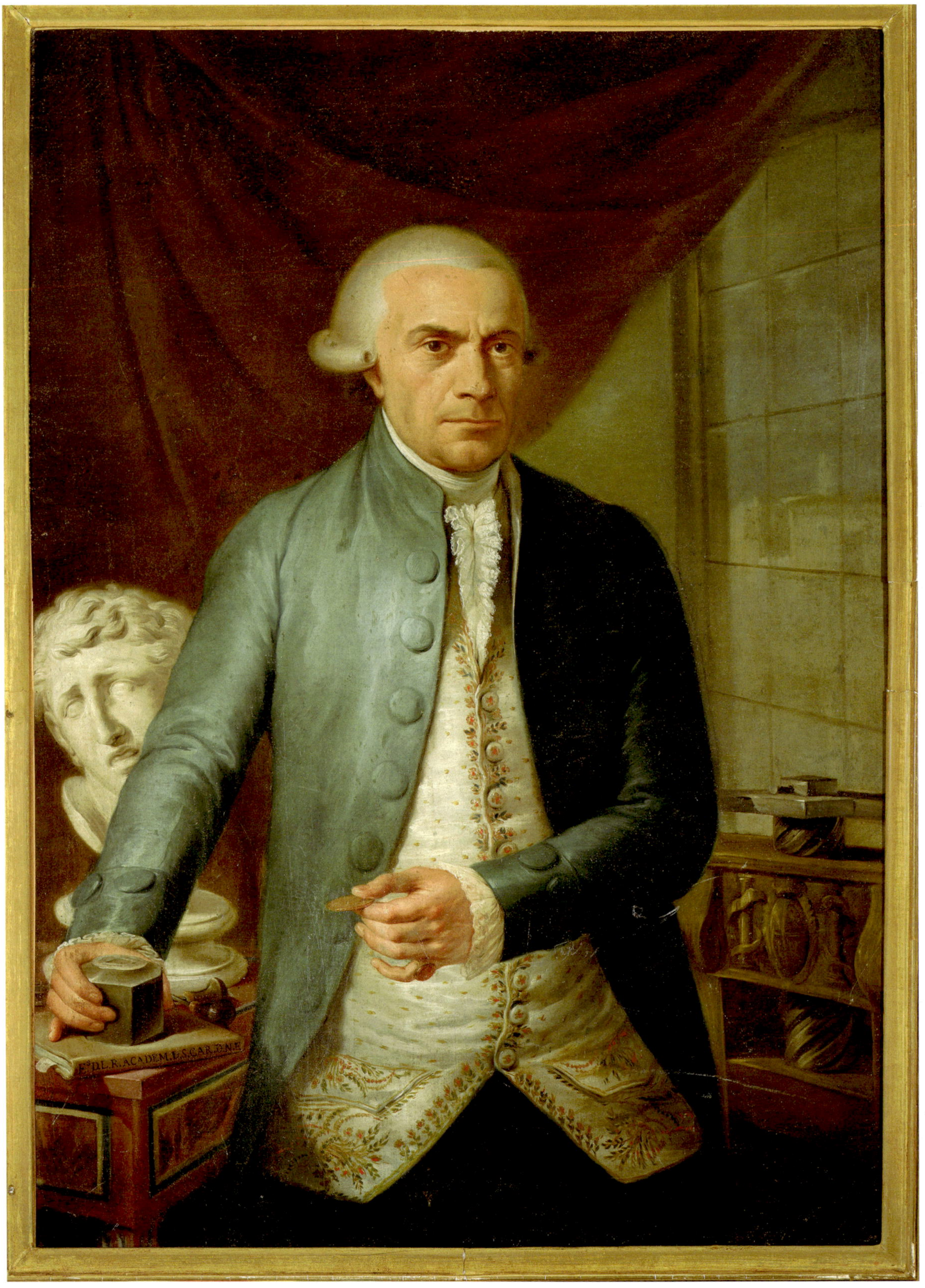

Fig. 7. Rafael Ximeno y Planes, *Portrait of Jerónimo Antonio Gil*. Mexico, 1795. Oil on canvas, $45^{2}/_{3}$ x $31^{7}/_{8}$ in. Museo Nacional de Arte, Mexico City, Mexico.

studios of guild masters. In return, Spain and New Spain would become manufacturing centers rather than merely sources of raw materials or consumers of imported fineries.

Prizes for academic progress were essential to this educational reform. In his influential text on improving Spanish industry, Pedro Rodríguez de Campomanes, the most powerful *ilustrado* in midcentury Spain—and, coincidentally, a friend and mentor of Jerónimo Antonio Gil—eloquently outlined their purpose: "The annual prize of a medal ... to one or two [disciples], applied with all justice to those who best excel, will excite the honorable emulation by all."[25] Prizes were consequently established at every type of institution, from the newly secularized and professionalized primary schools to the royal academies of law, language, history, and art. Jerónimo Antonio Gil, in fact, created many of these medals, as he would the Mexican academy's prizes once on American shores.

Corollary to this larger educational reform movement was the narrower, but no less important, goal to spur the Spanish nobility into putting their time, money, and energy into economic activity and industry. The Bourbon monarchs and their enlightened advisors viewed the Spanish *nobleza* as woefully undercontributing to the national good.[26] Hence the education reforms included the reform of elite behavior, as Campomanes and other *ilustrados* made their peers responsible to read, study, and publish about agriculture, technology, trades, and so on, and to join organizations such as the academies or economic societies wherein they had the opportunity to learn, debate, and mentor the next generation, and therefore to contribute to Spain's economic success. And to reward those nonnoble academicians who worked for the good of the state, all of Spain's newly established academies—Mexico's Academy of San Carlos included—conceded noble status to members who did not already possess titles, with the goal of swelling the noble ranks with productive intellectuals actively dedicated to national economic progress.[27]

Hence, when the Royal Academy of the Three Noble Arts of San Carlos opened in Mexico City, it represented much more than the improvement of art instruction, an attack on the guilds, a desire for a centralized bureaucracy, or the introduction of Neoclassical style to rid the viceroyalty of its Baroque tastes.[28] It represented the Bourbon aspiration for the transformation of manufacturing and of elite society, and embodied the imposition of new responsibilities on the Mexican nobility. If it is still correct to call the academy a ministry of taste, the notion of taste must be defined in the broad eighteenth-century sense—that is, of the elite man of taste, the courtier, the intellectual, the artist, the thinker who exercised his good judgment not just in matters of art, but in all aspects of life, public and private, particularly those benefitting the nation. San Carlos was about the transformation of members of the upper class into such men, and the creation of a larger population filled with active men of taste working for the good of the nation.

As it sought to transform this elite population, however, the Academy of San Carlos simultaneously depended upon it in a host of ways, not least financially. The *hombres nobles y ricos* of Mexico and regional cities—and the tribunals, councils, and bureaucracies to which they belonged—represented a substantial portion of the academy's financial resources. By the time the king committed 13,000 *pesos* of annual support, New Spain's *nobles y ricos* had already donated an equal amount, and the tribunals and city governments led by elite bureaucrats had committed more than 9,000 *pesos* more.[29] San Carlos likewise needed the cadre of local nobles and *ilustrados* to staff its councils, not to mention their support, either individually or collectively, as patrons for paintings, sculptures, and architectural monuments, and in the academy's effort to wrest training of young craftsmen away from the guilds. The academicians, the Crown, and the Bourbon reforms in general simply would not succeed without the full and active support of New Spain's elite and, more broadly, the 18 percent of New Spain's population who were identified as creoles and peninsular Spaniards.[30] And all of this was wrapped into San Carlos's foundation.

But how to reach this population? Let us recall that San Carlos, as a royal academy, was a very new and unfamiliar type of institution, both for its educational mission and for its central and prescribed role in transforming Mexican society and inserting New Spain into the international community of modern, progressive, and productive nations. Certainly no school or organization locally—with the possible exception of the newly created Royal Basque Society of Friends of the Nation—had previously had such lofty, totalizing goals and such a broad and ambitious reach.[31] And although Mexicans had ample familiarity with new concessions of nobility—sixty new noble titles were created in Mexico in the eighteenth century alone—the social promotion of academy faculty and students thanks to hard work and exemplary achievement, and not military service or personal wealth combined with charitable behavior, was a new concept.[32] In short, as the academy insinuated itself into the fabric of colonial life and its social hierarchies, the idea of the academy needed to be made familiar and normal if San Carlos were achieve its lofty goals.

And here we arrive at why Mexican academic award ceremonies developed distinctly from their Spanish counterparts. Comparing the Mexican situation to the Madrid *premio* events will help us to understand, beginning with the selection of royal birthdays and saints' days. The academy minutes read in Madrid at the San Fernando ceremonies are almost exclusively dedicated to the points of contact between the monarch and the institution—from the academicians' attendance at royal ceremonies, and their work completed on behalf of the state, to many, many examples of royal largess toward the school.[33] Seen in sum, the repeated examples of mutual assistance and affection demonstrated the intimacy of king and Spanish academy, and the centrality of the institution to the monarch's plans for the nation. San Fernando was, in essence, part of the body politic, a natural appendage working together with the head for the national good.[34]

The Academy of San Carlos in Mexico, using this metaphor, was therefore a severed limb.[35] Its relationship to the royal body was less clear, principally because it did not have the luxury of close physical proximity to the monarch and lacked the benefit of other local academies to model the intimate symbiosis of king and institution. For Mexican *ricos y nobles*, and, of course, the broader colonial society, San Carlos's relationship to the monarch was consequently undefined. It was a school, an institution of learning, trade preparation, and economic development, as the locals certainly understood. But less obvious to Mexican viewers was the intimate relationship between the monarch and his academies—a factor that was key to the king's reformist agenda. For the viewing public, the role of a drawing school in the operation of the state and the transformation of their own being and essence as nobles and men of taste was likely not immediately clear.

Hence, San Carlos's selection of the royal birthdays and saints' days bolstered the bodily, organic connection of the academy as appendage to the monarch as head of the national body.[36] It gave a biological imperative to the school, as if it too were born of the king's seed and the queen's womb—even on the same day as king, queen, or prince—to take its place in the body politic of the Spanish nation. The act of the *besamanos* that was part of the award ceremony, requiring attendees to touch the body of the king's alter ego in a choreographed display of homage, reinforced the message.[37] Rather than strive for eventual acceptance, the academy inserted itself into colonial society immediately by drawing upon the medieval metaphor of the king's body and lineage. By extension, it made itself a relative of each member of the extended familial network of Spanish and creole nobles, with the effect of being less an institution imposed from the outside than a newborn natural child of the imperial family to which they all belonged.

And while the selection of the birthdays and saints' days in part dictated the festival aspect of the *premio* ceremonies, this too was a strategy to promote the idea of the academy and what it represented. There was, as I have said, no precedent for this at the San Fernando Academy in Madrid, whereas in Mexico City, the San Carlos administration and governing councilors happily folded their awards into an event that included masses, processions, *paseos*, *besamanos*, illuminations, sound, pageantry, and theatrical productions. In other words, this institution that was the very symbol of enlightened modernity drew upon, but also manipulated, the familiar language of Baroque spectacle to insert itself into colonial society.

As Stephanie Merrim and Linda Curcio-Nagy have amply demonstrated, festivals embodied the spectacular Baroque expression of the colonial social order and filled the Mexican calendar.[38] The purpose, as Christoph Müller argues, was "cementing social relationships."[39] For example, the parade of the *Paseo del Pendón*—the Procession of Cortés's Banner—that anchored the celebration of New Spain's foundation, the solemn processions of the faithful on Corpus Christi, and the grand cavalcade that accompanied new viceroys or archbishops into Mexico City all consisted of carefully organized arrangements of guilds, confraternities, religious orders, bureaucrats, and dignitaries reenacting the colonial social hierarchy as they paraded past plebeian onlookers or were received in the royal palace. Their bodies and dress, and the festooned buildings and blazing torches past which they walked and rode on *paseo*, visually manifested their status and role within society, as did the ephemeral structures, floats, and processional images that filled parade routes. Even poetry competitions were sheathed in a festival atmosphere in colonial Mexico City, with lavish public processions, decorated city buildings, and performances.[40] As Merrim writes, "the society of the spectacle installed in the colonies hyperbolically ritualized events large and small, colonial and imperial, religious and secular, praiseworthy and shameful."[41]

The San Carlos award ceremonies performed similarly, even if, as late eighteenth-century festivals, the events took on a more modern cast, vividly demonstrated by the overall restraint and limited scope of the public displays, and the inclusion of enlightened theater.[42] Likewise, in this modern version of the Baroque festival, the role of the participating public was in some ways allegorized by the academy students, who received their medals from the viceroy in a polite exchange rather than in a hurly-burly rush forward to collect largess thrown from the royal balcony or carriage. Rather than cater directly to that kind of crush of humanity, the enlightened festival selected and celebrated its best and most exemplary representatives. But even in this altered form, the event was clearly a kind of festival that colonists would recognize, with processions, *paseos*, artillery salvos, and other traditional festival elements. Hence the academy became just one more organization within the colonial community, like church, *cabildo*, or confraternity. The festival aspect of the *premio* events consequently made the academy seem like a natural and familiar part of the viceregal "society of spectacle."[43]

At the same time, however, the academy's adjustments to the festival type clearly communicated its reformist goals and its purpose in the viceroyalty; that is, we have little difficulty seeing the events as part of the "guided culture" defined by Antonio Maravall.[44] Perhaps most vivid was its apparent elimination of guilds from the celebration. The academy was of course working hard to supplant these organizations, including requiring apprentices to attend academy classes and placing academic authority over guild hierarchies and processes.[45] Likewise, the school embodied the king's 1785 declaration of the free exercise of arts, without the need for guild affiliation, and the requirement that architectural projects in New Spain be approved by the academy, as had happened in 1777 in Spain.[46] Appropriating the procession, a type of performance that had once privileged the role of the guild in the colonial economic and social order, and keeping this population out of the parade—despite the fact that the event celebrated artisanal achievement—clearly communicated the new rule of the day. If guilds were the anchors of the traditional civic and religious festivals—and they remained so even during the ceremonies celebrating the coronation of Charles IV and the entry of a new viceroy in 1789—their absence from the academy event, including the public procession and the more private *besamanos*, could not have escaped notice.

By the same token, the award-winning and submitted entries displayed in the viceregal palace functioned as a parallel to the ephemeral objects of the traditional festival that offered the opportunity for guild and civic organization to visualize its relationship to the crown. The academic works displayed during the *premio* events were in this way allegories of the grand agenda of social and economic reform that San Carlos represented. And if, as Stephanie Merrim has argued, festival architecture and ornament "refocused and ideologized urban space ..., estheticizing the city," the award-winning works and other entries promised a new urban esthetic, one that reflected the values and tastes of the academy.[47] In turn, the Neoclassical buildings and monuments that would occupy this imagined city, with their rationality and orderliness, would symbolize the industry and modernity of the Mexican state.

The performance of the artists during the inauguration and award ceremony described above consequently takes on added significance. These artists activated the event, taking the place of the poets, dancers, and performers—both official and impromptu—of the Baroque festival. Performing their schooled work, in the open, for those in attendance was, like those performances, more than mere entertainment. It was a demonstration completed within the span of the ceremony to embody the advantages and possibilities of an academy unfettered by guild rules and bureaucracies and their glacial pace of change. Moreover, the objects were seen under the watchful eye of the king's representative and the king himself, in the form of the royal portrait hanging in the *Salón del Besamanos*. The link among monarch, academy, reform, industry, and progress was made clear again.

Finally, and although there are many more parallels to be explored between the Baroque festival and the academic award ceremony, the illumination of the city merits attention. As Carmen Montoya has written in the context of the festivals celebrating the ascension of King Charles IV in 1789, "If it is true that light was one of the elements of the Baroque festival that demonstrated the leader's imposition of his will on nature and to turn even the darkest night into bright day, it is also the glorious metaphor of the Enlightenment."[48] Likewise, as Linda Curcio-Nagy has noted, the control of light symbolized good and beneficent government during the Bourbon era, changing night to day to delight the public and to make city streets safer, at least temporarily.[49] Hence the award festivals connected the academy and the literal enlightenment of the city; and it was not just art that was illuminating, but every corner of the colonial context that was illuminated, as the reforms of the king and his academy touched the breadth of society and made life in the city better. Hence we see that while the academy readily embraced the festival to insinuate itself into colonial society, it took liberties to alter festivals in significant ways that embodied its purpose and goals.

By way of a conclusion, let us return to where we began, on the pages of the *Gazeta de México*, as this too was a means to introduce the academy into the colonial context. While the Mexican academy published sheets listing its award winners, including the smaller monthly recognition of exemplary works, the newspaper carried the greater burden of chronicling the academy festivals. As I have argued elsewhere, the significance of the *Gazeta de México*, its claim to be the gazette of New Spain, and its importance for formation of an elite identity are best understood in light of Benedict Anderson's writings on the nation as an imagined community of citizens shaped by their interaction rather than direct governmental intervention.[50] This imagined community—this notion of an "us" distinct from others—was articulated in the eighteenth-century newspaper, which juxtaposed stories, advertisements, and notices that collectively defined the nation. The stories that appeared on the *Gazeta* pages created the idea of New Spain for its readers; they defined the nation of the elite, literate person of taste. Hence academic award ceremonies and festivals, by their mere presence in the newspaper, operated, to paraphrase Anderson, as an imagined community that defined a specifically Mexican man of taste, expected to participate in and appreciate the academic ceremonies, and to help the academy transform Mexican industry. Like the choice of festival dates that drew upon medieval notions of kingship and lineage, and the displays of pageantry and spectacle that exploited the familiar language of festivals, the academy's use of the newspaper was yet one more strategy to secure its place and bolster its centrality within the Mexican nation in order to achieve the lofty goals of king and institution.

Notes

[1] The scholarship on the *Caballito* is rich. Some of the more significant work includes Clara Bargellini, "La lealtad americana: el significado de la estatua ecuestre de Carlos IV," in *Iconología y sociedad, arte colonial hispanoamericano*, XLIV Congreso Internacional de Americanistas (Mexico City: Universidad Nacional Autónoma de México, 1987), 207–220; Stacie G. Widdifield, "Manuel Tolsá's Equestrian Portrait of Charles IV: Art History, Patrimony, and the City," *Journal X*, 8 (2003): 61–83; and Clementina Díaz y de Ovando, "Manuel Tolsá en el inicio y fin de un nuevo mundo americano (1791–1816)," in *Manuel Tolsá. Nostalgia de lo 'antiguo' y arte ilustrado México-Valencia* (Valencia: Generalitat Valenciana, 1988), 196–214.

[2] "Description of the Festival Celebrated in the Imperial

Court of México for the Purpose of the Solemn Installation of an Equestrian Statue of Our August Sovereign ... Charles IV in the Principal Plaza," *Gazeta de México*, 8, December 28, 1796, p. 8.

[3] "El regocijo público que se hace con el concurso del pueblo, para que logre algún descanso de las fatigas comunes de la naturaleza." *Diccionario de la lengua española* (Madrid: Real Academia Española, 1780), 470.

[4] "El festejo que se hace en obsequio de alguna persona real, o en su presencia." *Diccionario*, 471.

[5] The literature on Spanish and Spanish colonial festivals is vast. A few of the more significant studies include Antonio Bonet Correa, *Fiesta, poder y arquitectura. Aproximaciones al barroco español* (Madrid: Akal, 1990); José Antonio Maravall, *La cultural del barroco. Análisis de una estructura histórica* (Barcelona: Ariel, 1996); Rafael Ramos Sosa, *Arte festivo en la Lima virreinal* (Sevilla: Junta de Andalucía, 1992); *Rituals of Rule, Rituals of Resistance: Public Celebrations and Popular Culture in Mexico*, ed. William H. Beezley, Cheryl English Martin, and William E. French (Wilmington: Scholarly Resources, 1994); and Linda Curcio-Nagy, *The Great Festivals of Colonial Mexico City: Performing Power and Identity* (Albuquerque: University of New Mexico Press, 2004).

[6] On the Mexican court, see Christoph Rosen Müller, *Patrons, Partisans, and Palace Intrigues: The Court Society of Colonial Mexico, 1702–1710* (Calgary: University of Calgary Press, 2008) and Alejandro Cañeque, *The King's Living Image: The Culture and Politics of Viceregal Power in Colonial Mexico* (New York and London: Routledge, 2004).

[7] Unfortunately, this aspect of the Royal Academy of the Three Noble Arts of San Carlos has yet to be thoroughly studied. Guillermo Tovar de Teresa, "Arquitectura efímera y fiestas reales: La jura de Carlos IV en la ciudad de México en 1789," *Boletín del Museo e Instituto Camón Aznar* 48–49 (1992): 353–378, exemplifies the studies done on specific events. Academic contributions to Mexican festivals more broadly are briefly addressed in *Manuel Tolsá. Nostalgia de lo "antiguo" y arte ilustrado México-Valencia*, exhibition catalog (Mexico City: Generalitat Valenciana, 1998); *Juegos de ingenio y agudeza. La pintura emblemática de la Nueva España*, exhibition catalog (Mexico City: Instituto Nacional de Bellas Artes/Patronato del Museo Nacional de Arte, A.C., 1995); Beatriz Berndt, "Memoria pictórica de la fiesta barroca en la Nueva España," in *Pinceles de la historia. De la patria criolla a la nación mexicana* (Mexico City: Banamex/Museo Nacional de Arte, 2000), 92–103; Victor Mínguez, Inmaculada Rodríguez Moya, Pedro González Tornel, and Juan Chiva Beltrán, *La fiesta barroca. Los Virreinatos americanos (1560–1808)*, Triunfos barrocos, vol. 2 (Castelló de la Plana: Universitat Jaume I, 2012); Inmaculada Rodríguez Moya, *El retrato en México: 1781–1867. Héroes, ciudadanos y emperadores para una nueva nación* (Sevilla: Universidad de Sevilla/Diputación de Sevilla, 2007); and Juan Chiva Beltrán, *El triunfo del virrey. Glorias novohispanas: origen, apogeo y ocaso de la entrada virreinal* (Castelló de la Plana: Universitat Jaume I, 2012).

[8] Stephanie Merrim, *The Spectacular City, Mexico, and Colonial Hispanic Literary Culture* (Austin: University of Texas Press, 2010), 24.

[9] William H. Beezley, Cheryl English Martin, and William E. French, "Introduction: Constructing Consent, Inciting Conflict," in *Rituals of Rule, Rituals of Resistance*, xiii.

[10] Again, as with the festivals, the relationship between the academy and Mexico City's newspapers remains ripe for further research. The fruitfulness of this line of inquiry is illustrated by Andrés Ubeda de los Cobos's discussions of the relationship between Madrid's Royal Academy of San Fernando and the city's newspapers in the era of burgeoning art criticism. Andrés Úbeda de los Cobos, *Pensamiento artístico español del siglo XVIII. De Antonio Palomino a Francisco de Goya* (Madrid: Museo Nacional del Prado, 2001).

[11] *Gazeta de México*, 1, June 30, 1784, p. 110.

[12] *Gazeta de México*, 1, November 8, 1785, p. 422.

[13] *Gazeta de México*, 2, September 11, 1787, pp. 403–404.

[14] The authoritative history of the San Fernando academy remains Claude Bedat, *La Real Academia de Bellas Artes de San Fernando (1744–1808)* (Madrid: Real Academia de Bellas Artes, 1989). A more specific study of aesthetics at the academy is Úbeda de los Cobos, *Pensamiento artístico*. The prize ceremonies in Madrid are described in many imprints published by the academy from 1752 on.

[15] The Spanish academy's exhibitions are discussed at length in Úbeda de los Cobos, *Pensamiento artístico*, especially 19–95.

[16] On the construction of Mexico City as "spectacular city" in the sixteenth and seventeenth centuries, see Merrim, *Spectacular City*, especially 23–29.

[17] *Gazeta de México*, 6, January 7, 1794, pp. 4–5.

[18] I am not suggesting that the Royal Academy of San Carlos was alone in choosing the king's birthday and saint's day for its ceremonies. The Economic Society of Madrid, for example, awarded its prizes on the king's birthday. See José Antonio Maravall, "The Idea and Function of Education in the Enlightenment," in *The Institutionalization of Literature in Spain*, ed. Wlad Godzich and Nicholas Spadaccini (Minneapolis: Prisma Institute, 1987), p. 85.

[19] The most complete history of the Royal Academy of San Carlos written to date is Eduardo Báez Macías, *Historia de la Escuela Nacional de Bellas Artes (Antigua Academia de San Carlos) 1781–1910* (Mexico City: Escuela Nacional de Artes Plásticas/Universidad Nacional Autónoma de México, 2009). Thomas A. Brown, *La Academia de San Carlos de la Nueva España*, 2 vols. (Mexico City: Secretaría de Educación Pública, 1976) remains useful as well. See also Clara Bargellini and Elizabeth Fuentes, *Guía que permite captar lo bello. Yesos y dibujos de la Academia de San Carlos 1778–1916* (Mexico City: Universidad Nacional Autónoma de México, 1989).

[20] Brown, *Academia*, 1:16.

[21] "La destreza y habitualidad en el dibujo, que es el principal fundamento de [estas nobles artes], influye al mismo tiempo en casi todas las [artes] que sirven no solo la mayor comodidad, sino aún a las necesidades de la vida civil a que estamos acostumbrados." Report directed to don Matías de Gálvez, May 22, 1783, as cited in Eduardo Báez Macías, *Guía del archivo de la Antigua Academia de San Carlos* (Mexico City: Universidad Nacional Autónoma de México/Instituto de Investigaciones Estéticas, 2003), 29.

[22] Brown, *Academia*, 1:18.

[23] This aspect of the San Carlos academy's foundation is also addressed in Susan Deans-Smith, "'A Natural and Voluntary Dependence': The Royal Academy of San Carlos and the

Cultural Politics of Art Education in Mexico City, 1786–1797," *Bulletin of Latin American Research* 29, no. 3 (2010): 278–295.

[24] The scholarship on Spanish educational reform in the eighteenth century is quite ample. I find José Antonio Maravall, *Estudios de la historia del pensamiento español (siglo XVIII)* (Madrid: Biblioteca Mondadori, 1991) a useful and accessible resource on the topic.

[25] "El *premio* anual a uno o dos aprendices de una medalla del busto del Rey, con las armas de la Provincia, aplicado con toda justicia a los que mas sobresaliesen; excitaria la emulacion honrada entre todos." Pedro Rodríguez de Campomanes, *Discurso sobre el fomento de la industria popular* (Madrid: Sancha, 1774), lxxxix–xc.

[26] On Spanish nobility in the eighteenth century, see William J. Callahan, *Honor, Commerce and Industry in Eighteenth-Century Spain* (Cambridge: Harvard Graduate School of Business Administration, 1972) and Eva Velasco Moreno, *La Real Academia de la Historia en el Siglo XVIII. Una Institución de sociabilidad* (Madrid: Boletín Oficial del Estado/Centro de Estudios Políticos y Constitucionales, 2000).

[27] While, as Eduardo Báez Macías and others have noted, the nobility of the blood may not have welcomed these new peers into their elite fold, the fact remained that the academic model grew and transformed this population in new and unfamiliar ways. Báez Macías, *Historia*, 39.

[28] In fact, many scholars today agree that the Mexican academy did not promote a doctrinaire Neoclassicism until nearly twenty years after its foundation. The style of art practiced at the academy from 1783 to late in the 1790s is a kind of classicizing late Baroque style, more like Boucher than like David. For a nuanced study of this issue, see Eloisa Uribe, "El dibujo, la Real Academia de San Carlos de Nueva España y las polémicas culturales del siglo XVIII," in *Arte de las academias. Francia y México. Siglos XVII–XIX*, exhibition catalog (Mexico City: Antiguo Colegio de San Ildefonso, 1999), 45–58.

[29] Báez Macías, *Historia*, 51.

[30] Sharon Bailey Glasco, *Constructing Mexico City: Colonial Conflicts over Culture, Space, and Authority* (New York: Palgrave Macmillan, 2010), 20. Mexico City's population of creoles and Spaniards in 1772 was 50 percent of 112,462.

[31] On the Real Sociedad Bascongada de Amigos del País in Mexico, see Josefina María Cristina Torales Pacheco, *Ilustrados en la Nueva España. Los socios de la Real Sociedad Bascongada de los Amigos del País* (Mexico City: Universidad Iberoamericana, 2001).

[32] On the Mexican nobility, Doris Ladd, *The Mexican Nobility at Independence, 1780–1826* (Austin: University of Texas Press, 1976) remains a standard resource.

[33] Published throughout the second half of the eighteenth century under the title *Distribución de los premios*, the Spanish award ceremony books recount in detail the sequence of events.

[34] I am of course using the metaphor of the royal body/body politic as defined in the European medieval and early modern context by Ernst Kantorowicz and applied to Latin America by Alejandro Cañeque in *The King's Living Image: The Culture and Politics of Viceregal Power in Colonial Mexico* (London and New York: Routledge, 2004), especially 20–28.

[35] Cañeque, *King's Living Image*, 142, notes that within the body politic, institutions also constituted bodies unto themselves.

[36] Victor Mínguez and colleagues note similarly how entry festivals held in the Americas for viceroys, archbishops, and bishops likewise served to counteract the distance between monarch and colony, "symbolizing with each new viceregal entry the arrival of Hispanic power in the Americas, the loyalty of the subjects towards their monarch who sent his *alter ego* to reign in his overseas territories." Mínguez et al., *La fiesta barroca*, 49. Translation mine.

[37] Müller, *Patrons, Partisans, and Palace Intrigues*, 44, briefly addresses the ritual of the *besamanos*.

[38] Merrim, *Spectacular City*, and Linda Curcio-Nagy, *Great Festivals*.

[39] Müller, *Patrons, Partisans, and Palace Intrigues*, 43.

[40] Merrim, *Spectacular City*, 196.

[41] Merrim, *Spectacular City*, 25.

[42] The reduced scale of viceregal festivals is attributed to Charles III and his reformist *visitador*, José de Gálvez, who ordered that the entries of viceroys, for example, be held only in Mexico City and at a much more modest cost. See Juan Chiva Beltrán, *El triunfo del virrey*, 204.

[43] Merrim, *Spectacular City*, 25.

[44] Maravall defines "guided culture" in the context of seventeenth-century Spain in *Culture of the Baroque: Analysis of a Historical Structure*, trans. Terry Cochran (Minneapolis: University of Minnesota Press, 1986) and applies it to the eighteenth century in *Estudios de la historia del pensamiento español.*

[45] For more detailed information on the academy and its relationship with the painters' guild, see Susan Deans-Smith, "'Dishonor in the Hands of Indians, Spaniards, and Blacks': The (Racial) Politics of Painting in Early Modern Mexico," in *Race and Classification: The Case of Mexican America*, ed. Ilona Katzew and Susan Deans-Smith (Palo Alto, CA: Stanford University Press, 2009), 43–72.

[46] *Distribución de los premios* (Madrid: Ibarra, 1787), 3.

[47] Merrim, *Spectacular City*, 26.

[48] "Si bien [la luz] había sido uno de los elementos de la fiesta barroca para mostrar el poder de las autoridades para sobreponerse a la naturaleza y tornar en luminoso día hasta la noche más oscura, es a la vez gloriosa metáfora de la Ilustración." María del Carmen Montoya Rodríguez, "Palabra, imagen y poder. Iconografía de las Casas Capitulares sevillanas para las fiestas de proclamación de Carlos IV," *I/C Revista científica de información y comunicación* 4 (2007): 260.

[49] Curcio-Nagy, *Great Festivals,* 71–72. The illumination of the city is also addressed by Solange Alberro in "Los efectos especiales en las fiestas virreinales de Nueva España y Perú," *Historia mexicana* 59, no. 3 (2010): 837–877, esp. 846–847.

[50] Benedict Anderson, *Imagined Communities: Reflections on the Origin and Spread of Nationalism*, rev. ed. (London and New York: Verso, 1991), 6. I apply Anderson's notion of the imagined community in Kelly Donahue-Wallace, "A Taste for Art in Late Colonial New Spain," in *Buen Gusto and Classicism in the Visual Cultures of Latin America, 1780–1910*, ed. Paul B. Niell and Stacie G. Widdifield (Albuquerque: University of New Mexico Press, forthcoming).

Transforming Status

The Genesis of the New World *Butaca*

Jorge F . Rivas Pérez

Although more than five centuries have passed since Columbus landed on the island of Hispaniola in 1492, our understanding of the material world from the early days of European expansion in the Caribbean is still very limited. Indeed, early modern Spanish Caribbean material culture remains an understudied subject, as most scholarly work on post-Conquest cultural issues has concentrated primarily on the viceroyalties of New Spain and Peru. The history of hybrid objects from the colonial period, such as the *butaca* chair that is the subject of this essay, can help us gain a better understanding of how Caribbean native American and mixed race (*mestizo*) colonial societies operated within the new cultural and social paradigms imposed by Europeans in the Americas, and realize how their material world mirrored the cultural adjustment, negotiation, and transformation that characterized early colonial times.

From the initial days of European exploration and conquest, the indigenous populations of the New World began to selectively incorporate European goods and manufacturing technologies into their material world. In the long run, this process resulted in a hybrid material culture that still thrives today in many regions. While hybridity emerged from a complex and protracted cultural exchange among natives, Spaniards, and, later, Africans as well, it is important to realize that the dynamic of interchange was considerably asymmetrical, because objects, and the production processes to manufacture them, had different economic value, use modes, and symbolic significance for each culture. The destruction, transformation, and forced assimilation of native cultures and their material worlds into a single new colonial reality operated within a highly mutable sociocultural context; change transformed both sides of the equation, although not in the same measure.

Colonial domestic spaces proved to be outstanding "laboratories" for experimenting with traditional and innovative object types placed in different sociocultural contexts. Households mirrored on a small scale the larger social landscape of the colonial society. Conquerors and conquered, masters and vassals coexisted under a single roof and interacted every day. Historical circumstances forced different material worlds to complement each other. The spontaneous emergence and subsequent evolution of new hybrid household objects, such as the *butaca* chair, and the evolving cultural practices associated with their use reflect the ways in which native and Spanish cultures managed change during the turbulent years after the Conquest. Change brought about a continuous reevaluation of the very essence of things: that is, their intrinsic nature, cultural significance, modes of use, and, above all, status in colonial society.

The *Butaca* Chair and Its Name

The word *butaca*, also spelled *butaque*, designates a low inclined easy chair with a high back, a type that is known in North America as a Campeche chair, or in Louisiana as a *boutaque*. Still today the *butaca* is commonly found in domestic environments all over Latin America, and particularly in the Caribbean. Its inclined design provides a very comfortable resting position while the high back gives an appropriate support for back and head. The type has proven to be so popular and adaptable over time that it has resisted the homogenizing forces of today's design globalization.

Although some scholars have claimed a European origin for *butacas* and associated types,[1] exclusively on the basis of formal similarities with the ancient Roman *sella curulis* (chair of state), there is enough evidence to demonstrate that *butacas* are in fact a hybrid Spanish Colonial type derived from Pre-Columbian ritual seats. The *butaca* emerged and evolved as a result of cultural transformation in post-Conquest colonial society in the Caribbean during the sixteenth and early seventeenth centuries.

The American origins of the name *butaca* are quite precise. It is derived from the word *putaca*, which means "seat" in the Cumanagoto tribal language. Related to the Arawak and Carib ethnic groups that populated the Caribbean, the

Cumanagoto peoples inhabited eastern Venezuela's coastal territories. Alexander von Humboldt (1769–1859), who visited the region in 1799, mentioned in his travel account that Indians of this group were still living near Cumaná—at that time the capital city of the eponymous province.[2] Cumanagoto is today an extinct language; however, a dictionary compiled by the Franciscan friar Mathías Ruiz Blanco, and published in 1683 in Burgos by Juan de Viar together with a grammar treatise by Manuel de Yangües, provides us with the precise origin of the term. In the dictionary, the word for seat (*asiento*) is paired with tool (*instrumento*), and two names are given for both, *aponto* and *putaca*.[3] Pronounced in Spanish, the words *putaca* and *butaca* sound quite similar.

Despite the fact that *butacas* and *butaques* are mentioned in early Venezuelan colonial documents—the earliest known mention is the "two *butaques*" listed in the 1632 will of Sebastian Hinojosa, a cabinetmaker in Caracas[4]—the word does not appear in the Royal Spanish Academy dictionary until 1843. In that edition, *butaca* was defined as "A big and very low inclined chair. It and its name are of American origin."[5] The word, spelled *butaque*, appears in the Royal Academy dictionary of 1927, here defined as a barbarism

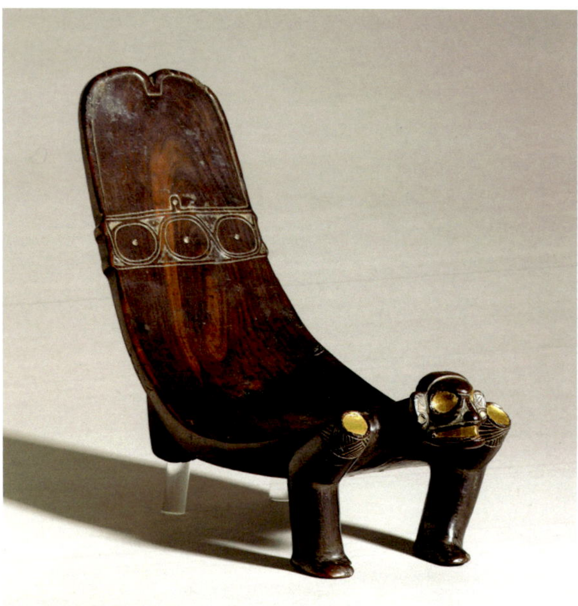

Fig. 1. Stool (*Duho*). Dominican Republic, 15th century. Wood and gold, 17⁵/₁₆ × 8⁵/₈ × 5½ in. (43.1 × 20.3 × 12.7 cm). British Museum, London. Photo: © The Trustees of the British Museum.

of *butaca*.[6] However, in colonial documents, the words *butaca* and *butaque* are used interchangeably, although *butaque* is the earliest and most common form. *Butaque* is found in sixteenth- and seventeenth-century documents, while *butaca*, which first appears in a 1650 inventory,[7] is employed later. Related names such as *butacón*, and diminutive forms like *butaquito* and *butaquillo*, are fairly common as well. In some inventories it is specified when *butacas* have arms. We can therefore deduce that although all surviving examples have arms, both types (with and without arms) were made.

Pre-Columbian Antecedents

The repertoire of Pre-Columbian chair types was very narrow, consisting mostly of low stools and, in some exceptional cases, high-back chairs such as the woven cane and sedge Mexican *tepotzoicpalli*, often depicted in ancient Mexican codices. High-back chairs in the Caribbean were generally used for ceremonial purposes, often for persons smoking tobacco or using hallucinogenic substances during social and religious functions,[8] and were reserved for *caciques* (Indian rulers) and high priests. The Caribbean high-back ceremonial seat, known as a *duho* among the Taíno peoples from Hispaniola, established the seat type that disseminated across the entire region (fig. 1).[9] The chair types found among Venezuela's native population, named in Venezuela *putacas* and *tures*, are associated with *duhos*. Regarded as elite objects par excellence, they were closely associated with social prestige and power; *duhos* and related chairs were fundamental components of ritual ceremonies. Thanks to early Spanish chroniclers such as Bartolomé de las Casas (1484–1566), we know the importance of *duhos* in Taíno rites and rituals. Besides describing ritual uses for *duhos*, de las Casas indicates that they were low and finely carved; in addition, he explains how the name should be pronounced.[10] Europeans quickly recognized the significance, extraordinary craftsmanship, and rarity of these ritual seats. *Duhos* were sent to Europe, where they were treasured as rare and valuable curiosities. In the 1620s, a Taíno *duho* is recorded in the famed collection of Nicolas-Claude Fabri de Peiresc (1580–1637), an influential French scholar and antiquarian active in French and Italian intellectual circles.[11] He most likely acquired the Taíno *duho* around 1600 during a trip to Rome, where he visited fellow scholars and collectors from the circle of Cardinal Francesco Barberini (1597–1679). Peiresc considered his *duho* such a precious piece that its record includes a detailed drawing (fig. 2).

In contrast with the high straight-backed European chair types prevalent in the sixteenth century, Pre-Columbian chairs were generally very low and designed for comfort. Galeotto Cey (1513–1579), a Florentine traveler who lived in Santo Domingo and in Venezuela in the 1540s, sat on these low seats and described them in his memoirs: "The Indians usually sit on the floor; however, some of them make seats, both small and large, and they call them *ture*. Some are made from a single piece of wood, others of wood and reeds, covered with a skin of deer, tiger, wildcat, or lion. Those seats are low, but very comfortable."[12] Cey complemented his description with a drawing (fig. 3). Archeological finds of Pre-Columbian seated ceramic figurines in Venezuela corroborate Cey's description and drawing (fig. 4).

The word *ture*, or in some regions *dure*, is still used in Venezuela to designate the same type of native low chair, usually of an x-shaped structure. The word first appears in a rare 1680 dictionary compiled by Francisco de Tauste (1626–1685), a Capuchin friar active in the province of Cumaná, where *ture* is defined as a small wooden seat.[13] In a 1789 manuscript, the "[Vocabulario] De Espanyol y Guaraúno"[14] (Guarauno is still spoken today by the Warao people living in Venezuela's Orinoco delta region), formerly in the Madrid Royal Palace library collection, the name *ture* is again mentioned to designate a seat. Therefore, from pre-Hispanic times the same type of chair, only with different names, was used by several Indian nations in northern Venezuela and the Caribbean islands. This native chair may have originated in eastern Venezuela, from where it probably disseminated with population migrations. It is important to remember that the early Taíno first inhabited South America, in the area of the Orinoco Delta in eastern Venezuela, and only later—circa 2000

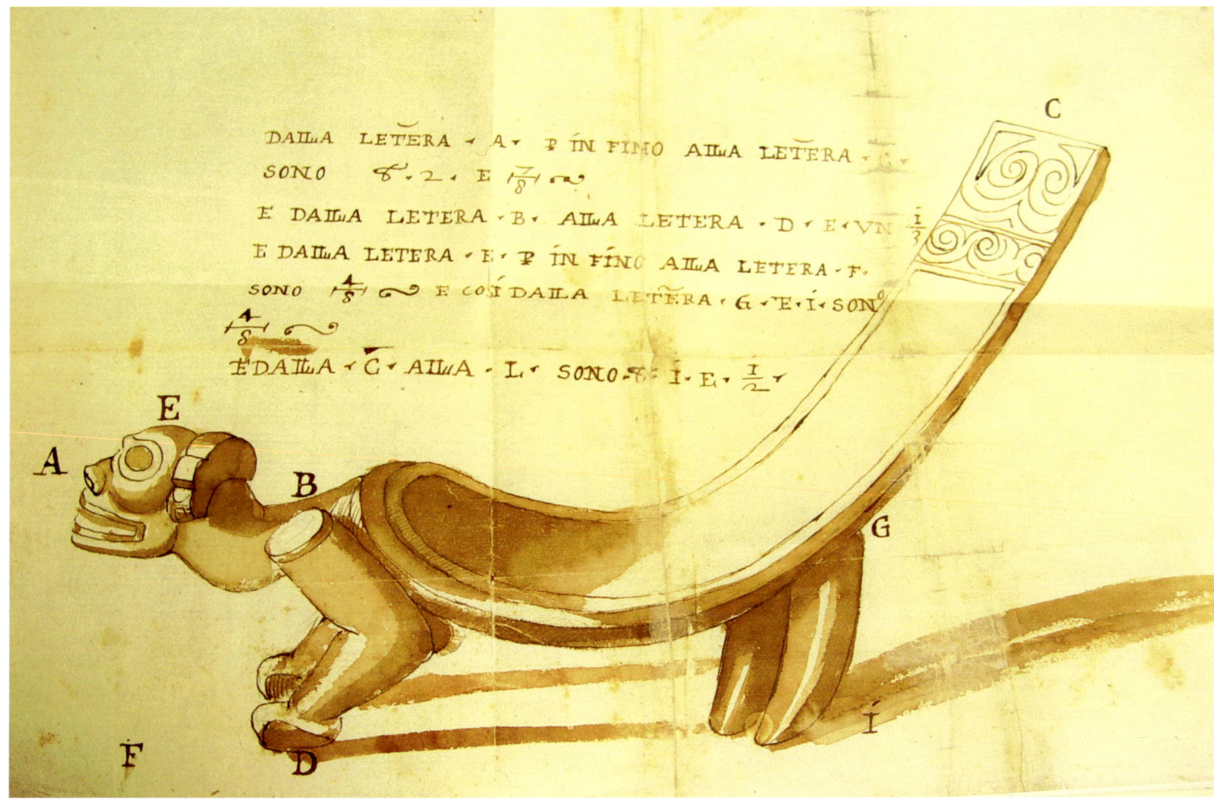

Fig. 2. Stool (*Duho*). Taíno, c. 1620. Nicolas-Claude Fabri de Peiresc, Manuscript 1821, fol. 21. Bibliothèque Inguimbertine, Archives et Musées de Carpentras (France). Courtesy of Peter N. Miller.

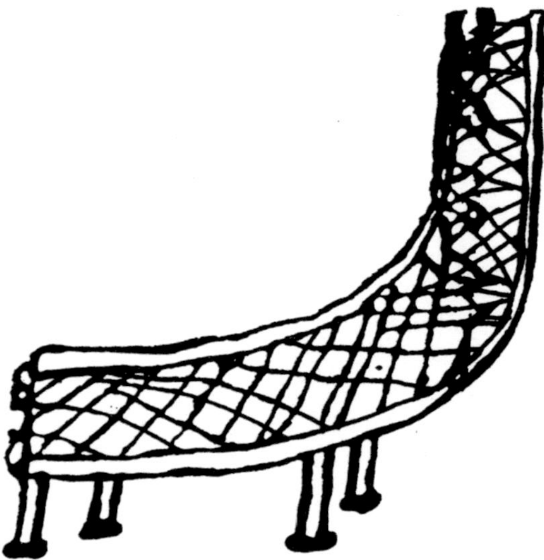

Fig. 3. Detail of a seat (*Ture*). From Galeotto Cey, *Viaje y Descripción de las Indias, 1539–1553* (Caracas: Fundación Banco Venezolano de Crédito, 1995), 113.

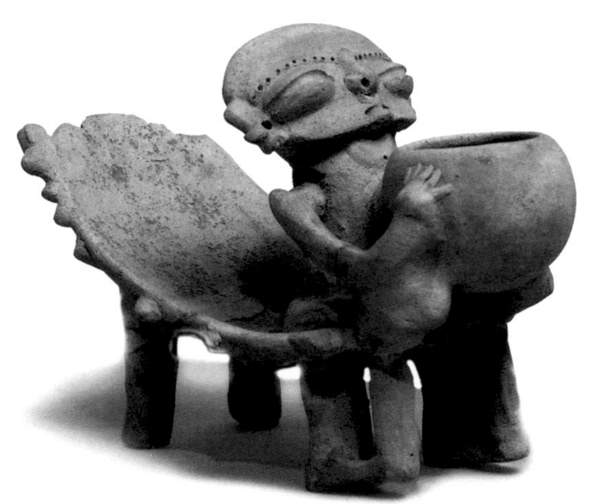

Fig. 4. *Seated male figure holding a vessel.* La Mata, Palo Negro, municipio Libertador, Aragua (Venezuela), 13th century. Grey clay ceramic with pink slip, 7½ × 10¼ × 5½ in. (19 × 26 × 14 cm). Museo Arqueológico de Maracay, colección Henriqueta Peñalver. From Carlos Duarte, *Un asiento venezolano llamado butaca*, exhibition catalog (Caracas: Centro de Arte La Estancia: Acción Cultural PDVSA, 1999).

BC—migrated to several islands of the Caribbean. This would explain the constant appearance of the native chair throughout the region.

These comfortable Pre-Columbian ritual low and small seats were different from the Spanish *silla de caderas* (X-shaped folding chair) (fig. 5), a chair type that from ancient times in Europe was associated with power and social prestige. Bernal Díaz del Castillo (1492–1585) recounts in his *True History of the Conquest of New Spain* that, on Easter in 1519, Hernán Cortés sent a carved and painted *silla de caderas* from San Juan de Ulúa to Mexico City as a special gift to Moctezuma.[15] Díaz del Castillo mentions how Cortés expected the Mexica ruler to use it while receiving him in Tenochtitlan. *Sillas de caderas* were often misrepresented with a distorted prospective view in ancient Mexican codices, as in the Lienzo de Tlaxcala, which represents the encounter between Cortés and Moctezuma. Inventories of important early Spanish Colonial households generally include *sillas de caderas* among the furniture items. These chairs were highly fashionable during the sixteenth century and were used as status symbols even in remote places such as the town of Nueva Cádiz on Cubagua, a desert island off the coast of eastern Venezuela.

By the early sixteenth century, starting from the 1510s, Nueva Cádiz was a small but very rich village, thanks to the plentiful pearl grounds of the region. The town had stone houses, a church, and a Franciscan monastery decorated with ceramic tiles imported from Seville. In 1528 Pedro de Barrionuevo had in his house on the island half a dozen *sillas de caderas*. That same year Martín Alonso Alemán was selling at his store in Nueva Cádiz several *sillas de caderas*.[16] Cubagua was a key point of departure for various expeditions organized to establish permanent settlements in mainland South America. From 1515 Franciscan and Dominican friars, with the help of Spanish authorities, tried to establish missions along the coast of Venezuela. After several failed or short-lived attempts, in 1569 the village of Cumaná, birthplace of the *butaca* chair, was finally permanently settled.

From its foundation, Cumaná had a troubled existence. Indians and pirates frequently attacked the village. Major earthquakes, the first of which

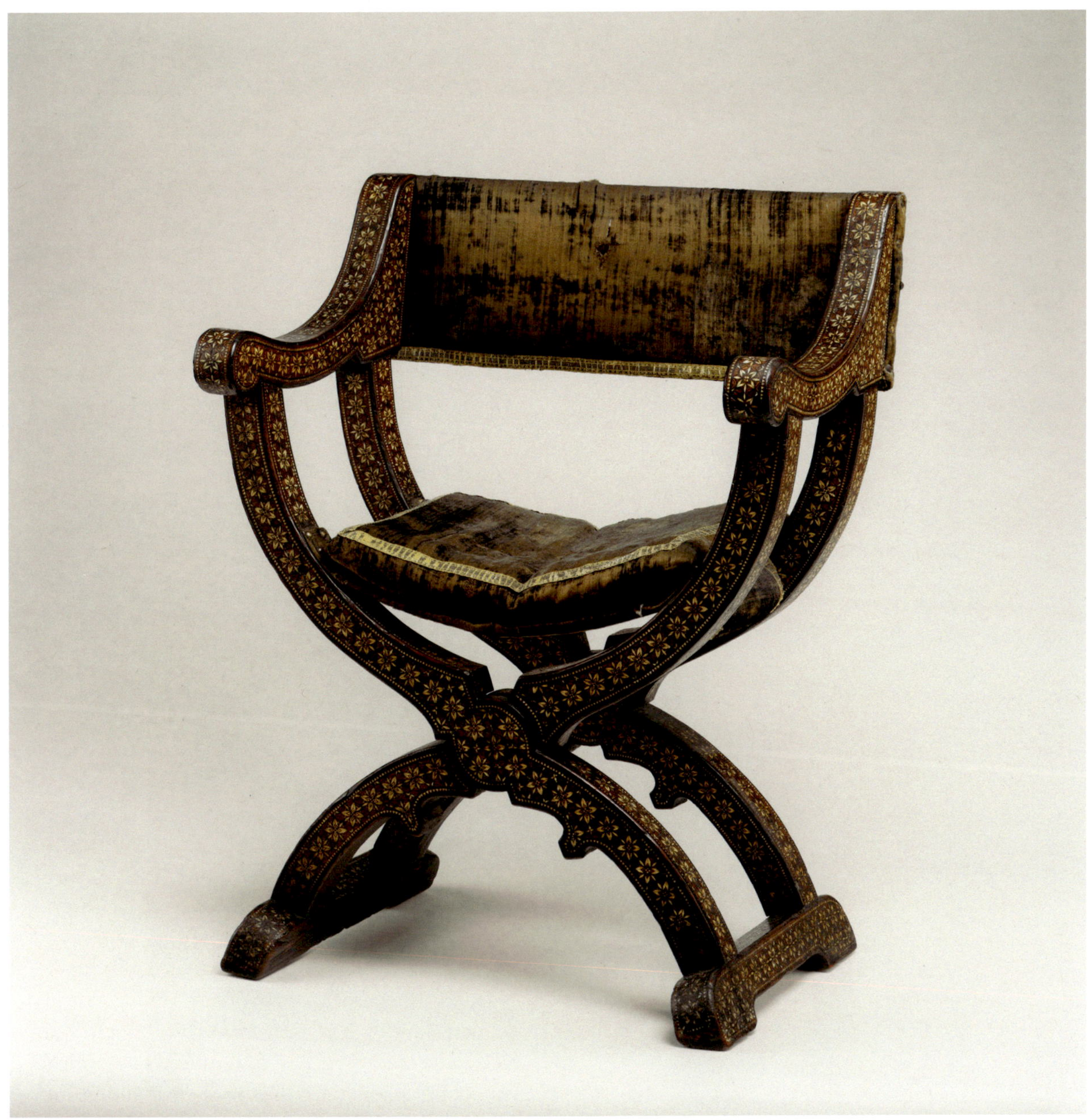

Fig. 5. Folding chair (*silla de caderas*). Granada (Spain), c. 1480–1500. Walnut and elm, partly veneered and inlaid with different woods, ivory, bone, and pewter, and covered in silk velvet not original to the armchair, 36½ × 24 × 19½ in. (92.7 × 61 × 49.5 cm). Metropolitan Museum of Art, New York, Fletcher Fund, 1945, 45.60.41a, b. Photo: Art Resource, NY.

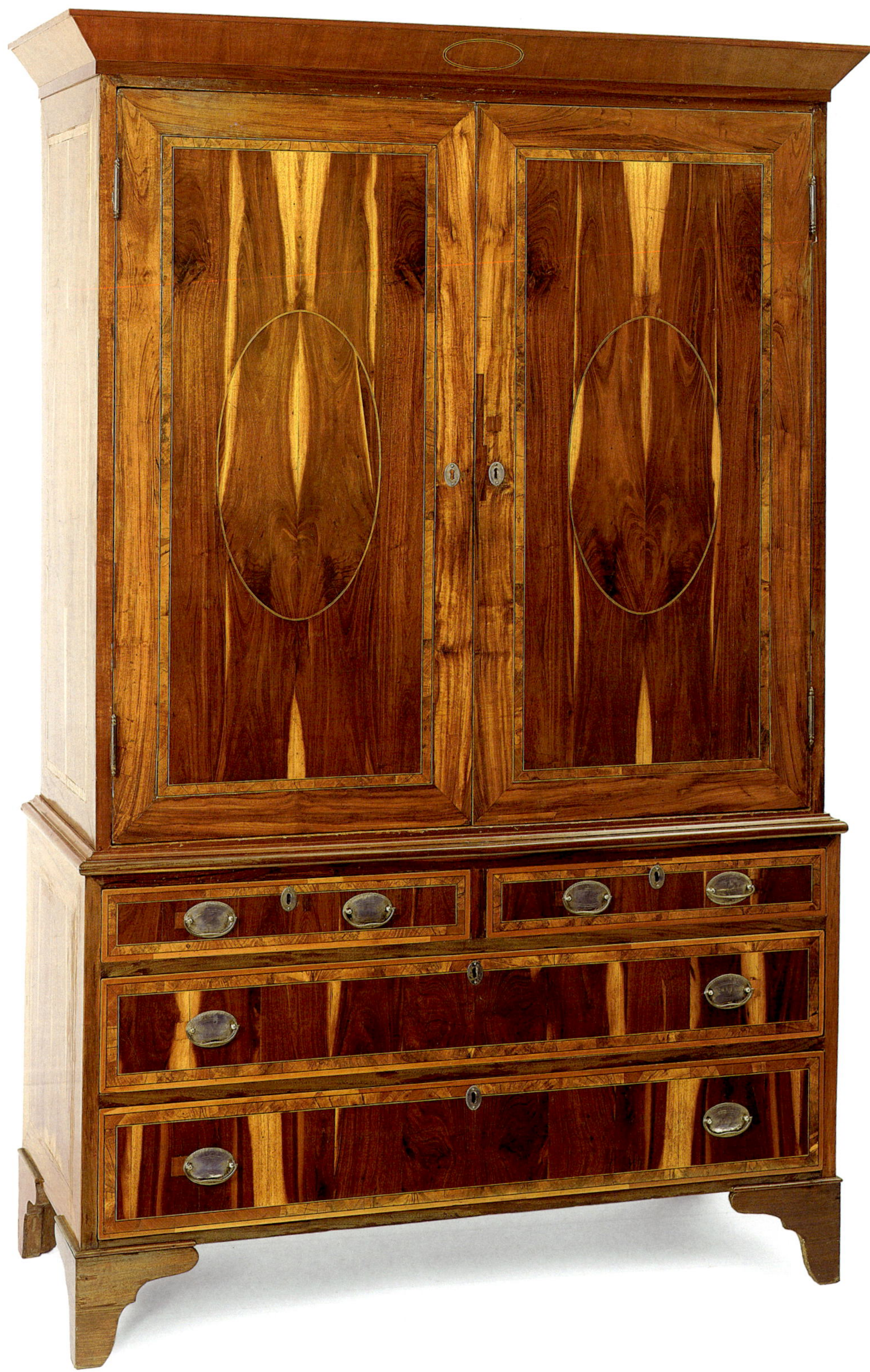

Fig. 6. Chest on chest. Cumaná (Venezuela), 1799. Veneers of *gateado* wood and *carreto* wood over a Spanish cedar base, silver hardware not original to the chest, 78³/₈ × 49¾ × 21¹/₁₆ in. (199 × 125.5 × 53.5 cm). Colección Patricia Phelps de Cisneros, 2005.21.

was recorded in 1530, periodically shattered its foundations. Records on early Cumaná woodworking have yet to be discovered. However, thanks to subsequent travelers' accounts, and a few surviving examples, we know that the town had a remarkable tradition of fine furniture making. In 1799, Alexander von Humboldt described the city as a provincial town and reported that "Mr. de Emparan [Don Vicente de Emparán y Orbe (1747–1820), the governor of the province of Cumaná] showed us cottons dyed with native plants, and fine furniture that was made exclusively with the wood of the country."[17] There is a rare surviving piece from that period (now in the Colección Patricia Phelps de Cisneros), a marquetry chest made in 1799 for Don Domingo Mauricio de Besoitagoena de Berrizbeitia y Zamalloa to commemorate his marriage to Doña María de los Dolores Mayz y Márquez de Valenzuela (fig. 6).[18] The fine construction and detailing of this chest testifies to the high level of craftsmanship reached by local cabinetmakers. Unfortunately, although *butacas* were consistently listed in colonial inventories from the second quarter of the seventeenth century, no early examples or depictions of the easy chair survive. The earliest surviving Venezuelan examples date from the second half of the eighteenth century.

Scholarly Research on the Subject

Since the late nineteenth century, Venezuelan scholars have been interested in the *butaca*, particularly in the chair's exact place of origin. The first to write on the history and etymology of the *butaca* chair was Arístides Rojas (1826–1894), a respected nineteenth-century Venezuelan scholar and collector. In his brief circa 1894 text on the subject,[19] published in a posthumous 1907 edition

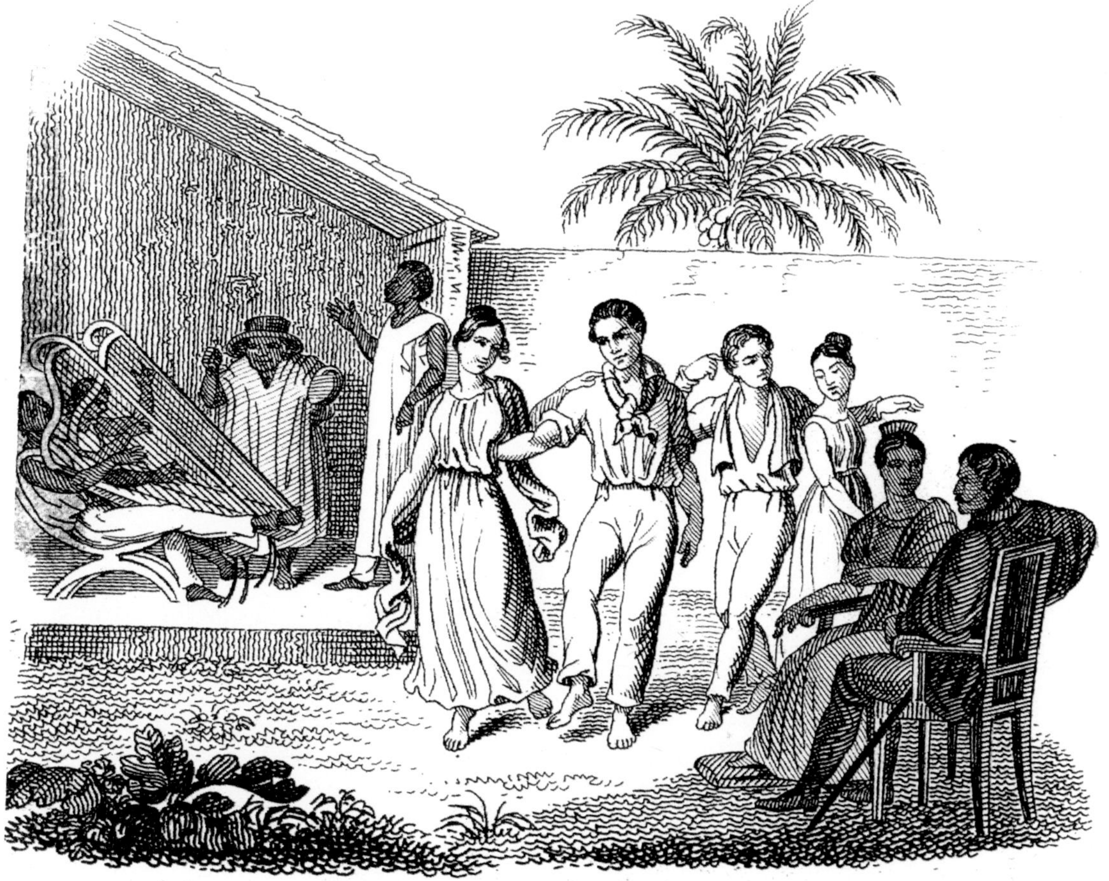

Fig. 7. *Creolentanz zu Cumana* (Creole Dance in Cumaná). From Alcide Dessalines d' Orbigny, *Malerische Reise in Süd-und Nordamerika: eine geordnete Zusammenstellung des Wissenswürdigsten von den Entdeckungsreisen …* (Leipzig: Baumgärtners Buchhandlung, 1839), pl. 6, fig. 2.

of a work he left unfinished at his death in 1894, he cites Ruiz Blanco's 1683 dictionary as well as Roque Bárcia (1821–1885), certainly in reference to his *Primer diccionario general etimológico de la lengua española*,[20] and Vicente Salvá Pérez (1786–1849) for his numerous works on Spanish grammar and etymology—key figures to support Rojas's thesis. Bárcia's dictionary is the first of its kind in Spanish, and Salvá Pérez and Andrés Bello (1781–1865) are considered the fundamental pillars of modern Spanish grammar. Rojas's work was followed by texts by other scholars, namely Juan Röhl (1892–1974) in 1946, Angel Rosemblat (1902–1984) in 1953, Carlos Manuel Möller (1896–1966) in 1960, and Carlos Duarte (b. 1939) in 1999.[21] However, all these later authors departed from Rojas's etymological approach without including much additional documentation to justify their departure.

I have been able to locate the original source of a previously unidentified nineteenth-century German print that includes a pair of *butacas* (fig. 7).[22] The engraving, entitled "Creolentanz zu Cumana,"[23] belongs to the 1839 German translation of a well-known 1836 French travel diary, *Voyage pittoresque dans les deux Amériques,* by Alcide Dessalines d' Orbigny (1802–1857), a French traveler who in 1826 visited the city of Cumaná. The original print "Danse Créole à Cumana,"[24] (fig. 8), which is nearly identical to the German engraving, features the same pair of *butacas*, of which Dessalines d' Orbigny wrote: "The harp-players sat gently reclined in a buttaca [sic] or priest's chair, a seat whose form is prior to the conquest, and that is claimed to have been found in the country by the Spanish."[25] This accurate description, accompanied by the illustration, confirms the Pre-Columbian origin

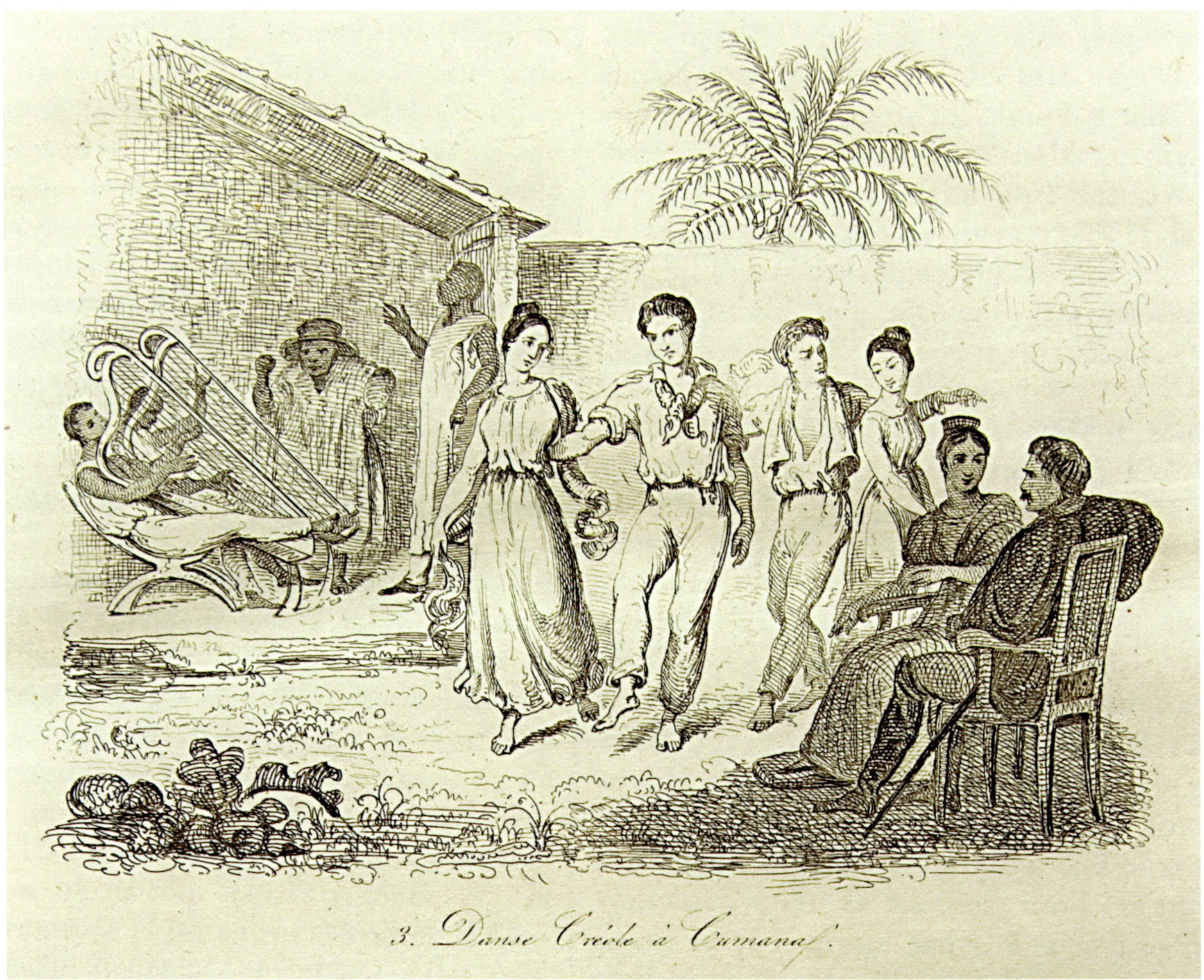

Fig. 8. *Danse Créole à Cumana* (Creole Dance in Cumaná). From Alcide Dessalines d' Orbigny, *Voyage pittoresque dans les deux Amériques: Résumé général de tous les voyages …* (Paris: L. Tenré [etc.], 1836), pl. 6-3. Colección Patricia Phelps de Cisneros.

for *butacas*, Cumaná as their birthplace, and the inclined position determined by the shape of the chair. The French traveler's description of the chair as a "*chaise de prêtre*" (priest's chair) is also important, revealing that even in 1826 the *butaca*, or its name, was still associated with ancient Pre-Columbian religious practices. A *butaca* depicted in a drawing in the travel notebook of Ferdinand Bellermann (1814–1889), a Prussian painter who in 1843 lived in Cumaná (fig. 9), further confirms the prevalence of *butacas* in mid-nineteenth-century Cumaná private interiors.

Hybrid multicultural societies, such as the Spanish Colonial, frequently require new types of objects appropriate for the new social reality that characterizes them. In such cases original hybrid artifacts, such as the *butaca*, are created by adopting, recombining, and adapting various design components taken from different cultural backgrounds. The overall shape of the *butaca* and its low height are of Pre-Columbian origin. The rigid frame derives from the Spanish *silla de caderas* (though, unlike *sillas de caderas*, *butacas* do not fold), but it is rotated ninety degrees and its shape is substantially modified to fit the *butaca* design program. The technology and utensils necessary to build *butacas* also came from Spain; complex wood joinery, iron nails, and tools unknown in America before the arrival of Europeans.[26] A fundamental element differentiating the *butaca* from its Spanish and native design components was its function, which was dictated by the new use context. Colonial *butacas* were neither ritual seats for special functions like their Pre-Columbian predecessors, nor chairs of state like the Spanish *sillas de caderas* and their classical antecedents, the *sellae curules*, which symbolized authority and power. Stripped of the symbolism and ceremonial

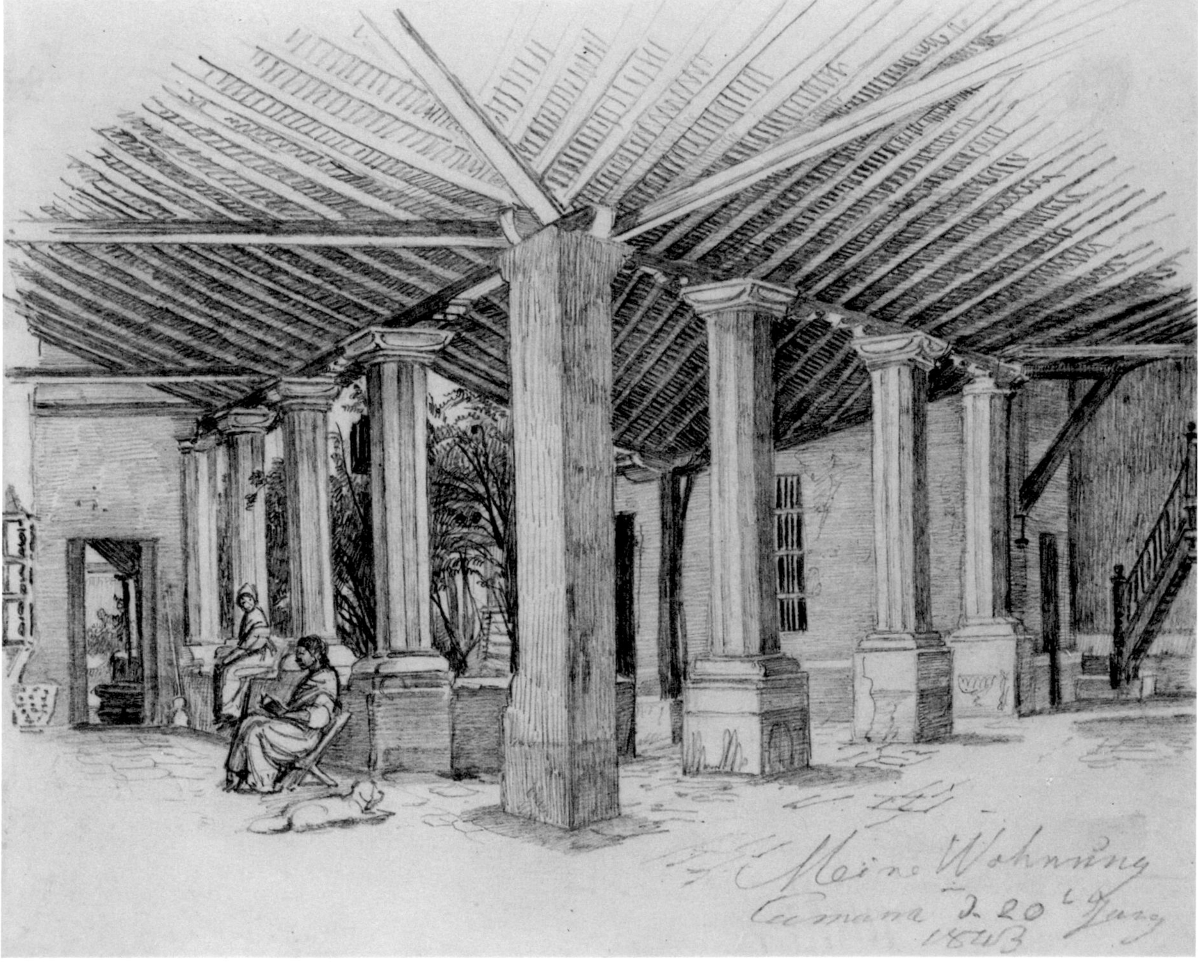

Fig. 9. Ferdinand Bellermann (Prussian, 1814–1889), *Apartment of the artist in Cumaná*. Venezuela, 1843. Drawing, 7¾ x 9¾ in. (20.0 x 24.7 cm). Kupferstichkabinett, Staatliche Museen, Berlin, Germany. Inventory no. SZ Bellermann 116. Photo: bpk, Berlin / Art Resource, NYImage.

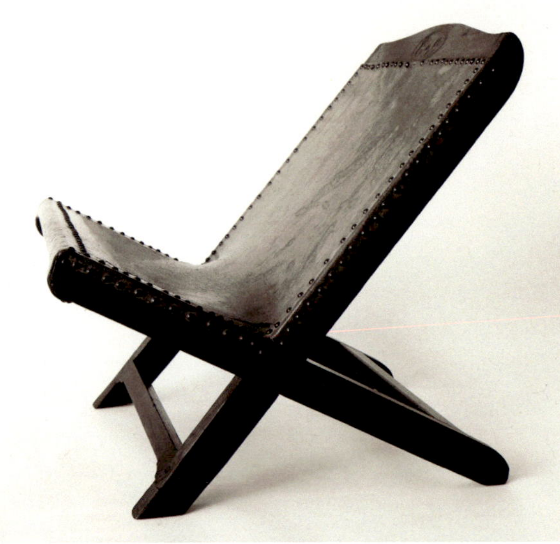

Fig. 10. *Ture*. Venezuela, 19th century. Wood, leather, and iron nails, 20⅞ x 13¾ x 27⅛ in. (53 x 35 x 69 cm). Private collection. Photo: Carlos Germán Rojas, Caracas.

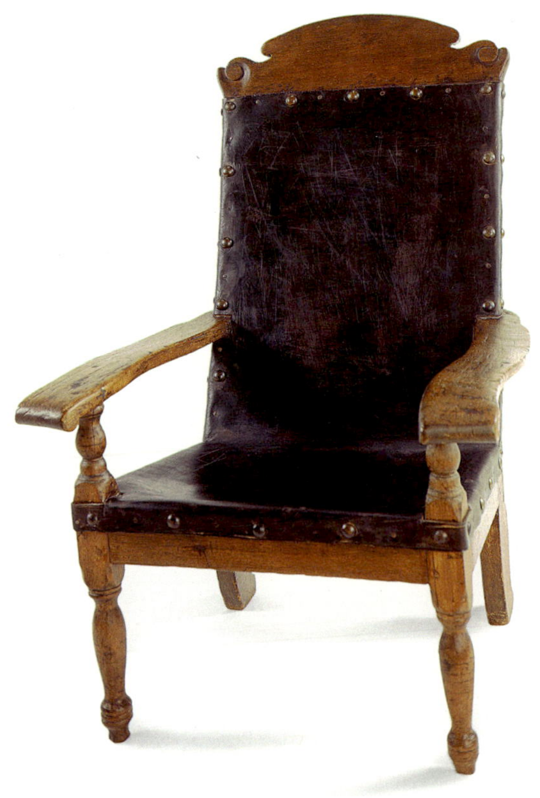

Fig. 11. *Butaca*. Venezuela, c. 1800–1812. Spanish cedar with new leather upholstery, 41⅜ × 28 × 15 in. (105 × 71 × 38 cm). Colección Patricia Phelps de Cisneros, 2001.66.

functions of its predecessors, the *butaca* simply became a resting chair expressly designed to provide a comfortable reclined posture, and it was recorded as such in colonial documents.

Initially *butacas* and *tures* were used in colonial Venezuela among the lower levels of society. For the Indians, who were converted to Catholicism and forced to adopt Spanish customs, the change broke their ancestral cultural link with artifacts of the pagan past, among them ritual chairs, and recontextualized such objects under new social and cultural paradigms, those of colonial society. Comfortable low seats of hybrid design, now constructed with European technology, became part of the colonial domestic material world. Yet, as Dessalines d'Orbigny reported, in the early nineteenth century they still were redolent of ancestral Pre-Columbian heritage.

Possibly because it was in part European and had long lost its Pre-Columbian ritual component, from the seventeenth century onwards the colonial *butaca* was also adopted by the upper classes, which further modified its original design by adding arms, associating elements taken from European decorative repertoires, and manufacturing it in more luxurious materials suitable for their own higher social status. *Butacas* became archetypal easy chairs in Caribbean Spanish America. They served as seats for personal use and were reserved for the most intimate domestic spaces, the only places where a reclining position was socially acceptable under strict Spanish Habsburg etiquette, which forbade a reclined seating posture in public. Although most *butacas* have a characteristic continuous seat and back in the profile of an inclined J that recalls Galeotto Cey's drawing of a *ture*, some examples have an inclined-L configuration. In both variations, the shape forces the user to sit in a reclining position.

Design Features

The colonial *butaca*'s main design features are the wide, low inclined seat and reclined high back; most high-end examples are adorned with wide flat straight or serpentine arms that often end with a scroll shape. A distinctive design element of the chair is its structural frame, in most cases based on a pair of X-shaped side supports joined by rails and stretchers. To this frame is nailed a piece of rawhide, skin, or leather—*guadamecí* (tooled leather) in the more luxurious examples—that serves as a continuous seat and back, as in Venezuelan *tures* (fig. 10). In Venezuela, some of the more refined eighteenth-century examples retain the inclined seat and high back but adopt a more traditional European seat design with four legs (fig. 11). The type evolved by incorporating fashionable European-style decorative features. Eighteenth-century Rococo pieces from the 1770s and 1780s, for example, usually have carved rocaille decoration as well as front cabriole legs with claw-and-ball or pad feet. Rear legs on these examples are usually flat with an S-shaped profile that reproduces a cabriole leg contour; in old inventories this type of leg is named "*de recorte*" (cut).[27] This four-legged design with an inclined-L configuration, wide flat arms, and upholstered seat and back, which probably first appeared in the 1760s,[28] may be the type referred to as a "*butacón*" in colonial documents (fig. 12). Although no examples have survived, records mention *butacones* that incorporated a small adjustable writing table or a bookstand, while other examples had wings that probably were similar to the ones of a Cuban *butaque* of the 1840s, today in the Brooklyn Museum's collection (fig. 13).[29] Starting in the late 1760s, instead of rawhide and skin, finer leathers such as cordovans and *badana* (tanned sheepskin) were used to upholster *butacas*, usually in bright colors like red or yellow, and fixed to the frame with gilt nail heads. In the same period *butacones* were upholstered in velvet and other types of fine fabrics.[30]

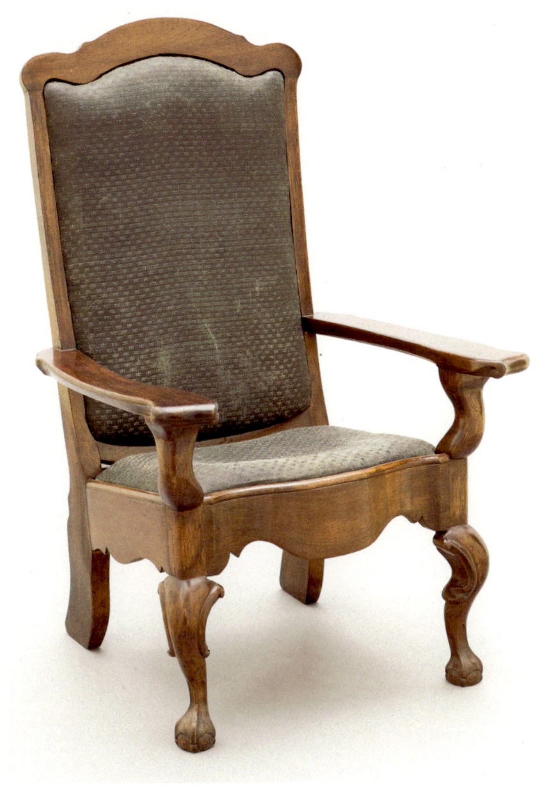

Fig. 12. *Butacón*. Venezuela, c. 1760–1770. Mahogany and *pardillo* wood, upholstery in horsehair over frames not original to the piece, 40^3/16 × 25^3/16 × 26^3/4 in. (102 × 64 × 68 cm). Los Angeles County Museum of Art. Gift of Adriana Cisneros in honor of Gustavo Dudamel (M.2013.209).

Arístides Rojas declares that "the seat of many of the Indians from Venezuela was an X-shaped, concave, and leather-upholstered piece of furniture; this was the old *butaquito* without a back that was used in children's schools," adding, "later, this piece of furniture became augmented and it turned into the *butaques* or *butacones* for elderly ladies."[31] His opinion is important not only because it coincides with Dessalines d' Orbigny on the native origin of the type, but also because Rojas had firsthand knowledge of Venezuelan colonial uses and traditions, as he lived in a society in transition from the colonial traditions into a modern nation. Thanks to several surviving inventories, we now know that both types (Indian and Spanish)

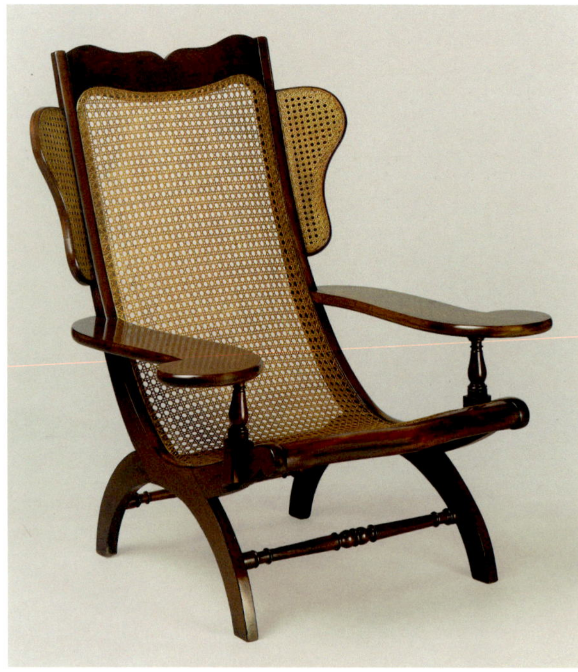

Fig. 13. *Butaque*. Cuba, second quarter of the 19th century. Mahogany and old and new cane, 43 × 35$^{3}/_{4}$ × 35⅜ in. (109.2 × 90.8 × 89.9 cm). Brooklyn Museum, Gift of Mrs. J. Fuller Feder, by exchange and Brooklyn Museum Collection, 2011.58.1.

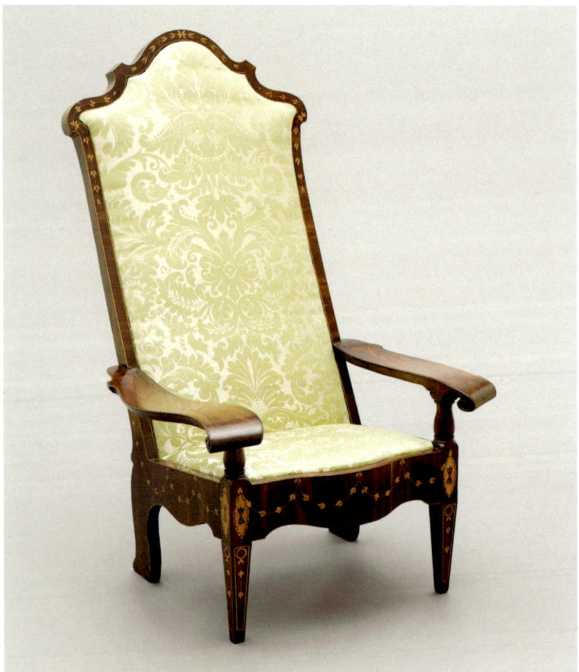

Fig. 14. Serafín Antonio Almeida (Venezuela, 1752–1822), *Butacón*. Caracas (Venezuela), c. 1795–1812. Veneers of *gateado* wood and *carreto* wood over a Spanish cedar base, with new cloth upholstery over frames, 49 x 30$^{5}/_{16}$ x 31$^{1}/_{2}$ in. (124.46 x 76.99 x 80.01 cm). Colección Patricia Phelps de Cisneros, 2006.21.

coexisted in households. For example, Doña Lucía Puncel in 1778 in Caracas had "one large *butaque* with its back and seat in black sole (thick leather)" as well as "four of the small ones of the type made by the Indians at half a *real* each."[32] Therefore, we can conclude that small *butaquitos*, upholstered in rawhide or skin fixed to the frame with iron nails, and probably manufactured by Indians, were closer to the original hybrid type, while the larger and costlier *butacas*, *butaques,* and *butacones*, made in fine woods, upholstered in fine materials, and bearing European-style ornament, were the high-end versions of the type developed by colonial cabinetmakers for the elite.

Butaca design routinely appropriated elements from established fashionable European furniture styles. As I previously mentioned, pieces from the second half of the eighteenth century generally include Rococo elements. Early nineteenth-century Neoclassical *butacas* incorporate Classical features and ornament, such as the semicircular crest with marquetry decoration and the turned finials, poles, and stretchers seen on a Campeche chair in the Metropolitan Museum of Art's collection,[33] or the classical-themed marquetry on the *butacón* by Serafín Antonio Almeida (1752–1822) in the Patricia Phelps de Cisneros Collection (fig. 14).[34] As unique, custom-made pieces, *butacas* sometimes have personalized decorative details; these might include the owner's initials on the crest, or attributes such as a carved dog's head and bird on the legs on a Rococo example here illustrated, which may allude to the owner's pets or his interest in animals (fig. 15).[35]

Diffusion of the Type

The *butaca* type traveled throughout the extensive network of Spanish trade routes that encompassed the Americas, the Iberian Peninsula, the Canary Islands, and Asia, but above all, in the Caribbean and key ports along the Gulf of Mexico. The diffusion of the type increased particularly after Charles III signed the 1778 decree of free trade, which allowed the Spanish American ports to trade directly with one another and with most ports in Spain. The *butaque* depicted in the right foreground of Francisco Oller's 1893 masterpiece *El velorio* (*The Wake*) illustrates how the native chair had evolved and spread to Puerto Rico, among other islands, becoming a key part of Caribbean material culture (fig. 16).[36] A *butaque* production is recorded as well in Cuba (see fig. 13).

In the late eighteenth and early nineteenth centuries, the port city of Campeche, in Yucatán, was the most important manufacturing center in New Spain for *butacas*, called there *butaques*, which were exported from there (via Veracruz) to other American and Spanish cities. Campeche had a long tradition in fine furniture making. In the seventeenth century it was famous for its production of bone and ebony inlaid furniture, especially writing desks, boxes, and other types of small case furniture. In the following century, solid mahogany and marquetry furniture, in particular chairs, settees, and case furniture such as chests of drawers, constituted the more relevant furniture export items. From the 1780s onward we find large numbers of *butaques* in cargo manifests from Campeche to Veracruz. In some cases these shipments reached Veracruz in transit to other destinations such as Havana, New Orleans, Maracaibo, La Guaira, and several cities in Spain. We should note that for most of the colonial period, because of Spanish monopoly trade policies, the trade of the Gulf was centralized in Veracruz, with mandatory stops for any type of ship involved in trade activities. Export furniture was shipped from Campeche to Veracruz in small boats; then, once administrative procedures had been performed, it would be sent to the final destination in larger ships. For example, a cargo manifest dated January 25, 1792, from Veracruz to La Guaira (Venezuela), lists five *butaques* on the brig *El Victorioso*.[37] Another record dated January 27, 1789, from Veracruz to Cádiz and Málaga (both in Spain), lists "2 [boxes] with 2 *butaques*" on the frigate *Prosperidad*.[38] A Mexican *butaque* (incorrectly classified in the book) illustrated in Rafael Doménech and Luis Pérez-Bueno's *Muebles Antiquos Españoles* (1921) confirms *butaque* trade with Spain (fig. 17).[39]

Because Veracruz was the principal port of the region, in addition to fine furniture from Campeche, we find furniture in transit from other

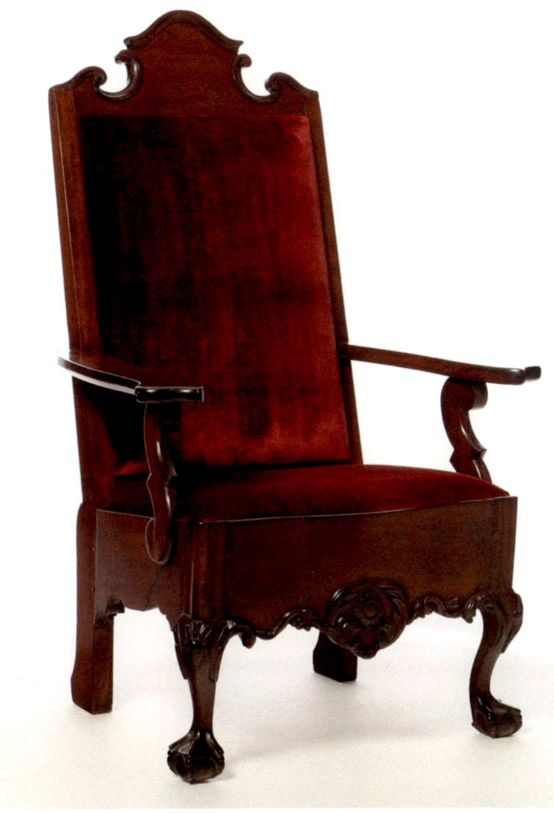

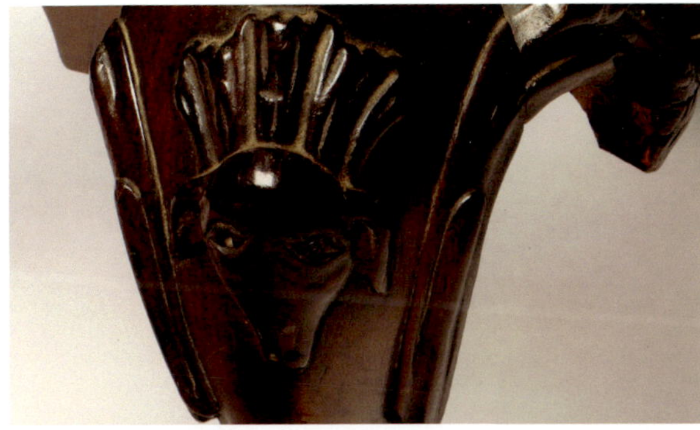

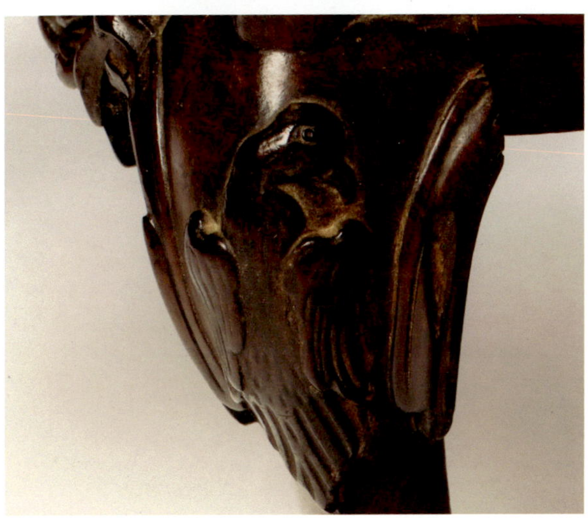

Fig. 15. *Butaca*. Venezuela, mid-18th century. Mahogany with new velvet upholstery, 45¼ × 28⅜ × 16$^{15}/_{16}$ in. (115 × 72 × 43 cm). Colección Patricia Phelps de Cisneros, 2004.7.

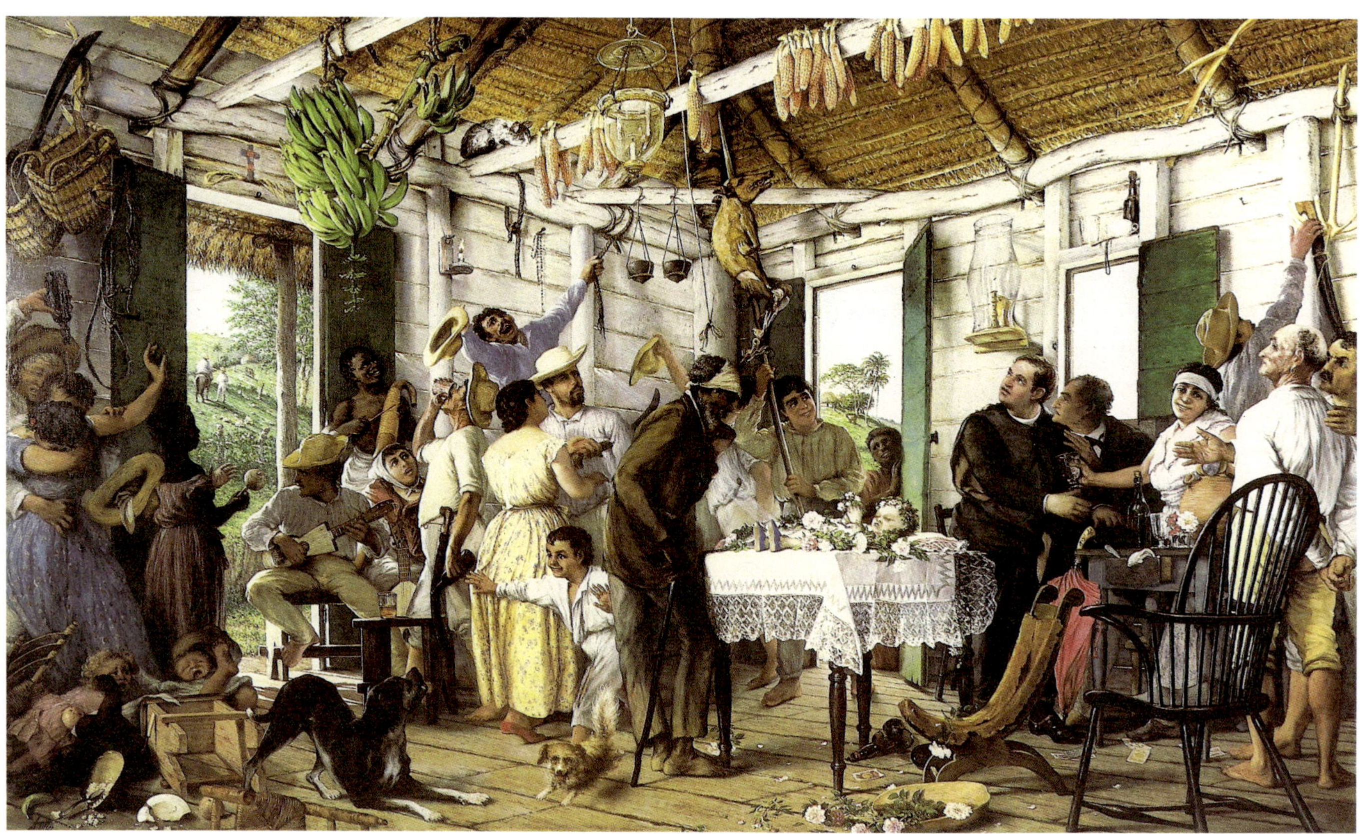

Fig. 16. Francisco Oller (Puerto Rican, 1833–1917), *El Velorio* (The Wake). Puerto Rico, 1893. Oil on canvas, 96 x 156½ in. (224 x 397.5 cm). Museo de Historia, Antropología y Arte de la Universidad de Puerto Rico. From *Francisco Oller un Realista del Impressionismo: exposición organizada por el Museo de Arte de Ponce en conmemoración del sesquicentenario del natalicio del pintor puertorriqueño Francisco Oller (1833–1917)*, edited by Marimar Benítez (Ponce: Museo de Arte de Ponce, 1983), 18, pl. 10.

places with outstanding traditions in fine furniture making such as Havana.[40] Cargo manifests also record materials and tools required for furniture making, including wood (mahogany, cedar, ebony, and ordinary wood), precious materials such as tortoiseshell and mother of pearl, and tools for the trade.[41]

Surprisingly, *butaques* have not yet been found in early colonial Mexican inventories, nor do early twentieth-century Mexican furniture scholars such as Manuel Romero de Terreros and Abelardo Carrillo y Gariel mention them as part of domestic New Spain furniture repertoires.[42] That may indicate that the production and consumption of *butaques* during the colonial period in Mexico was a local phenomenon most likely restricted to the Gulf Coast, especially to the ports of Campeche and Veracruz. More recent Mexican scholarship on the subject is scarce. Carlos de Ovando illustrates a Campeche *butaque* in "Taracea Mexicana," a 1969 article in *Artes de Mexico*, but he does not refer to it in the text (fig. 18).[43] Teresa Castelló Iturbide briefly mentions *butaques* in "Mueble Popular," a chapter in the 1985 catalogue *El Mueble Mexicano*.[44] Iturbide links them to the *jamuga*, a Spanish women's chair-saddle of Moorish origin.

Butacas further evolved in the first quarter of the nineteenth century, when numerous local variations on the type appeared. During that period most Latin American nations gained independence from Spain, and local societies experienced deep changes as a result of the war and their new independent status. In opposition to the old and rigid Spanish protocol, identified with the ancient regime, less formal social customs that allowed more relaxed seating postures on semipublic occasions were adopted. Although still relegated to private spaces and used for informal occasions, the *butaca* gained further popularity and conquered additional spaces at home. In those years *butaca* design was also influenced by the expansion of trade and immigration in the Caribbean, to include the United States, France, England, Prussia, and other European powers. European and North American cabinetmakers who immigrated to the Spanish Caribbean in this period, and brought with them their own decorative repertoires, produced *butacas* and related types that often blended local traditions with their own. For example, Joseph P.

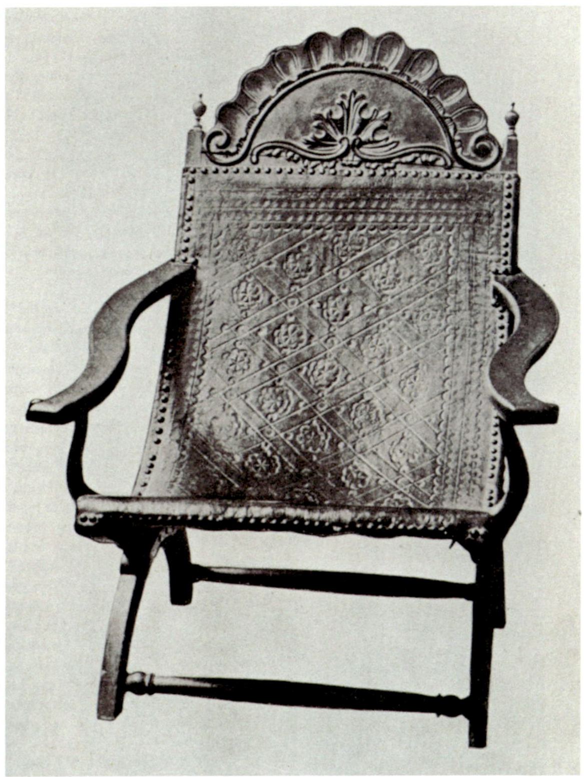

Fig. 17. *Butaque*. From Rafael Domenech and Luis Pérez Bueno, *Muebles antiguos españoles* (Barcelona: M. Bayés, 1921), pl. 12, fig. 29.

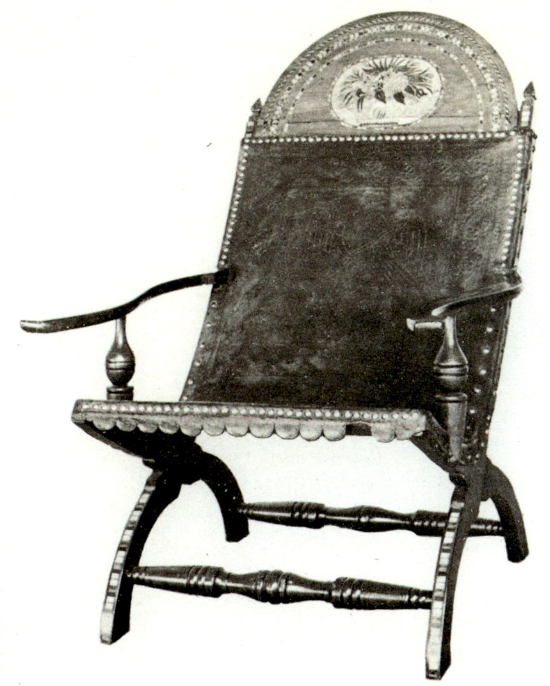

Fig. 18. Campeche *Butaque*. From Carlos de Ovando, "La taracea mexicana," *Artes de México* 118 (El mueble mexicano) (1969): 73.

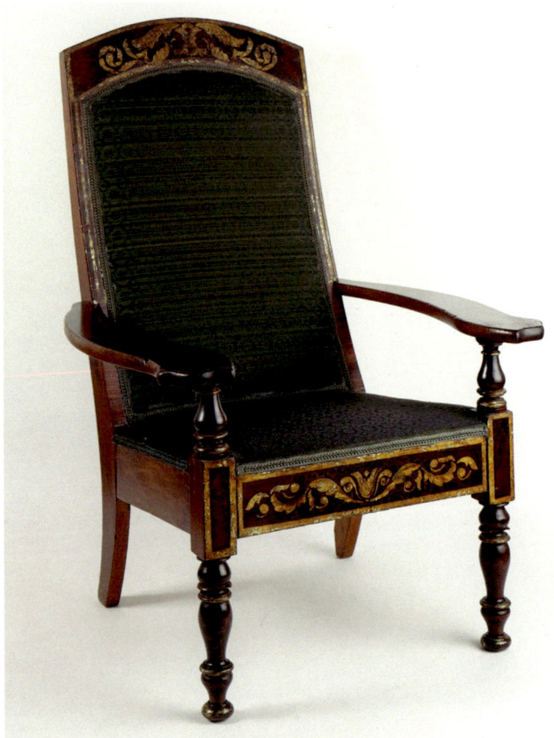

Fig. 19. Joseph P. Whiting (American, 1800–1849), *Butaca*. Caracas (Venezuela), circa 1823–1845. Mahogany and mahogany veneer on Spanish cedar, gilt stencil decoration, with new horsehair upholstery, 35⁷/16 × 27 × 27¹/16 in. (90 × 68.5 × 69 cm). Colección Patricia Phelps de Cisneros, 2000.62.

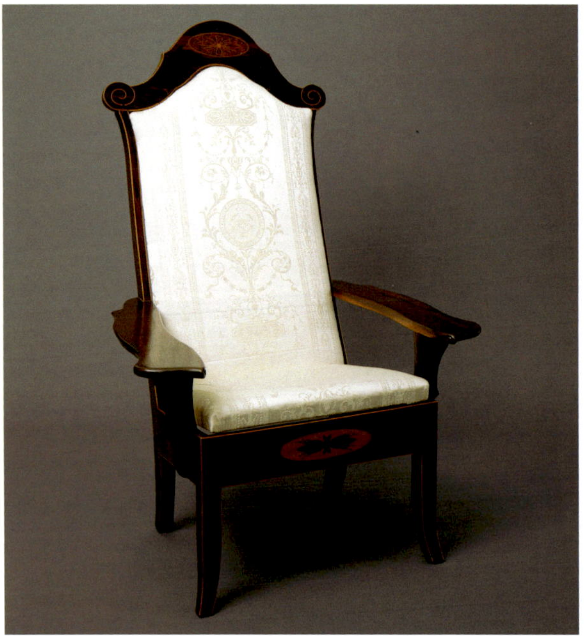

Fig. 20. *Butacón*. Caracas (Venezuela), c. 1825–1835. *Gateado* wood and veneers of *gateado* wood and *carreto* wood over a Spanish cedar base, with new cloth upholstery over frames, 45¹/4 × 28⅜ × 16¹⁵/16 in. (122 × 79 × 49.5 cm). Colección Patricia Phelps de Cisneros, 2001.77.

Whiting (1800–1849), from Baltimore, who was active in Caracas between 1824 and 1845, produced *butacas* decorated in the Baltimore fashion with gilded and stenciled classical figures and foliage (fig. 19).[45] Another foreign cabinetmaker active in Caracas in the same period—possibly from Prussia or northern Europe—manufactured Empire style marquetry *butacas* with upholstered seat and back, like the example illustrated here (fig. 20).[46]

It was in the same period, at the turn of the nineteenth century, that the *butaca*, under the name *boutaque* or Campeche chair, landed in the United States and became part of southern plantation material culture. The type, appreciated because of its comfort, gained enthusiasm among prominent Americans such as Thomas Jefferson, who owned one of the chairs.[47]

The twentieth century saw a growing interest in *butacas*, particularly during the interwar period, which was certainly linked to the flourishing of Neocolonial and Neobaroque architecture movements that spread across Latin America. Although most examples from this period are Neocolonial adaptations of antique pieces, some examples of a slightly later date, such as the ones designed by the Cuban-born Mexican designer Clara Porset (1932–1981), William Spratling (1900–1967), an American designer active in Mexico, and the Venezuelan designer Miguel Arroyo (1920–2004), are more overtly modern versions of the type.

Perhaps relegated to quiet private corners, the shade of verandas, or the intimacy of bedrooms, *butacas*, stripped of ancient ritual connotations, and without announcing their illustrious history, still endure in many Caribbean homes as witnesses of the transforming hybrid material world in the region.

Notes

[1]For more on this subject, see Cybèle Trione Gontar, "The Campeche Chair in the Metropolitan Museum of Art," *Metropolitan Museum Journal* 38 (2003): 183–212; Gontar, "The American Campeche Chair," *Magazine Antiques* 175, no. 5 (May 2009): 88–95, Gontar, "The Campeche Chair in Louisiana," in *Furnishing Louisiana: Creole and Acadian Furniture, 1735–1835*, ed. Jessica Dorman and Sarah R. Doerries (New Orleans: Historic New Orleans Collection, 2010), 330–343, and Gontar, "Spanish Chairs in the New Republic," *Magazine Antiques* 176, no. 4 (Summer 2010): 78–82.

[2] Alexander von Humboldt and Aimé Bonpland, *Personal Narrative of Travels to the Equinoctial Regions of the New Continent during the Years 1799–1804*, trans. Helen Marie Williams (London: Longman, Hurst, Rees, Orme, and Brown, 1818), 3:283–284.

[3] Manuel de Yangues and Mathías Ruiz Blanco, *Principios y reglas de la lengua cummanagota, general en varias naciones que habitan en la Provincia de Cummana en las Indias Occidentales* (Burgos: Juan de Viar, 1683), 93.

[4] Carlos Duarte, *Grandes carpinteros del período hispánico venezolano* (Caracas: CANTV, 2004), 112.

[5] "Silla grande muy baja y tendida. Ella y su nombre son de procedencia Americana." See Real Academia Española, *Diccionario de la lengua castellana por la Academia Española* (Madrid: Imprenta de D. Francisco María Fernández, 1843), 118.

[6] Real Academia Española, *Diccionario manual e ilustrado de la lengua española* (Madrid: Espasa-Calpe, 1927), 318.

[7] Carlos Duarte, *Un asiento venezolano llamado butaca*, exhibition catalog (Caracas: Centro de Arte La Estancia: Acción Cultural PDVSA, 1999), 7.

[8] "El primero que la comenzaba era el señor, y en tanto que él la hacía todos callaban; tomada su cohoba (que es sorber por las narices aquellos polvos, como está dicho), y tomábase asentados en unos banquetes bajos, pero muy bien labrados, que llamaban duohos (la primera sílaba luenga)...." See Bartolome de las Casas in Ramón Pané and José Juan Arrom, *Relación acerca de las antigüedades de los indios: el primer tratado escrito en América* (Mexico City: Siglo XXI Editores, 1974), 113.

[9] For further reading on *duhos*, see Joanna M. Ostapkowicz, "To Be Seated with 'Great Courtesy and Veneration': Contextual Aspects of the Taino Duho," in *Taíno: Pre-Columbian Art and Culture from the Caribbean*, ed. Fatima Bercht and Estrellita Brodsky, exhibition catalog (New York: El Museo del Barrio, 1997), 56–67, and Henri Lehmann, "Un 'duho' de la civilisation Taino au Musée de l'Homme," *Journal de la Société des Américanistes* 40 (1951): 153–162.

[10] See note 8.

[11] I am grateful to Peter N. Miller for sharing this information with me.

[12] Galeotto Cey, *Viaje y descripción de las Indias, 1539–1553*, ed. José Rafael Lovera, trans. Marisa Vannini de Gerulewicz (Caracas: Fundación Banco Venezolano de Crédito, 1995), 113. English translation by the author.

[13] Francisco de Tauste, *Arte y bocabulario de la lengua de los indios Chaymas, Cumanagotos, Cores, Parias y otros diversos de la Provincia de Cumana o Nueva Andalucia: con un tratado a lo ultimo de la doctrina christiana y catecismo de la doctrina de nuestra Santa Fe traducido de castellano en la dicha lengua Indiana* (1680; Leipzig: Julius Platzmann, 1888), 7.

[14] *[Vocabulario] de Aspanyol y Guaraúno*, 1789, Lenguas de América, Manuscritos de la Real Biblioteca, 1:441–452, Royal Library, Madrid.

[15] Bernal Díaz del Castillo, *Historia verdadera de la conquista de la Nueva España* (Barcelona: Círculo de Lectores, 1971), 111.

[16] Enrique Otte, *Las perlas del Caribe: Nueva Cádiz de Cubagua* (Caracas: Fundación John Boulton, 1977), 507, 511.

[17] Humboldt and Bonpland, *Personal Narrative of Travels*, 2:180.

[18] Colección Patricia Phelps de Cisneros, accession number 2005.21.

[19] Arístides Rojas, *Obras escogidas de Arístides Rojas* (Paris: Garnier Hermanos, 1907), 769.

[20] Roque Bárcia, *Primer diccionario general etimológico de la lengua española* (Madrid: Álvarez hermanos, 1881–1883).

[21] Juan Röhl, *Historias viejas y cuentos nuevos, colección de escritos sobre historia, arte y otros temas* (Caracas: Elite, 1946), 101; Angel Rosemblat, "Butacas y butaques," *Papel Literario de El Nacional*, August 27, 1953; Carlos Manuel Möller "La arquitectura y el mobiliario venezolano en la época de la independencia," *Revista Shell* 8, no. 34 (March 1960), republished in Carlos Manuel Möller, *Páginas coloniales* (Caracas: Editorial Arte, 1962), 172–181; Carlos Duarte, *Un asiento venezolano.*

[22] The print was originally found by Carlos Duarte, a Caracas scholar. It has been subsequently reproduced in several texts on the subject. See Gontar, "The Campeche Chair in the Metropolitan Museum of Art," 200, and Gontar, "The Campeche Chair in Louisiana."

[23] Alcide Dessalines d' Orbigny, *Malerische Reise in Süd- und Nordamerika: eine geordnete Zusammenstellung des Wissenswürdigsten von den Entdeckungsreisen ...* (Leipzig: Baumgärtners Buchhandlung, 1839), pl. 6, fig. 2.

[24] Alcide Dessalines d' Orbigny, *Voyage pittoresque dans les deux Amériques: Résumé général de tous les voyages . . .* (Paris: L. Tenré [etc.], 1836), pl. 6-3.

[25] " Les joueurs de harpe se tenaient mollement renversés sur une *buttaca* [sic] o chaise de prêtre, siége dont la forme est antérieure a la conquête, et qu'on assure avoir été trouvé dans le pays par les Espagnols." Ibid., 54. Translation by the author.

[26] See Jorge F. Rivas Pérez, "Observations on the Origin, Development, and Manufacture of Latin American Furniture," in *The Arts in Latin America, 1492–1820*, organized by Joseph J. Rishel with Suzanne Stratton-Pruitt, exhibition catalog (Philadelphia: Philadelphia Museum of Art; Mexico City: Antiguo Colegio de San Ildefonso; Los Angeles: Los Angeles County Museum of Art; New Haven: Yale University Press, 2006), 476–507.

[27] See Duarte, *Un asiento venezolano,* 4.

[28] Ibid., 7.

[29] Ibid., 8–9. Cuban *butaca* at the Brooklyn Museum, accession number 2011.58.1.

[30] On *butaca* upholstery see Duarte, *Un asiento venezolano,* 8–9.

[31] "El asiento de muchos de los indios de Venezuela consistía en un mueble, armado en forma de tijereta, cóncavo, y forrado de cuero; este era el antiguo butaquito, sin espaldar del que se hacia uso en las escuelas de niños. Mas tarde, este mueble tomó creces y se hicieron los butaques o butacones para las señoras ancianas." Rojas, *Obras escogidas*, 769.
[32] Carlos Duarte, *Mobiliario y decoración interior durante la época hispánica en Venezuela* (Caracas: Armitano Editores, 1996), 293. Translation by the author.
[33] Metropolitan Museum of Art, accession number 2000.451.
[34] Colección Patricia Phelps de Cisneros, accession number 2006.21.
[35] Colección Patricia Phelps de Cisneros, accession number 2004.7.
[36] Note also the height difference between the Spanish American *butaque* and the higher British American Windsor chair depicted next to it.
[37] *Gazeta de Mexico* 5, no. 3 (February 7, 1792): 119.
[38] *Gazeta de Mexico* 3, no. 45 (February 17, 1789): 249.
[39] Rafael Domenech and Luis Pérez Bueno, *Muebles antiguos españoles* (Barcelona: M Bayés, 1921), pl. 12, fig. 29. Juan José Junquera y Mato correctly identifies the type in his 1999 essay "Mobiliario," in *Artes decorativas II, Summa Artis: Historia general del arte*, ed. Alberto Bartolomé Arraiza (Madrid: Espasa Calpe, 1999), 45:399.
[40] For instance, a cargo manifest from January 27, 1789 from Habana to Veracruz on the frigate *Nsa. Sra. de la Concepción* lists "1 mahogany canapé." *Gazeta de Mexico* 3, no. 24 (January 20, 1789): 249.
[41] For example, a 1788 compilation of the cargo manifests from America to Spain from August 1759 to December 1787 lists 160,695 boards of mahogany and cedar, 96 of ebony, and 20,711 of ordinary wood, 469 arrobas and 9 ½ pounds of tortoiseshell, and 2 boxes of mother of pearl. *Gazeta de Mexico* 3, no. 32 (May 26, 1789): 317–318. Regarding tools, January 12, 1792, the ship *El Cazador* from Santander (Spain) to Veracruz listed "60 adzes and 250 carpenter's saws." *Gazeta de Mexico* 5, no. 2 (January 24, 1792): 11.
[42] Manuel Romero de Terreros, *Las artes industriales en la Nueva España* (Mexico City: Libreria de P. Robredo, 1923); Abelardo Carrillo y Gariel, *Evolución del mueble en México* (Mexico City: Instituto Nacional de Antropología e Historia, 1957).
[43] Carlos de Ovando, "La taracea mexicana," *Artes de México* 118 (1969): 73.
[44] Teresa Castelló Iturbide, "Mueble Popular," in *El mueble mexicano: historia, evolución e influencias*, ed. María del Carmen Aguilera García et al., exhibition catalog (Mexico City: Fomento Cultural Banamex, 1985), 103–114.
[45] On Joseph P. Whiting see Carlos F. Duarte, "El mobiliario de la época republicana en Venezuela," *Armitano Arte* 1 (December 1982): 11–42; Jorge F. Rivas Pérez, *El repertorio clásico en el mobiliario venezolano, siglos XVIII y XIX* (Caracas: Fundación Cisneros, 2007). This example is from the Colección Patricia Phelps de Cisneros, accession number 2000.52.
[46] On Venezuelan furniture from this period see Rivas Pérez, *El repertorio clásico.* This example is from the Colección Patricia Phelps de Cisneros, accession number 2001.77.
[47] Gontar, "The Campeche Chair in Louisiana," 183.

Women's Fashion in Colonial Buenos Aires

Susan Migden Socolow

Several problems make the study of women's fashion in colonial Río de la Plata a challenging endeavor. Chief among them is a paucity of visual sources. Unlike more mature viceregal capitals such as Mexico City or Lima, Buenos Aires has left us few paintings, drawings, or descriptions of colonial women's dress.

Thus, this discussion is based mainly on travelers' writings and a sample of dowries and inventories of women living in Buenos Aires during the eighteenth century. The documents reflect a range of women from different socioeconomic backgrounds and show change over time. But poor women, slaves, and indigenous women rarely owned enough property to appear in these records. Moreover, those relatively few poor women who drew up a will often failed to mention any items of clothing in their list of property.

Fashion in the Río de la Plata did not stand still. Historians have noted important stylistic changes in women's dress during the colonial period. Colonial fashion was based foremost on European models, reflecting both fashion in the mother country and that in other European countries. In the Río de la Plata (and probably in all of colonial Spanish America), different styles coexisted and complemented each other.[1]

From the founding of the colony, Spain provided the model for women's clothing. Spanish fashion was based on somber use of color and sobriety of line. Dark, long capes, wide skirts, and shawls were the hallmarks of this style. Most clothing was black or dark blue, offset by a white neck ruff and frilly sleeves. The complete dress for an elite woman consisted of a jerkin, which functioned as a rigid bodice and was held close to the body, and two skirts held in place by cords. The wide bottom skirt was made of anywhere from five to eight panels of a highly adorned fabric; it was covered by a simpler and more somber top skirt which could be either open or closed in front. In the Río de la Plata, two skirts were used on the street. The top skirt was removed in more private settings so that the richness of the underskirt could be appreciated. The well-dressed woman also wore a shawl or cloak, either silk or woolen serge (depending on the season), that covered part of her face and her body (fig. 1a). For gala occasions, the

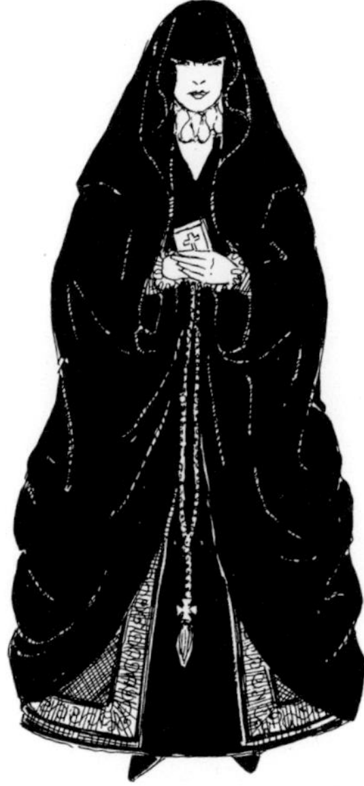

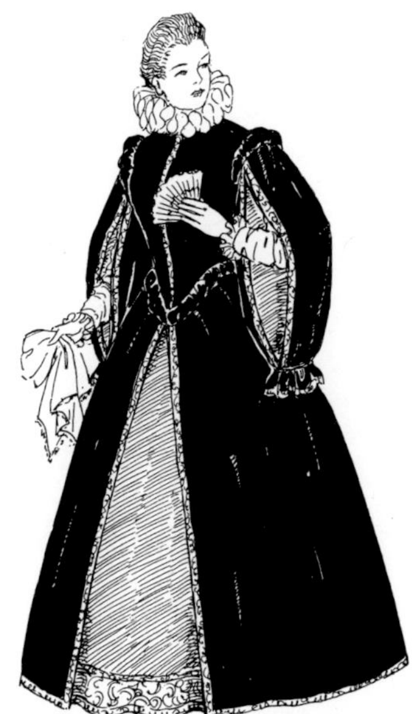

Fig. 1a. (left) Spanish dress of a young girl, dressed in black with a white ruff and sleeve frills and a cloak of fine black wool.
Fig. 1b. (right) A Spanish lady in a wasp-waisted corset, hoop-gown, hanging sleeves, and a lace-edged handkerchief.
From R. Turner Wilcox, *Five Centuries of American Costume,* 2nd ed. (New York: Dover, 2004).

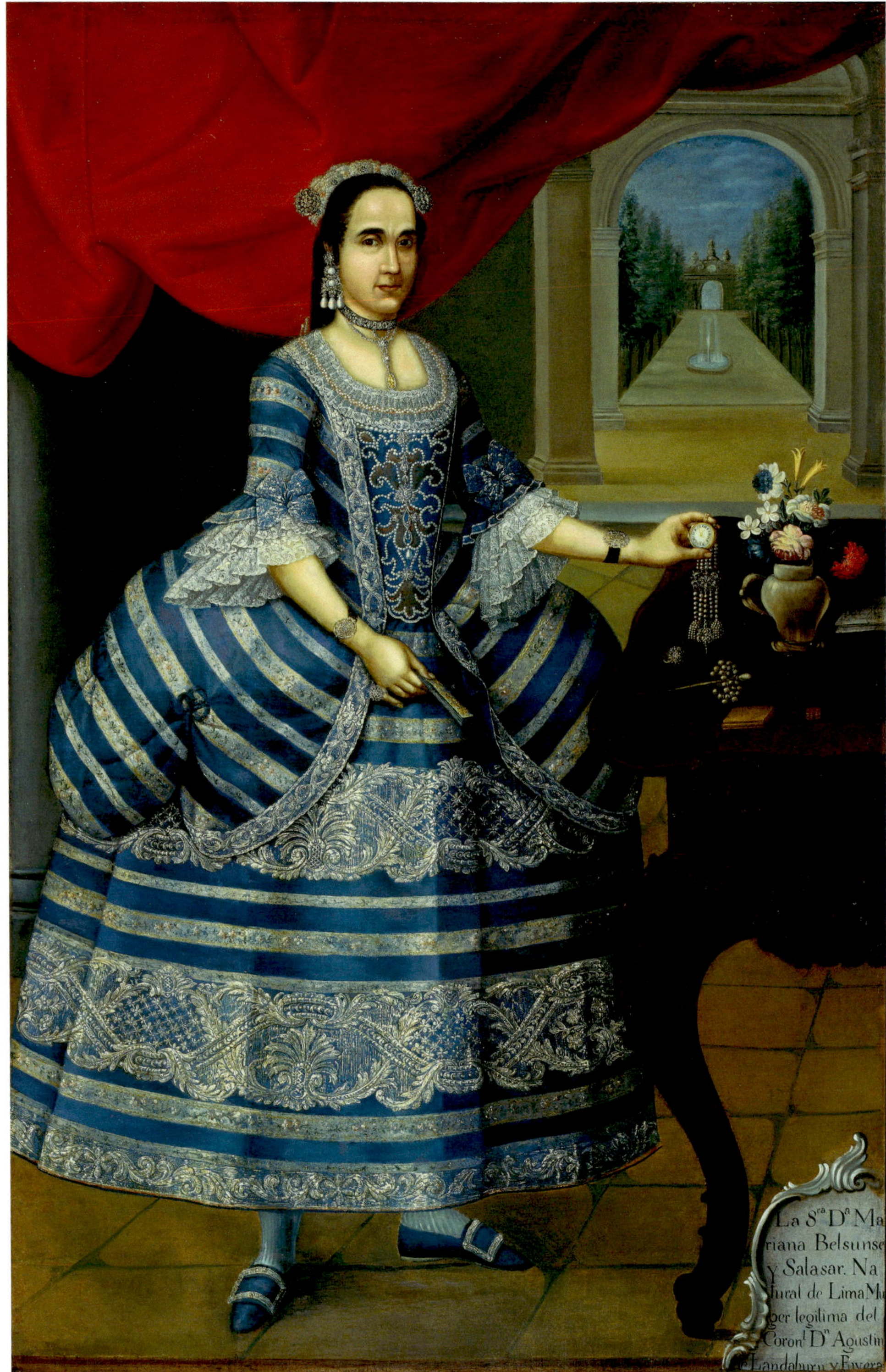

(Above and opposite) These two examples are of late 18th-century party dresses worn by elite *Limeño* women. Both paintings are similar in composition, and possibly were painted by the same artist.

Fig. 2a. The dress shown is embellished with copious amounts of lace. The shoes feature diamond buckles and match the color of the dress. The inscription in the cartouche to the lower right reads "La Sra. Da Mariana Belsunse y Salasar. Natural de Lima Mujer legítima de Coronel Agustín de Landaluru y Rivera." José Joaquín Bermejo (Peruvian, active c. 1760–92) or Pedro José Díaz (Peruvian, active 1770–1810), *Doña Mariana Belsunse y Salasar*. Peru, c. 1780. Oil on canvas, 78½ x 50 in. (198.4 x 127 cm). Brooklyn Museum, Gift of Mrs. L.H. Shearman, 1992.212.

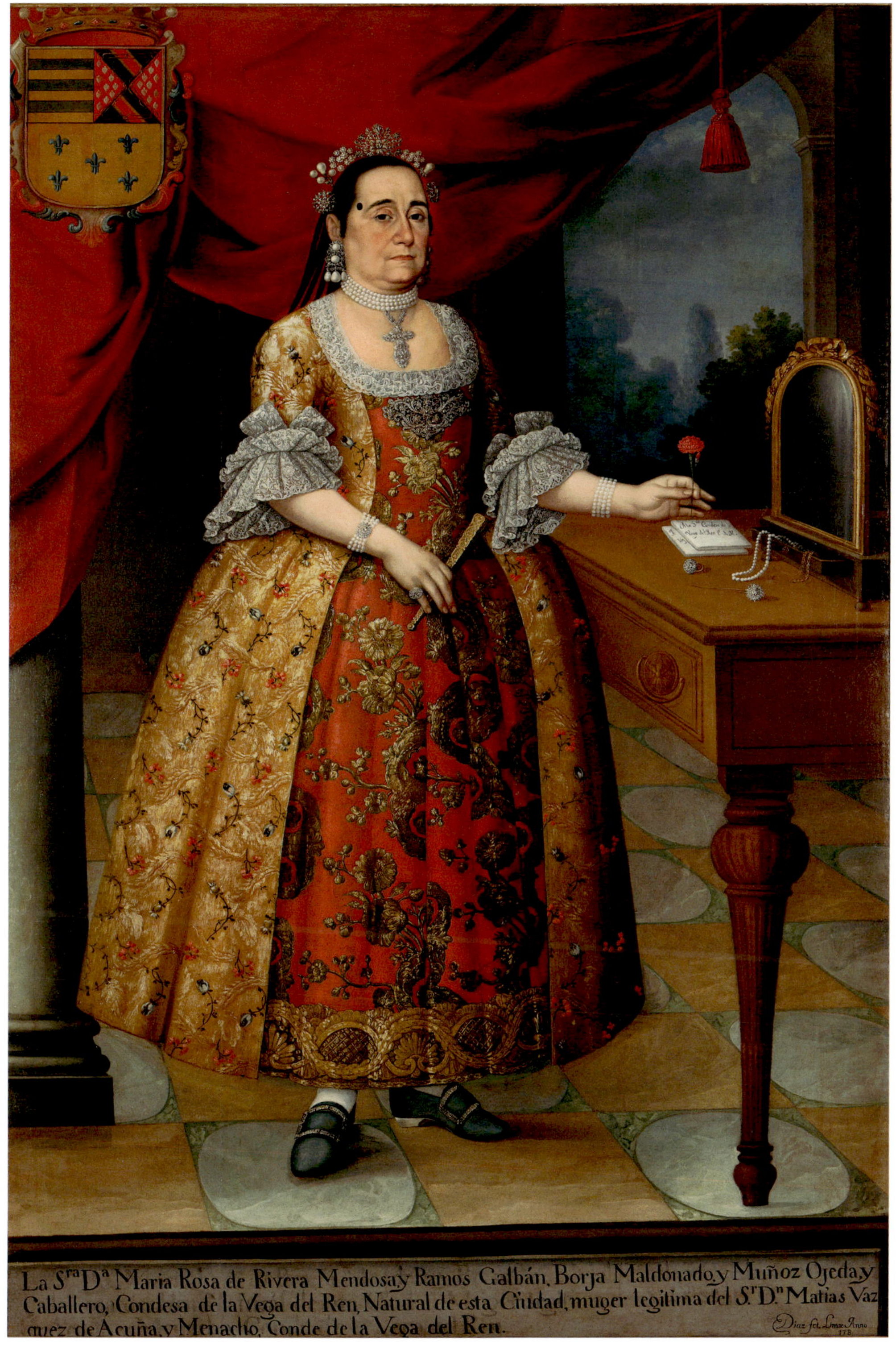

Fig. 2b. Portrait depicts a much older woman who has chosen more sedate brocaded satin for her costume. Pedro José Díaz (active 1770–1810), *Portrait of Doña María Rosa de Rivera, Countess of Vega del Ren*. Lima, Peru, c. 1780. Oil on canvas, 78¼ x 51 in. (198.8 x 129.5 cm). Marilynn and Carl Thoma Collection, Chicago, Illinois. Photo: Jeff Wells, Denver Art Museum.

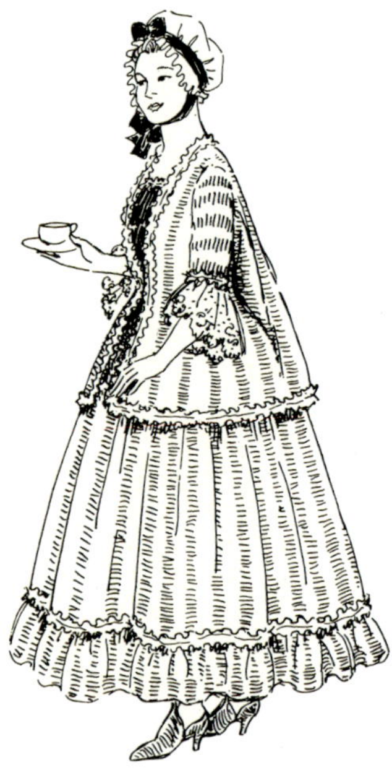

Fig. 3. French-style Watteau dress and matching sacque. From R. Turner Wilcox, *Five Centuries of American Costume*, 2nd ed. (New York: Dover, 2004).

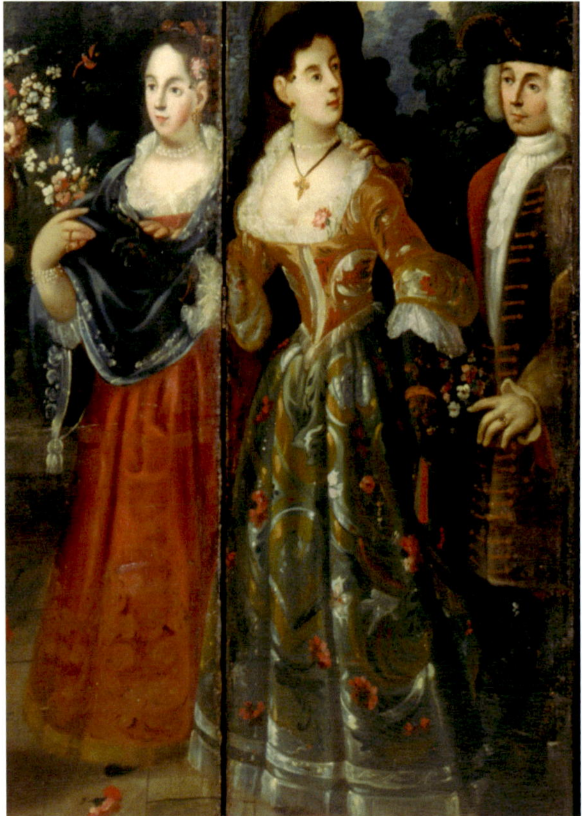

Fig. 4. The daytime dresses of the Mexican elite are made of elaborate fabrics trimmed in lace and feature décolleté necklines. (Detail) *Garden Party on the Terrace of a Country Home* folding screen. Mexico, c. 1725. Oil on canvas, 87 x 219 in. Denver Art Museum; Gift of Frederick and Jan Mayer.

Spanish style for women consisted of a neck ruff, a wasp-waisted corset, a farthingale or hoop-gown of velvet or cloth over satin, hanging sleeves topped with wings, white lawn undersleeves edged in lace, and a lace-edged handkerchief (fig. 1b). Examples of the modified Spanish style can be seen in two paintings from mid-eighteenth-century Peru (figs. 2a and 2b).

During the latter half of the eighteenth century, no doubt reflecting the period of Bourbon rule in Spain and Spanish America, French models became fashionable, especially for party clothing. The French style was based on the so-called Watteau gown, a dress with a wide back pleat flowing from the neck of the garment to its hem. These dresses emphasized a bosom pushed high by a corset. Attached to the corset below the waistline were small tabs with eyelets to which an underskirt, a small hoop, or embroidered petticoats could be laced (fig. 3).

In addition to the Watteau gown, the wide Spanish skirt was replaced by a shorter and less voluminous French skirt. In place of the Spanish jerkin, for her upper body a woman of fashion could wear a blouse wrap, a short-sleeved tunic, or, at home, a shorter version of the wrap called a *sevillé*. Jackets were increasingly made of rich, ornate fabrics such as brocade or undulating velvet (fig. 4). They were usually closed with laces or buttoned up the front. A flowing tail in back of the jacket varied from short to long; the longer lengths were often decorated at the lower edge with pearl tassels. Sleeve length also varied from elbow length decorated with ample ruffles to tight sleeves that ended at the wrist in a cuff closed with buttons.

French style introduced transparent fabrics, ornate fabrics reflecting the French Rococo, oriental themes and floral designs, lavish trimmings (fine lace, silver and gold embroideries, braids and ribbons bedecked in shining sequins), decorative handkerchiefs, and wide, plunging necklines. French style also featured a wider array of color than the Spanish black, ranging from pastels to vivid tones. Light blue, pink, carnation, pearl, and dawn blue, as well as turquoise blue, yellow, several reds, and greens were used widely in garments.

By the end of the eighteenth and beginning of the nineteenth century, as a direct result of the anti-monarchical French Revolution, there was a gradual rejection of all things French, and the adoption of elements of English style (figs. 5 a–c). Thus, French style was replaced with the silhouette of the Roman Republic in the form of the English robe, a frock of soft cotton. English-styled garments tended to be short-waisted, featuring a slim, shorter skirt, and several petticoats edged with frills showing below the skirt. English style was a simplification of French style using English textiles such as lawn, muslin, batiste, chintz, or light silk. In essence, English woven cloth came to replace luxurious French fabrics.

Changing fashion can be seen by comparing the garments listed in two inventories thirty-three years apart. The earlier document, the will of María Martínez,[2] drawn up in 1776, listed a black skirt with flowers and its shimmering cloak; three jackets (one of brocade, one of black velvet, and the third of green velvet decorated with gold); three petticoats (a red one embellished with silver, a taffeta one in the same color with a ribbon decoration, and another one in blazing red taffeta); and a green damask bustier with its silver hook, decorated with French stones in different colors. These garments, especially the three jackets and the three petticoats, closely reflected French fashion, as did the use of strong colors in the clothing (black, red, and green), the luxurious fabrics (brocade, velvet, taffeta, and damask), and the embellishment of fabric with silver adornments. But a Spanish element was still present in her black skirt and cloak.

The later list appeared in the estate inventory of the clothing of María Josefa Ruiz de Gaona, drawn up in 1809.[3] Doña María Josefa, wife of a Buenos Aires merchant (José Santos de Incháurregui), left a longer list of garments. Her wardrobe consisted of five skirts (one of satin with two rows of fringes, a second of satin with trimming, a white cotton skirt, a silk open-weave skirt with ruffles, and a skirt with pink trimming); nine blouses of French Brittany linen, two pink dressing gowns, four petticoats (one of pink open-weave silk; two taffeta petticoats, one pink and the other light blue; and another of pink Lyonnaise heavy taffeta); a cashmere shawl, and a used fur shawl lined with baize. Her more intimate wardrobe contained three robes (one of white satin with silk lace trimming, the same robe in black, and a third robe in pink with half sleeves), two silk bodices,

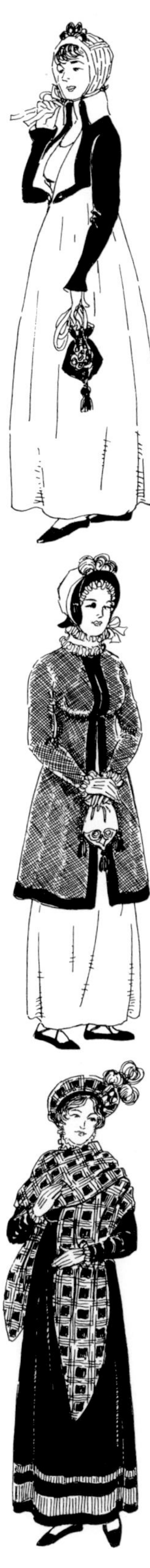

Figs. 5a–c. English walking costume of cloth coat edged in velvet and plain light-colored skirt (top); English white frock of twill muslin and short Spencer jacket (middle); English dress of cloth with plaid shawl and matching hat (bottom). From R. Turner Wilcox, *Five Centuries of American Costume*, 2nd ed. (New York: Dover, 2004).

two nightgowns of the same fabric, and twenty-two used handkerchiefs of various quality and design. This inventory reflects the use of lighter colors (white, pink, and light blue) and a greater variety of fabrics, frilled petticoats, and relatively less ornamentation on the garments.

Regardless of fashion, there were four ways to acquire clothing in colonial Buenos Aires: have it made by local tailors or seamstresses, purchase garments and ready-to-sew clothing in shops or general stores, make it yourself, or remake used clothing. These ways to obtain clothing more or less corresponded to one's social group, although according to Concolorcorvo, a Spanish visitor to the region in the 1770s,

> all the common people and a large part of the principal ladies do not provide any work for the tailors because the women cut, sew and decorate their dresses and other garments with perfection, for they themselves are inventive and skillful seamstresses. Without prejudice to the many others that today one considers to have great skill in Buenos Aires, I observed during several days the great art, discretion and talent of the beautiful and prolific Spanish woman Doña Gracia Ana, having seen her imitate the best sewing and embroidery that can be found in Spain and France.
>
> Middle-group women, and even the poor, women that I don't want to call second or third class, because they would get angry, do not only make and mend their own clothing, they also make that of their husbands, children and brothers ....[4]

The earliest traveler to remark on women's fashion was the Frenchman Martin du Bassin, who in 1708 wrote,

> The clothing of the women is more sumptuous than that of the men, and when they want to really shine they look very beautiful in their skirts of gold and silver cloth, mixed at times with colors, or skirts of silk and lovely brocades. On top of these garments, they wear a short masculine styled jacket done in a light fabric. As for their hair, they don't waste money as in France. Most Spanish ladies and the local women too, go about with their head uncovered and their beautiful hair braided in back. They protect their hair with a sweep of taffeta that falls almost to their ankles and which, gathered at the waist, forms a type of second dress with its squared, wide train, producing an effect that is very pretty. Over this taffeta cloak, they have a thin, transparent veil that they lower over their faces when they are walking in the street to protect themselves from the dust.[5]

According to Captain William Trotter, an American ship captain and smuggler who spent more than a month in Buenos Aires in the summer of 1800–1801,

> The genteel people of both sexes dress very gay and rich. The clothing is exceeding high [expensive]. They, in general, wear the best of super fine broadcloth and cashmere of all colours with the waistcoats richly embroidered with gold and silver. The ladies wear the finest Muslins, all white with openwork and sprig are their favorites. And the price is here not looked at, if the articles suit the taste of the buyer. They wear the finest of Muslin handkerchiefs and shawls, all of which have fancy borders of needle work round them. The hair, in general, is tied up on the top of the head and then braided down the whole length, the end turned up and secure with a comb and a ribbon bound around the head and the flowers then in bloom put in under the ribbon together with some aromatic sprig and which plenty are here to be found.[6]

In 1807, another visitor, the Englishman Samuel Hull Wilcocke, described the *porteño* women:

> The ladies of Buenos Ayres are reckoned the most agreeable and handsome of all South America. An English traveler has not, however, considered them as equally his countrywomen in beauty, yet the playful voluptuousness of their manners, conversation, and dress, contrasting with the gravity of taciturnity of the men, are described as calculated to please and

> designed to ensnare. The usual dress is of light silk, and fine cotton, with a profusion of lace, which rather displays than conceals the contour of the bosom. No head-dress or cap confines or encumbers their long and flowing black hair. A petticoat that descends scarcely below the knee, is lengthened by folds of deep lace, which seldom hide from view even the gold fringe of their tasseled garters. At their parties [assemblies], the brilliancy of their appearance excites admiration. A petticoat of various coloured taffeta, ornamented with gold lace, or fringe, richly tasseled, though carried down to the feet, is worn with sufficient art of conceal, and with sufficient address, at intervals to display, the shape of the leg, which is encircled by a silk stocking with a fanciful and luxuriant display of gold embroidery. Slippers of embroidered silk, or gold brocade, with diamond buckles or clasps, but unpleasantly high-heeled, and sometimes with heels of solid silver, adorn the feet. A kind of jacket of rich velvet is fitted tight to the shape, and laced or buttoned in front, with long points hanging down quite round the petticoat, and trimmed at the ends with pearl tassels. A cloak of gauze, or very fine cotton, hanging down to the ground, and occasionally fastened to the side by a clasp of jewels, is thrown over the shoulders, which would be otherwise wholly uncovered; as would also be the beauties of the bosom, but for the innumerable trinkets, jewels, necklaces and crosses with which its luxuriance is hidden; the principal of these is a large oval or round gold plate in the middle, connected with a broad ribbon that passes over the shoulders, and under the arms and returning, forms a sash round the waist. A head-dress, consisting of a handkerchief of gold gauze with braids of diamonds, or of chains of gold twisted in and out of their shining black hair, complete the attire of ceremony of a lady of rank.[7]

Emeric Essex Vidal, a 25-year-old Englishman in Buenos Aires from 1816 to 1818, provided one of the richest sources of descriptions and illustrations of the city. Borrowing heavily from the work of Wilcocke, he wrote,

> Within these few years, however, the ladies of Buenos Ayres have adopted a style of dress between the English and French, retaining indeed the mantilla, which still gives it a peculiar character. No hat or bonnet is ever seen on a native lady, unless she be on horseback, when she wears a beaver hat and feather, with a riding-habit.
>
> The mantilla is usually a piece of silk, about half a yard wide in the middle, and a yard and a half long, sloping to a point at each end, which is terminated by a tassel. It is worn over the head and back of the neck, and being brought over the shoulders, the ends hang down in front. No broche or pin is used to secure it; but it is artfully and gracefully confined under the chin by one hand, or by the end of the fan, without which no woman ever stirs, and made to conceal all but the eyes, or to discover the whole face, at the pleasure of the wearer.
>
> In cold weather, or when they pay visits at night, they use the rebozo, which is a piece of cloth a yard wide, as long as the mantilla, and worn in the same manner. The mantilla belongs exclusively to the mistresses; and the rebozo is always worn by servants, whose little vanity is displayed in this part of their dress, which they are solicitous to have, if possible, of the finest cloth and the most delicate colour, sometimes embroidered, or bordered with velvet or satin ribbons.
>
> ... The children of both sexes are generally beautiful, but after the age of fourteen years the girls cease to improve in appearance; they marry from that age upwards, and at twenty-five few retain any appearance of youth.
>
> ... The ladies of Buenos Ayres wear for ornament the natural flowers of a small bush which grows in the neighbourhood of that city, and is very common in the plains of Monte Video. These flowers are numerous, and instead of petals they have silken fibres, two or three inches long, of a very brilliant red. In its general figure the flower resembles a bottle-brush, and at Buenos Ayres it is called *plumerito*.[8]

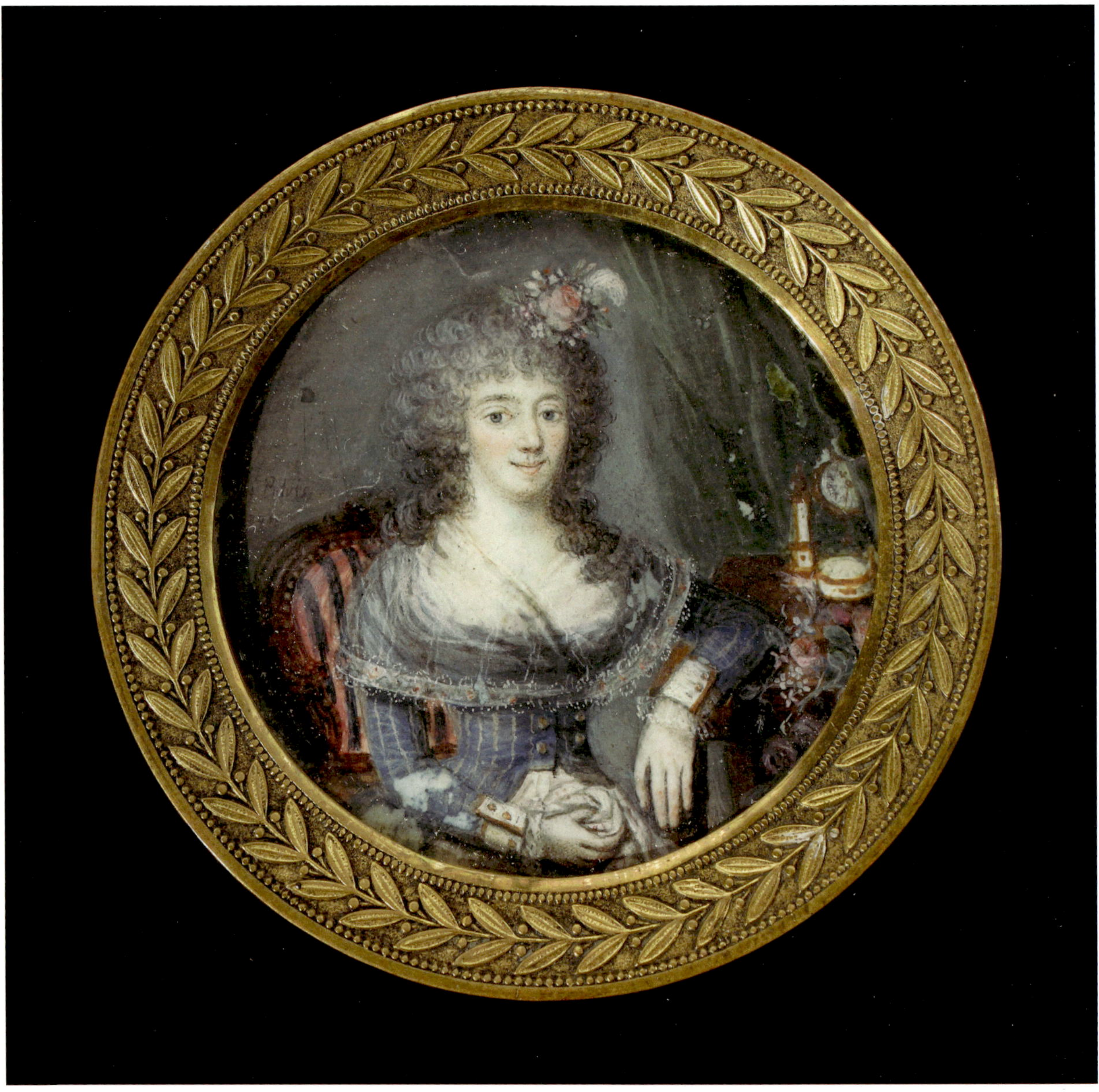

Fig. 6. Martín de Petris, *Portrait of Francisca Silveyra de Ibarrola*. Buenos Aires, Argentina, 1794. Miniature on ivory, $2^{1}/_{3}$ x $2^{1}/_{3}$ in. (60 x 62 cm). Museo Histórico Nacional, Buenos Aires, Argentina.

About five years later, Samuel Haigh, an Englishman who traveled in Argentina and Chile in the 1820s, remarked about *porteña* women and their dress.

> ... Most of the women are very good-looking, and some are perfect beauties in the exquisite outline of their features; their complexions are usually pale and incline to olive; the nose aquiline, and there is much sweetness about the mouth. The large dark eyes, for which the Spanish beauties are so deservedly celebrated, occasionally shoot forth a volley of expression not often to be met with in more northern climes. Their figures are extremely good, and they know how to set them off by great attention to gracefulness of carriage. They invariably dance and walk well, and with such apparent ease that not the least tinge of affectation is visible.... I must not omit to notice, also, the taste they display in the disposal of the glossy ringlets of their "raven hair," which is never disfigured by either cap or bonnet; the sole ornaments are a comb, and sometimes a flower, the dark clustering curls are left flowing on the neck down to the shoulders.[9]

Haigh was even more enraptured by the *porteñas* he encountered at a party.

> The evening dresses of the ladies are very tasteful, and I believe the French fashions are preferred. At balls and public assemblies, they are decorated with the finest fabrics that England, France, or the "georgeous East" can produce.
>
> There are in Buenos Aires both French and English tailors, cloak-makers, and milliners who follow close upon the best fashions in Europe: and there can be no doubt that it is a city considerable in advance of old Spain, with regard to modern stile and improvement; the manners of the inhabitants assimilate more to those of the two great capitals, London and Paris, than to those of their more sedate and silent neighbours the Dutch.[10]

How dependable are these sources? We can compare the descriptions given by Concolorcorvo and others with one of the very few visual sources for women's fashion in colonial Buenos Aires, a small portrait of Francisca Silveyra de Ibarrola, painted in 1794 (fig. 6).[11] We see Francisca wearing a snug blue striped jacket, with a deep round neckline. The cuffs of the jacket are edged in a gold-colored fabric, enhanced by the gold buttons on the cuff and the jacket itself. At the edges of the cuffs we can see lace trimming, lace that is echoed in the transparent lace shown around her shoulders. She is holding a handkerchief in her right hand. The little that we can see of the white skirt seems to have a figured design. Her hair ornament is made of flowers and a feather, not unlike those described by the travelers mentioned above. So too is her hair style, featuring clusters of curls flowing on the neck down to the shoulders.

In general, women's ability to amass clothing and jewelry was closely tied to the wealth of their fathers and husbands. Fathers were not required to dower their daughters. Husbands might squander the wives' dowry or inheritance, and fortune (or perhaps fortune hunters) could always change one's economic situation. In her will, Doña Magdalena de Arévalo made clear that her second husband had wasted all the property that her first husband had left her. She limited her profligate husband's inheritance to 300 *pesos*, included a lengthy list of the property that he had no right to claim, and added a codicil stating that "her husband should never have any say in her affairs after death because one can never depend on anything he says." Her meager clothing (a sugar-cane-colored velvet dress, another dress, a gauze cloak, and a fan made of openworked ivory) and one piece of jewelry, a topaz ring made of gold, were the only surviving remnants of a fine wardrobe.[12]

The amount and quality of the clothing a woman owned also reflected her social class. For elite women, their clothing might include everyday home garments, church clothing, street clothing, party or gala clothing, riding costumes, and mourning dress. Elite women would have at least a few skirts to wear at home, as well as frilly ruffled blouses, a whale-boned girdle that cinched the body, a sleeveless bodice jacket that closed with enameled buttons and secured the silk stockings with garters, white or black stockings, petticoats trimmed with fine Flemish lace, and finely adorned nightgowns made of Brittany linen, cotton, or muslin.

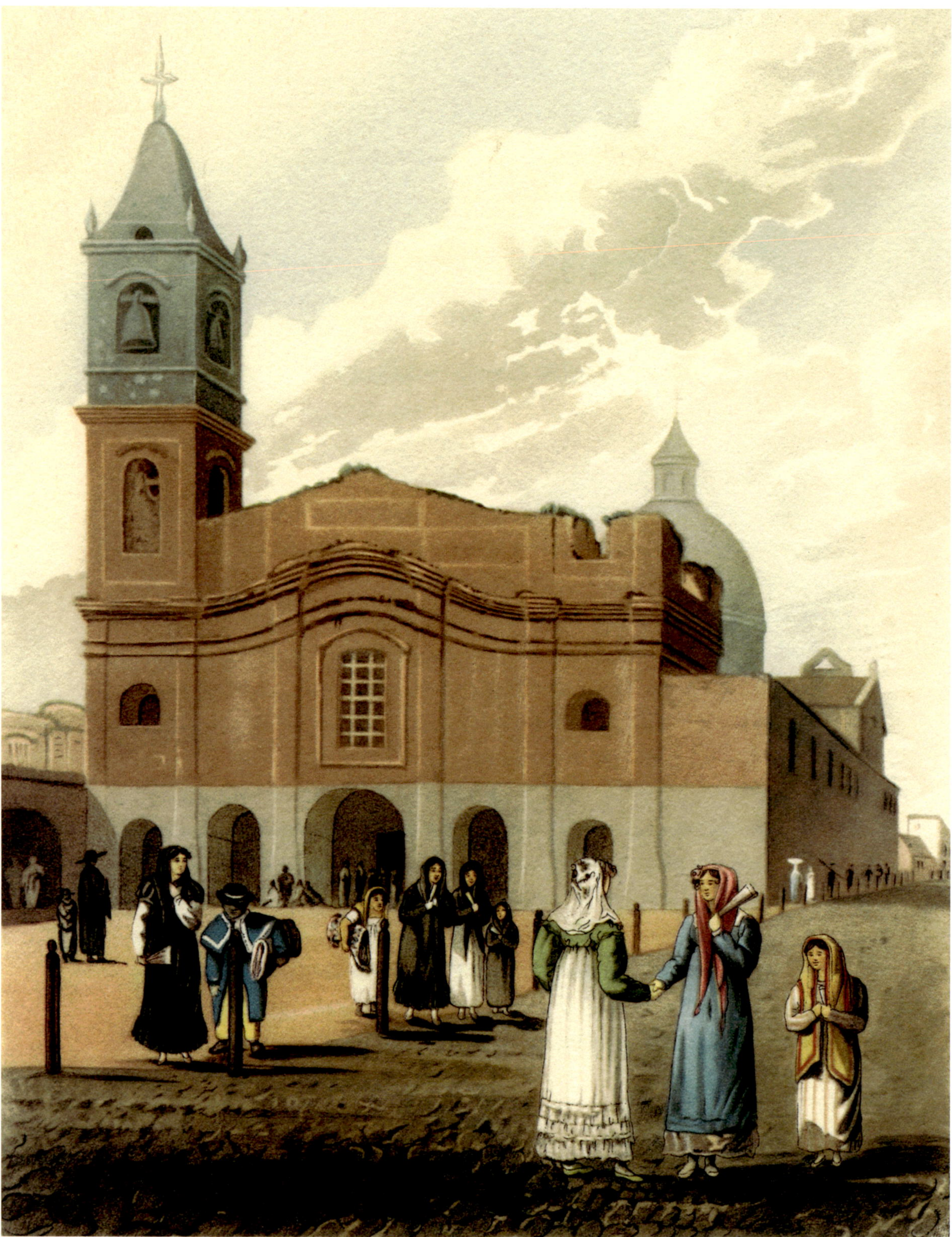

Fig. 7. Women's street and church clothing. A woman in church clothing is accompanied by a male servant or slave holding her church rug (left). A mother and her two daughters accompanied by a servant are leaving the church (center). Two women in street clothing are accompanied by a young servant (right). *Church of San Domingo, and Female Costumes.* From E.E. Vidal, *Buenos Aires and Monte Video* (London: R. Ackerman, 1820).

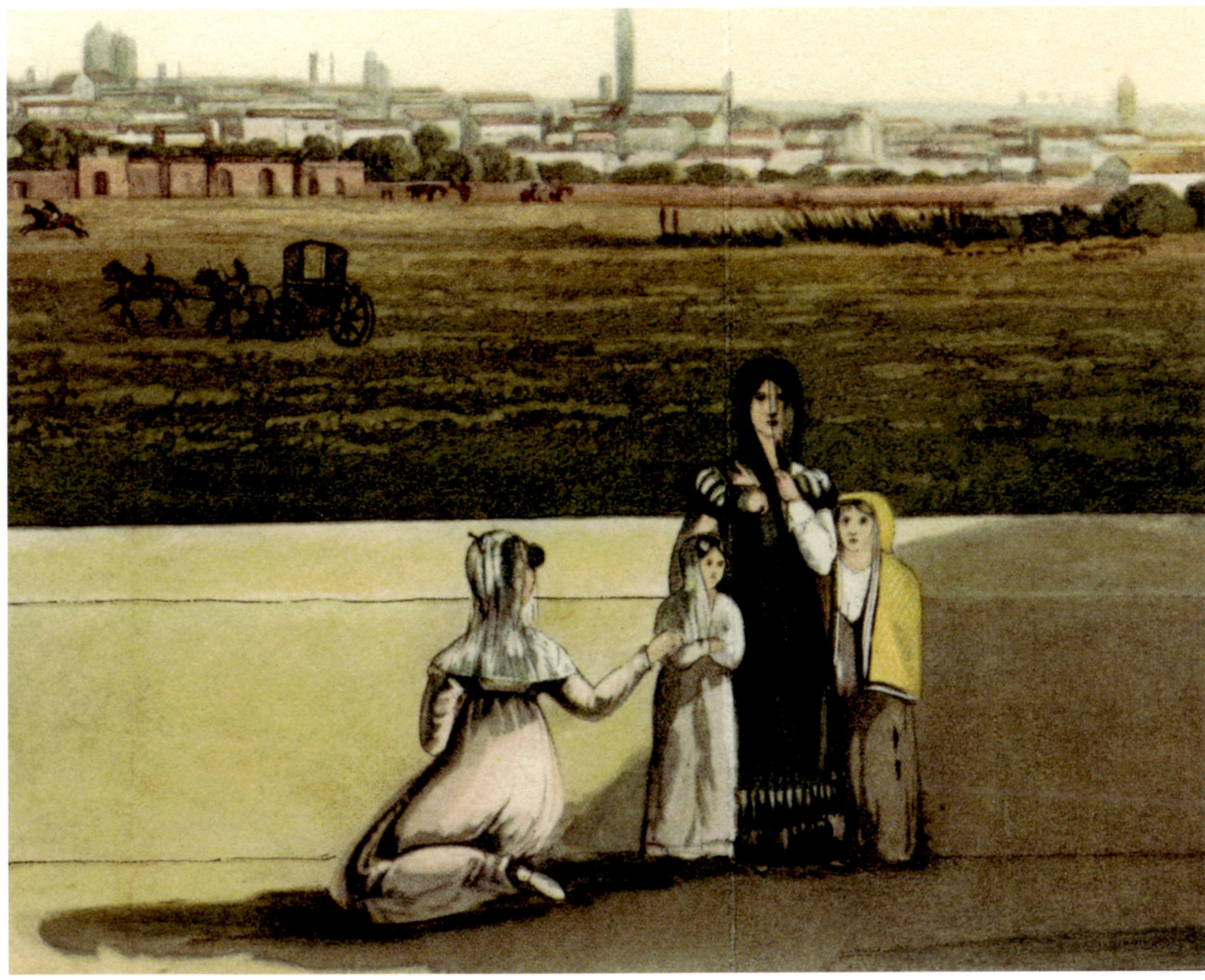

Fig. 8. A kneeling woman wearing a white mantilla and a standing woman wearing a black mantilla with her two daughters. (Detail) *General View of Buenos Aires from the Plaza de Toros*. From E.E. Vidal, *Buenos Aires and Monte Video* (London: R. Ackerman, 1820).

In his drawing of the Church of San Domingo, Vidal provides us with a good illustration of the church clothing worn by *porteña* women (fig. 7). In the foreground are exhibited the varieties of church and street costume. We also have two literary descriptions of what women wore to go to church. According to Vidal,

> The church dress had not undergone any change, but retains its Spanish character, and is always made of black silk, worn with white silk stockings and white satin shoes. It is considered indecorous to attend mass in coloured attire. Sometimes a white veil is used, and a little white is introduced into the dress of the young girls, whose clothes, being made in all respects like those of grown persons, give them an air of extreme formality.[13]

His fellow countryman Haigh also commented about the clothing women wore to attend Mass:

> A Spanish belle shows off to great advantage in the mass-dress, which is of black silk, perfectly adjusted to the shape of the body; a black or white lace veil is thrown gracefully over the head, and is sometimes contrasted with a bright-coloured silk shawl worn over the shoulders; the shoes and stockings are of white silk, for the Spanish ladies never wear either black or blue stockings, and they take great pride in their feet, which is not to be wondered at, as they generally display a very small foot and a neatly turned ankle.[14]

For church, a black velvet skirt trimmed with cotton or silk lace was mandatory in winter. In summer, a similar skirt in a lighter fabric such as silk was the fashion.

Street clothing featured a long jacket, a *mantilla*, and a *rebozo* or shawl—a rectangular piece of fine or medium weight wool decorated with ribbons that was wrapped around one's body (fig. 8). This shawl was a somewhat suspect garment because it could be used by a woman to act with impunity while covering her face.

Gala dresses most reflected the influence of European fashion. Among the dresses that were worn to the festivities celebrating the coronation of Carlos IV as king of Spain (1789) was a costume consisting of a rose-colored brocade French jacket and skirt, and another of a skirt and a pink bib with silver flowers, and an apron of gold raised work.[15]

Riding dress for women was usually a skirt, a blouse, and a vest or jacket. Also required for both men and women was a poncho, often embroidered or covered with decorative elements. Several types of poncho were found throughout *porteño* society, including long ponchos of heavy wool (the most expensive ponchos), short cape-like ponchos, ponchos of striped wool, and ponchos of double-faced wool. Ponchos were always made of cloth woven in the northwestern region of the viceroyalty.[16]

In spite of Concolorcorvo's opinion, most of the clothing worn by the elite women of Buenos Aires was increasingly produced by the numerous seamstresses of the city. Some garments were copies of foreign models; others were purchased ready to sew, such as the "fabric for a black church skirt, six panels wide with trimming consisting of a satin border" described in the dowry of Doña María de la Paz Lezica.[17]

The most detailed dowry found in colonial notary registers is that of 16-year-old Doña Flora de Azcuenaga, daughter of the powerful merchant Vicente de Azcuenaga.[18] On June 8, 1781, five days before her marriage to the merchant Don Gaspar de Santa Coloma, her parents registered and detailed her sumptuous dowry, valued at more than 20,000 *pesos*.[19] The new clothing gifted to her included underwear and three dressing gowns ("six petticoats of the genuine wide Brittany linen," "a dressing gown with a green-edged skirt, trimmed with fine lace," "another dressing gown, identical to that above but in pink," and "a silk brocade dressing gown and skirt, sea green"). There were also some everyday garments: "a suit of genuine wide Brittany linen, with flounces of fine cambric and a little Flemish lace at the borders," "a black satin skirt, with narrow lace trimming," "two jackets of smooth satin," "twelve shirts of genuine wide Brittany linen with sleeves of fine linen [valued at 7 *pesos* apiece]," and a gala "dress of silver and gold silk tissue, with its jacket and matching accessories". Other accessories included a pair of fine cambric ruffles with fine Flemish lace edges, two mantillas ("a black mantilla of embroidered silk serge" and "a white mantilla of silk serge and flowered silk"), "a wool gauze shawl with fine wide lace trim," "a pink cape open on both sides to put one's arms through," and three cloaks ("a cloak with bone lace," "one pink satin sleeveless cloak with silk lace trim," and "another satin sleeveless cloak lined with fur"). Lastly, Flora was given three handkerchiefs ("two fine cambric handkerchiefs with the same lace trim," "one handkerchief of silk serge with figured lace trim") and six aprons ("an apron of fine cambric with Flemish lace" and "five fine linen aprons"). The total value of her clothing, all garments made of the finest imported fabrics, was 1,208 *pesos*.

Flora's jewelry, an important accessory and adornment, was even more sumptuous than her clothing. She was given a set of diamond and gold jewelry; six diamond rings (a diamond ring set in gold; a topaz ring with diamond chips; a ring with three stones, the largest stone set among diamonds; a diamond ring with eight stones set in a circle, one in the center and two at the sides; another ring with ten stones set in a circle and one center rose-colored diamond; and a ring with two stones at the sides and one in the center); and a set of gold buttons set with diamonds for shirt cuffs. In addition she received two fans (one made of mother-of pearl with gold encrustations and the other of tortoise-shell), a topaz hair ornament with diamond chips, three strings of pearls, and four strings of Baroque pearls.

The most sumptuous pieces in her jewelry collection were made in Europe. One necklace, in the shape of a diamond branch with stems, flowers, and branches, contained more than 200 diamonds, including a 3¼-carat rose diamond, and was valued at 1,369 *pesos*. Another necklace, a double strand of silver with gold links, was embellished by two hanging pendants shaped like leaves and flowers, 180 pink slender diamonds, and six large diamonds in the center of the piece. It was worth 777 *pesos*.

A tiara, worth 884 *pesos*, was made of silver and gold, and again used a leaf and flower motif. In the center was a bird placed on a gold trunk and covered with 135 rose-colored diamonds, with an almond-shaped diamond hanging from its beak, and a ruby eye. Several large diamonds embellished the piece, the largest of which weighed 2¼-carats. A pair of chatelaines (waist ornaments), again using the trunk, leaf, and flower motif, was set with 160 slender rose diamonds and two larger stones. Lastly, Flora was given a rosary containing 5 ounces of new gold, described as having seven heavy beads mounted in gold, smaller beads of marbled glass, and a mother-of-pearl cross. This collection of extraordinary jewelry was worth 3,773 *pesos*, 5 *reales*—three times as much as Flora's clothing.

Flora Azcuenaga was not the only elite young woman to be dowered, but no other dowry came near the opulence of hers. For example, in 1780 Doña María Magdalena Carrera, about to marry Don Martín de Alzaga, a Basque merchant resident in Buenos Aires, received more than 19,000 *pesos* in furniture, slaves, and household goods, but was given only "a woman's dress of blue silk with silver adornment made up of a jacket and a skirt" worth 75.2 *pesos*.[20]

María Magdalena did receive some jewelry: a matching set of gold jewelry including a cross and bracelets with entwined table and rose diamonds (60 *pesos*); a ring with two flat diamonds and a damaged emerald in the middle (8 *pesos*); another ring with a topaz in the middle and ten diamonds adorned with leaves (18 *pesos*); and a ring of openwork brass encrusted with silver with three brilliant diamonds set in gold (240 *pesos*).

Urban women of middling condition owned far more modest clothing, although there was great variation within the group. (figs. 9–10). Prosperous middling women such as Doña Luisa Barbosa, widow of the successful ship captain Vicente Pérez de Otalora, left lavish wardrobes. Upon her death in 1700, Doña Luisa left a woman's blouse made of new wide Brittany linen with cuffs embroidered with silk; a dress skirt and a bodice of old wool with flowers embroidered in gold thread; a piece of blue cotton cloth in which the dress above was wrapped; a new blue bodice of camel hair and wool; some white Brittany linen underpants embroidered with coarse thread from an agave plant; a black ribbed silk jacket without buttonholes; an old jacket of double-shaded taffeta; a used cotton combing towel; a new black shawl of double taffeta; two new cloaks; an old beaver hat; an apron of green wool from Naples

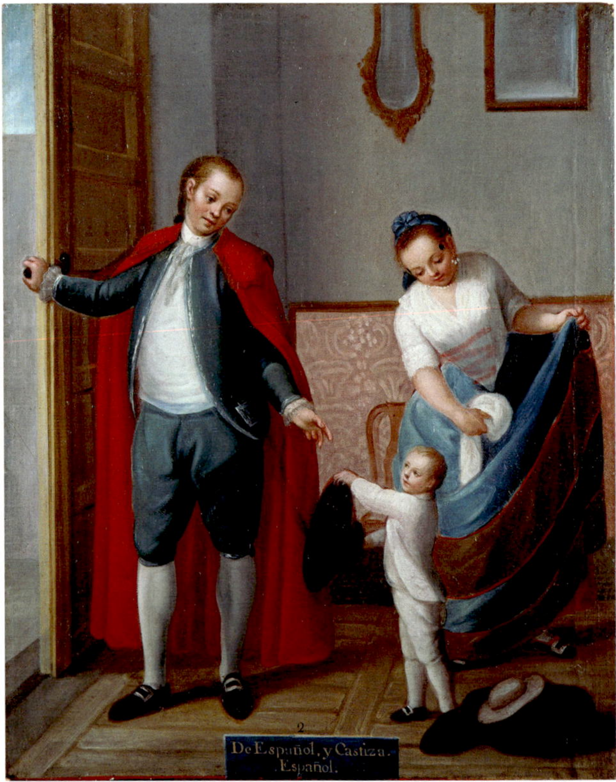

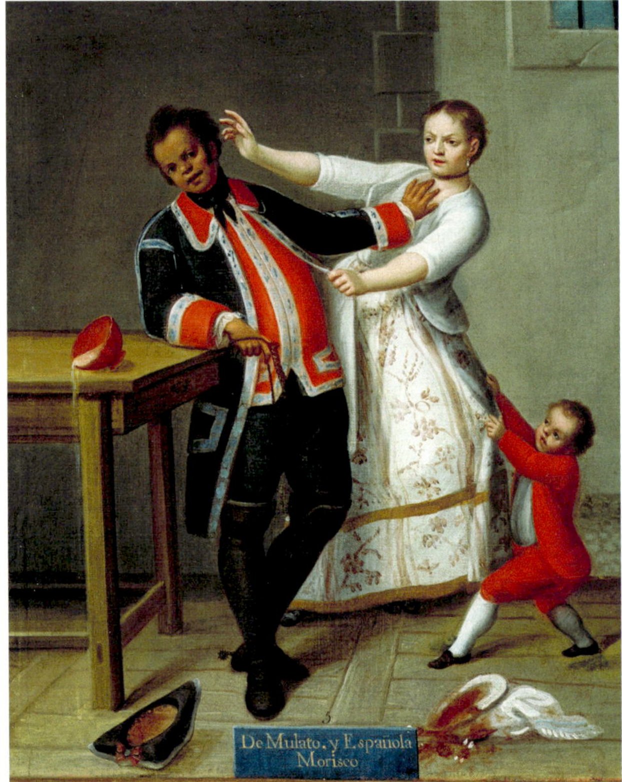

From a series of sixteen *casta* paintings by Francisco Clapera. Mexico, c. 1785. Oil on canvas, each canvas measures approximately 20 1/8 x 15 5/8 in. Denver Art Museum; Gift of Frederick and Jan Mayer, 2011.428.
Fig. 9. (top) *De Mulato y Española, Morisco*. The woman's lavish dress suggests that this is a prosperous middle-group couple.
Fig. 10. (bottom) *De Español y Castiza, Español*. An example of the dress of a middle-group woman.

decorated with wide lace embroidered with fine silver and fine gold thread; a used blue skirt of camel hair with false lace edging; a green camel hair and wool skirt with fine gold lace; a red apron from Castile with fine gold lace; six doublets (a woman's black doublet made of Castilian baize, another new doublet made of white cotton sheeting, a used white doublet of Brittany linen with sleeves of Cambray, another doublet of Brittany linen with white Flemish lace, another new doublet made of dimity, a cut of white Brittany linen for a doublet); a pair of new Brittany plain linen gloves; and four handkerchiefs (two handkerchiefs of fine French linen covered with blue embroidery, a used linen handkerchief with fine points, and a new linen handkerchief with no lace trimming). Her jewelry consisted of a gold crucifix with a pendant adorned with pearls and blue enamel, a gold ring with eight medium-sized pearls, a double strand of red beads, another double strand of smaller red beads, a ring with three stones, some small gold earrings, a pair of small gold earrings with pearls and two false blue stones, and a gold lighter with pearl buttons.[21]

In addition to this generous collection of clothing and jewelry, Doña Luisa also had a collection of fabrics and findings probably inherited from her late husband. These included a large pile of new Chamberg lace; a stack of Brittany linen edged with Lorena lace; four yards of new white lace, six inches wide; fourteen yards of Lorena lace; fourteen ounces of white thread; half a pound of Flemish thread; half a gross of black silk buttons; three-fourths of a pound of fine silver lace; ten yards of blue ribbon; a bodice of new baize; and some old short sleeves of Cambray lace.

Doña Luisa's wardrobe clearly shows that Buenos Aires was involved in foreign commerce (lace from France, silk from China) well before the free trade regulations of 1778. In theory, until the end of the eighteenth century, Buenos Aires was not supposed to participate in transatlantic trade. Instead, goods being sent to Buenos Aires were to be shipped from Seville or Cádiz to Havana, transshipped to Portobelo, unloaded and moved across the isthmus of Panama on mule back, reloaded onto ships in Panama City, and transported to Cartagena and on to Lima, one of the three officially recognized points of trade in the Americas. From Lima, these Buenos Aires-bound goods were again carried overland, this time on llamas, through the Peruvian Andes to Potosí and Charcas and then via Salta and Córdoba to Buenos Aires.

This long, circuitous route was time-consuming and costly. It was also frustrating for a city that sat on the edge of the Atlantic Ocean. Within years of the second founding of the city, its inhabitants began to trade extra legally with Brazil, the Iberian Peninsula, and eventually the rest of Europe and the world, usually working closely with local authorities who were more than willing to turn a blind eye for a price.

Candy maker Ana María González, another middle-group woman, at the time of her death in 1765 owned a green skirt of camel hair and wool, a deep red skirt of the same fabric, a chintz skirt, and a buttoned jacket of deep red closely woven cloth, a yellow cloak with silk undulating ribbons, a jacket, fabric for a velvet jacket, a bib of silver *lamé* in three sections, a smock of flowered fine linen, a supporting garment of common cloth, a white poncho, three handkerchiefs of fine linen, three-and-a-half yards of lace, and a fan, as well as a pair of silver buckles and a pair of gold earrings with pearls, garments not unlike those worn by the woman in figure 10.[22]

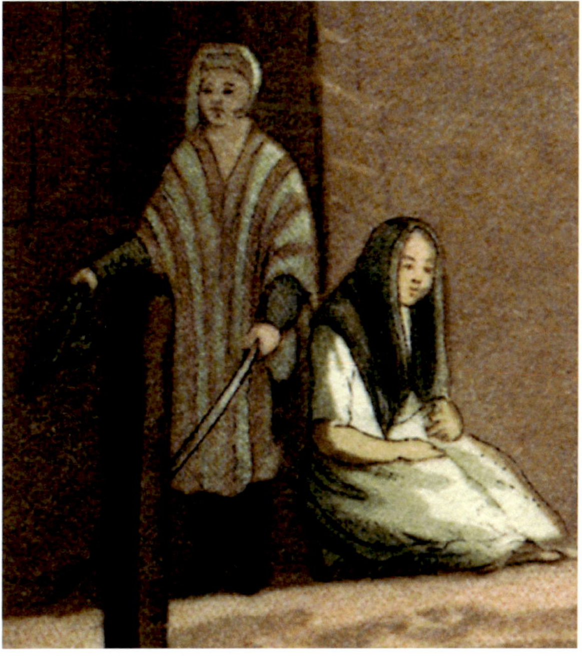

Fig. 11. A poor woman reduced to begging is dressed in modest clothing. (Detail) *Beggar on Horseback*. From E.E. Vidal, *Buenos Aires and Monte Video*, (London: R. Ackerman, 1820).

A less affluent member of the middle group, Doña María Isabel Rodríguez, wife of the owner of a small farm (*quinta*) not far from the city, owned "five old blouses, five handkerchiefs for the face and nose, a used bodice, two used petticoats, three used colored skirts, a black skirt with a silk fringe for church, a black thin wool cloak, a pair of ordinary ruffles, three summer bathrobes in different colors, a red thin wool shawl, two pairs of used white silk stockings, and one pair of used shoes" when she died in March 1797.[23] Doña Ana María Rodríguez, wife of the *pardo* (mulatto) violinist Francisco Pozo, left even fewer garments when she died in November of the same year. Her clothing consisted of two skirts of coarse cloth, a robe of the same fabric, a thin wool shawl, a used blouse, and a used pair of petticoats.[24]

Poorer women purchased ready-made garments sold in urban and rural general stores (*pulperías*). Here the quality of the fabric was more important than the cut of the garment, although this clothing was of rougher quality fabric (fig. 11). They also remade clothing from used garments.

Doña María Rosa Rocha, thrice married widow and the owner of a small *estancia* and some cattle in the Pago de la Matanza, mentioned in her will that she had owned "some jewelry of used metal that I sold in order to provide for my children." Although she mentioned no clothing or jewelry in her will, she had previously given "a new yellow damask skirt" as a marriage gift to one daughter, and another marriage gift of a complete mourning costume that she had used when she was widowed and some earrings to another daughter.[25] Upon her death in 1764, Eugenia Basualdo, wife of a middling rural ranch owner in Las Conchas, listed a ring worth 2 *pesos* and some silver buckles worth 4 *pesos*.[26] The lack of any mention of clothing in the inventory of her goods suggests that all her garments were too old to have any value.

This was not unusual. Poor Spanish women often failed to mention any items of clothing in their wills. The urban street vendors, washerwomen, both slave and free, and the rural poor owned even fewer garments (figs. 12–16). Doña María

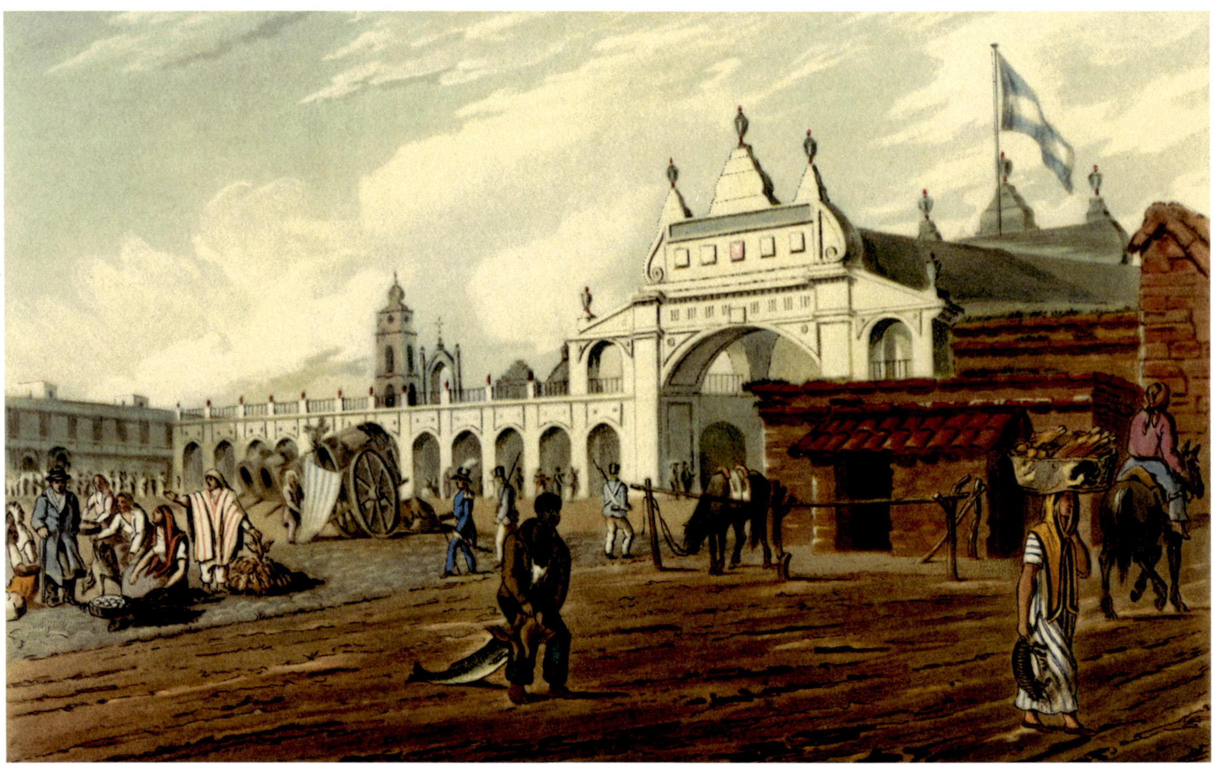

Fig. 12. On the left, market women dressed in plain skirts and blouses are selling eggs, partridges, and armadillos. To the right, a servant carries her purchase (an armadillo) in her right hand while balancing a basket of bread and fruit on her head. Her dress and stockings suggest that she works for an affluent family, but her head scarf is similar to those of the market vendors. (Detail) *Market Place*. From E.E. Vidal, *Buenos Aires and Monte Video*, (London: R. Ackerman, 1820).

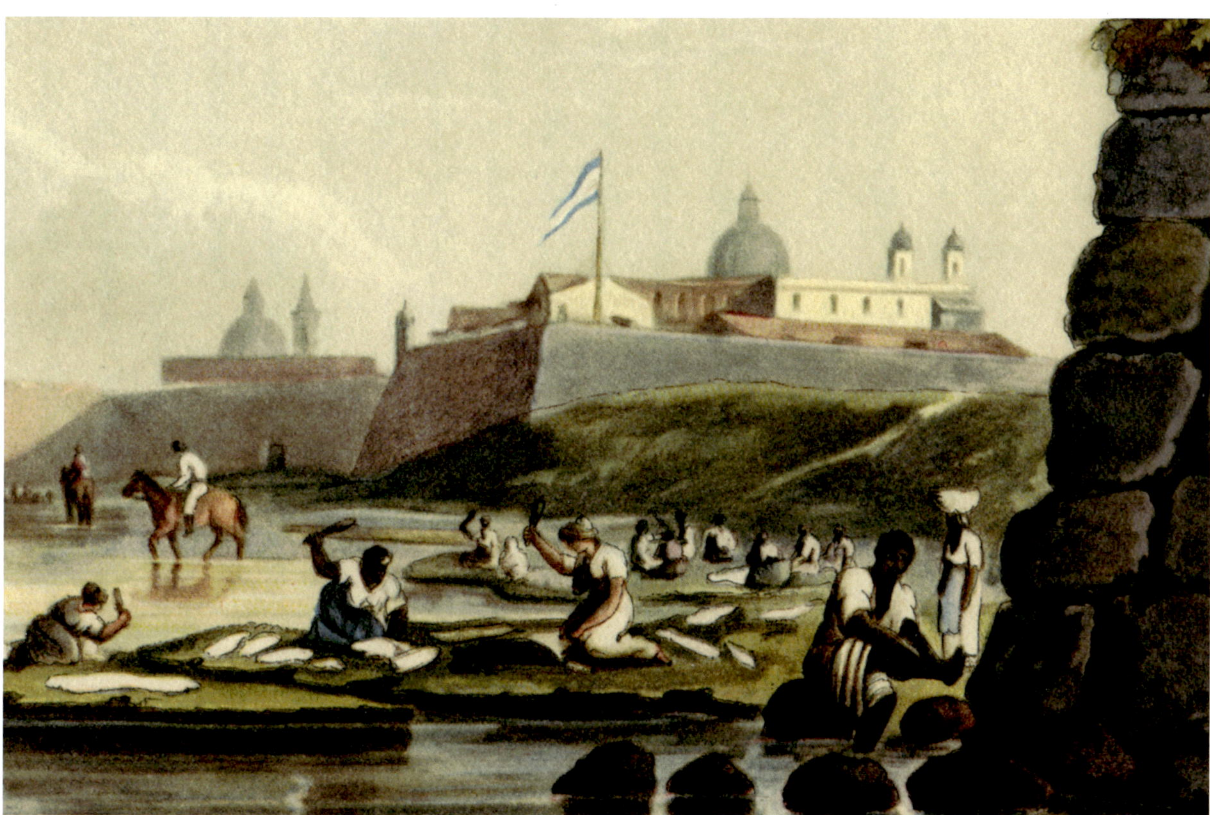

Fig. 13. Black and white washerwomen beating clothing in the river beneath the fort. (Detail) *The Fort*. From E.E. Vidal, *Buenos Aires and Monte Video*, (London: R. Ackerman, 1820).

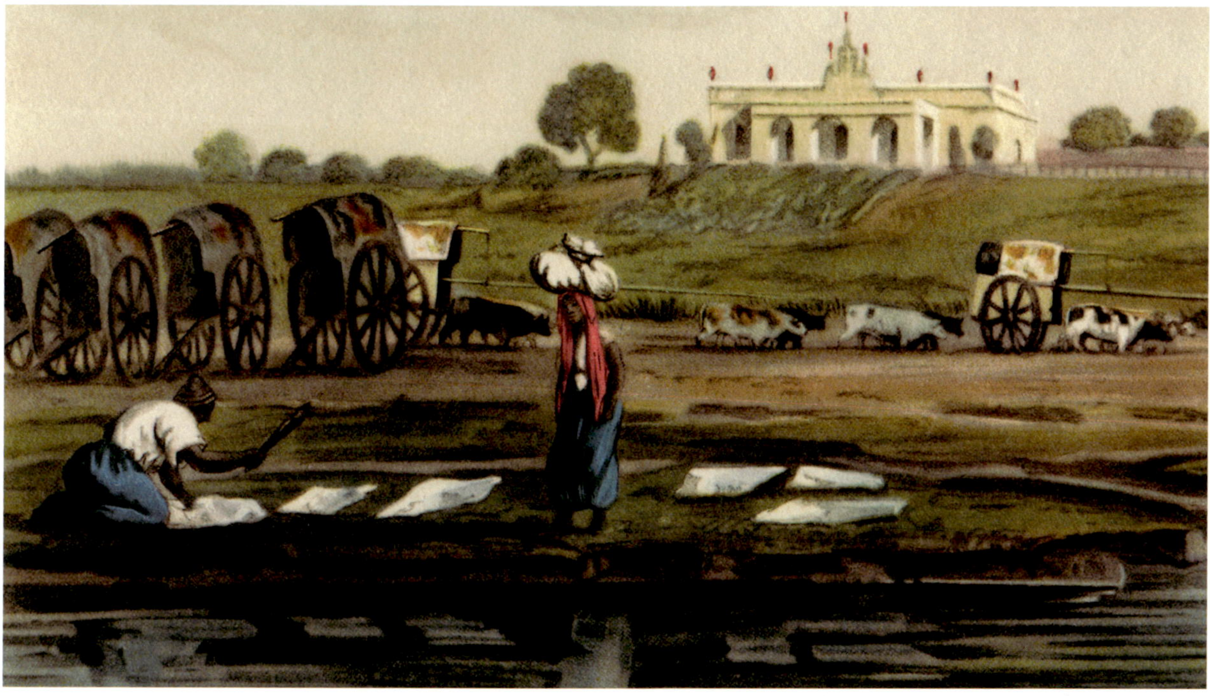

Fig. 14. One woman beats the clothing, while a second carries a bundle of more clothing on her head. Both are dressed like the washerwomen in Buenos Aires. (Detail) *Washerwomen in an* estancia. From E.E. Vidal, *Buenos Aires and Monte Video*, (London: R. Ackerman, 1820).

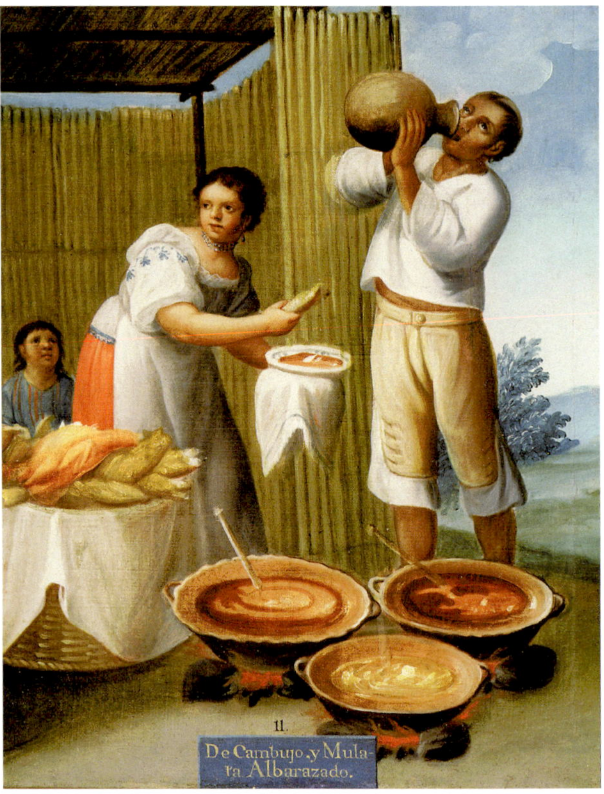

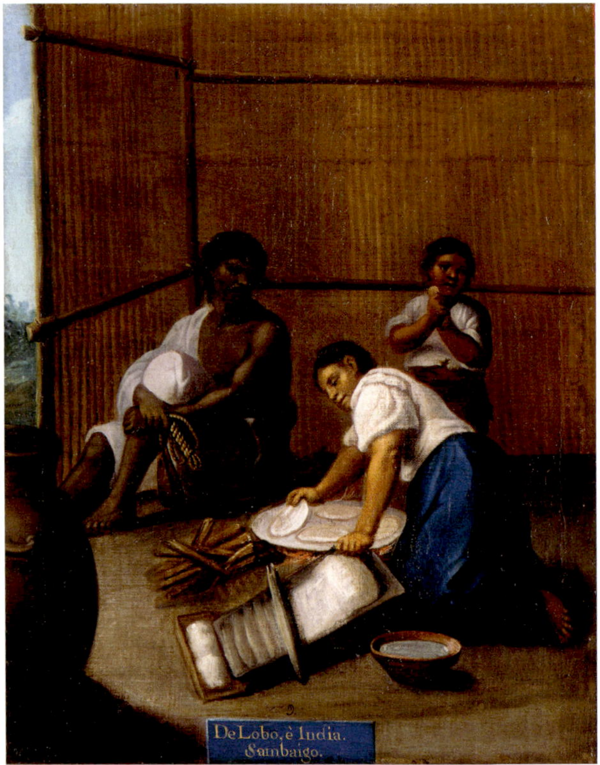

From a series of sixteen *casta* paintings by Francisco Clapera. Mexico, c. 1785. Oil on canvas, each canvas measures approximately $20^{1}/_{8}$ x $15^{5}/_{8}$ in. Denver Art Museum; Gift of Frederick and Jan Mayer, 2011.428.

Fig. 15 (top). *De Cambujo y Mulata, Albarazado.* A market vendor dressed in an embroidered blouse, skirt, and apron.

Fig. 16 (bottom). *De Lobo y India, Sambaigo.* A poorly dressed Mexican tortilla maker at work, while her husband and child look on. The family lives in a straw hut with a mud floor.

Alberta Cisneros de Pérez of Luján, the wife of a poor herdsman and mother of two small children, left only one garment, a silk bodice (*un corpiño de seda*) valued at one *peso*, when she died in 1787 (fig. 17).[27]

Like the poor, older women tended to list several "used" garments among their possessions. The wealthy widow Doña María Josefa Ruiz owned a large house "in the old fashion" in the Merced neighborhood of Buenos Aires, a small house along the heights along the River Plate, and a small farm in the Santa Recolección neighborhood. Among her clothes were a skirt made of plain black satin with old trimming, a used cotton skirt of fabric from India, three old bodices given to the servants, two pairs of unusable silk stockings, two old pairs of cotton stockings also given to the servants, and a used silk gauze smock.[28]

From time to time, women's wills inadvertently contain indirect information about clothing and jewelry. Such a case is that of the will drawn up by Petrona Cavezas, an unmarried woman who left her entire estate to set up chaplaincies to pray for her soul. Deeply religious, in her will Petrona also left the Dominican convent "an undressed statue of Saint Catalina, virgin and martyr," as well as "three silk dresses for the saint, including one, adorned with red lace, and a palm leaf of flowers (the insignia of virginity), a string of fine pearls, a gold cross with some emeralds and a false topaz jewel in the middle surrounded by false pearls, and silver flowers."[29]

Clothing, always a mark of social status, continued to serve as a status symbol after death. Both male and female members of the third orders, religious institutions tied to monasteries and convents, requested burial in the "sacred habit of the order." Thus when Doña Magdalena de Arévalo, widow of the late Don Lorenzo Pérez and wife of Don José Cernadas, drew up her last will and testament, she specified that she be buried in the Church of the Santo Domingo Convent in the "habit of its venerable third order as a member of that order that I am."[30] Two months later, Doña Juana Francisca de Rocha, wife of Don Vizente Porsel de Peralta, also drew up her last will and testament. The second clause of that document requested that she "be buried in the Church of the convent of Our Mother and Lady of Mercy in the

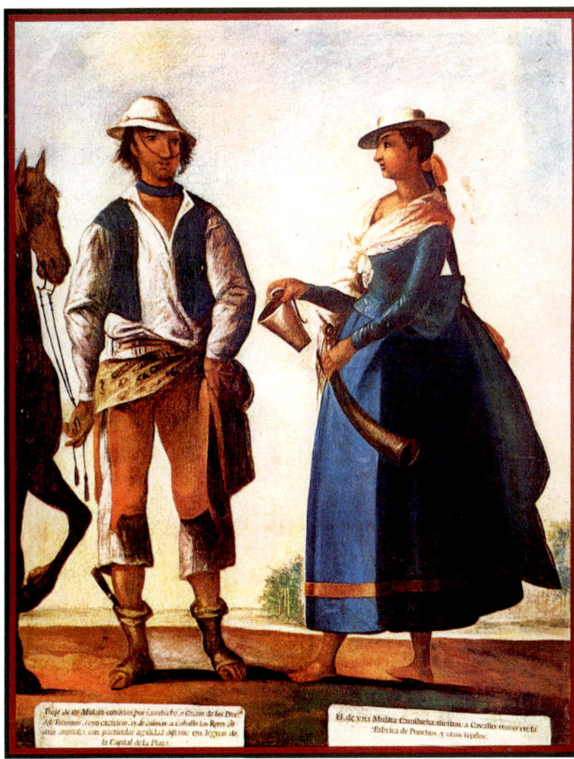

Fig. 17. The dress of a rural gaucho and his woman. The inscription below this rural woman reads, "The mixed-race *camilucha* is as skilled on horseback as in weaving ponchos and other cloth." Anonymous, *Camilucho y camilucha del Tucumán*. La Gaceta/Archivo.

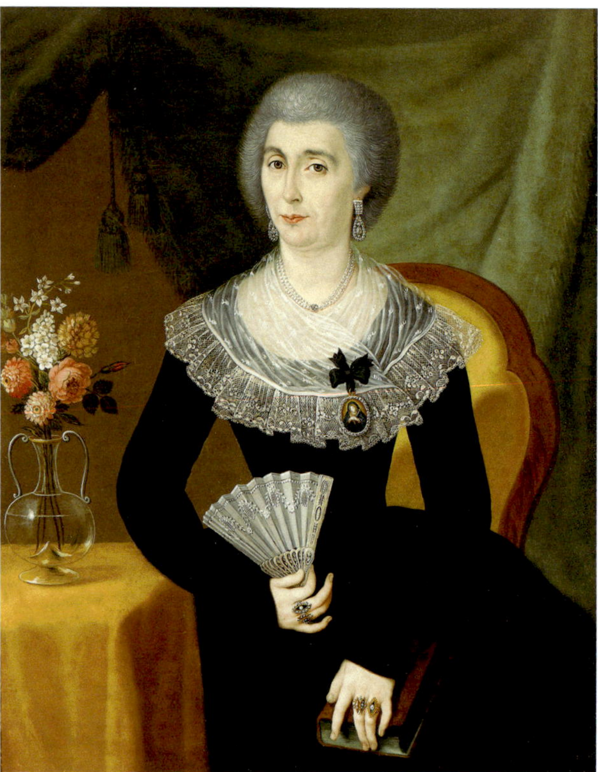

Fig. 18. This wealthy widow dressed in black is wearing a mourning brooch with an image of the Virgin of Sorrows. José Campeche (1751–1805), *Portrait of a Woman in Mourning*. Puerto Rico, c. 1807. Oil on canvas, 39 x 30²/₃ in. (99.1 x 77.9 cm). Marilynn and Carl Thoma Collection, Chicago, Illinois.

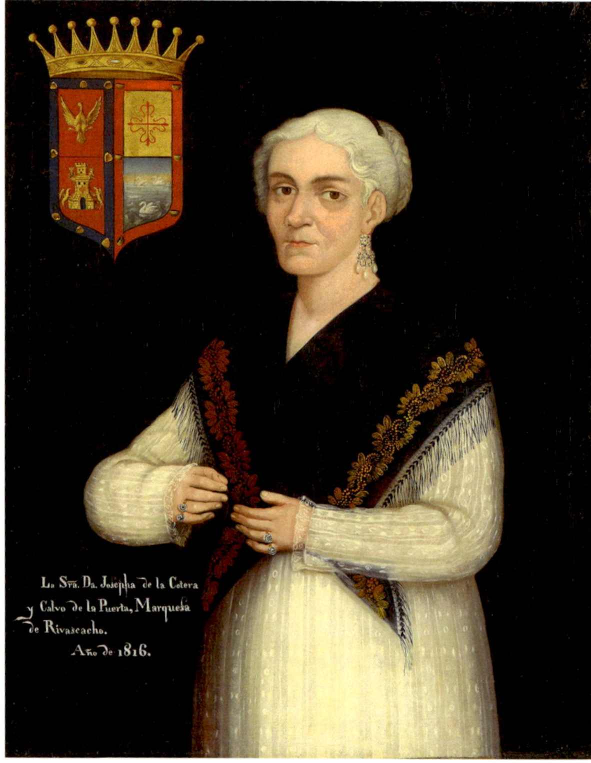

Fig. 19. Because the titled Doña Josefa, Marquesa de Rivas Cacho, had passed the required mourning period, she could dress in white with a blue shawl embroidered around the edges and fringed in gold. She also wears elaborate earrings and rings on both fingers. *Portrait of the Widow Doña Josefa de la Cotera y Calvo de la Puerta, Marquesa de Rivas Cacho*. Mexico, 1816. Oil on canvas, 33 x 25½ in. (83.8 x 64.7 cm). Brooklyn Museum, Museum Collection Fund and the Dick S. Ramsay Fund, 52.166.5.

place that I should have as a member of the third order, my cadaver enshrouded in the sacred habit of Our Lady of Mercy."[31] Later the same year, although she made no mention in her will that she was a member of the Mercedarian Third Order, Doña Juana Paula Blasini, natural daughter (*hija natural*) of Don Tomás Seco and Doña Francisca Gutiérrez, and wife of the Englishman Don Juan Francisco Ubaldon, also requested that she be buried "in the habit of our Lady of Mercy and buried in the Church of her convent."[32] The request to be buried in the habit of the decedent's third order continued throughout the colonial period. The requisite shroud usually cost 25 *pesos*.

In addition to the garments worn by middling and elite corpses, the official mourners also had a required dress. Mourning clothing, often made by local seamstresses, was always black and usually made of fine wool, although less fine black woolen cloth, heavier wool lining, or black silk could also be used (figs. 18–19). Other mourning accessories, all in black, such as earrings, buckles, silk fans, and silk handkerchiefs were sold in local shops.[33]

Some final words about fabrics. There were at least a hundred different fabrics used for women's clothing during the eighteenth century. There were classic fabrics, winter fabrics, summer fabrics, fabrics for underwear and outerwear, fancy fabrics, and plain ones too. Just in wool, there were more than thirty varieties, ranging from the locally domestically produced to the imported machine made. The garment that had the greatest variation in fabric was the skirt, which was listed in more than forty different fabrics in colonial dowries and inventories. Many fabrics were especially prized for their ability to shine and attract attention.

There was also a great diversity in the prices of different fabrics. In general the least costly textiles, the fabrics that made up most of the clothing of the poor and lower middling groups, were woven goods produced in Córdoba (Argentina). Plain white linen cloth from Cochabamba (in present-day Bolivia), the so-called "*tucuyos,*" and colored linens, called "*pintados*" and costing twice as much as the white linen, were very popular for skirts. The embroidered cloth of Salta (Argentina) was also in large demand.

The preferred fabric for shirts and nightgowns was Brittany linen imported from France, the so-called "legitimate linen." During periods of warfare in Europe, this cloth was often impossible to obtain, so Hamburg linen or local fine muslin was used as a substitute.[34]

Paradoxically, the 1790s, years of almost non-stop European wars, saw a large number of new fabrics introduced into Buenos Aires, including cashmere, serge, stamped wool, and very fine mantilla wool. New varieties of silk including heavy Chinese silk and stamped silk were now added to traditional silks such as velvet, taffeta, and double satin taffeta. New fabrics always appeared first in women's clothing before being adopted by men.

Notes

[1] N. R. Porro, J. E. Astiz, and M. M. Rospide, *Aspectos de la vida cotidiana en el Buenos Aires Virreinal* (Buenos Aires: Universidad de Buenos Aires, 1982), 367–368.

[2] Archivo General de la Nación Argentina, Buenos Aires (hereafter AGNA), Testamento de María Martínez, Registro 4, 1776–1777, December 9, 1776.

[3] AGNA, Tasación de la ropa usada de la finada María Josefa Ruiz de Gaona, Sucesiones, legajo 7779, August 17, 1809.

[4] Concolorcorvo, *El lazarillo de ciegos caminantes desde Buenos Aires a Lima* (Guijon, 1773), 34–35.

[5] Martin du Bassin, "Relación del viaje hecho al Río de la Plata [1708]," in *Viajeros al Río de la Plata, 1701–1725,* ed. Daisy Ripodas Ardanaz (Buenos Aires: Union Académique Internationale and Academia Nacional de la Historia, 2002), 148–149.

[6] "Captain Trotter's Description of Buenos Aires (1800)," in Maryanne Tefft Force, *Eighteenth-Century Global Trade: The Logs of Captain William Trotter*, ed. Nan McCowan Sumner-Mack (Providence: Estate of Maryanne Tefft Force, 2012), 215–236.

[7] Samuel Hull Wilcocke, *History of the Viceroyalty of Buenos Aires* (London, 1807), 393–394.

[8] E. E. Vidal, *Buenos Ayres and Monte Video consisting of Twenty-four Views accompanied with descriptions of the scenery and of the Costumes, Manners, &c. of the Inhabitants of those Cities and their environs* (London: R. Ackerman, 1820), 49–50.

[9] Samuel Haigh, *Sketches of Buenos Aires and Chile* (London: J. Carpenter and Son, 1829), 16.

[10] Ibid., 20–21.

[11] Museo Histórico Nacional, Buenos Aires, *Portrait of Señora Doña Francisco Silveyra de Ibarrola,* painted in 1794 by De Pelvis.

[12] AGNA, Registro 5, 1785, Testamento de Doña Magdalena de Arévalo, February 9, 1785.

[13] Vidal, *Buenos Ayres and Monte Video*, 50.

[14] Haigh, *Sketches*, 16.

[15] AGNA, Tribunales, Sucesiones, legajo 8139, Bienes de María Martina Pereyra de Lucena, September 9, 1799.

[16] For more information about ponchos, see N. R. Porro, J. E. Astiz and M. M. Rospide, *Aspectos de la vida cotidiana,* 425–426.

[17] AGNA, Dote de Doña María de la Paz Lezica, Registro de escribano 2, 1798.
[18] AGNA, Registro de escribano 5, Carta de Dotte de Doña Flora de Azcuenaga, June 8, 1781.
[19] As a point of comparison, the average price for an adult slave was 300 *pesos*.
[20] AGNA, Registro 5, 1780, Carta de Dote de Doña Josefa de Inda, a favor de su Hija Da. María Magdalena Carrera, September 11, 1780.
[21] AGNA, Tribunales, Sucesiones 7712, Inventario de los bienes que han quedado por fin y muerte de Doña Luisa Barbosa, difunta, April 3, 1700. The lighting mechanism was a cord coated with sulphur that was then used to light candles.
[22] AGNA, Sucesiones 6264, Cuenta de división y partición de los bienes que quedaron por fallecimiento de Ana María González, May 4, 1761.
[23] AGNA, Tribunales 8125, Auto de quema de los bienes de Doña María Isabel Rodríguez, March 4, 1797.
[24] AGNA, Tribunales 8125, Diligencia de quema de los bienes contaxiados que quedaron por muerte de Doña Ana María Rodríguez, November 14, 1797. The goods belonging to both Rodríguez women were burned because of the fear that they had died of a contagious disease.
[25] AGNA, Registro 5, 1780, Testamento de Doña María Rosa Rocha, August 1, 1780.
[26] AGNA, Tribunales, Sucesiones 7712, Inventario de Doña Eugenia Basualdo, November 18, 1794.
[27] AGNA, Tribunales, Sucesiones 8125, Inventario de los bienes dejados por muerte de Doña María Alberta Cisneros de Pérez, September 25, 1787.
[28] AGNA, Sucesiones 8125, Inbentarios de la finada Da. María Josefa Ruis, April 3, 1791.
[29] AGNA, Registro 5, 1785, Testamento de Petrona Cavezas, September 19, 1785.
[30] AGNA, Registro 5, 1785, Testamento de Doña Magdalena de Arévalo, February 12, 1785.
[31] AGNA, Registro 5, 1785, Testamento de Doña Juana Francisca de Rocha, April 4, 1785.
[32] AGNA, Registro 5, 1785, Testamento de Doña Juana Paula Blasini, July 2, 1785.
[33] AGNA, Tribunales, Sucesiones 7712, Cuenta de lo que se gastó en el entierro y funerales de Da Luisa Bernarda del Pino, 1799.
[34] In 1790, Lázaro de Ribera, the governor of Moxos (in present-day Bolivia), informed Viceroy Arredondo that the native people of his jurisdiction were able to imitate the best quality European fabrics such as muslin and cotton.

Colonial Images

Tipos y costumbres of Ecuador Revisited in the 19th and Early 20th Centuries

Alexandra Kennedy-Troya

The persistent representation of native Indians—their costumes, types of labor, and festivities—has been key to understanding nation building and the construction of identities in Latin America since the 1820s. Let me bring to mind a map of Nueva Granada, the governing unit that comprised present-day Venezuela, Colombia, and Ecuador during early republican times. It was used to illustrate French historian Guillaume N. Lallement's book *Historia de Colombia,* published in 1827 (fig. 1).[1] Independence hero Simón Bolívar, seen in the upper center, is surrounded by emblematic landscapes pertaining to the three unified nations along with generic types (*tipos*) of men, women, priests, and a Muisca Indian family shown in two images: one of a man and one of a woman with a child. It is well known that both Bolívar and his compatriot Antonio José de Sucre believed in the power of images to influence important changes in the newly created independent nations. In this context one can understand the hasty creation of the Cuenca School of Arts in 1822, where students were expected to make war instruments as well as to design new artistic images for the republics (fig. 2).[2]

As Peruvian colleague Natalia Majluf noted in a remarkable essay concerning Pancho Fierros´s colonial-era *costumbrista* watercolors, the antecedents of *costumbrista* images of the nineteenth century have to do with the vigorous international industry of producing paintings and engravings for illustrated travel and costume books, as well as for series dedicated to trades related to street commerce and industry, which enjoyed a resurgence in the late eighteenth century.[3] Peruvian Bishop Baltasar Martínez Compañón´s images done in 1780 and 1785 come to mind.[4] In a broad sense of the word, these publications fulfilled the Enlightenment-era desire for images in order to pursue, compile, and organize knowledge. Illustrations were a vital part of these visual encyclopedias—first on a continental level, later for the nations, and finally for and about specific regions.

Integrated into an official map in a major history manual such as Lallement's *Historia de Colombia,* intended to circulate on a worldwide level so as to reinforce the newly formed and independent nations, the so-called *tipos* y *costumbres* (types of people and customs) and landscapes seem to tell us a different story from the earlier illustrated genre. These images relate not to the pursuit of knowledge but to local Latin American politics and interests in a new republican context. The indigenous figures portrayed still remain at the lower bottom of the map, and of society, although their labor was crucial to the economy of the new nations. They seem to depict the order in which Bolívar was trying to visualize free Latin America.

Besides the printed plates combined with maps, dozens of painters in Quito, Mexico City, or Lima from the 1830s to the 1920s were still being commissioned by international and local leisure travelers and scientists to make inexpensive small watercolors similar to the prototypes that had been established in the previous century.[5] Examples can be seen in Gaetano Osculati's *Costumes of Quito,* painted by Ramón Salas in Quito (fig. 3),[6] or Le Moyne´s *Antioqueña.*[7]

Therefore, in accord with Majluf´s proposal, nineteenth-century *tipos* and *costumbrista* renderings based on the earlier tradition were not an invention of Latin American artists as a means to present or discuss local identities, although, I argue, they were *used* later in other contexts to do so. These kinds of representations in the first and second halves of the nineteenth century—most of them anonymous—follow quite closely the late colonial tradition, although most of the scientific discourses that characterized the previous genre were lost as other interests, mainly political, arose. The most coveted images were copied, simplified, and decontextualized in order to meet a demand for souvenirs and illustrations for travel journals and diaries (figs. 4a, b, and c).

We must also remember that these representations were not memoirs of a colonial past but were still related to present-day life—life that changed very little in the Andean region until around the 1870s (fig. 5). They served as a sort of *carte postale*

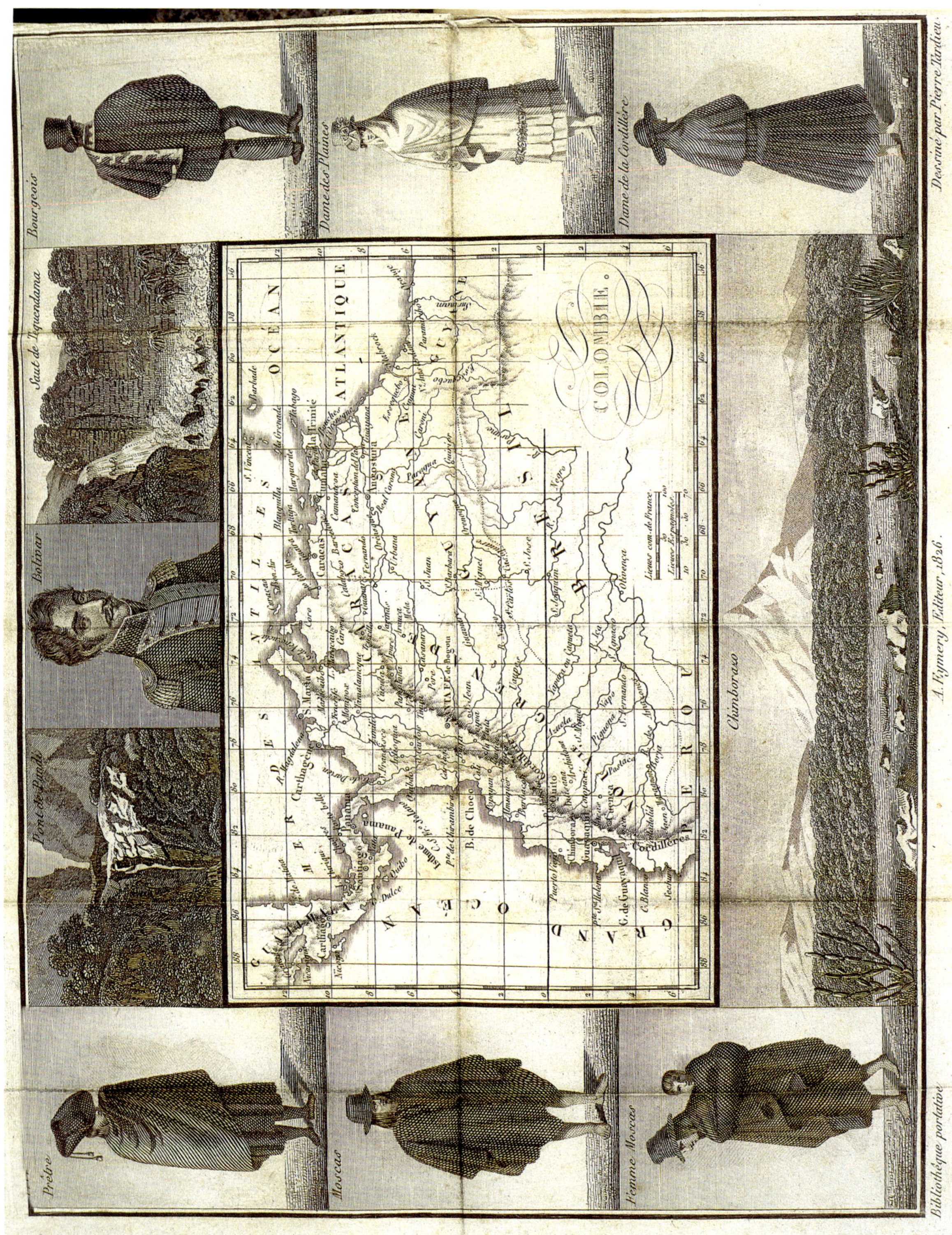

Fig. 1. *Map of Colombia.* From Guillaume N. Lallement, *Historia de Colombia* (Paris: Imprenta y Fundición J. Pinard, 1827).

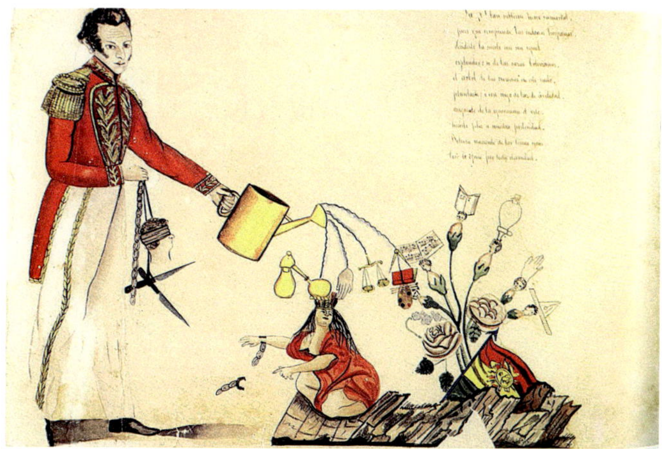

Fig. 2. *Sucre Making the Arts and Sciences Be Born from Bolivia's Head*. From Melchor María Mercado, *Melchor María Mercado, álbum de paisajes, tipos humanos y costumbres de Bolivia (1841–1869)* (La Paz: Banco Central de Bolivia/Archivo Nacional de Bolivia/Biblioteca Nacional de Bolivia, 1991).

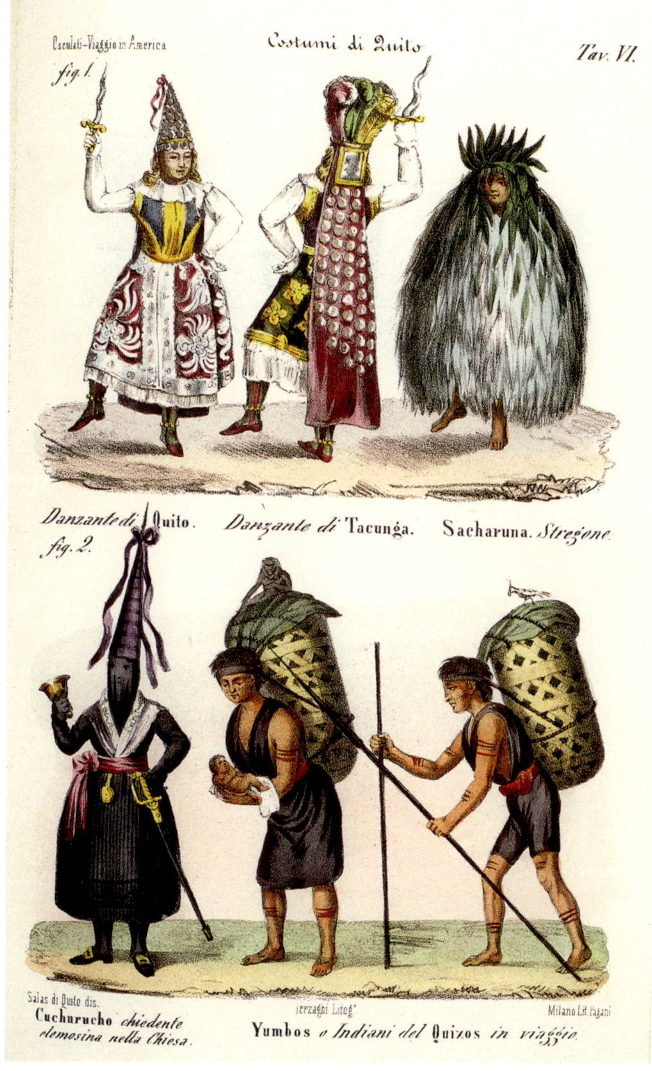

Fig. 3. Ramón Salas, *Costumes of Quito*. From Gaetano Osculati, *Esplorazione delle regioni equatoriali lungo il Napo ed il fiume delle Amazzoni. fiammento di un viagio fatto nelle due Americhe negli anni 1846–7–8*, 2nd. ed. (Milan: Fratelli Centenari e Comp., 1854).

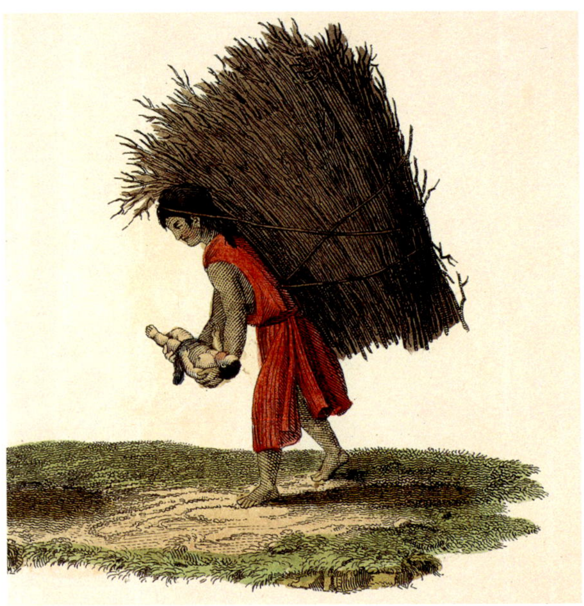

Fig. 4a. (detail) *Woman and Man from Quito*. From William Bennett Stevenson, *Relation historique et descriptive d'un séjour de vingt ans dans l'Amérique du Sud ou voyage en Araucane, au Chili, au Pérou et dans la Colombie* [1809–1810 in Quito] (Paris: A. J. Filian Libraire, 1826).

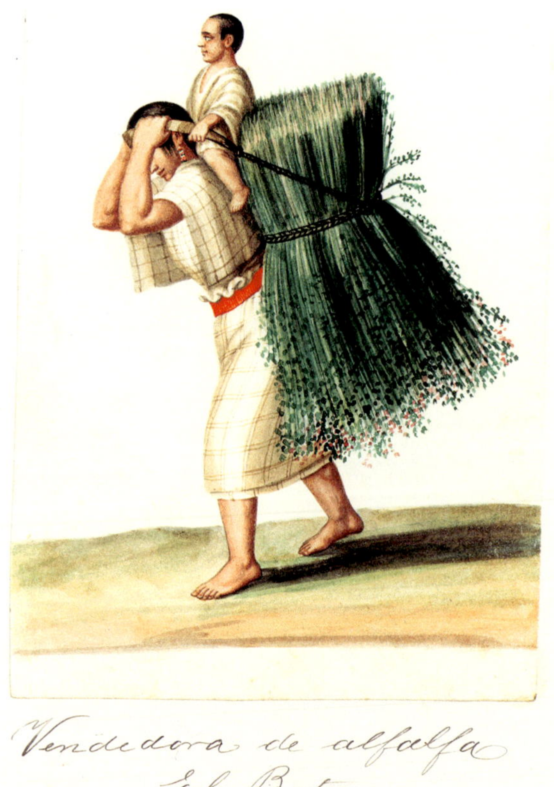

Fig. 4b. Ramón Salas, *Alfalfa Vendor, El Batán*. Ecuador, c. 1855–1865. Watercolor on paper. From *Album de costumbres ecuatorianas: paisajes, tipos y costumbres*. Biblioteca Nacional de España, inv.# 15-90, Madrid. Reproduced in *Imágenes de identidad. Acuarelas quiteñas del siglo XIX*, ed. Alfonso Ortiz, Biblioteca Básica de Quito 6 (Quito: FONSAL, 2005), 350–351.

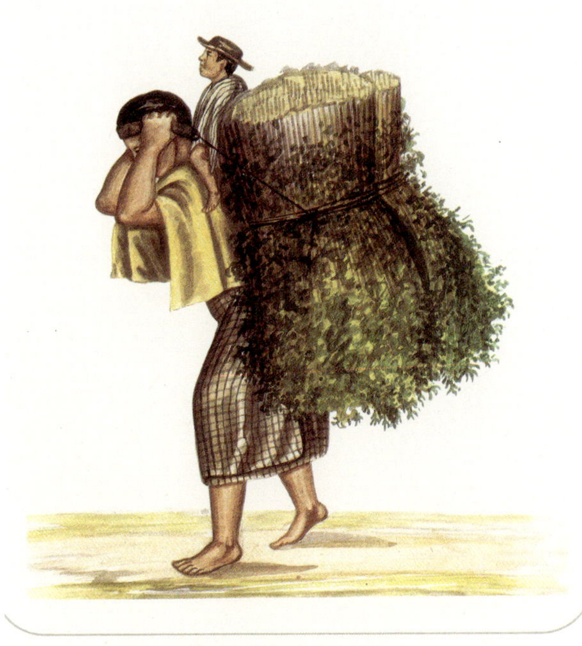

Yndia vendedora de Yerva.

Fig. 4c. Juan Agustín Guerrero, *Indian Herb Vendor*. Ecuador, 1852. Watercolor on paper. From *Imágenes del Ecuador siglo XIX. Juan Agustín Guerrero 1818–1880*, texts by Wilson Hallo (Quito/Madrid: Ediciones del Sol/Espasa-Calpe, 1981).

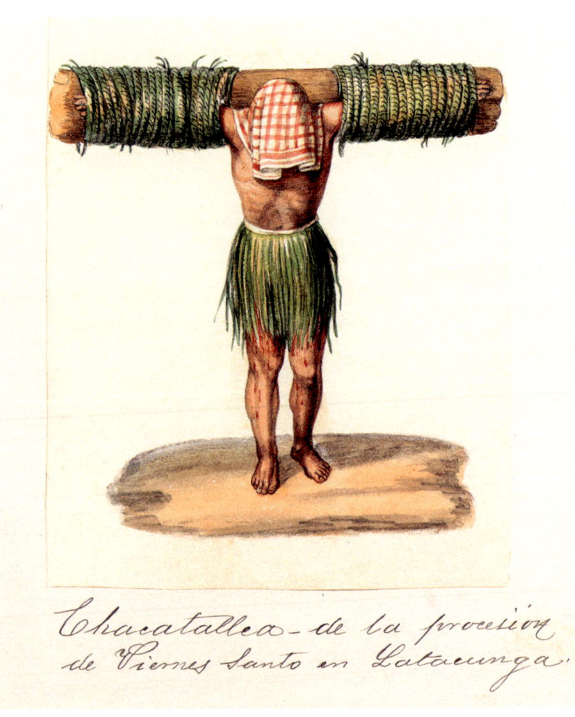

Fig. 5. Ramón Salas, *Chacatallca in the Holy Friday Procession in Latacunga*. Ecuador, c. 1855–1865. Watercolor on paper. From *Album de costumbres ecuatorianas: paisajes, tipos y costumbres*, Biblioteca Nacional de España, inv.# 15-90, Madrid. Reproduced in *Imágenes de identidad. Acuarelas quiteñas del siglo XIX*, ed. Alfonso Ortiz, Biblioteca Básica de Quito 6 (Quito: FONSAL, 2005), 274–275.

that depicted contemporary life in the ex-colonies, elaborated under the gaze of a colonial local eye.[8] Eventually, late-nineteenth-century photography of *tipos* displaced laborious watercoloring and gave this genre a new stance, something we shall go back to.

This was the way to represent (and collect)—in a very European fashion—what was occurring in the newly independent Latin American nations, with the intention to attribute the backwardness of these ex-colonies to the ill treatment of the native population by Spanish and Portuguese administrators and by the clergy of the Catholic Church. These new discourses would be a major platform upon which to defend and promote neocolonialism in the minds of British or U.S. politicians and businessmen.

As time went by, these images became more and more sophisticated and showed a greater diversity of trades and types of people—in both cases mostly representing indigenous life and costumes—as well as urban and rural landscapes, which sometimes included active volcanoes (fig. 6). Although some of these new images were created or promoted by nineteenth-century foreign travelers, the information incorporated into visual and written texts/narratives came from well-informed local Latin American elite groups, as well as from the popular classes.

A resurgent demand in the 1850s originated from within the new American republics, specifically Ecuador (fig. 7). To mention only one of many cases, the Brazilian ambassador Miguel María Lisboa, upon arrival in the Ecuadorian capital in 1853, located Ramón Salas (1815–1885), son of the famous painter Antonio Salas (active 1790–1860), and commissioned him to produce a "collection of national costumes." Some days, he recalled, he would have seven or eight people in his waiting room expecting to sell their watercolors.[9] Circulation and recirculation of these watercolors provided income for many people. The

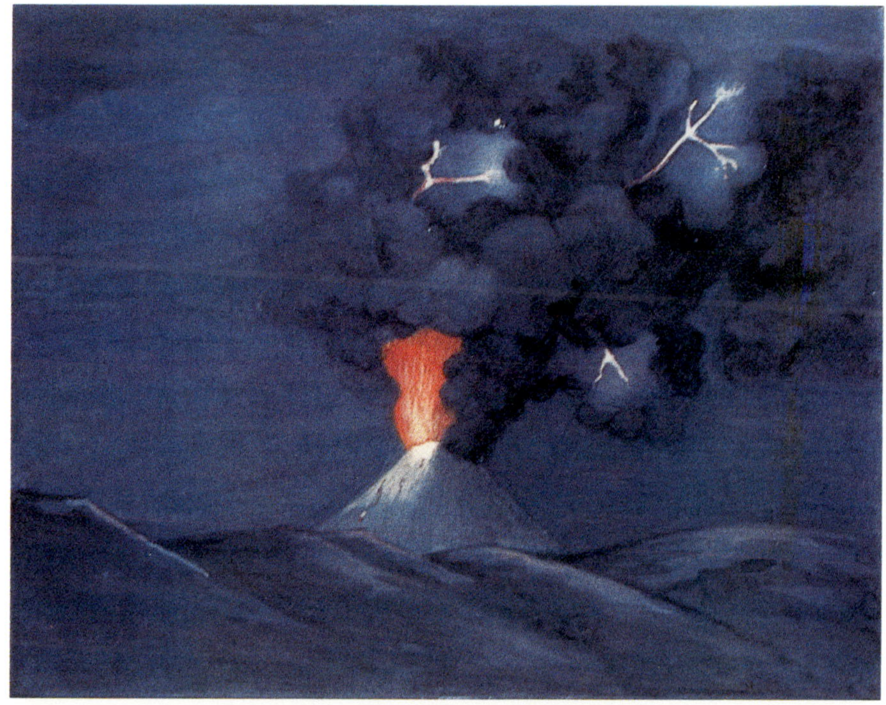

El cotopaxi.

Visto de Quito el 23 de agosto de 1878 por la noche.

Fig. 6. Juan Agustín Guerrero, *Cotopaxi as Seen from Quito on August 23rd, 1878 at Night.* Watercolor on paper. From *Imágenes del Ecuador siglo XIX. Juan Agustín Guerrero 1818–1880*, texts by Wilson Hallo (Quito/Madrid: Ediciones del Sol/Espasa-Calpe, 1981). Title of watercolor was given much later, as was customary.

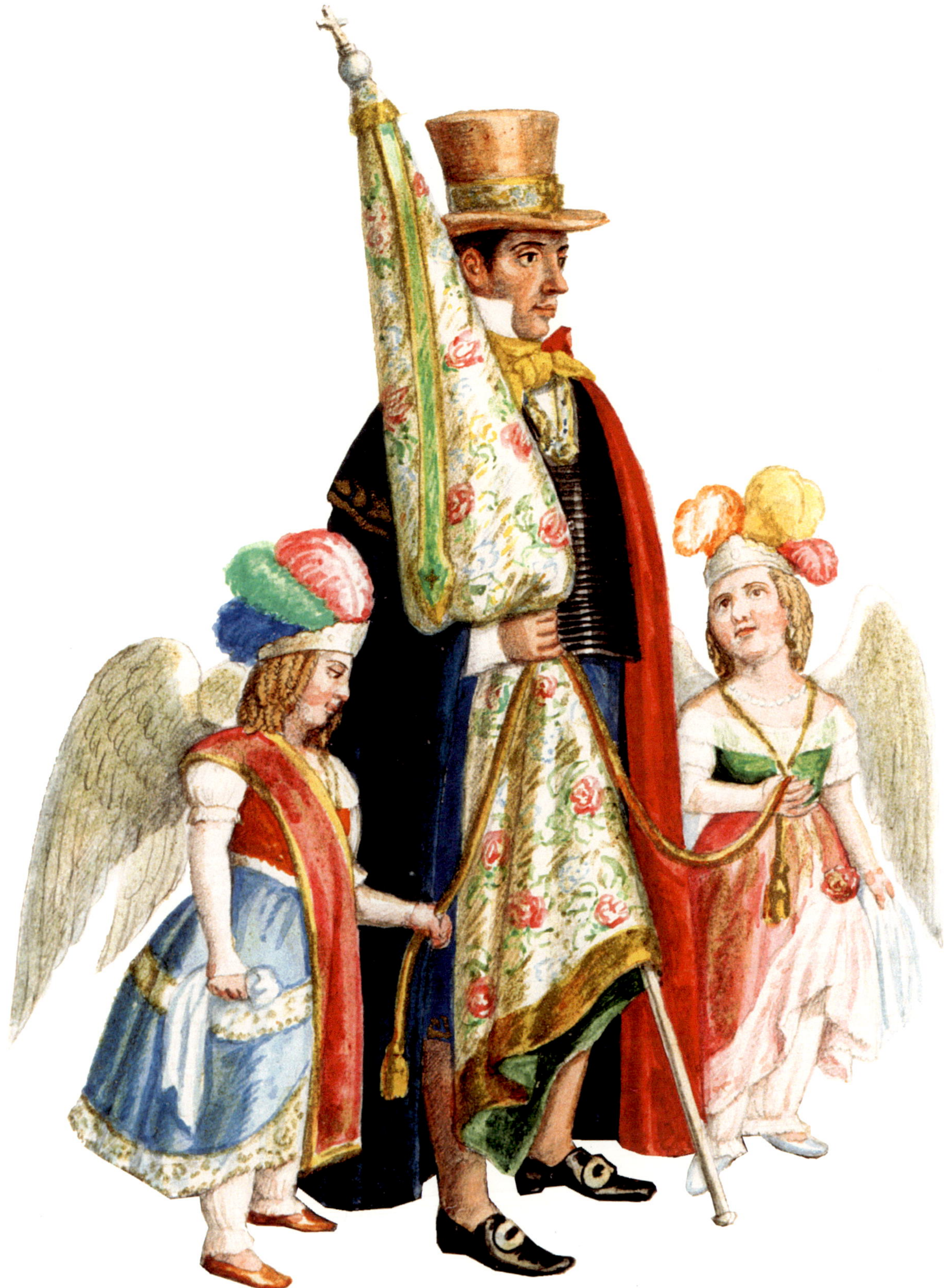

Fig. 7. Ramón Salas, *Indian Governor Carrying the Standard*. Ecuador, c. 1855–1865. Watercolor on paper. From *Album de costumbres ecuatorianas: paisajes, tipos y costumbres*, Biblioteca Nacional de España, inv.# 15-90, Madrid. Reproduced in *Imágenes de identidad. Acuarelas quiteñas del siglo XIX*, ed. Alfonso Ortiz, Biblioteca Básica de Quito 6 (Quito: FONSAL, 2005), 278–279.

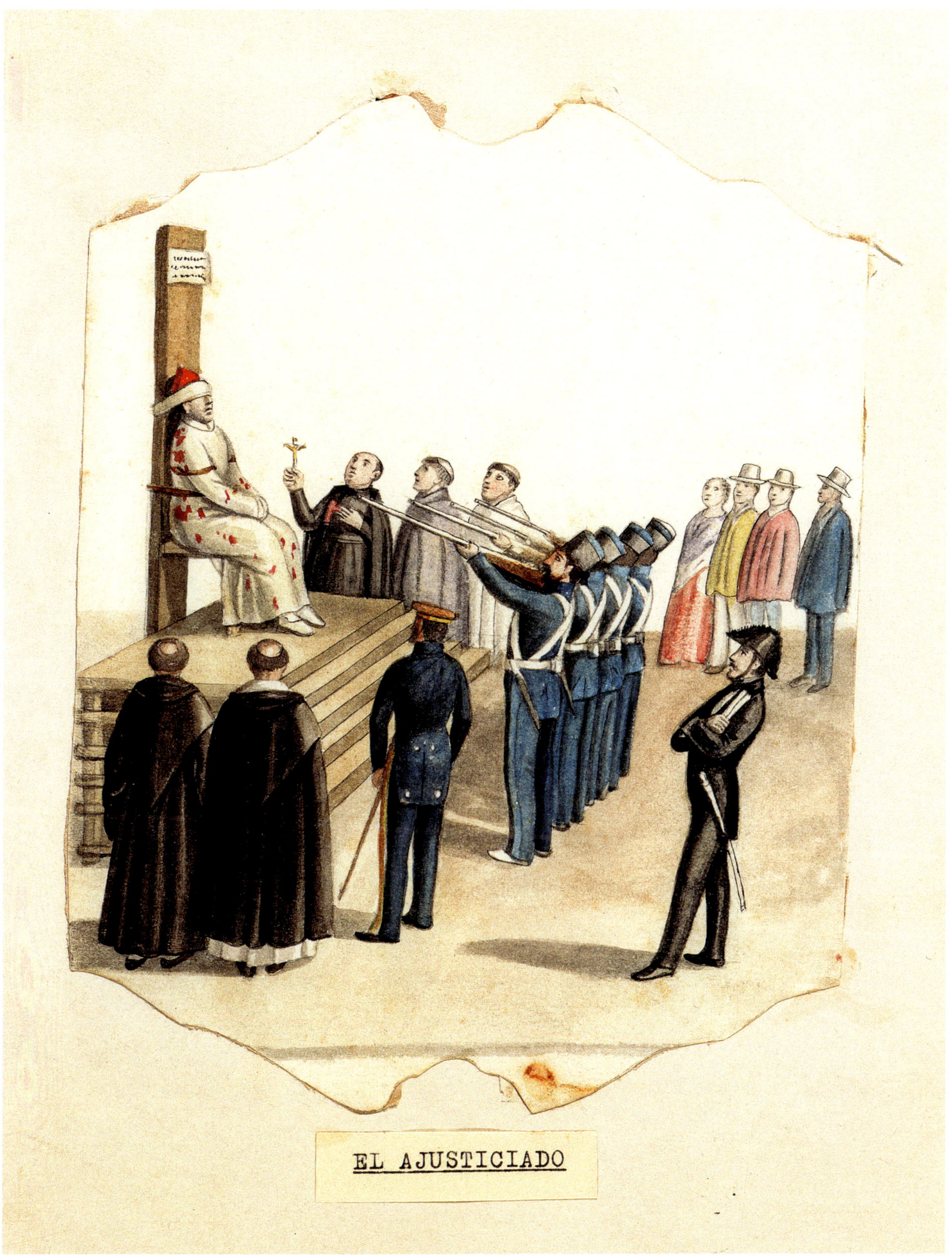

Fig. 8. Ramón Salas, *The Executed*. Ecuador, c. 1855–1865. Watercolor on paper. From *Album de costumbres ecuatorianas: paisajes, tipos y costumbres*, Biblioteca Nacional de España, inv.# 15-90, Madrid. Reproduced in *Imágenes de identidad. Acuarelas quiteñas del siglo XIX*, ed. Alfonso Ortiz, Biblioteca Básica de Quito 6 (Quito: FONSAL, 2005), 414–415.

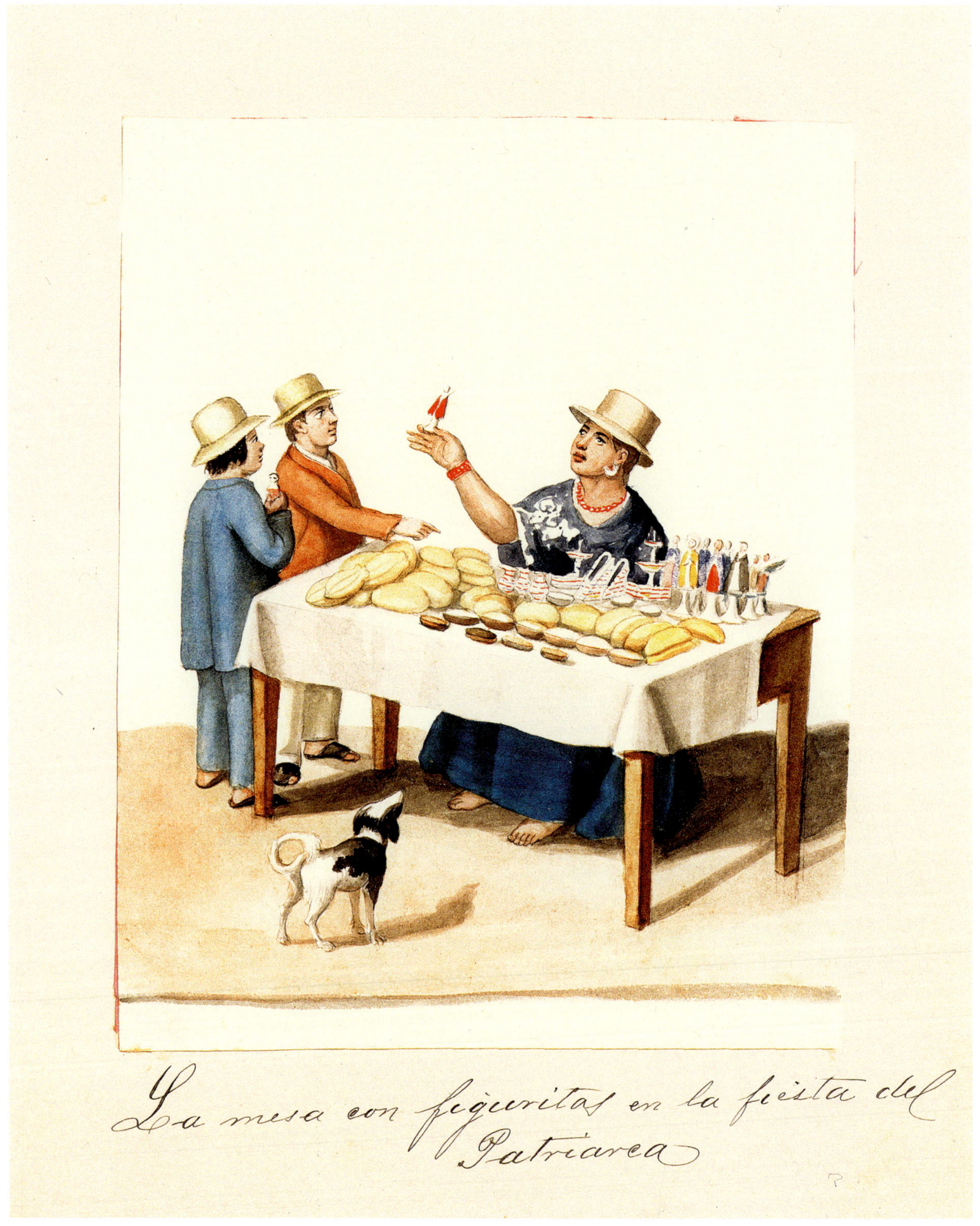

Fig. 9. Ramón Salas, *Table with Figurines at the St. Francis Celebration*. Ecuador, c. 1855–1865. Watercolor on paper. From *Album de costumbres ecuatorianas: paisajes, tipos y costumbres*, Biblioteca Nacional de España, inv.# 15-90, Madrid. Reproduced in *Imágenes de identidad. Acuarelas quiteñas del siglo XIX*, ed. Alfonso Ortiz, Biblioteca Básica de Quito 6 (Quito: FONSAL, 2005), 302–303.

lack of engraving workshops in Quito, Lima, or Potosí, in contrast to Mexico City, induced artists and artisans to hand-copy established models over and over, and, as was to be expected, the quality of these images varied enormously.

But there were other one-of-a-kind images painted and photographed[10] for new commissioners linked more to the *costumbrista* genre, which explicitly showed the stagnation and corruption of the new nation under local rulers (fig. 8). These unique plates must have been significant primarily to local citizens involved in politics and interested in changing the course of history. As much as I am interested in these plates as images, I am inclined to look at them in the context of a collection, as an organized narrative sequence. In this essay I am concerned with the impact these images had as a whole—as well as in the collecting of such images in albums in the late nineteenth and early twentieth centuries—in the hands of local Latin American progressive politicians and image makers. They were reinterpreted or re-read in late Romantic, Modernist, and Indigenist Latin American contexts up to the 1930s, moments in which nation building and national identities were again at stake, although faced in very different ways.

To uncover such re-readings I have chosen an exceptional album of Ecuadorian watercolors with a beautiful cover inlaid with mother-of-pearl, put together around the 1920s and now held by the National Library of Spain in Madrid.[11] It contains 165 anonymous watercolors of Ecuadorian types (*tipos*), *costumbrista* scenes, and landscapes. The first 141, apparently intentionally organized, have been dated around 1855–1865 (fig. 9). These are followed by much later watercolors and ink drawings, dated around 1900–1920s and done by less accomplished hands. What is most intriguing is that the album starts with two photographs taken

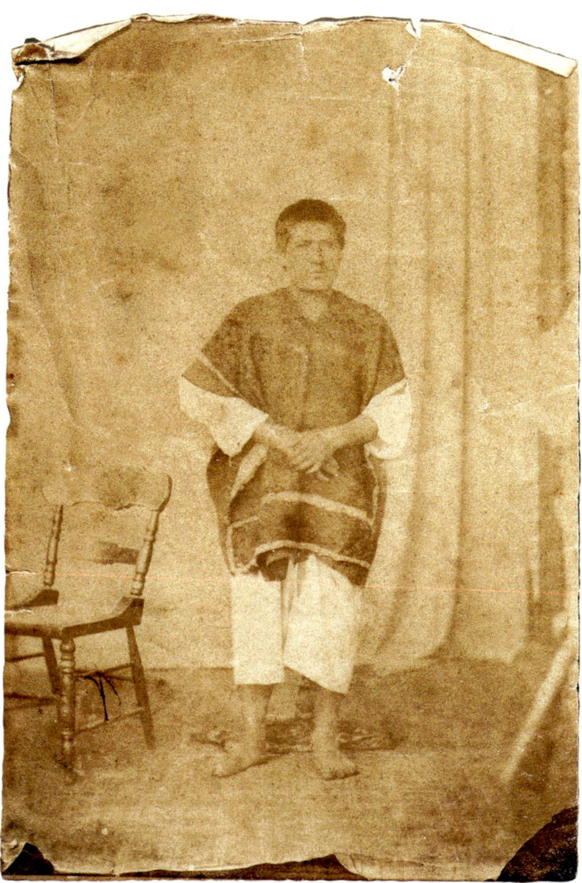

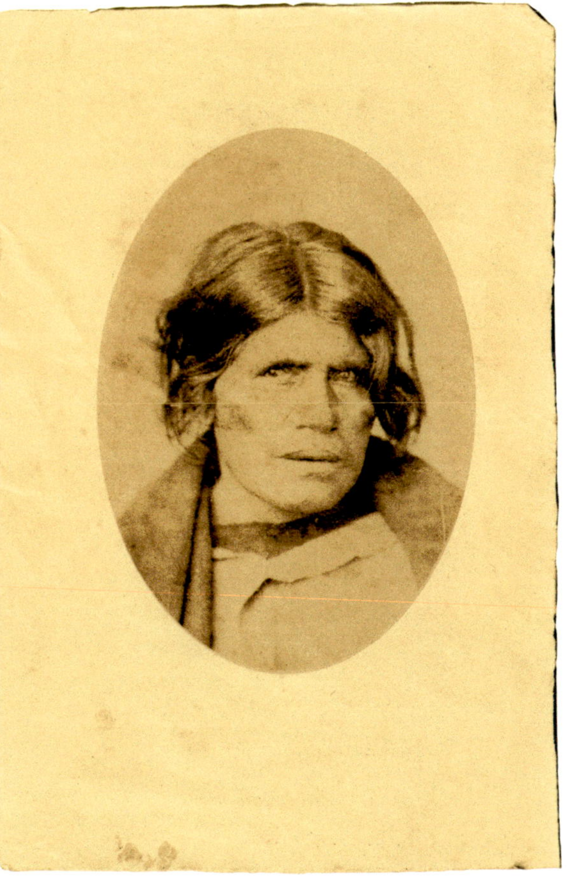

Figs. 10a, b. Pedro José Vargas, *Fernando Daquilema* (left) and *Manuela León* (?) (right). Ecuador, c. 1870. Photograph. From *Album de costumbres ecuatorianas: paisajes, tipos y costumbres*, Biblioteca Nacional de España, inv.# 15-90, Madrid. Reproduced in *Imágenes de identidad. Acuarelas quiteñas del siglo XIX*, ed. Alfonso Ortiz, Biblioteca Básica de Quito 6 (Quito: FONSAL, 2005), 160–161.

around 1870 (figs. 10a and 10b), of two Indian leaders who were involved in the most important indigenous uprisings of Ecuador in the 1870s, in Azuay and Chimbo provinces. The subjects are Daquilema de Cachi, of Incan descent, who was executed in April 1872, and a woman, probably Manuela León, his wife.[12] Real, fierce, and "savage" looking, these photographs have a totally different feeling from the picturesque, unmenacing watercolors in the album. All the items in this album—passed on generation after generation—seem to have been organized by the final owner at the end of the 1920s, when Indigenism as a strong political movement was on its way. The collector must have been involved or at least heavily interested in the new left-wing ideologies. Unfortunately, there is no information on how or when the Madrid Album became part of the Spanish National Library.

Collecting and assembling albums was quite common from the 1850s onwards, and they have to be treated as important cultural objects in themselves.[13] Read as a collection, the Madrid Album represents social and public affairs more than the familial or domestic aspects of society. It comprises images of wide circulation at the time: characters, landscapes, or events that were socially visible and probably valued by the community, as historian Rosemarie Terán observed.[14] This and other albums I have studied emphasize the popular aspects of a regional society situated around Quito. The album opens with "Vista del Antiguo Quito" (View of Old Quito, fig. 11). At that time the city had 50,000 inhabitants, many of whom regarded its recent colonial past as "antique" history and viewed its mythic aboriginal history as linked to Shyris and Incas, cultures that had been systematically denigrated by foreign visitors.

This "regional" album portraying craftsmen and free peasants, administrators, and traders from the highlands of Ecuador north of Quito becomes a sort of national manifesto. The nation considered

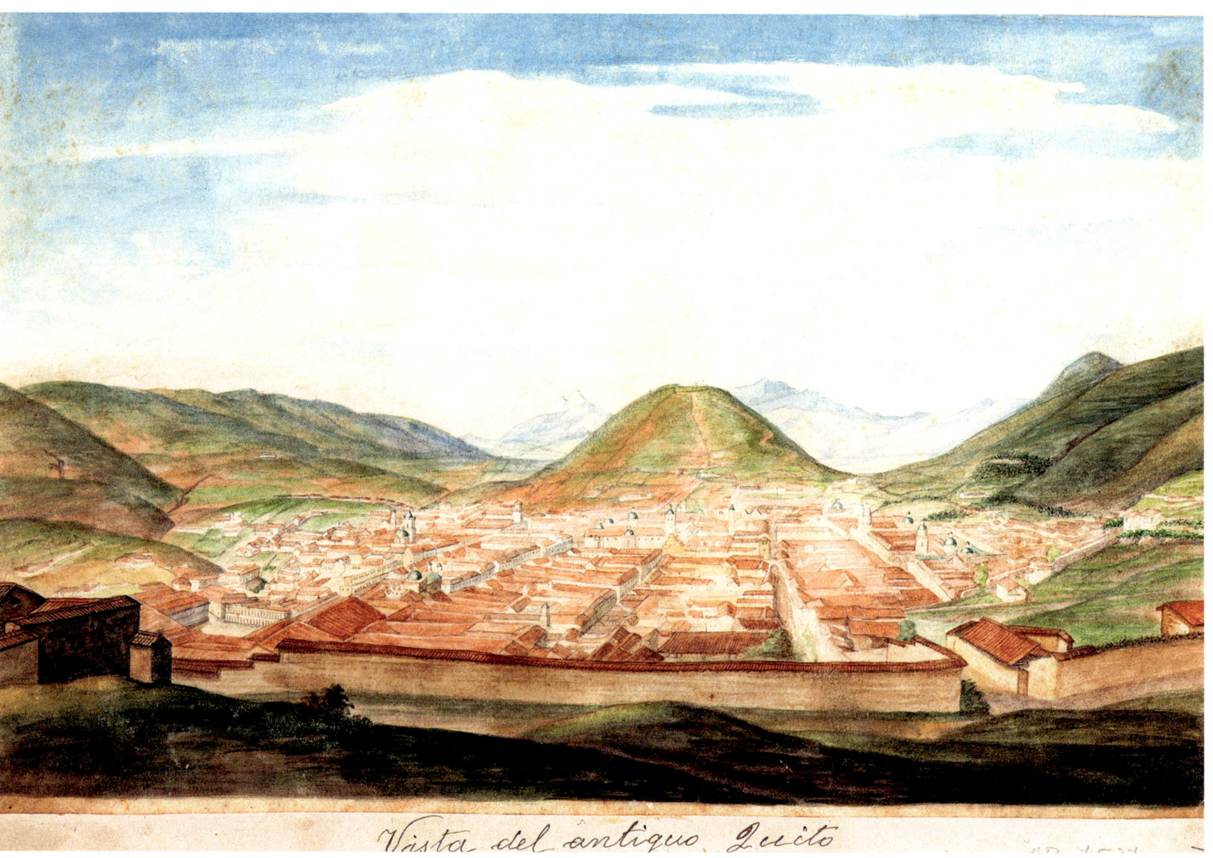

Fig. 11. Ramón Salas, *View of Old Quito*. Ecuador, c. 1855–1865. Watercolor on paper. From *Album de costumbres ecuatorianas: paisajes, tipos y costumbres*, Biblioteca Nacional de España, inv.# 15-90, Madrid. Reproduced in *Imágenes de identidad. Acuarelas quiteñas del siglo XIX*, ed. Alfonso Ortiz, Biblioteca Básica de Quito 6 (Quito: FONSAL, 2005), 163.

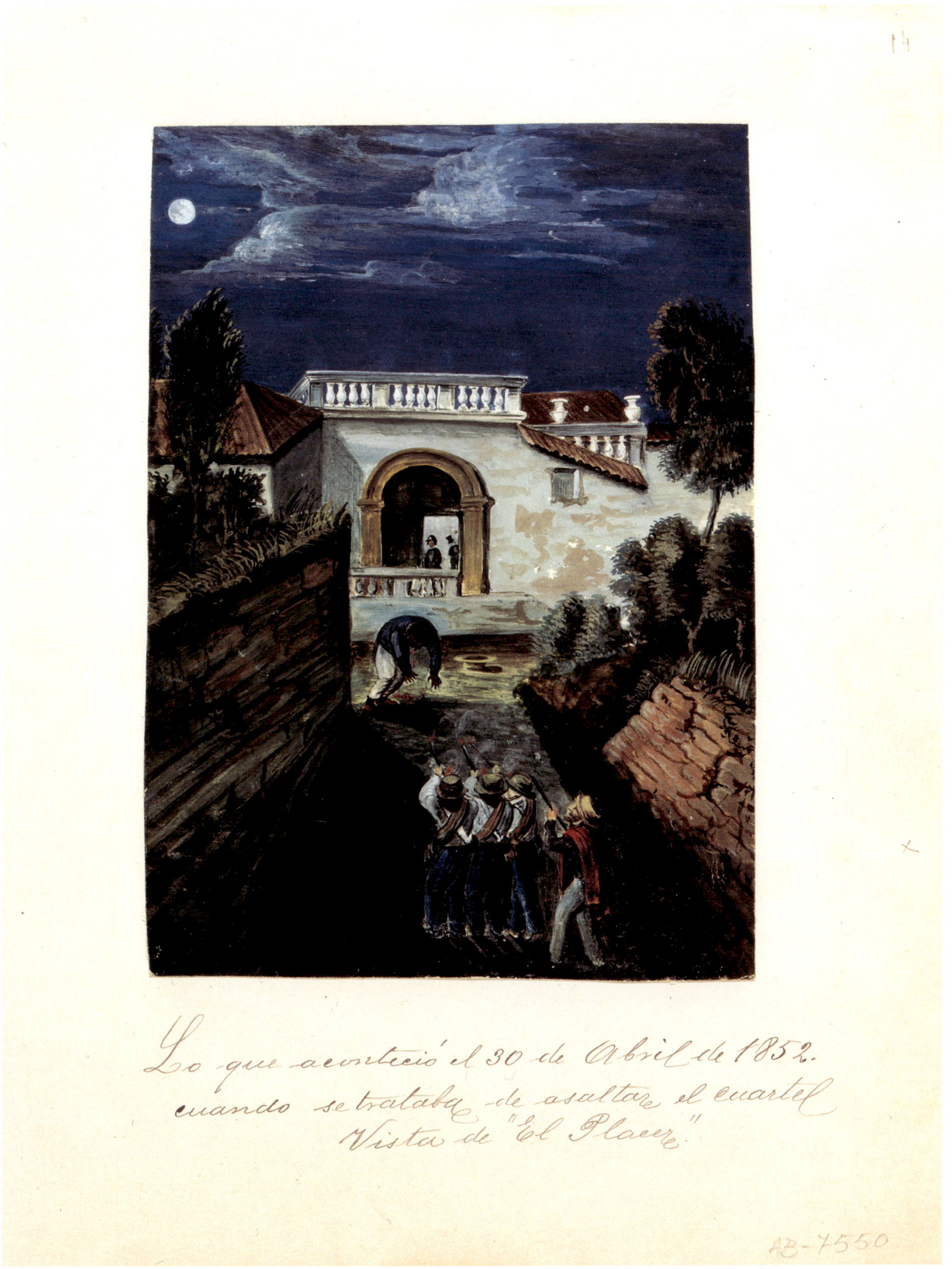

Fig. 12. Ramón Salas, *What Happened on April 13th, 1852*. Ecuador, c. 1855–1865. Watercolor on paper. From *Album de costumbres ecuatorianas: paisajes, tipos y costumbres*, Biblioteca Nacional de España, inv.# 15-90, Madrid. Reproduced in *Imágenes de identidad. Acuarelas quiteñas del siglo XIX*, ed. Alfonso Ortiz, Biblioteca Básica de Quito 6 (Quito: FONSAL, 2005), 192–193.

its capital to be a unifying force.[15] Behind the scenes the Catholic Church, as an institution, played an ambiguous role as shaper of the nation but also as the great landowner in the Sierra. It encouraged its members to be active participants in politics.[16] Many images show its relevance in daily life and annual festivities; in contrast, very few show the strong presence of military forces, and when they do, it is in a satirical fashion. An appropriate question seems to be: Was/were the collector/collectors antimilitarists?

Ramón Salas, to whom I have attributed most of the watercolors in the Madrid Album,[17] had been strongly involved in the political changes that took place from the 1830s to what is known as the Revolución Marcist (March Revolution), a revolution that began on March 6, 1845, and overthrew Venezuelan military officer Juan José Flores, the first president of independent Ecuador. Salas was a member of many art-promoting societies such as the Sociedad Democrática Miguel de Santiago (Democratic Society of Miguel de Santiago), the first art school founded after the Revolution, which aimed to promote free art in a freed nation. Its members declared themselves antimilitarists and anticlericalists. In one of the discourses at the inauguration, it was said that painting should represent the "image of Ecuadorian nature," as well as "virtues and vices, deformity and beauty, all of the passions, all of the events, uses, habits and costumes" of the new nation.[18] These were images created to set examples.

Some of the watercolors inserted in the album appear to have been commissioned by local intellectuals. These have to do with specific political events or are more general political satires, criticisms of Catholic priests and their abuses, such as "What Happened on April 13th, 1852" (fig. 12), "Child Jesus Mass" (fig. 13), "Satire of the Republic in the Times of (President) Urbina" (fig. 14), and "The Executed" (fig. 8).[19] They are intermingled with other images of Indian types or costumes, which, if seen in a decontextualized fashion, we could think of as symbols of the

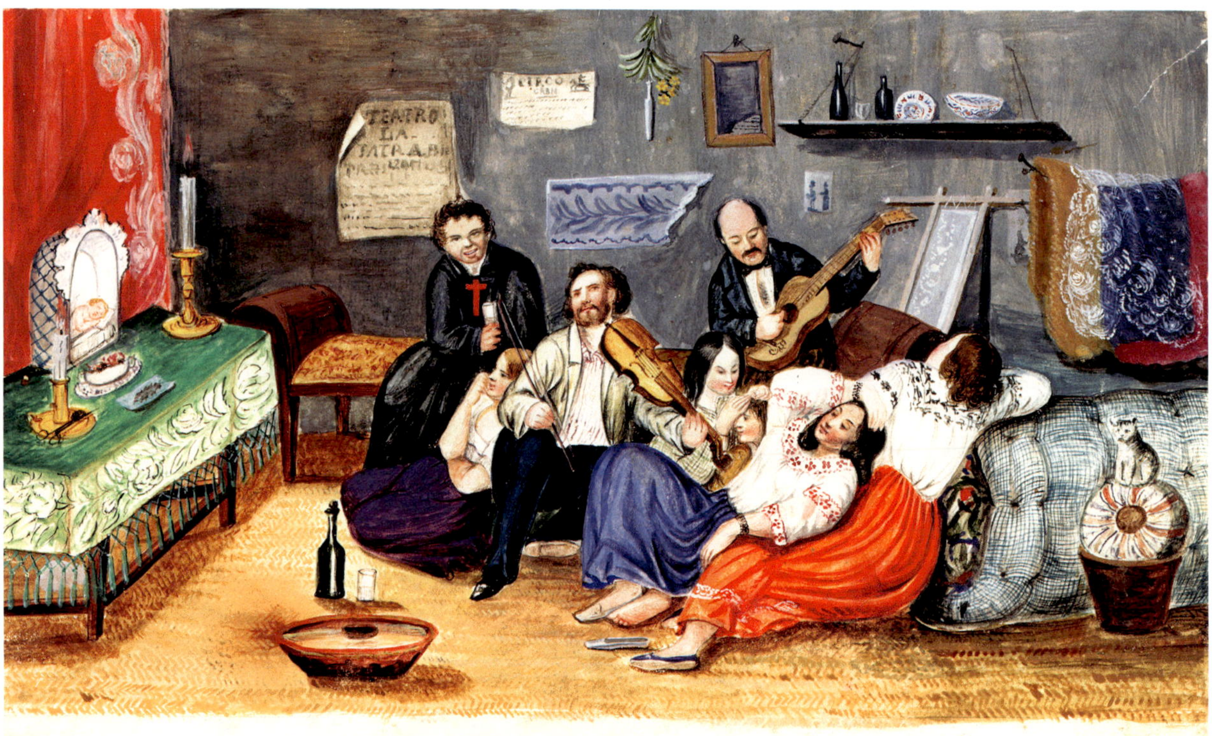

MISA DEL NIÑO

Fig. 13. Ramón Salas, *Child Jesus Mass*. Ecuador, c. 1855–1865. Watercolor on paper. From *Album de costumbres ecuatorianas: paisajes, tipos y costumbres*, Biblioteca Nacional de España, inv.# 15-90, Madrid. Reproduced in *Imágenes de identidad. Acuarelas quiteñas del siglo XIX*, ed. Alfonso Ortiz, Biblioteca Básica de Quito 6 (Quito: FONSAL, 2005), 242–243.

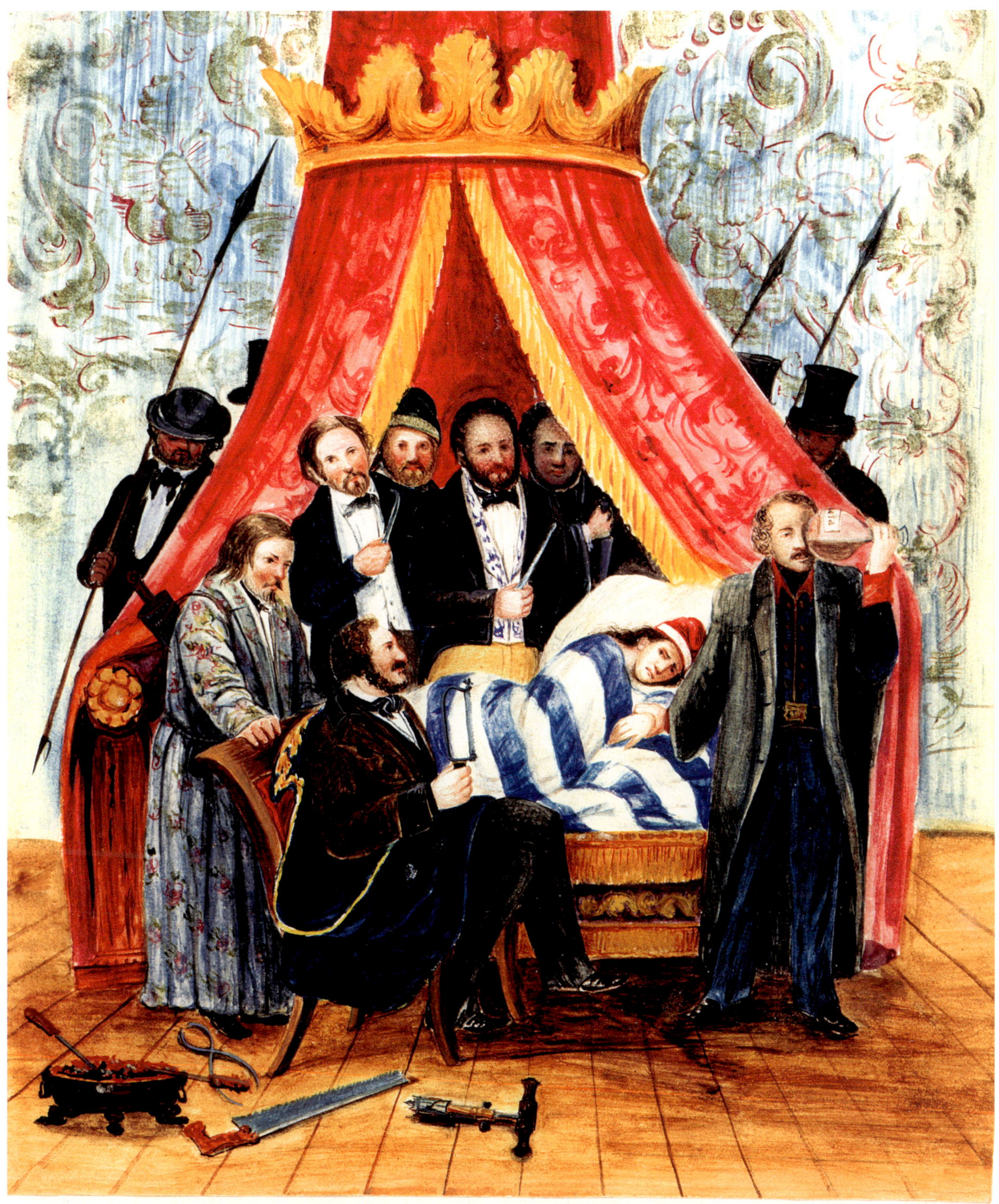

Fig. 14. Ramón Salas, *Satire of the [Ecuadorian] Republic in the Times of [President] Urbina*. Ecuador, c. 1855–1865. Watercolor on paper. From *Album de costumbres ecuatorianas: paisajes, tipos y costumbres, Biblioteca Nacional de España*, inv.# 15-90, Madrid. Reproduced in *Imágenes de identidad. Acuarelas quiteñas del siglo XIX*, ed. Alfonso Ortiz, Biblioteca Básica de Quito 6 (Quito: FONSAL, 2005), 298–299.

politics of exclusion, neutralizing social and ethnic inequalities that could menace the new mestizo orders being established. But I believe that they were afterwards literally tied to the album in a very special kind of political narrative.

The above example and other albums exhibit popular classes—mainly indigenous—about whom leading progressive politicians, diplomats, and lawyers such as Pedro Moncayo (1807–1888)[20] were concerned. Another peer of Ramón Salas and Pedro Moncayo was visual artist, musician, and politician Juan Agustín Guerrero (1818–1880), who had also been part of the Escuela Democrática Miguel de Santiago. In 1852 Guerrero finished his thesis presenting a collection of *tipos* and indigenous musical scores. He dedicated this work to Pedro Moncayo. When Moncayo was exiled to Valparaiso, Chile, around 1870, he took with him this album/thesis, which was passed on to his son Pedro. Later inscriptions—including a dedication in the album—show that Pedro, the son, gave it as a present to Peruvian Indigenist painter Julia Codesido de Mora (1883–1979).[21] This must have been a cherished gift, as it included models to be used in her own painting, with direct references to a neighboring country that suffered from the same "illness": mistreatment of indigenous people.

As another example, in the 1870s Italian musician Pedro Traversari was hired by conservative president Gabriel García Moreno as a flute professor at the new National Music Conservatory in Quito. It is known that he left for Chile with his Quiteñan wife, Alegría Salazar, to whom he dedicated another such album of watercolors compiled by him.[22] His son, Pedro Pablo (1874–1956), who moved to Chile with his parents at age ten and also trained as a musician (in the Conservatorio de Santiago de Chile), was an enthusiastic collector of indigenous instruments. We might assume that Pedro Pablo kept this album for some years, as many of these plates showed Indians playing

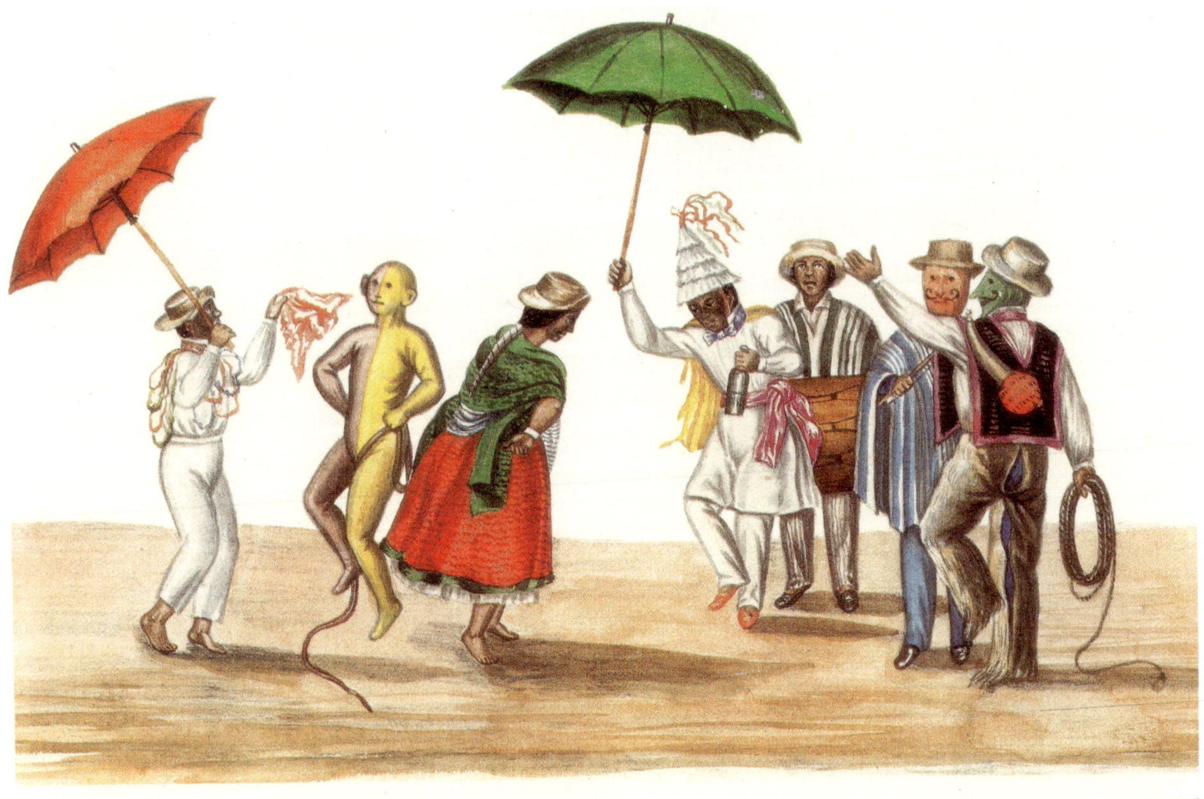

Fig. 15. Juan Agustín Guerrero, *Indians Dancing in Costumes on Reyes (Kings) Day*. Ecuador, 1852. Watercolor on paper. From *Imágenes del Ecuador siglo XIX. Juan Agustín Guerrero 1818–1880*, texts by Wilson Hallo (Quito/Madrid: Ediciones del Sol/Espasa-Calpe, 1981), 77.

quenas, horns, *zampoñas*, and other musical instruments (fig.15). Again, this album played the role of a visual encyclopedia of the country, which was probably used as a reminder of what should be collected and valued in modern times. Pedro Pablo went back to Quito in the 1900s to direct the Conservatorio de Música, reopened by liberal president Eloy Alfaro, and his collection was ultimately donated to the Casa de la Cultural Ecuatoriana in Quito.

These originally colonial images of *tipos* and *costumbres* were still present around the turn of the twentieth century (figs. 16a and 16b). Some of these small collectible images were used as models and reworked by renowned Romantic painters such as Joaquín Pinto (1842–1906), Juan Manosalvas (1840–1906), and Antonio Salguero (1864–1935), many of whom illustrated essays on indigenous life and popular characters in modern journals such as *Vejeces y Novedades*. They were also linked to politician and writer Juan León

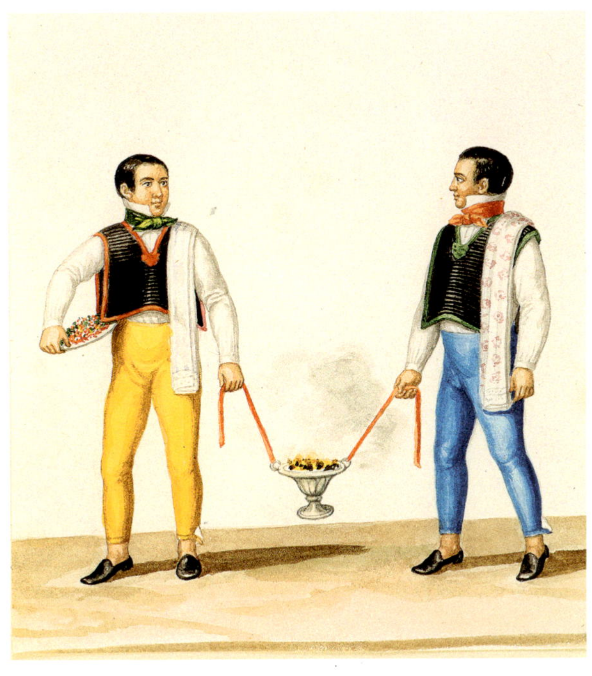

Fig. 16a. Ernest Charton, *Incense Burners in Procession*. Museo Nacional, Quito.

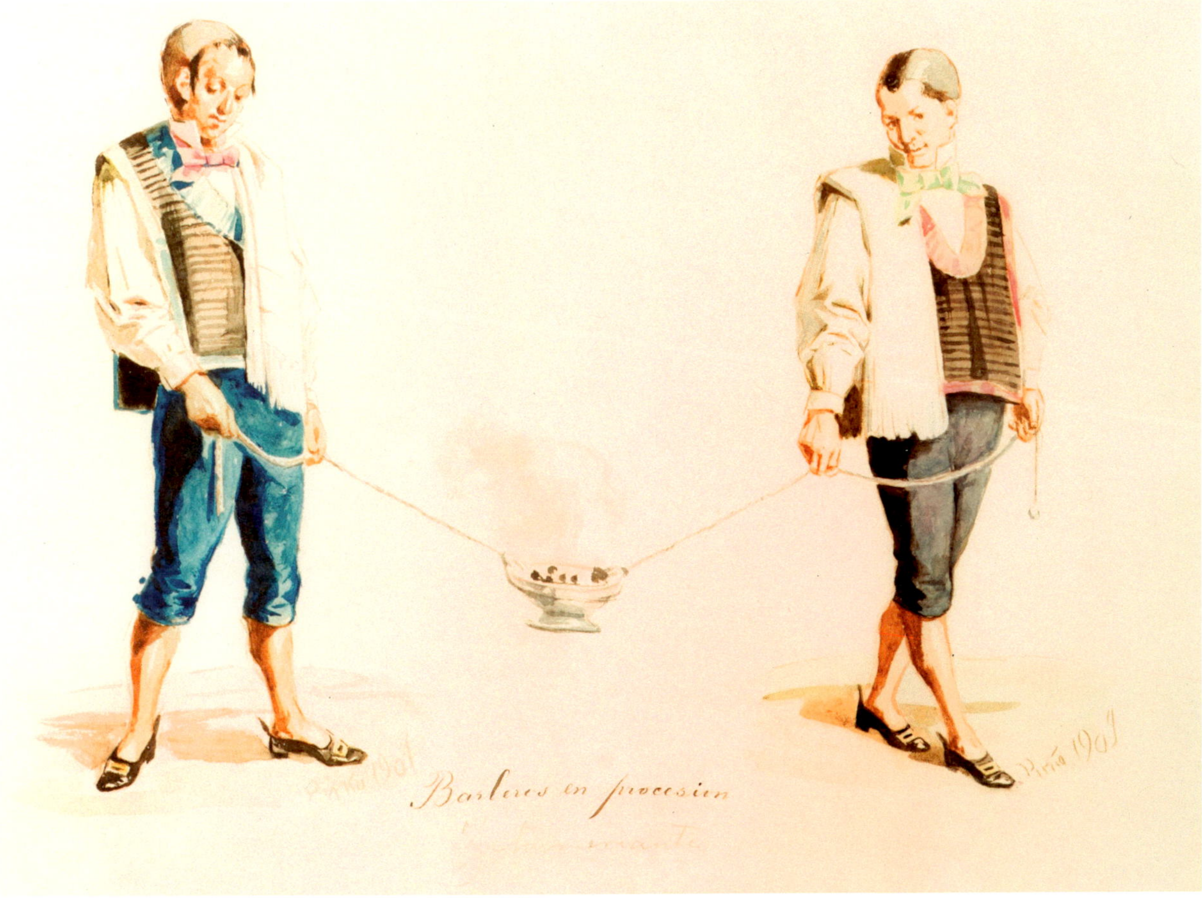

Fig. 16b. Joaquín Pinto, *Barbers in Procession*. Ecuador, 1909. Watercolor on paper, $10\,^{5}/_{8}$ x $13\,^{5}/_{8}$ in. (27 x 35 cm). In album by Joaquín Pinto, private collection, Quito. Photo: Christoph Hirtz.

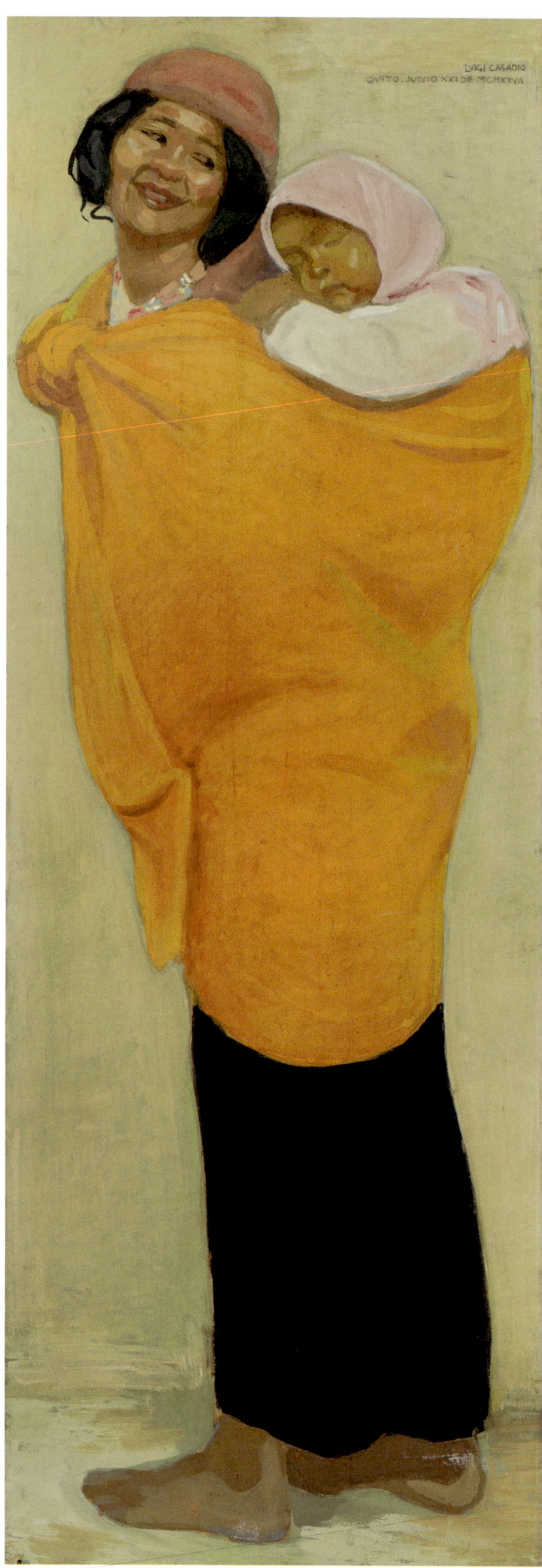

Fig. 17. Luigi Cassadio, *Indian Mother*. Ecuador, 1928. Tempera on cardboard, 39 1/3 x 13½ in. (100 x 34 cm). Museo de la Casa de la Cultura Benjamín Carrión, Quito. Photo: Christoph Hirtz.

Mera´s (1832–1894) compilation of popular poetry published in 1892 as *Cantares del pueblo ecuatoriano*. In this case, artists and writer were focused upon dignifying and preserving popular culture in a society that was starting to change dramatically. Modernity was on its way, as was a feeling of the loss of an arcadian life on the part of local Romantic artists, whose minds and hands exoticized the indigenous and popular communities with their closeness to Mother Earth and their moaning music and verses.

At the same time, the School of Arts in Quito was opened in 1904, with its main goal being to train students to become modern artists for a modern nation. While its first director, the Spanish artist Víctor Puig, was key to the initial organization of the institution, his successor from 1911 until 1920, José Gabriel Navarro (1881–1965), was fully committed to modernizing its curriculum by bringing in professors who could teach the know-how of European modern art *and* introduce themes that were typically Ecuadorian, thereby distancing the School of Arts from the main art centers.[23] One such "imported" teacher was Italian sculptor Luigi Cassadio (active in Ecuador 1915–1933), who would insistently recommend that his students explore their own surroundings, the landscape, and especially the Indians. Unfortunately very few of his works have remained, and those that we know of have little or nothing to do with what he preached, the exception being *Madre india* (Indian mother), dated 1928, a large sketch that shows a young Indian woman carrying a baby, who turns around to see him with a smiling face (fig. 17).[24] This gesture had never been present in depictions of the Indian race, which was always shown in a severe mode and related to its historically remote past.

In this new scenario, the colonial *tipos* still served as models to the new modern artists. A very good example is the large-format oil painting *India de Zámbiza* (Indian from Zámbiza) (fig. 18) by Víctor Mideros (1888–1965), dated around 1925–1930. But the *tipo* has undergone a dramatic change. This barefoot Indian young woman is beautifully dressed in her best gown and is presented in a realistic way looking firmly into the beholder's eye. She protects herself from the sun. The impressive white backdrop reminds us of

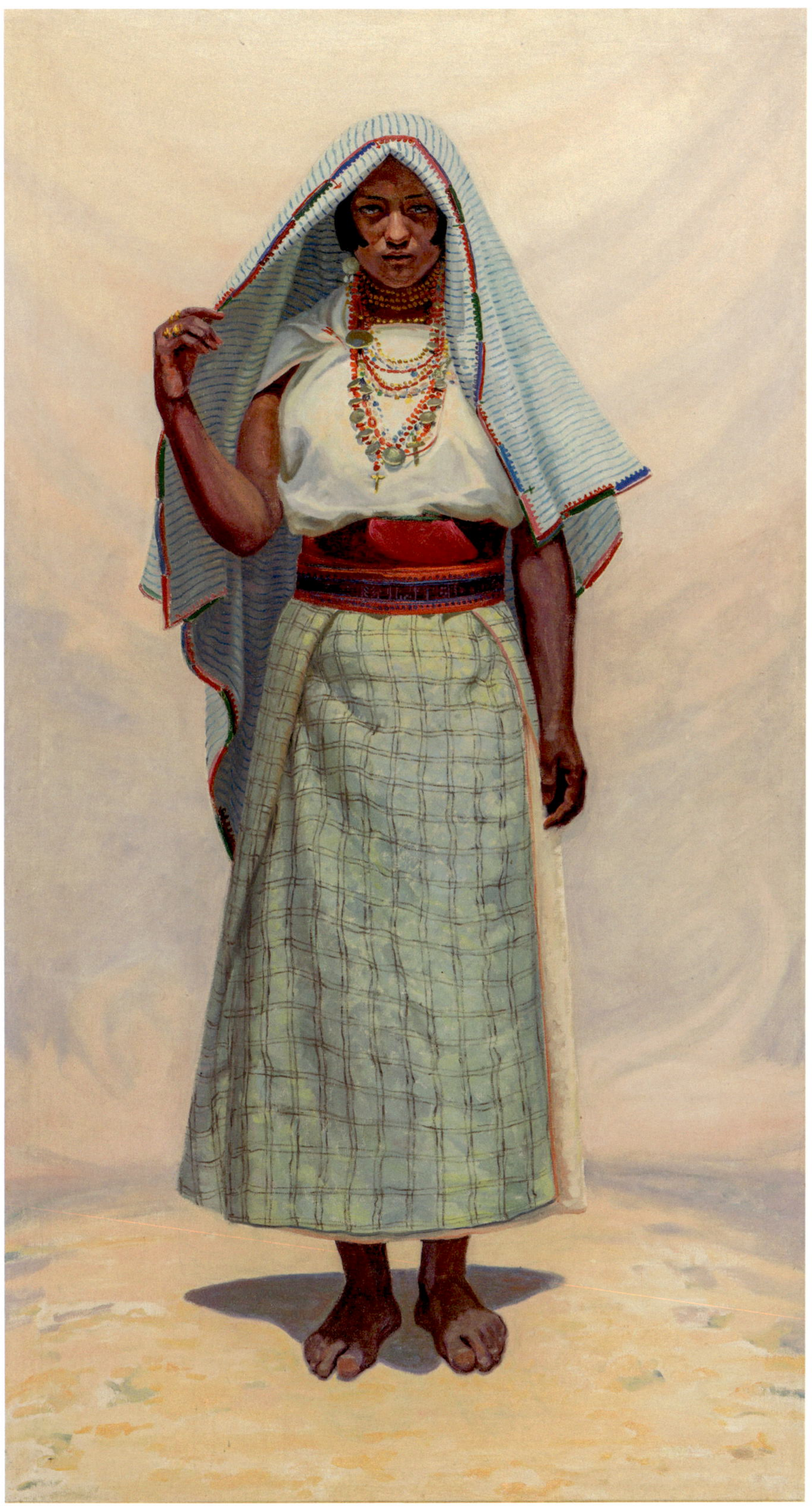

Fig. 18. Víctor Mideros, *Indian from Zámbiza*. Ecuador, c. 1925. Oil on canvas, 74 x 39½ in. (188 x 99.6 cm). Fondo de Arte Moderno-Contemporáneo del Ministerio de Cultura y Patrimonio del Ecuador, Guayaquil. Photo: Christoph Hirtz.

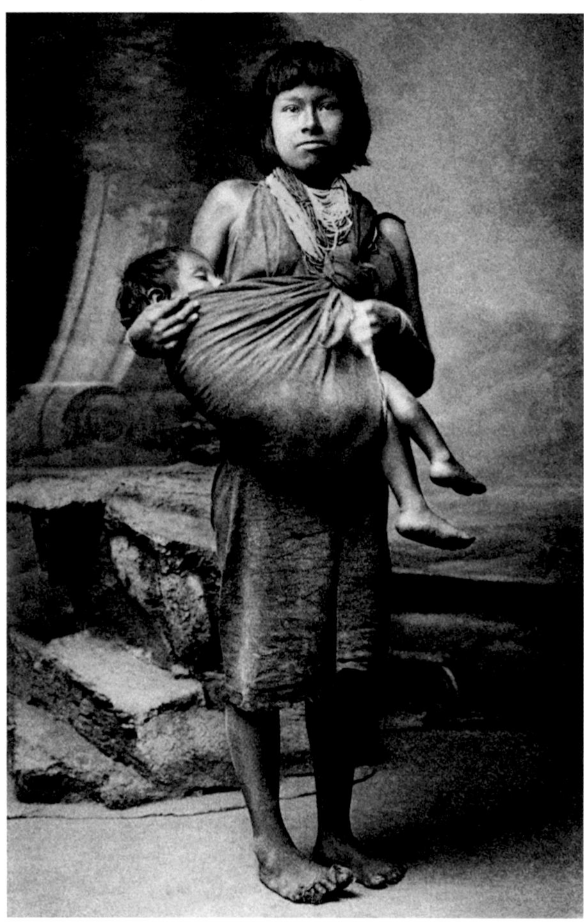

Fig. 19. José Domingo Laso, *Types and Costumes of Amazonian Indians. Studio Portrait: Indigenous Girl Carrying a Baby.* Ecuador, c. 1920. Photograph, 5½ x 4 in. (14 x 8.97 cm). Taller Visual, Quito.

Whistler. Mideros, a former student at the school, then a teacher, and many years later, director of the institution for several terms, aestheticized and humanized the Indian woman so that she seemed real, as in Cassadio´s *Indian Mother.* The latter and other representations of indigenous characters of the time are also related to Symbolist visual art and ideas and the recovery of national pride and soul.[25]

This same path was followed by outstanding Quiteñan photographer José Domingo Laso (1870–?), who portrayed Indian *tipos* in his studio, often using neoclassical European landscapes as backdrops (fig. 19). Again, the notion of modernizing and dignifying the subject is present. Individually or in a group, Indians from different tribes and regions of Ecuador are shown as real people, sometimes showing their deformed members caused by malnutrition or overwork, at other times smiling, talking to each other, or breastfeeding.[26]

But such attractive and dignified depictions of indigenous peoples were by no means common practice in Ecuador—far from it. By the end of the 1920s leftwing *mestizo* intellectuals were condemning the way Ecuadorians had ill-treated this group. Many of these thinkers were inspired by Peruvian Juan Carlos Mariátegui´s 1928 book *Siete ensayos de interpretación de la realidad peruana* (Seven essays for interpreting Peruvian reality). Similar voices were heard across Latin America in countries that had large indigenous populations such as Mexico, Guatemala, and nations throughout the Andean region.

The *costumbrista* and *tipo* watercolors from the eighteenth century, welcomed by scientists and voyagers, had lost their original purpose and meaning. Romantic practitioners had imbued them with a picturesque and nostalgic aura, and in turn, in modern times, paintings, sculptures, and photographs had lost their picturesque character. The people represented began to be recognized as icons of national identity—specifically, of national modern art and culture that gave character to local art.

As a result of social unrest, the difficult situation of the indigenous peoples was harshly denounced by left-wing politicians and Indigenist artists, such as former Modernists Pedro León (1894–1956) or Camilo Egas (1895–1962), during the latter years of the 1920s, the same time in which the Madrid Album was put together.[27] Did our collector share this important political stance? Apparently, in this new context, the original objects were re-semanticized, and these nineteenth-century watercolors, collected in the late 1920s, served to recall a highly segregated population that had to be empowered, as it was many decades later.

Notes

[1] Guillaume N. Lallement, *Historia de Colombia* (Paris: Imprenta y Fundición J. Pinard, 1827).

[2] See José María Vargas, O.P., *El arte religioso en Cuenca* (Quito: Editorial Santo Domingo, 1967); Alexandra Kennedy, "Del taller a la academia: educación artística en el siglo XIX en Ecuador," *Procesos. Revista Ecuatoriana de Historia* (Quito) 2 (1992): 119–134.

[3] Natalia Majluf, "Pancho Fierro, entre el mito y la historia," in *Tipos del Perú. La Lima criolla de Pancho Fierro*, ed. Marcus Burke and Natalia Majluf (Madrid: Ediciones El Viso and the Hispanic Society of America, 2008), 17–50.

[4] See Pablo Macera, Arturo Jiménez Borja, and Irma Franke, *Trujillo del Perú: Baltazar Jaime Martínez Compañón–Acuarelas siglos XVIII* (Lima: Fundación del Banco Continental para el Fomento de la Educación y la Cultura, EDUBANCO, 1997).

[5] See *América exótica. Panorámicas, tipos y costumbres del siglo XIX. Obras sobre papel en colecciones de la banca central de Colombia, Ecuador, Mexico, Perú y Venezuela*, curated by Patricia Londoño Vega (Bogotá: Biblioteca Luis Angel Arango/Banco de la República, 2004).

[6] In Gaetano Osculati, *Esplorazione delle Regioni Equatoriali lungo il Napo ed il fiume delle Amazzoni frammento di un viaggio fatto nelle due Americhe negli anni 1846–47–48*, 2nd ed. (Milano: Fratelli Cantenari, 1854).

[7] See *Donación Carlos Botero, Nora Restrepo. Augusto Le Moyne en Colombia 1828–1841*, exhibition catalogue, December 16, 2003–February 29, 2004 (Bogotá: Museo Nacional de Colombia).

[8] Rosemarie Terán Najas, "Facetas de la historia del siglo XIX, a propósito de las estampas y relaciones de viajeros," in *Imágenes de identidad. Acuarelas quiteñas del siglo XIX*, ed. Alfonso Ortiz, Biblioteca Básica de Quito 6 (Quito: FONSAL, 2005), 64–65.

[9] Manuel María Lisboa, *Relación de un viaje a Venezuela, Nueva Granada y Ecuador* (Caracas: Ediciones de la Presidencia de la República, 1954), 405, cited by Patricia Londoño Vega, "El arte documental en la era del viajero y de la imagen impresa," in *America exótica*, 36.

[10] *Tipos* were also represented—a couple of decades later—by photographers in the same fashion as watercolorists. See Lucía Chiriboga and Silvana Caparrini, *El retrato iluminado. Fotografía y república en el siglo XIX* (Quito: Museo de la Ciudad/Taller Visual, 2005), 40.

[11] A thorough study of this document was undertaken by four Ecuadorian specialists: architectural historian Alfonso Ortiz, historian Rosemarie Terán, anthropologist Jorge Trujillo, and art historian Alexandra Kennedy-Troya, and was published as *Imágenes de identidad. Acuarelas quiteñas del siglo XIX*, ed. Alfonso Ortiz, Biblioteca Básica de Quito 6 (Quito: FONSAL, 2005).

[12] This photograph was taken by P. J. Vargas. See Lucía Chiriboga and Silvana Caparrini, *El retrato iluminado*, 104 ff.

[13] I highly recommend Susan M. Pearce´s book *On Collecting* (London: Routledge, 1995).

[14] Terán Najas, "Facetas de la historia del siglo XIX," 72.

[15] Alexandra Kennedy-Troya, "Formas de construir la nación ecuatoriana. Acuarelas de tipos, costumbres y paisajes," in *Imágenes de identidad. Acuarelas quiteñas del siglo XIX*, 62.

[16] Terán Najas, "Facetas de la historia del siglo XIX," 64.

[17] As we saw before, he was the person who illustrated Gaetano Osculati's book published after his visit to the Amazonian jungle in Ecuador. Many watercolors by Ramón Salas, some signed, can be found in the Museo de la Casa de la Cultura in Quito.

[18] *Sociedades Democráticas de Ilustración, De Miguel de Santiago y Filarmónica. Discursos pronunciados en la sesión pública efectuada el 6 de marzo de 1852* [1852], in *Fuentes y documentos para la historia de la música en el Ecuador*, vol. 2 (Quito: Banco Central del Ecuador, 1984), 5. See also Alexandra Kennedy, "Del taller a la academia. Educación artística en el siglo XIX en el Ecuador," *Procesos. Revista Ecuatoriana de Historia* (Quito) 2 (1992): 119–134.

[19] "The Executed" became a prototype image of popular members of the opposition regularly executed by firing squads in public squares from the time of President Vicente Rocafuerte. In contrast, President Urbina became known as a statesman who defied militarism; he expelled the Jesuit order from the country, abolished slavery, limited taxes on indigenous people, and became very popular among subordinate sectors of society.

[20] Moncayo and many other progressive leaders—such as Miguel Riofrío (1822–1881) and famous writer Juan Montalvo (1832–1889)—were Masons and openly criticized the government. Many had to go into exile, Moncayo among them.

[21] Wilson Hallo (comp.), *Imágenes del Ecuador en el siglo XIX* (Quito: Ediciones del Sol/Espasa Calpe S.A., 1981), 21 ff. Codesido was the daughter of Peruvian Bernardino Codesido Oyaque, who was sent to Europe as a consul and remained there with his family for 18 years. Julia Codesido went back to Lima in 1918 and, at the Escuela Nacional de Bellas Artes del Perú, asked to be transferred to José Sabogal´s workshop in 1922. She then became one of many good Peruvian Indigenist painters. See Eduardo Moll, *Julia Codesido (1883–1979)* (Lima: Ed. Navarrete, 1990).

[22] At present this album belongs to a descendant of his in Quito, Mario Ribadeneira. It contains 56 watercolors.

[23] See Trinidad Pérez Arias, "La construcción del campo moderno del arte en el Ecuador, 1860–1925: geopolíticas del arte y eurocentrismo" (doctoral thesis, Universidad Andina Simón Bolívar, Estudios Culturales Latinoamericanos, Quito, 2012).

[24] *Madre india* was discovered in the course of research for an exhibition curated by Kennedy and Rodrigo Gutiérrez: ALMA MIA. Simbolismo y modernidad en Ecuador, 1900–

1930. Seen through the lenses of Symbolism and Modernism, the Indian image gained a new status in art and society. See essays by Fausto Ramírez, Rodrigo Gutiérrez, Alexandra Kennedy, and Trinidad Pérez in *ALMA MIA. Simbolismo y modernidad en Ecuador, 1900–1930* (Quito: Fundación Museos de la Ciudad, 2014).

[25] Alexandra Kennedy, "Modernidad y gestos simbolistas en la cultura visual ecuatoriana," in *ALMA MIA*, 94–96.

[26] Lucía Chiriboga and Silvana Caparrini, *Identidades desnudas. Ecuador 1860–1920. La temprana fotografía del indio en los Andes* (Quito: Taller Visual/ILDIS/Abya-Yala, 1994); Francois Laso-Chenut, "Fotografía de Quito de José Domingo Laso: lo posible y lo real," *La fotografía en el Ecuador. Ciudades, retratos y memorias, Revista Nacional de Cultura* (Quito) 12 (2008).

[27] Michele Greet, *Beyond National Identity: Pictorial Indigenism as a Modernist Strategy in Andean Art, 1920–1960* (University Park, PA: Pennsylvania State University Press, 2009).